WEB SITE PROGRAMMING WITH JAVA™

http://www.mts.net/~dharms/websitejava/index.html

WEB SITE PROGRAMMING WITH JAVA™

David Harms
Barton C. Fiske
Jeffrey C. Rice

McGraw-Hill
New York San Francisco
Washington, D.C. Auckland Bogotá
Caracas Lisbon London Madrid Mexico City
Milan Montreal New Delhi San Juan Singapore Sydney Tokyo Toronto

The title page graphic is courtesy of Planet Art, 505 S. Beverly Drive, Suite 242, Beverly Hills, CA 90212, (213) 651-3405.

Published by The McGraw-Hill Companies, Inc.

pbk 2 3 4 5 6 7 8 9 10 FGR/FGR 9 0 0 9 8 7 6

Library of Congress Cataloging-in-Publication Data

Harms, David.
Web site programming with Java / by David Harms, Barton C. Fiske & Jeffrey C. Rice.
p. cm.
Includes index.
ISBN 0-07-912986-2 (pbk.)
1. World Wide Web (Information retrieval system) 2. Java (Computer program language) 3. Internet (Computer network) I. Fiske, Barton C. II. Rice, Jeffrey C. III. Title.
TK5105.888.H37 1996
005.2—dc20 96-4679
CIP

Acquisitions editor: Brad Schepp
Editorial team: Robert E. Ostrander, Executive Editor
John C. Baker, Book Editor
Production team: Katherine G. Brown, Director
Jan Fisher, Desktop Operator
Jodi L. Tyler, Indexer
Design team: Jaclyn J. Boone, Designer
Katherine Lukasczewicz, Associate Designer

WK3
9129862

DEDICATIONS

For Bonny

— Dave Harms

For Suzanne, Sean, Jack, and Mom

— Barton C. Fiske

For my family: Rhonda and Clifton

— Jeffrey C. Rice

ACKNOWLEDGMENTS

We owe a large debt of gratitude to the many people who made this book possible. Without Lisa Swayne, who proposed the collaboration and provided continuing encouragement, there wouldn't have been a book at all. Brad Schepp guided us from proposal to final product, and John Baker put in long days behind his editor's desk, beating the manuscript into shape. Stephen Jacobs was both technical editor and design consultant, helping us see beyond our own vision of the book.

We'd also like to thank our reviewers: Patrick Andrew Palmer, Jimmy Torres, Rich Schaefer, Laura Owens, and Donald Rogers. Prasad Wagle assisted us with Web site content, and Rick Levine graciously allowed us use of the style guide. Phil Parkman was an unwavering moral support. Thanks also to Mike Peck for his support and patience, to Irving Salisbury III for the initial version of the Linked list code, and to Marianne Mueller and Lisa Friendly of the JavaSoft group.

Above all, thanks to our families and friends for their patience, encouragement, and support.

CONTENTS AT A GLANCE

CONTENTS

INTRODUCTION

FOR SUN MICROSYSTEMS, 1995 was a remarkable year. In the spring of that year, Sun released the alpha version of the Java™ language and the HotJava browser. By summer, Netscape had licensed Java technology for use in its market-leading Web browser. By fall, the Java language was in beta testing amid excited industry speculation. By year's end, the press releases were coming thick and fast as software industry giants lined up behind Java, signing licenses and letters of intent to support and embody Java technology in their own products. A few weeks into 1996, Java 1.0 shipped.

It's doubtful whether any programming language has ever generated so much enthusiasm in so short a time, both in the software industry and in the popular media. In part, the excitement was due to Java's suitability to Internet programming. To understand that significance of Internet programming, you have to go back a few years to the summer of 1991, the year of the of the first World Wide Web (WWW) software.

In the same way that the Macintosh computer changed the personal computer interface, this Internet software, the first Web browser, transformed the representation of information on the Internet. Instead of requiring users to type in arcane commands, the Web browser interpreted and displayed HyperText Markup Language (HTML) documents, which were provided to the browser by a Web server running at the Internet site. Terminal screens gave way to graphics-laden, hypertext documents. File transfers became as easy as clicking

with a mouse. Users could see the Internet before their very eyes, as Web browsers revealed the Net in hyperlinks of seemingly limitless information.

THE INTERNET: A PROBLEM IN SEARCH OF JAVA

The World Wide Web now is the fastest growing part of the Internet and continues to gain in popularity. It is what many people now think of as *the* Internet. However, success has brought another set of problems to light, including security and data encryption, support of Web software across multiple platforms and operating systems, and the difficulty of extending that software in ways not anticipated by its authors. These issues cannot be solved with just another hypertext format specification. They are of sufficient magnitude that an Internet-aware language is required. That language is Java, from Sun Microsystems, Inc.

The HotJava browser and, more importantly, the Java language, take the fusion of audio, video, and hypertext to a new level by allowing actual program code to be incorporated into existing HTML documents. This means that any capability that a Web information provider wants the browser to have can be made available to the consumer via Java applets (a term for small, portable Java applications). There's no need to make sure that the browser is a current version with the ability to execute some complex set of instructions, perhaps transfer data using a specialized protocol, or display a particular kind of image. The code (the Java applet) is embedded in the HTML document, and the Java-capable browser runs the applet locally, no matter which platform the browser is running on.

This ability to distribute program code has real benefits. For example, the secure transaction mechanism in Netscape Communication's Web browser was recently found to be flawed. This mechanism encrypts sensitive data (such as credit card information) so that individuals and companies can do business on the Internet, despite the Net's essentially public nature. Hackers at a California State college were able to crack the code in a few days. Because this security code ships with Netscape Navigator, the only solution is to replace all of those copies of the software currently in use.

In a Java-based security system, the Web server provides the actual program code to the browser, so in the event of a security breach, there is no need to ship new software; the updated code is automatically transmitted when the user logs into the Web server. Privacy-conscious administrators can change security options as often as they like.

Java effectively removes the limitations ordinarily associated with the HTML specification, and it solves the problem of updating browser software to take advantage of whatever new feature the Web page author wants to incorporate. As much as the introduction of HTML altered the Internet, the widespread use of Java will mean an even greater change in the way that information is presented over the Web.

For example, one trading company now is experimenting with an applet that will do queries on historical data while delivering a ticker-tape style readout of current bond prices. Java can be used to deliver the same kind of real-time information provided by dedicated online trading systems.

Another possibility is classified advertising. With Java, for-sale ads could take on a three-dimensional representation more like a market than a two-dimensional printed page. When you go into a store to buy something, you have a number of visual clues that tell you where to find what you're looking for. Java classifieds could provide those same kinds of visual clues, and more. Users could query the author of the ad for more information or submit a bid (in the case of an "or best offer" price). For an additional price, the ad page vendor could provide Java applets designed to attract attention to the ad, much as newspapers now charge for bold type.

Newsgroups and "chat" areas also could benefit from a dose of Java. Any current browser can give you a list of your chosen newsgroups and, for each of those, a list of new messages. A Java applet could scan your newsgroups and show you the activity in those groups as, for example, a rural scene with each newsgroup appearing as a woodlot and each conversational thread a tree. Tree height could be determined by the rate at which messages are arriving on that thread, and the number of branches by the number of messages. One glance at the size and composition of the woodlots in your "newsgroup forest" would give you a good idea of the conversations going on in the group.

Most of us rely heavily on visual clues to understand our world. The World Wide Web has become immensely popular because it makes the Internet visual, but the images that it uses are static. It lacks a landscape—a virtual geography. Java brings Web documents to life and makes them representational of the Net's ever-changing data.

HOW TO USE THIS BOOK

In this book, you will explore the origins, purpose, and use of Java (and HotJava). As is the case with many new technologies, the full potential of Java is not immediately obvious. We'd also be overstating our case if we said we fully understood Java's potential; only time, and the creative minds that use Java, will tell that story. Accordingly, we've tried to give you not just the mechanics of using Java, but also something of the Web programming mindset that Java inspires.

WHO THIS BOOK IS FOR

Broadly put, this book is for anyone who would like to learn how to use Java to create applets and applications. You'll find things a bit easier if you have some programming experience and even more straightforward if you're a C++ programmer, but the basics of Java are easy enough to learn that, even if you've had next to no exposure to programming, you should be able to get started.

More specifically, this book is for anyone who sees a future in developing Internet software with Java. We've focused on applet programming and application programming from the perspective of creating applications that serve applets. Whether you're just planning on jazzing up your personal home page or you're a Webmaster looking to create the ultimate Java game server, this book can help.

PART 1: LAYING THE GROUNDWORK

Part 1 of this book is an introduction to what Java is all about and how Java works. If you're a beginning Java programmer, are relatively new to the Internet, or just want to make sure that you have a solid

conceptual understanding of Java and its place in the programming world, you'll want to read these chapters. If you're particularly eager to start programming, you might want to skip ahead to Part 2 and come back to Part 1 at your leisure.

In chapter 1, "*The Java quick start,*" you'll see a Java applet go from source code to running on a Web page. You'll also take a tour of some of the more popular World Wide Web sites where Java programmers go for products and support.

Chapter 2, "*Essential Internet concepts,*" is a short history and discussion of the Internet and the World Wide Web, with a view to those features of the Internet that apply to Java programmers. This chapter will be particularly useful to you if you're new to the idea of Internet programming.

Chapter 3 takes you "*Behind the scenes at a Java session.*" The process of putting an applet on a Web page and running that applet from a Web browser running on any number of different hardware platforms is deceptively simple. Learn what's really involved in loading and executing an applet. This chapter builds on some of the Internet concepts from chapter 2.

In chapter 4, "*Java language concepts,*" you'll learn about Java's origins and its unique design. Some of the Java language's key features—including object orientation, automatic garbage collection, and portability—are discussed here.

Chapter 5, "*The Java development environment,*" rounds out the discussion of Java concepts. Although the development environment still is fairly basic as compared to the environments for more mature languages like C++, you'll find that Java provides all of the essentials for applet and application programming and even for linking in native methods.

PART 2: INTRODUCTION TO JAVA PROGRAMMING

Part 2 of this book teaches essential Java programming skills. Java programming can be roughly divided into two camps: applet

programming and application programming. Applets (usually) are small Java programs that are designed to run in the context of an HTML page, while applications are standalone Java programs. While the focus of this book is on applets, applications also are discussed, particularly as they interact with applets across a client (applet)/server (application) connection. Most applet programming techniques can be equally well applied to applications, and vice versa.

Chapter 6, "*Essential Java applet programming,*" is an introduction to Java programming via the ubiquitous "Hello World" (or, in this case, "Hello WebWorld") program. You'll learn about the basic structure of Java applets and get a fundamental understanding of Java's object orientation.

All programs work with data in some form. In chapter 7, "*Declaring and evaluating data,*" you'll learn how to declare and work with Java's data types, from integers to strings to arrays.

Chapter 8, "*Statements, expressions, and control flow,*" covers statement structure, expressions, and the constructs used to control Java program flow. You'll learn how to make Java code do loops, splits, and plenty of other circus tricks.

Java is a programming language with a high level of support for graphical user interface elements. Chapter 9, "*Applets: Getting user input,*" shows you how to easily create buttons, check boxes, text fields, and more.

Components like buttons and text fields are even more useful when you exercise some control over where they appear. Chapter 10, "*Writing Java Applets: Panels, layouts, and canvases,*" shows you how to organize your components on frames and panels by using layout managers. This chapter also discusses the use of canvases for isolating graphics operations.

By the time that you reach chapter 11, you should have a good practical understanding of Java programming. However, there are many nuances to object-oriented programming, and this chapter, "*Using Java classes,*" builds on your experience in the first half of Part 2 and demonstrates some of the finer points of class use.

Chapter 12, "*Error and exception handling,*" takes you through Java's facilities for handling critical program errors. You'll learn how to test for, catch, and even define critical errors.

Java applications require a little more work from the programmer than applets do. Chapter 13, "*Writing Java applications,*" takes you through the basics of application programming as it differs from applet programming.

Chapter 14, "*The Java debugger,*" shows you how to get inside your code, whether applet or application. Learn how to set breakpoints, examine variables, and understand the messages the debugger displays.

Java is a multithreaded language, and in chapter 15, "*Threads for applications and applets,*" you'll learn how, when, and why to create multiple threads of execution. Multithreading is one of Java's most useful and powerful features.

Although Java is a full-featured language, there might be times when you want to link in some platform-specific (native) code. It's not that difficult to do, and chapter 16, "*Linking native C code,*" shows you how and explains the restrictions native methods impose.

PART 3: PRACTICAL JAVA APPLICATIONS

Once you have the basics of Java under your belt, you'll be ready for some more involved programming. In Part 3, you'll know how to write real-world Java applets and applications that go beyond simple applet functionality.

Chapter 17, "*Designing Java applets and applications,*" looks at some of the issues that can make or break any program, long before the coding is finished. You'll also learn about design issues that affect Java specifically.

On the pre-Java Web, getting data from existing information systems is a kludgy process, involving CGI scripts that create custom HTML pages.

Java revolutionizes this process, bringing true client/server functionality to the Web. In chapter 18, "*Client/server, Java style,*" you'll learn all about a client Java applet and a server Java application that you can tailor to your own needs.

Chapter 19, "*More client/server: The Commodity Trading game,*" takes the client/server model established in chapter 18 to a new level, in the form of a multiplayer game that demonstrates real-time transaction processing and data encryption.

Chapter 20, "*Animation with Java,*" dissects the animator applet that comes with the development kit. You'll learn some things that you probably didn't suspect about the animator, and you'll get a solid foundation for your own animation efforts.

Chapter 21, "*Transforming the Web with Java,*" wraps up Part 3 with a look at where Java already is taking the World Wide Web and what the future might hold. Be part of the revolution!

PART 4: BUILDING A JAVA-READY WEB SERVER

Java programming can be highly addictive, and there's no doubt that Java's horizons stretch further when you can program for the Web server, as well as for the browser client. Even if you're just writing for your own home page now, there's a good chance that you'll start writing for the server side soon. Accordingly, we've devoted one part of the book to teaching you how to get the kind of Web site that you need and even how to set up your own Java-powered Web server.

Chapter 22, "*Introduction to Web site planning,*" starts off Part 4 with a brief introduction of the topics that will be covered in the remaining chapters in the part.

Chapter 23, "*Choosing a Web site type,*" outlines the various site options and gives you a good understanding of the pros and cons of each type. You might find that you don't need your own server and that using space on an existing server will suffice. If you decide that you need your own server, however, read on.

In chapter 24, "*Choosing a Web site platform,*" you'll learn about the standard platforms and how to evaluate the hardware and software against your needs. Java's availability for various platforms also is discussed.

So you've decided on a server platform, and you probably have a good idea of what you want to put on it. Web publishing is like other publishing; there are good ways and bad ways to go about it. Chapter 25, "*Creating content,*" guides you through the process of designing the content of your Web site.

One of the hottest issues on the World Wide Web is security, and no one cares about this more than the Webmaster. Java introduces both solutions and some new areas of concern, and these are addressed in chapter 26, "*Security.*"

Chapter 27, "*Implementation: Bringing it all together,*" integrates the various topics discussed in Part 4 into a 10-step process that you can use as a guideline for getting your Web site up and running and keeping it there.

SUMMARY

Java has something for every programmer, whether you're just looking for some nifty applets or wiring your entire business for a presence on the Web. If you're a Webmaster, this book should provide all of the information and tools that you would need to make your site fully Java fluent. If you're just interested in jazzing up your home page, this book will teach you Java concepts and ideas and show you how to start developing Java applets and applications of your own or integrating other existing Java content.

We hope you'll find as much enjoyment working with Java as we have!

THE JAVA QUICK START

THIS CHAPTER will introduce you to the basic concepts and practices of Java programming for the World Wide Web. If you already have some experience with Java programming, then you probably can skip the first part of this chapter, but you at least might want to scan the "Java tour" section in the second part of the chapter, which covers some of the Java-powered places on the Web as well as places to go for further information.

This book covers both applet and application programming (the difference between applets and applications is discussed in detail in chapter 6, "Essential Java applet programming"). However, because most users are likely to start with applet programming, that's what this chapter sticks with.

CREATING AND USING JAVA APPLETS

Creating and using Java applets usually is a three-stage process. You need to create the applet, you have to create a tag for that applet in your HTML document, and then you have to copy the applet and the document to your Web site. Once you've done that, anyone who visits your site with a Java-powered Web browser (like Netscape's Navigator, version 2 or higher) will be able to see your applets in action.

CREATING A JAVA APPLET

Java applets start life as simple text files. It's quite common for a single applet to consist of only one source file, even if the applet is fairly large. Having all of the code in one place makes applets easier to maintain and easier to share with other developers.

Figure 1-1 shows the source code for a small applet that will be the demonstration applet for this chapter. Don't worry about understanding the source code right now; that will come soon enough. Although Java source code does show C++ roots, Java is much more forgiving than C++ and is a lot easier to learn.

Figure 1-1 The ColorBox applet source code.

```
import java.applet.Applet;
import java.awt.*;
import java.lang.Math;

public class ColorBox extends java.applet.Applet
implements Runnable {

  Thread aThread = null;
  boolean threadSuspended = false;
  int boxCount = 0;
  int red,green,blue = 100;
  int c,h,w,x,y = 0;
  int stepSize = 33;

  public void init() {
    resize(100,100);
  }

  public void start() {
    if(aThread == null) {
      aThread = new Thread(this);
      aThread.start();
    }
  }

  public void stop() {
    aThread.stop();
  }

  public void run() {
    while (aThread != null) {
    try {Thread.sleep(50);} catch (InterruptedException e){}
    repaint();
    }
    aThread = null;
  }

  public void update(Graphics g){
    paint(g);
  }

  public void paint(Graphics g) {
    boxCount++;
    if (boxCount > 50)  boxCount = 1;
    red =  red + stepSize;
    if (red >  255) {
      red =  (int)(Math.random()*stepSize);
```

Figure 1-1 Continued.

```
      green = green + stepSize;
      if (green > 255) {
        green =  (int)(Math.random()*stepSize);
        blue = blue + stepSize;
        if (blue > 255)  blue = (int)(Math.random()*stepSize);
      }
    }
    x = 50 - boxCount;
    g.setColor(new Color(red,green,blue));
    g.drawRect(x,x,(boxCount * 2),(boxCount * 2));
  }

  public boolean mouseDown(java.awt.Event evt, int x, int y) {
    if (threadSuspended) {
      aThread.resume();
    }
    else {
      aThread.suspend();
    }
    threadSuspended = !threadSuspended;
    return true;
  }
}
```

The ColorBox applet has only one function: it displays an outward-expanding box that changes color as it expands, and when the box reaches the bounds of the applet's window, the display begins again from the center of the box. In other words, this applet is just a widget.

Java applet source files all have the extension .java, and the name of the file is the same as the name of the applet. The ColorBox applet source file shown in Figure 1-1 has the filename ColorBox.java.

After creating the source file, which you can do with any plain text-file editor, you need to compile the source into a binary format called a *class file*. Class files have the extension .class.

To compile ColorBox.java, you use the command:

```
$ javac ColorBox.java
```

In Java, case sensitivity is important. If you renamed this source file to Colorbox.java, the compiler would give you an error message. Also note that the example here is running on a Unix system, hence the $ prompt. If you're running on a Windows system, for instance, your prompt might look something like:

```
c:\java\demo>
```

If the compile succeeds, you'll now have a file named ColorBox.class sitting in the current directory. This file is the applet and will be less than 2K in size. It's really impossible to create any kind of a windowed application with 2K of code, so you can be sure that there is other Java code that this applet will need before it can work, but you don't have to be concerned about that code, because anyone who visits your Web site with a Java-powered browser will by definition have the necessary support code.

CREATING AN HTML DOCUMENT

Now that you have an applet that's ready to run, you need some way of making it visible to a Web browser. The answer is insert a special applet tag in an HTML document. Figure 1-2 shows a short HTML document that contains an applet tag.

The key lines from index.html are the following:

```
<applet code="ColorBox.class" width=100 height=100>
</applet>
```

Figure 1-2 The index.html document.

```
<head>
<title>A Java Demo</title>
</head>
<body>
<h1>The ColorBox Applet Demo</h1>
<hr>
<body>
<p>This is a test of a small Java applet.
<p>
<applet code="ColorBox.class" width=100 height=100>
</applet>
<p>
<h3>Click on the applet to pause/resume display.</h3>
```

These lines will be read and understood by any Java-powered Web browser as an instruction to retrieve the ColorBox.class file from the Web server and execute the class file.

Once you have an HTML document with an applet tag and the applet's .class file, you're ready to upload the files to your Web site. (Actually, you'd probably want to do some local testing first, but that subject is covered in chapter 6, "Essential Java applet programming.")

UPLOAD THE FILES TO YOUR WEB SITE

You'll need to upload at least one HTML document and one class file to your Web site to have an applet available to your site's visitors. You'll typically use one or another of the FTP programs to send these files.

> The example HTML document is called INDEX.HTML, which is the filename that Web browsers default to if you don't specify a file when visiting a site. Your site should have one file called INDEX.HTML that contains links to all other HTML files that people want to use. In this case, INDEX.HTML and ColorBox.class will be the only two files on the site.

Follow the instructions for your FTP software. If you're using a command-line version of FTP, your session could look something like this:

```
ftp> binary
200 Type set to I.
ftp> send g:\cwjava\thread\index.html
200 PORT command successful.
150 Opening BINARY mode data connection for index.html.
226 Transfer complete.
277 bytes sent in 0.00 seconds (277000.00 Kbytes/sec)
ftp> send g:\cwjava\thread\ColorBox.class
200 PORT command successful.
150 Opening BINARY mode data connection for ColorBox.class.
226 Transfer complete.
1854 bytes sent in 0.00 seconds (1854000.00 Kbytes/sec)
ftp>
```

Note the use of the **binary** command to set the transfer mode. If you transfer .class files as text, they will become corrupted. If the files transferred successfully, you're ready to visit your site!

VIEW THE APPLET!

To view your new Java applet, surf to your Web site. There will be a short delay while the browser retrieves INDEX.HTML and then the applet,

Figure 1-3 The ColorBox applet running under Netscape's Navigator.

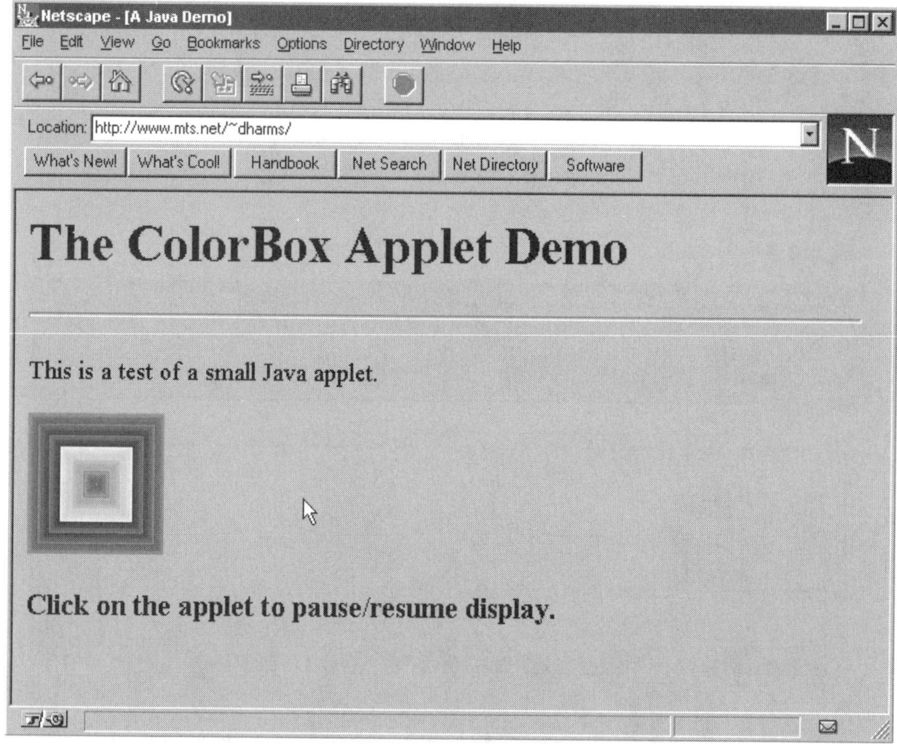

in the form of ColorBox.class. Once the applet has started, you'll see the colored box start growing out of a spot on the page. (See Figure 1-3.)

That's all there is to getting Java working on your Web site. Of course, this is a very simple applet (though not the simplest possible applet, by a long stretch) and not particularly useful. You'll undoubtedly want to do something a little more useful with your applets. So what can you do? For now, just sit back and enjoy the tour.

THE JAVA TOUR

Because Java is an Internet programming language, it stands to reason that many of the best resources for Java programming (aside from this book, of course) are on the 'Net. The most logical place to begin is with the originator of Java, Sun Microsystems.

JAVA.SUN.COM

The Java home page on the World Wide Web is at *http://java.sun.com*. As of early 1996, this home page looked like Figure 1-4. Even the site name is of note here. Rather than prefix the site with *www*, as is common, the good people at Sun decided to prefix the site name with *java*, in light of Java's potential to transform the World Wide Web.

Figure 1-4 The Java home page at *http://java.sun.com*.

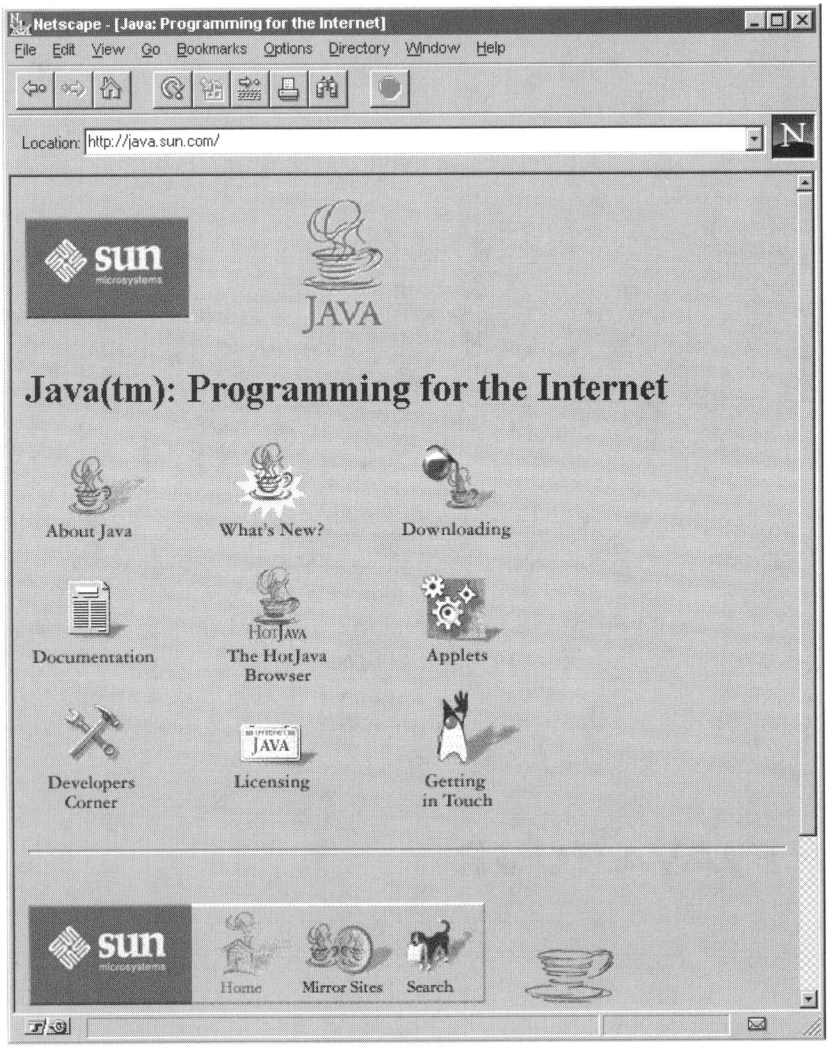

That animated coffee cup (well, you can't *tell* it's animated in the book, but trust me, it is) is another example of a Java applet. However, if you'd like to see a much wider range of applets, click on the Applets icon. This icon takes you to *http://java.sun.com/applets/index.html*, which will ask you which version of the applets you'd like to view. Java was prereleased in alpha in early 1995, in beta in late 1995, and version 1.0 in early 1996. As there were substantial changes in version 1.0 that broke a lot of alpha applets, Sun has been maintaining alpha applets for those users who still are working with the alpha HotJava browser. You'll want to look at the version 1.0 (or beta) applets.

Find your way to *http://java.sun.com/applets/applets/StockDemo/index.html* and you'll see a set of applets shown in Figure 1-5.

Figure 1-5 The stock ticker and stock graph applets.

Netscape - [Financial Portfolio Demonstration]
File Edit View Go Bookmarks Options Directory Window Help
Location: http://java.sun.com/applets/applets/StockDemo/index.html
The first applet is a stock ticker. It shows new quotes in green and old quotes in white.
TO 26 7/8 +1 5/8 SUNW 99 3/4 +6 1/2 HWP 86 7/8 +4 3/4 SGI 37 +1 3/4
The source for this applet uses the StockTicker, StockStreamParser, and StockWatcher classes.
If you want to keep better track of a stock, you might use a graph showing some historical quotes. These quotes can be obtained (via a URL) from any HTTP server that keeps a database of stock quotes. The NEATO quotes shown below are randomly faked every 5 seconds.
SUNW = 99 3/4 +6 1/2
Netscape = 128 1/2 -5
NEATO = 25 13/16 +9/16
The source for this applet uses the QuoteChart, StockStreamParser, and StockWatcher classes.
100% of 16K (at 173 bytes/sec)

As you can see, the difference between these applets and the same information delivered via a static HTML document is that the applets are constantly updated with new data and change their output based on that data. There's no need to retrieve and redisplay a new document each time.

Applets can be highly interactive. Visit *http://java.sun.com/applets/applets/WireFrame/example1.html* to see a simple wire-frame 3D model that you can rotate in three dimensions by moving the mouse. (See Figure 1-6.)

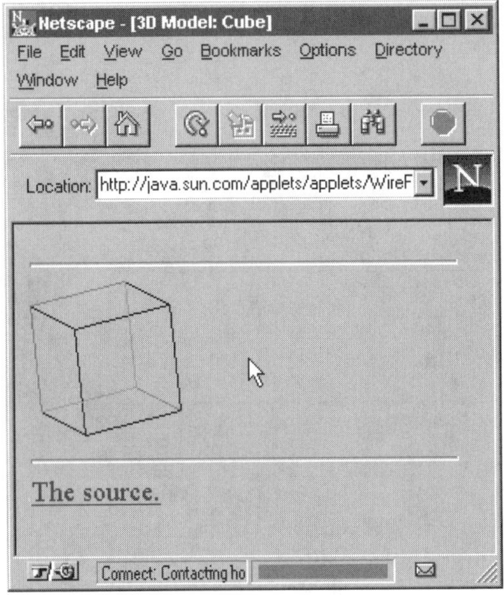

Figure 1-6
The WireFrame applet.

Java is well-suited to educational purposes. At *http://java.sun.com/applets/applets/SortDemo/example1.html*, you'll find an applet that not only displays images describing three different types of sorting used in software (Figure 1-7), but also animates the sorts so that you can see, graphically, just how the different sorting algorithms proceed and also observe their relative speed. (This applet also demonstrates Java's multithreading capabilities.)

Java is used regularly for animation. The TumblingItem applet, at *http://java.sun.com/applets/applets/TumblingDuke/example1.html*, sends

Figure 1-7 The SortDemo applet.

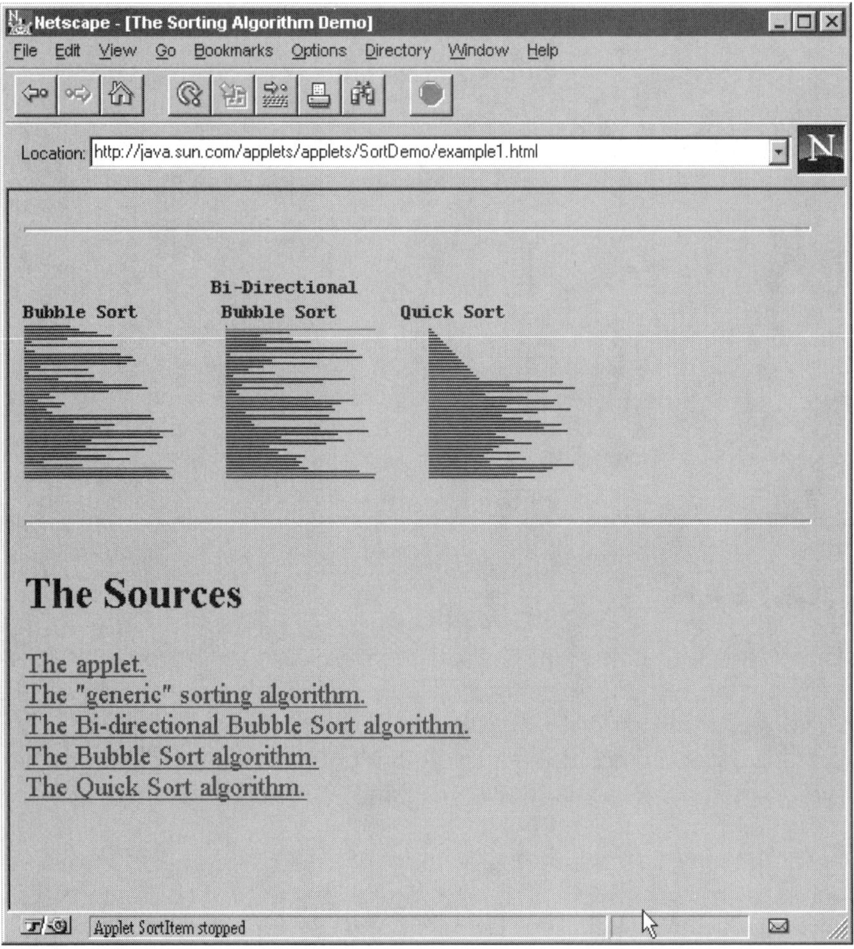

Duke, the Java mascot, doing somersaults across the top of the page. (See Figure 1-8.) In Java, it's also easy to cue sounds to animation. Although sounds are not played here, a number of the other animations at the Sun site do have sound.

Aside from being a good source of applets, the Sun Java site also is an excellent place to get information and updates on the Java language. If you go back to the home page at *http://java.sun.com*, you'll see there are areas on the site for downloading the Java Development Kit, getting the latest news about Java and the HotJava browser, obtaining developer documentation, and more.

Figure 1-8 The TumblingItem applet.

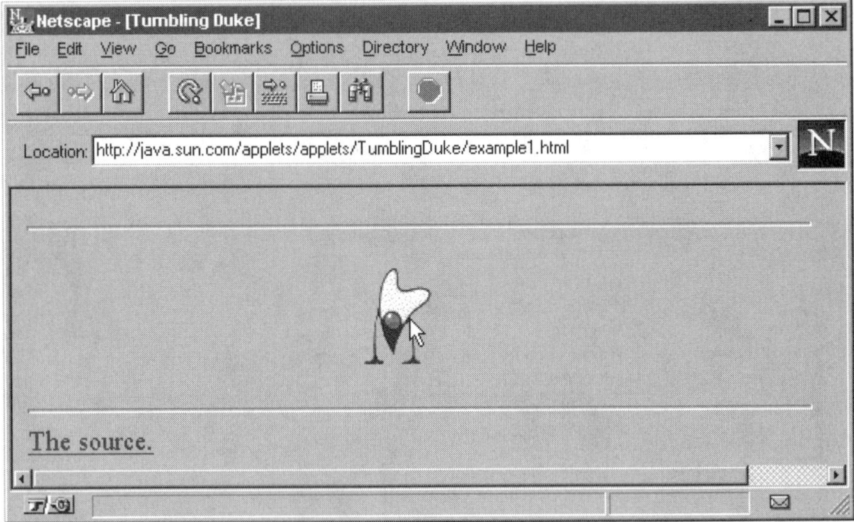

GAMELAN

Next to the Java home page, one of the best Java resources on the Internet is the Gamelan site, at *http://www.gamelan.com*. Gamelan is a directory of Java applets, applications, home pages, mirror sites, and more. It's a good place to go exploring if you'd like to see what other developers are doing with Java.

One of the well-designed sites available from Gamelan is the Dave Matthews Band home page at *http://www.ids.net/~reddog/dmb/*. This page includes a really nice animated band picture and a scrolling LED sign applet. (See Figure 1-9.)

Another interesting site is the SeaLevel home page, at *http://www.sealevelsoftware.com/sealevel/javademo.html*. (See Figure 1-10.) This page has a Java animation with a twist. The animation shows a logo on a background image, with raindrops falling on *both* sides of the logo. You'll also occasionally hear seagulls. It is nicely done.

Figure 1-9 The Dave Matthews Band home page.

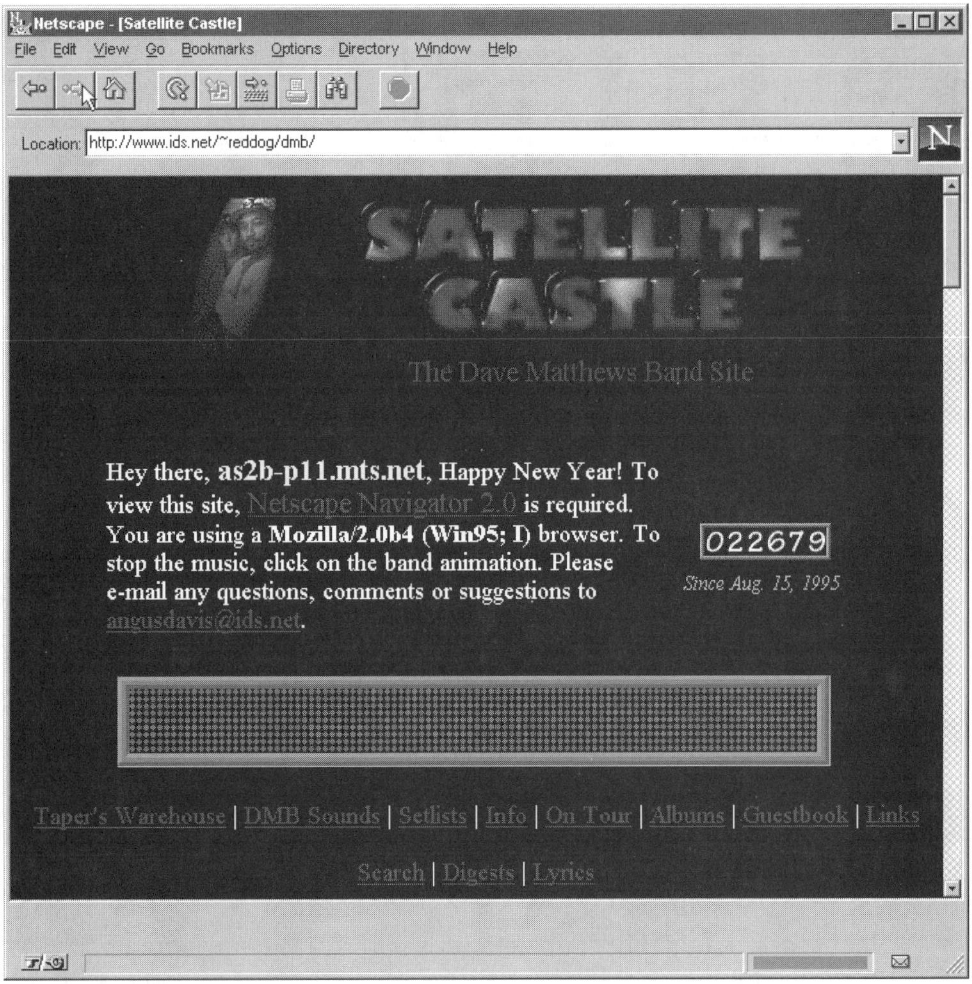

COMP.LANG.JAVA

For day-to-day information on Java, the *comp.lang.java* newsgroup is a wealth of information (even if you do have to do a bit of digging now and then). Keep an eye out for announcements of freely available applets, and surf the home pages of the participants. Discussions here cover everything from getting started with Java (though "newbie" questions usually are referred to the FAQ) to truly arcane Java lore. Pick the end of the pool that you like and dive in.

Figure 1-10 The SeaLevel Home Page.

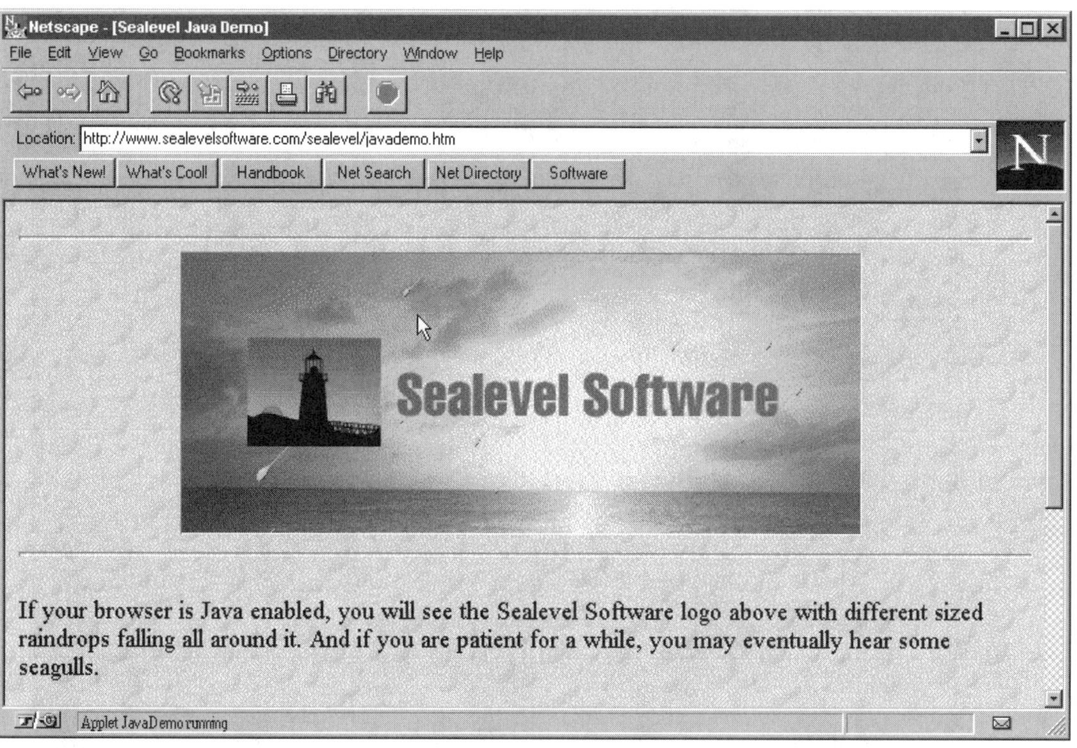

SUMMARY

That concludes the Java quick start. As you can see, Java programming opens up the World WIde Web in ways never before possible. In this book, you'll learn how to design and write Java applets and applications and take part in the transformation of the Web.

ESSENTIAL INTERNET CONCEPTS

THIS BOOK is about the Java language and the HotJava browser and their role in the transformation of the World Wide Web from a passive hypertext medium into an interactive, multidimensional medium. As such, this book is not a tutorial on the World Wide Web or the Internet in general but is an exploration of what Java is and does and how you can take part in the Java revolution.

The more you know about the Internet, however, the better you'll be able to take advantage of what Java and HotJava have to offer. This chapter discusses the Internet's history and essential concepts and the evolution of the World Wide Web as a service of the Internet, all from the perspective of the Java/HotJava user. Later chapters will refer back to many of the concepts discussed here.

If you already know about the structure of the Internet, the birth of the Web, the various protocols that tie the Internet together, Internet addressing, HTML, and the many Internet services such as Gopher and Archie, then you can safely skip this chapter.

If, on the other hand, the previous paragraph makes about as much sense to you as a foreign film without subtitles, read on.

THE INTERNET: A BRIEF HISTORY

You might have noticed that the names *Internet* and *World Wide Web* (or *WWW*, or just the *Web*) often are used interchangeably. In fact, the Web is a service on the Internet. This service allows for the exchange of specific kinds of data, particularly hypertext and graphic images, irrespective of requesting hardware platforms, operating systems, or even the format of the data itself.

The Web is important because it's the part of the Internet that the HotJava browser deals with and that the Java language extends. The Web also can't exist apart from the Internet, so any discussion of Java, and the World Wide Web, must begin with a look at the origins and nature of the Internet.

ARPANET

The Internet began life in the 1960s as ARPANET, a project of the U.S. Department of Defense's Advanced Research Projects Agency. There are any number of theories as to the driving force behind the development of the first computer network, but certainly one factor was the cold war—the prospect of massive nuclear destruction had researchers thinking about new ways to carry military information around the country. Another, and possibly more compelling, factor was the cost of computer resources. In the 1960s, computers were big, expensive, and not particularly fast. It was a waste of money to have a computer sitting idle when somebody somewhere could be using it.

Early experiments linked computers over the phone lines, in much the same way as two PCs can connect over the phone lines if both have a modem and the appropriate software. The trick to interconnection, however, is not really wiring a couple of computers together but determining what standards, or *protocols*, the computers will use when communicating. How does one computer tell another computer to expect information? How does the receiving computer know when all the information has been sent, and sent correctly? How does one computer identify itself to another computer? And so on. As this chapter goes on to describe, a number of protocols have evolved over the years to handle the various kinds of communication demanded by applications that use the Internet.

INTERNETWORKING PROTOCOLS

In the early 1970s, experiments in networking computers became experiments in networking networks of computers. This internetworking was a special problem because different networks from different vendors used different standards for communication. The researchers needed a way to deal with various protocols and/or hardware to conduct communications between geographically diverse systems and to sustain communication despite the failure of individual data links. The result of their work was something called the Transmission Control Protocol/Internet Protocol, or TCP/IP.

Of course, the TCP/IP protocol suite did not emerge from somebody's office one day fully formed. At first, it was known as the Kahn-Cerf

protocol, named for Bob Kahn and Vinton Cerf, who were the prime movers behind the protocol's development (although many individuals were involved in the evolution of TCP/IP).

It's useful to know that, in the early days of the Internet, the focus of development was far more on cooperation than on competition. There were internetworking standards that competed with TCP/IP, but the developers' concern was more with getting a solution that worked than with getting a solution that would sell or otherwise get the developers a competitive advantage over another group. For one thing, there really wasn't a market for internetworking software—the personal computer still was just a gleam in science-fiction writers' eyes, and the computers that did exist were so expensive that only governments and very large corporations could afford them. For another, there was a certain euphoria about the computer that transcended mere commercial interests and brought people together.

In an age when computer stores are almost as common as corner stores, it's easy to forget the magic of the computer. In the early 1970s, everyone was a pioneer, and every field of endeavor was a frontier. Imagine connecting two computers in different states for the first time in history. Imagine the excitement of sending electronic mail when only a handful of people even knew the concept existed. People wanted to work together, and the computing community still was small enough that many of these people shared the same interests.

It's fair to say that the individuals working on the early development of the Internet were an elite and somewhat privileged group. They were well-educated, dedicated, and often driven to achieve. Certainly what they achieved was to some extent determined by the technology they had at their disposal, but their achievements also came out of their personalities. They were the kind of people who would make it possible for computers to communicate with each other, but they also were the kind of people who would design this internetwork to function even if segments of it blacked out from time to time. They could have designed a monolithic system, entirely dependent on a powerful central authority, but they didn't. It's unlikely that a monolithic system would have flourished the way the Internet has.

The Internet, or ARPANET as it was then known, continued to grow throughout the 1970s. By the middle of the decade, the Internet had developed beyond the experiment stage and become a full-fledged Department of Defense (DOD) computer network. Actually, at this time, ARPANET was using a number of other protocols in addition to TCP/IP and would do so until 1983 when the network switched over to TCP/IP exclusively.

The world computing community also was aware of the trend toward TCP/IP and had been for some time. The International Organization for Standardization (ISO) proposed a modified TCP/IP standard in the late 1970s. (The changes were both to add useful new functionality and to take the edge off American manufacturers' competitive advantage). This standard, along with the inclusion of TCP/IP in Berkeley UNIX in the 1980s, clinched TCP/IP's place in computing history. Also, in the early 1980s, the ARPANET spawned MILNET, which took over ARPANET's military functions, leaving research and development on ARPANET.

THE NATIONAL SCIENCE FOUNDATION

In mid- to late-1980s, the National Science Foundation in Washington, DC began promoting ARPANET to universities and eventually funded NSFNET, which supplanted ARPANET in 1990. By that time, a number of other U.S. government agencies, as well as other organizations worldwide, were contributing resources to the Internet, so the loss of ARPANET did not have any significant, lasting impact on Internet users.

By 1990, the Internet was being used for more than just remote logins, electronic mail, and file transfer. The amount of information available on the Internet grew dramatically as more institutions and organizations joined up. Because information is useful only if it can be found, researchers developed a number of new services to manage this data—one of which is the World Wide Web, which is discussed later in this chapter.

HOW THE INTERNET WORKS

In some respects, this section could be entitled "Why the Internet works." With all these seemingly disparate services and so many different kinds

of hardware and software involved, it does seem a bit miraculous that the Internet hangs together at all. As the first part of this chapter indicated, the trick in making it all work is establishing protocols that allow the various components of the Internet to talk with each other.

INTERNET ADDRESSES

One key part of the TCP/IP protocol is the addressing system that the Internet uses. Every computer that's connected to the Internet, whether that connection is momentary or permanent, must have a unique number, or *IP address*.

Currently, this IP address is a 32-bit value, which is made up of four eight-bit values, or *octets*, with a minimum value of 0.0.0.0 and a maximum value of 255.255.255.255. This address notation is hierarchical in much the same way that postal addresses are hierarchical. The first part of a postal address usually specifies a building or unit number, followed by street information, followed by city and state or province, followed by some sort of postal code and possibly a country designation. IP addresses are similar, although they begin with the most general part of the address and become more specific towards the end. Just as letter addressing conventions make it possible to send letters between countries, so the hierarchical nature of IP addresses makes it easy to send an information packet to an IP address when the local computer recognizes only the first part of the address. Without a hierarchical system, each computer involved in passing along information would need a complete and current database of IP addresses, which is quite impractical if for no other reason than the disk space involved.

Under the 32-bit addressing scheme, there is a logical maximum of a little less than 4,300,000,000 IP addresses. In reality, the number is somewhat less, because some addresses have reserved purposes, and others simply are not used because of the hierarchical structure of the addressing system. Given that there are well over 7,000,000,000 people on the planet, the current addressing scheme will not support concurrent IP addresses for all of us, which is what has forced the IETF (Internet Engineering Task Force) to redesign the Internet addressing scheme to use a variation of the 32-bit design, called *octet addressing*. This redesigned specification is referred to as *IPNG* (Internet Protocol, Next Generation) and will be phased in gradually over time. Figure 2-1 diagrams the IPNG header format.

Figure 2-1 The IPNG header format.

<table>
<tr><td>Version</td><td>Priority</td><td colspan="3">Flow Label</td></tr>
<tr><td colspan="3">Payload Length</td><td>Next Header</td><td>Hop Limit</td></tr>
<tr><td colspan="5">Source Address</td></tr>
<tr><td colspan="5">Destination Address</td></tr>
</table>

The IPng protocol consists of two parts, the basic IPng header and IPng extension headers.

The "Version" field is a 4-bit Internet Protocol version number (default = 6). The "Priority" field is a 4-bit priority value. The "Flow Label" field is a 24-bit field.

The "Payload Length" field is a 16-bit unsigned integer. It is the length of the payload (i.e., the rest of the packet following the IPng header) in octets. The "Next Header" field is an 8-bit selector that identifies the type of header immediately following the IPng header. It uses the same values as the IPv4 Protocol field. The "Hop Limit" field is an 8-bit unsigned integer. It is decremented by 1 by each node that forwards the packet. The packet is discarded if Hop Limit is decremented to zero.

The "Source Address" field contains 128 bits. It holds the address of the initial sender of the packet. The "Destination Address" field contains 128 bits. It holds the address of the intended recipient of the packet (possibly not the ultimate recipient, if an optional Routing Header is present).

DOMAIN NAME SERVERS

While an IP address like 255.255.255.255 is quite easy to remember, a number like 205.200.16.65, the address of one of the Internet

computers at the Manitoba Telephone Service, lacks a certain mnemonic flair, not to mention soul. Accordingly, IP addresses usually are written as strings (like *dharms@mts.net*, *barton.fiske@east*, or *java.sun.com*). A specialized computer, referred to as a *name server*, is given the task of translating these strings, or *host names*, to IP addresses. Such a machine provides a *Domain Name Service*, or DNS (and often is referred to as a *Domain Name Server*), because, given a specific name, it serves the IP address of the machine or network that corresponds to that name.

The DNS is a list of IP addresses cross-referenced to hostname and network names. This list will contain complete IP addresses for local users, but much of the list will be made up of what look like partial addresses. These are domain addresses, much as a city and state is a partial address that greatly narrows the options for delivering regular postal mail. Name servers are kept updated with the most general name information, so even if the server can't fully resolve *mts.net*, it will have enough information to make a request to another name server that either will know what the address is or that can find out by passing the request along.

The real-world analog of DNS is the local directory information service offered by your phone company. You call a local number (such as 411), give the directory information operator a name, and receive back a phone number. Sun Microsystems used to refer to its naming services as *Yellow Pages*, or *YP* for short, until a British phone information company made legal objection to the practice. Today, YP has been renamed to *NIS* (*Network Information Services*), even though some of the commands still retain their YP origins, such as the **ypwhich** command, which returns the name of the current name server acting on your behalf.

The most important thing to know about naming services is that you will need to be aware of which ones you are using when configuring and working with HotJava and/or Java, as the operating system (OS) that you are using will require some means of resolving hyperlink references and applet references. If you always use the same Internet service, it is unlikely that you will need to change your name server, although this does happen from time to time. Your Internet service provider should provide you with all of the required addresses for name servers.

ASSIGNING IP ADDRESSES

Because of the potential for confusion if two computers share an IP address, all addresses used on the Internet are assigned by various authorities, all under the aegis of the Internet Assigned Numbers Authority. In most cases, organizations rather than individuals request IP addresses, and a range of numbers is assigned to the requester. This range usually accommodates a subnetwork of machines.

If you connect to the Internet via a dial-in server, you most likely do not have a permanent IP address. Your Internet provider will assign you a temporary IP address from its pool of available numbers and map your Internet address to that IP address for the duration of that session. Incoming messages, such as those containing e-mail addressed to your host name, are resolved to your current IP address by, you guessed it, the name server. There's really no need for a provider to assign a permanent ID to each subscriber if only a small fraction are connected up at any one time (and certainly no provider will go to the unnecessary expense of installing one dial-in line for each subscriber).

While anyone can access your temporary IP address while you are attached to the Internet, there's no way of knowing ahead of time which IP address you will get. This implies that you would have to explicitly tell someone what your current IP address is should they want to log in to your machine. While this might be advantageous from a security standpoint, it's about as practical as having your phone number change several times a day, forcing everyone who wishes to reach you to ask the operator for your current number.

Just as mail without an address can't be delivered, so it is that information without an IP address cannot be delivered across the Internet. Simple addressing isn't enough, however. There also must be a mechanism for actually delivering the information.

TCP AND IP: THE PACKAGE CARRIERS OF THE INTERNET

Information delivery on the Internet is handled by the TCP/IP set of protocols. TCP and IP are both "packet" communications protocols.

Information is passed from computer to computer in blocks, or *packets*, and each packet of data can be divided further into the header and the data section. A *header* is of fixed size and known composition; the receiving computer understands that the first few bytes (or bits) have a certain meaning, the next another meaning, and so on. An IP header, for example, contains information such as the packet's origin, its destination, the length of the data component, the type of information contained, a checksum of the header (to verify that the header has not been corrupted during transmission), and so on.

TCP is a higher-level protocol than IP. When a block of data is transmitted using TCP, the actual information that gets sent over the network consists of an IP header, which contains the addressing information); a TCP header, which contains among other things a sequence number (the actual data sent usually is far too large for a single TCP data block, so it has to be broken up into segments); a checksum (again to help detect any header corruption); and a variety of options and flags for different processes that can be used to optimize the protocol for speed or security.

The sequencing number in particular is important because packets can arrive out of sequence. This is why TCP is referred to as a *connectionless protocol*. There is no explicit requirement that a permanent, dedicated connection be made. If a network experiences some transmission difficulty (perhaps for only the smallest fraction of a second) one or more packets might not be transmitted. This does not necessarily interrupt the entire data stream; it just causes a slight hiccup, and the unsent packets are reintroduced into the stream at a later time and ultimately resequenced correctly at the destination machine.

Packet communication protocols give the Internet its resiliency. If you've ever received e-mail over the Internet, you've probably seen a long section of apparent gibberish at the top of the message, describing in detail the various host computers your message encountered as it made its way from the sender to you. It would be almost impossible for these computers to form a dedicated line of communication ensuring that the message would be sent in a single stream of data. By breaking up the data into packets, each with the required address and handling instructions, these same computers have no difficulty delivery a message, even if that message has to travel from the other side of the globe.

TCP/IP has to function under highly variable conditions. You might have the impression, while you're on the Internet, that you're the only one engaged in a certain activity and that the computer that you're connected to is giving you its full attention. This is almost never the case. At the same time as the information that you are requesting is traveling across the network to your computer, tens of thousands of other data streams might be flowing on the same network. TCP/IP manages this data flow, splitting up large blocks of data into manageable packets, carrying them across the network in the midst of a mass of other packets of data, and then reassembling those packets back into a useful block of data.

You can benefit from this ability to handle multiple data streams as well. As soon as your computer establishes a TCP/IP connection with the Internet, you're part of the network. If your operating system is multitasking, you can check your mail while downloading a file via FTP, or browse the Web while getting the latest messages from your favorite USENET newsgroup. Depending on how close you are to using the maximum bandwidth available to your machine, you might notice a slowdown, but in many cases, the performance penalty is not an onerous one.

ROUTING PROTOCOLS

While the Internet does have some permanent pathways for information, new computers are being added constantly, and connections that existed yesterday might be gone today (or they might be overloaded for the moment). When a computer transmits a packet of information or receives a packet to be forwarded, it often has a number of delivery pathways to choose between. These choices are the job of routing protocols.

There are lots of routing protocols, as well as devices such as *bridges* (which link different types of network hardware), that have their own protocols. Because all computers on the Internet are (by definition) in some way connected, the trick is to make the connection from point A to point B (or point Z) in as few hops as possible. A particularly good routing protocol might connect you to a computer on another continent in a half-dozen or fewer hops. A particularly bad protocol (you can be assured that none like this actually exist) theoretically could force you

through thousands of connections just to get to the mainframe down the street. All routing protocols work to minimize the number of hops and maximize the user of fast connections to get the best overall performance.

Routing protocols use databases of known point-to-point connections and apply a variety of methodologies to achieve the best possible route. Quite often, however, your packets of data might go through several different networks each with its own routing protocol, making it more difficult to achieve an optimal connection.

In any case, routing data is one of those little miracles that Internet users usually take for granted. Like the Internet itself, sometimes the remarkable thing is not so much that routing works well, it's that it works at all.

INTERNET TOOLS

So you've faithfully followed all of your Internet service provider's instructions and your computer now is hooked up to the world. What next? To do anything on the Internet, you need software running on your own computer that knows how to talk to the Internet. Over the years, a number of tools have been developed to perform various useful tasks. In general, these tools are implementations of one or more Internet protocols, and they're often known by the name of that protocol no matter which vendor they come from.

TELNET

Telnet is one of the oldest Internet tools, and its purpose is to let you log onto a host computer. It's essentially a terminal program, but one that knows how to connect with and talk to Telnet servers.

In the early years of the Internet, Telnet was the most common means of connecting to a host computer. A Telnet session duplicated the kind of experience that a user would have at a dumb terminal wired directly to the host computer, although the rate of data transfer probably would be a little slower because of the speed of the connection (usually made via telephone line).

With the introduction of the World Wide Web, Telnet use has declined. However, just as there's still a place for command-line interfaces in GUI operating systems, there probably will always be a place for Telnet on the Internet.

SENDING FILES WITH FTP

Files—such as nonhypertext documents, software, and most binary data—are sent from computer to computer across the Internet using the *File Transfer Protocol*, or *FTP*. FTP is more than just a means for sending files; it's a complete toolset for connecting to a host computer, browsing the host's directory tree, and sending/retrieving files. In its original incarnation, FTP was a text-mode, command-line application. Later versions (and there are a number available as freeware, shareware, and commercial software) have added such niceties as graphical directory displays and point-and-click file transfers.

FTP allows for four different file transfer types: ASCII, EBCDIC, IMAGE, and LOCAL. ASCII files are text-only files, and all implementations of the FTP protocol must support this type. EBCDIC is a mainframe data-encoding standard but is seldom used on desktop PCs except when translating data obtained from a mainframe. IMAGE is used for all binary file types, whether they contain graphic images, program code, or something else entirely. Most FTP implementations use the term *binary* rather than IMAGE. LOCAL allows for varying byte lengths and again is of no concern to most Internet users.

SENDING MAIL WITH SMTP

The *Simple Mail Transfer Protocol* is the standard way of sending e-mail on the Internet. In most cases, applications that support e-mail do so without the user having to know any SMTP commands, even though these commands aren't particularly difficult to learn. Usually the only requirement is to specify the Internet address of the recipient, and the application handles the connection to the mail server and the transfer of the document. Recipient names can be actual IP addresses or IDs (host names). If the latter, they will need to be looked up by a Domain Name Server, and DNS support is part of the SMTP standard. SMTP supports multiple recipients, so it's easy to broadcast a single message to a number of people.

SMTP also is designed to handle verification of mail. Because the message can travel to any number of hosts on the way to its destination, there's often no point in the initial mail server reporting that it successfully sent the message, because failure might occur on a later hop. Instead, SMTP mail servers ordinarily report back if they are unable to deliver a message. A failure report might take some time to materialize if a number of servers are involved.

INTERNET SERVICES

The line between tools and services on the Internet is a somewhat blurry one. However, for purposes of this discussion, *tools* are actual programs that you can obtain and run on your computer, while *services* are programs (or protocols) that generally are hosted on computers that are permanently connected to the Internet, and sometimes even spread out over a number of computers. You might use a tool such as Telnet (or a Web browser—browsers are discussed later in this chapter in the section on the World Wide Web) to access an Internet service, such as Internet Relay Chat (IRC).

USENET NEWSGROUPS

USENET is a part of the Internet devoted to bulletin-board style communications. USENET began in 1979 as a UNIX-based messaging system intended for users of the UNIX operating system. It quickly grew beyond those narrow confines, particularly after it became a part of the Internet in the early 1980s. There are thousands of newsgroups, covering topics from alien vampires to Zen Buddhism and just about everything in between. USENET groups work most like discussion areas on bulletin-board systems; news reader software lets you see a list of messages posted since your last visit, and you can read and reply to individual messages.

ARCHIE

With millions of files currently available for download by FTP across the Internet, the biggest problem that you're likely to have is finding the files that you want. A group of students at McGill University had the same problem and did something about it. The result was *Archie*, a

searchable database of downloadable files. Unfortunately, the only information in this database is the name and location of the file, so you really are at the mercy of the system administrator who is responsible for naming the file that you're looking for and/or the directory in which the file can be found. If you put files on the Internet for others to download, be nice and give them descriptive names.

Because of the vast numbers of files available on the Internet and the rate at which new files are added, it isn't practical to maintain a copy of the Archie database on every Web server. On the other hand, because the Internet lets you easily connect to a server that does have Archie, that's usually not a problem.

GOPHER

While Archie is a special-purpose tool for finding downloadable files, *Gopher* is a general-purpose tool for searching a variety of services on the Internet. Gopher was developed by the computer services group at the University of Minnesota as an aid to students using the Internet.

A Gopher server indexes files, documents, and available services by storing a single-line description of each item in a hierarchical database. When you access a Gopher server, you see this information as a series of menus. The top-level menu is the most general organization of data. By working your way down through the menus, you'll eventually get to a menu item that points to a resource, rather than another menu. This resource might be on the Gopher server, or it might be on the other side of the planet; it really doesn't matter.

There are a number of Gopher servers in use, and these servers can share information. This network of Gopher services is known as *Gopherspace*. That means that there's yet another pool of information with a cutesy name that you might want to search, but to do the job, you'll need another tool: Veronica.

VERONICA

VERONICA stands for Very Easy Rodent-Oriented Net-wide Index of Computerized Archives. Veronica makes use of a small number of

Internet sites that collect Gopher menus from around the Net. You can use multiple keywords when doing a Veronica search. Be warned that the Boolean "OR" operator is assumed, and there is no way to repeatedly narrow a search. Your only shot at success is choosing the right keywords. For certain common words, Veronica will petulantly respond that it has found too many items, so won't display any of them.

WIDE AREA INFORMATION SERVICES

Wide Area Information Services, or *WAIS* databases, really are databases of other databases on the Web. You can use a WAIS server to search any number of Internet databases to find out if those databases contain the information that you are looking for. Once you've found your list of suitable databases, however, you will need to search each database in turn.

THE WORLD WIDE WEB

Before the introduction of the first World Wide Web browser, Internet communications consisted of hooking up to the Internet via a TCP/IP connection, issuing text-mode commands, and reading text or sending/retrieving files. While the information might be interesting, the presentation had all the userfriendliness of the cockpit of an F-16 fighter jet. Consequently, most of the people who used the Internet were researchers, students, and various species of hackers.

The first Web browser, developed in 1991 by researchers at the CERN particle physics laboratory in Geneva, Switzerland, changed the face of the Internet dramatically. Instead of displaying simple text, the browser retrieved hypertext documents from the host computer and displayed these documents in glorious color, in a variety of fonts, and with embedded graphics. Much as the Macintosh computer revolutionized the personal computer interface, the Web browser, and the growing World Wide Web service, revolutionized the Internet interface. While the Internet still offers many non-Web services such as e-mail, newsgroups (discussion areas), and file transfer, the Web is the single most popular service and the most recognizable face of the Internet.

There now are a number of Web browsers available, as freeware, shareware, and commercial software. The browser with the longest pedigree is the National Center for Supercomputing Applications' (NCSA) MOSAIC. All Web browsers have essentially the same function: They retrieve and display hypertext documents. The heart of the hypertext document is the *HyperText Markup Language*, or *HTML*.

HTML: THE LANGUAGE OF THE WEB

One of the problems with the text-only Internet interface was the limited kinds of information that could be presented. In particular, researchers in high-energy physics, who were the prime users of the Internet, dealt with information that could not be easily represented in ASCII (some might say that the subject matter of theoretical physics cannot be easily represented at all). While it was possible to send nontext data by binary file, that wasn't an ideal solution. The Internet needed some kind of unified point of access that could deal with various kinds of media: text, graphics, sound, even access to other Internet services like file transfers and database search engines.

In 1989, Tim Berners-Lee of CERN proposed the first HyperText Markup Language specification. As a document language, HTML works a lot like a word-processor document, except that *tags* can be embedded in the text. These tags contain instructions to perform some action, such as format the text or display an image. Figure 2-2 shows a simple HTML document.

Because the tags are just ordinary text characters enclosed in angle brackets, HTML documents can be prepared on any word processor. You don't need to have special software (although there are a number of products available that greatly simplify the process. The prepared document is stored on the Web server. When the user requests the document, it's retrieved by the Web browser and displayed, as shown in Figure 2-3.

The Web browser interprets the tags in the document and displays the page accordingly. However, not all Web browsers display HTML documents in exactly the same way. Some, like MOSAIC, display

Figure 2-2 An example of an HTML document as viewed in a word processor.

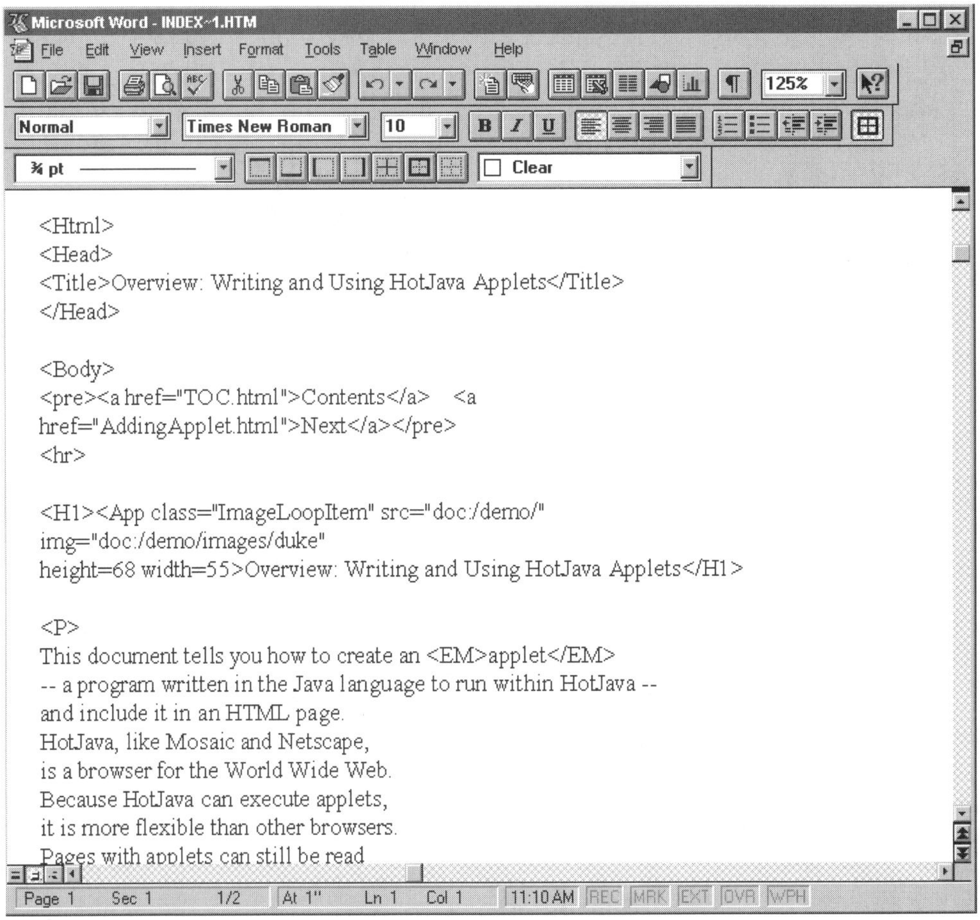

Microsoft Word - INDEX~1.HTM
File Edit View Insert Format Tools Table Window Help
125%
Normal
Times New Roman
10
¾ pt
Clear
<Html>
<Head>
<Title>Overview: Writing and Using HotJava Applets</Title>
</Head>
<Body>
<pre><a href="TOC.html">Contents</a> <a
href="AddingApplet.html">Next</a></pre>
<hr>
<H1><App class="ImageLoopItem" src="doc:/demo/"
img="doc:/demo/images/duke"
height=68 width=55>Overview: Writing and Using HotJava Applets</H1>
<P>
This document tells you how to create an <EM>applet</EM>
-- a program written in the Java language to run within HotJava --
and include it in an HTML page.
HotJava, like Mosaic and Netscape,
is a browser for the World Wide Web.
Because HotJava can execute applets,
it is more flexible than other browsers.
Pages with applets can still be read
Page 1 Sec 1 1/2 At 1" Ln 1 Col 1 11:10 AM REC MRK EXT OVR WPH

images at the left margin by default; others, like Netscape's Navigator, display images on the center of the page by default. Line spacing also is up to the browser, so with some products, you might get more information on a single screen. You've probably noticed that HTML documents can be much longer than the height of the computer screen. Document scrolling also is handled by the browser; you don't have to worry about how much real-estate exists on your reader's desktop.

HTML tags can occur either singly or in pairs. Single tags are elements like paragraph breaks (represented by the text **<P>**) or line breaks (**
**). They are used to mark features that occur at exactly one point

Figure 2-3 The HTML document from Figure 2-2, as displayed by the HotJava Web browser.

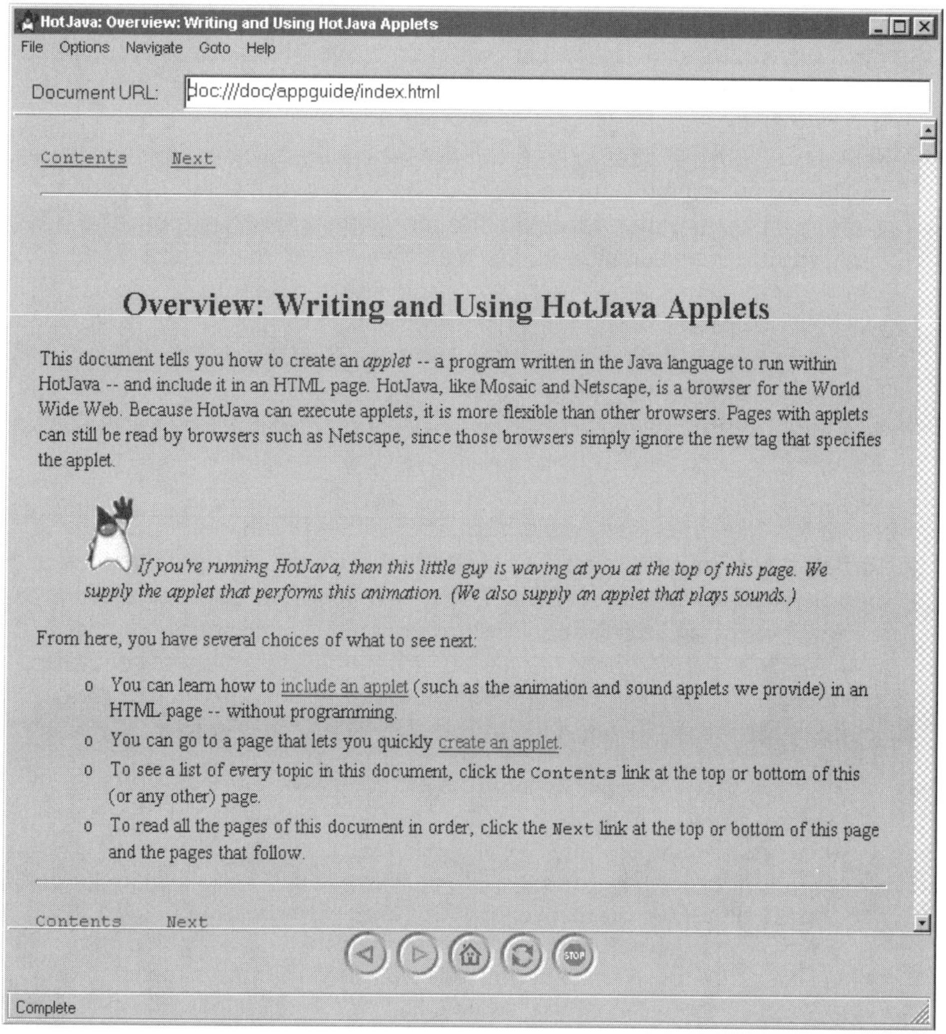

HotJava: Overview: Writing and Using HotJava Applets

File Options Navigate Goto Help

Document URL: doc:///doc/appguide/index.html

Contents Next

Overview: Writing and Using HotJava Applets

This document tells you how to create an *applet* -- a program written in the Java language to run within HotJava -- and include it in an HTML page. HotJava, like Mosaic and Netscape, is a browser for the World Wide Web. Because HotJava can execute applets, it is more flexible than other browsers. Pages with applets can still be read by browsers such as Netscape, since those browsers simply ignore the new tag that specifies the applet.

If you're running HotJava, then this little guy is waving at you at the top of this page. We supply the applet that performs this animation. (We also supply an applet that plays sounds.)

From here, you have several choices of what to see next:

- You can learn how to include an applet (such as the animation and sound applets we provide) in an HTML page -- without programming.
- You can go to a page that lets you quickly create an applet.
- To see a list of every topic in this document, click the `Contents` link at the top or bottom of this (or any other) page.
- To read all the pages of this document in order, click the `Next` link at the top or bottom of this page and the pages that follow.

Contents Next

Complete

in the text. Paired tags are used to mark features that cover a block of text, such as a heading (for example: **<H1>This text will appear as a heading</H1>**). Tags also are used to create links to other documents, collect user input, and display graphics, menus, and even lists of items.

HTML VERSIONS

HTML also has been through several revisions, or *Document Type Definitions* (*DTDs*). The earliest and most basic DTD is Level 0, followed by Levels 1 and 2. Most HTML documents today conform to Level 2 or an unofficial superset of Level 2. As with all other aspects of the computer industry, standards are a blessing and a curse. Standards make communication between various hardware and software platforms possible, but they also tend to stifle innovation. There is a Level 3 HTML specification in the works, but it's not official as of the time of this writing. In the meantime, vendors have created a variety of unofficial extensions to the Level 2 specification.

Chief among these innovators is Netscape Corporation, which gained the lion's share of the browser market by creating a fast, innovative product. Many of Netscape's extensions seem to be making their way into the HTML 3.0 specification.

Nonetheless, there is confusion over what the next standard will be, and you can be sure that HTML 3.0 will be obsolete approximately three months before the specification actually is published. As later chapters will show in detail, Java circumvents the problem of "unofficial" standards by making it practical to deliver actual program code that implements whatever "standard" the Web author wants to implement.

> HTML actually is a subset of yet another language: the *Standardized General Markup Language* (*SGML*). SGML predates HTML and is a lot "closer to the machine" than HTML. You need more skill and programming experience to use SGML effectively, but the flip side is that you also have greater control over the documents that you create with SGML. If you're just getting started in Web page authoring, you will almost certainly be better off sticking with HTML and expending all that extra energy on getting the most out of Java.

IDENTIFYING HYPERTEXT DOCUMENTS: URLS

For a hypertext document to be accessible, it has to have a name that identifies it across the entire breadth of the Internet. This name, which is called a *URL*, or *Uniform Resource Locator*, might look something like

http://java.sun.com/contest/winners.html, which is a document that appeared on the Sun web site in the fall of 1995 and listed the winners of a Java programming contest.

URLs can look complicated until you know how to break them down. In this example *java.sun.com* will resolve to an IP address, and */contest/winners.html* specifies the directory and name of the requested file.

Although URLs can have varying formats, when used for hypertext documents, they all begin with *http*, indicating that something called the HTTP protocol is to be used to retrieve the document.

HTTP: A WAY TO SEND HYPERTEXT DOCUMENTS

TCP and IP might be the core protocols of the Internet, but they're only the tip of the iceberg. It would appear that, for the architects of the Internet, every new data type warranted another approach to transferring that data, and the result is more protocols than you'll find at a United Nations cocktail party. Hypertext documents are no exception; they are transferred using the *HyperText Transfer Protocol*, or *HTTP*.

Just as TCP runs "on top of" IP, HTTP runs on top of TCP. HTTP ensures that the document that is sent will be correctly identified as a hypertext document. HTTP also specifies what portions of the document are to be transmitted, and therefore displayed, first (text before graphics), or specifies what portions are to be displayed at all. HTTP also is used to invoke other Web services, such as FTP file transfers, Telnet sessions, and Gopher searches.

When you specify a Web page to view, your Web browser communicates with the Web server over the TCP/IP connection and attempts to locate the requested page. In many cases, the Web page will not exist on the host computer that you are communicating with directly. Typically, that host will have to communicate with one or more other computers, forming a communication link extending between your computer and the host that contains the desired document. That host computer could be anywhere on the planet.

To build up this link, the computers involved use the addresses specified in the IP header packets. As you might recall from earlier in this chapter, a typical Internet Protocol, or IP address, looks like this: 192.9.186.155. A Domain Name Server looks up as much of the destination as it can resolve, and the routine protocols kick in to start ferrying TCP/IP packets of information around the Net.

If you come from the DOS/Windows 3.*x* world, you might be a bit surprised to see document and directory names that are considerably longer than you are used to. Unlike Internet IDs that translate to IP addresses, these directory and filenames really are the same directories and files that you would see if you were working at the host computer's console.

HOME PAGES

Because the World Wide Web is a hyperlinked system that allows you to jump from point to point, there is, in theory, no need to impose any particular structure on the hypertext documents that make up any given Web site. In practice, however, most servers (or organizations using space on a server) have a single document that is called the *Home Page*. The Home Page typically describes the nature and purpose of the site and contains a number of links to the other pages on the server, as well as interesting pages on other Web servers. It can be helpful to have a loosely hierarchical structure so that a users can start with the home page and quickly work their way down a series of hypertext links until they reach the desired document.

THE WEB IN ACTION

Let's say you're logged into your local Internet connection, and you're about to use the HotJava Web browser, or perhaps Netscape's Navigator, to look at a hypertext document. What's actually happening? On the surface, you're going to be retrieving and displaying a document. Below the surface, there's a great deal more information being communicated than you might realize.

With your browser running, enter the URL *http://java.sun.com* to go to the Java home page on Sun Microsystems' Web site (Figure 2-4). If you're running HotJava, the information page that is loaded when HotJava starts will have a link to this page.

Figure 2-4 Selecting the HotJava home page from the HotJava information page.

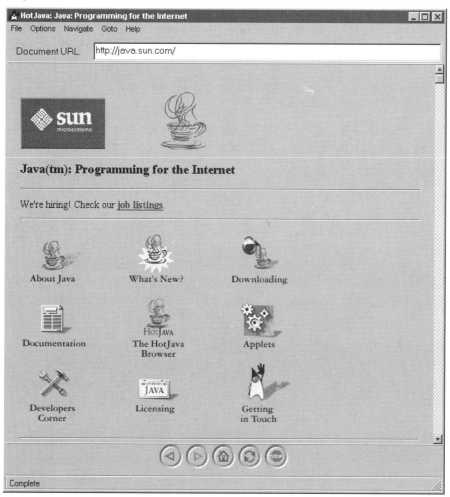

As we mentioned earlier in this chapter, one of the chief problems faced by the developers of the Internet was establishing a protocol that would allow different computer systems to communicate reliably, and the solution to this problem was the TCP/IP protocols. The computer that you are using might be Intel-based, running the Windows 95 operating system, or a Sparcstation running Solaris, or just about any other platform. The first thing that has to happen, then, is for all of the information going to and from the browser to be routed through the

TCP/IP software installed on your computer. The browser never communicates with the Internet directly.

When you click on **The Java/HotJava Programmer's Guide**, the browser reads the information associated with that link from the HTML document. The link is in the form of an HTML tag, and it looks like this:

```
<a href="http://java.sun.com/progGuide/index.html">The
   Java/HotJava Programmer's Guide</a>
```

Note that this link contains a URL that points to the Programmer's Guide index page (*/progGuide/index.html*) on Sun's Web server. Because the URL specifies that this document is to be transferred via HTTP, the browser will pass a request for the document through the TCP/IP stack to the HTTP server. This server, which actually is a process running on the computer that you're directly connected to, will make use of DNS to resolve *java.sun.com* into an IP address, or it will resolve as much of an address as is necessary to route the request a little closer to the Sun server where there is a higher likelihood that the request can be fully resolved. Eventually, unless you happen to be directly connected to the Sun server, the HTTP server will establish a link through one or more intermediate servers until it has a clear path to the Sun HTTP server.

The Sun HTTP server receives a request to send the document *index.html*, which is located in the *progGuide* directory, to your computer's IP address. The server begins streaming out the HTML document as data via its own TCP/IP stack, using the HTTP protocol. This protocol prioritizes the various blocks of data that make up the document, and these blocks then are broken down into manageable, individually addressed packets by TCP/IP.

The Sun server doesn't care at all how those packets of data get to your computer. That's the job of routing protocols, which were discussed earlier in this chapter. A number of computers (depending on the number of connections required to complete the circuit between your computer and Sun's computer) begin passing TCP/IP packets, containing HTTP headers and of course the actual hypertext document data, back to your computer. At the same time, these computers are handing any number of other packets of information belonging to other Internet users. There's a constant crossflow and counterflow of information of sometimes mind-boggling complexity.

INTERPRETING THE DATA STREAM

Let's assume the best has happened, and after a few seconds, during which many thousands of dollars of hardware have busily processed your request for a hypertext document, the document begins to arrive at your computer. The TCP/IP stack receives the data and assembles it into the kind of data stream that HotJava is expecting.

Because this was an HTTP request, HotJava knows to interpret the data stream according to HTTP rules. As the data comes in, HotJava begins to show text, and most likely graphics, on the screen. The document is transferred in a continuous stream, but it is displayed piece by piece, so you don't have to wait for an entire document to arrive before you begin reading it.

If, for the sake of speed, you've selected **Delay Image Loading** under **Options**¦Properties (see appendix A for more information on setting up HotJava), the Sun HTTP server will have received that information as part of the document request and will transmit the text portion first. Some browsers let you turn off image loading entirely (you'll usually see some sort of marker, such as a box, in place of the image, and you might be able to click on that box to retrieve the image manually), which speeds up the transfer of most Web pages tremendously.

Once the document has arrived in its entirety, the TCP/IP software becomes idle. Some Web browsers monitor the state of the TCP/IP connection and notify you if it goes down. HotJava (at least in the version we're using at the time of this writing) does not, so it's possible (at least under Windows 95 and Windows NT) to disconnect from your Internet provider after receiving a document, read the document, then re-establish the connection at some later time and select another document, all without any noticeable interruption to the browser.

TCP/IP was designed as a base for multiple higher-level protocols, all running at the same time. This means that, while TCP/IP is handling an HTTP request from HotJava, it also could be taking care of an FTP file transfer request and sending messages from your electronic mail software. Within individual protocols, however, tasks usually are handled one at a time.

HotJava is written in Java, a threaded language, and can run multiple instances of the same kind of transfer protocol at the same time, so you will, for example, sometimes see multiple images being retrieved at the same time.

SUMMARY

The Internet is a remarkably successful internetworking of many different computers and kinds of computers, across a great variety of devices and communication links. There are a number of communication protocols that make this happen, not all of which have been discussed here. From a user perspective, the most important set of protocols is TCP/IP, which handles all of the Internet addressing needs. For users of the World Wide Web, the most significant protocol, after TCP/IP, is HTTP, which moves Web documents across the Internet.

Java and HotJava are designed explicitly to run within the Internet/World Wide Web environment. As such, they make use of, and interact with, the various protocols and services of the Internet and the Web. The more you know about how the Internet works, the greater your opportunities as a Java Web site programmer will be.

BEHIND THE SCENES AT A JAVA SESSION

IF YOU'VE BEEN THROUGH the exercises in chapter 1, you already have a good idea of what Java can do. If you intend to do any Java programming, however, you'll also want to know why Java is able to do what it can do. This chapter will take a look at what's actually going on behind the scenes during a Java session. You'll learn how the Java-compatible browser obtains the Java applet, what form the applet is in, and how the Java applet code executes on the browser, no matter which computer platform the browser happens to be running on.

THE <APPLET> HTML TAG

When a Web browser retrieves an HTML document from a Web server, it begins interpreting the document as soon as it begins to arrive. It does not wait until the entire document has arrived. Each tag that the browser encounters is read and interpreted. When the browser reaches an **<applet>** tag, it either ignores it, if it doesn't understand Java, or it sends a request to the server to retrieve the applet code in the location specified in the tag.

The full format of the <applet> tag is as follows:

```
<applet=
  [codebase=URL]
  code=AppletClass
  alt=AlternateText
  name=AppletInstanceName
  [width=WidthInPixels height=HeightInPixels]
  [align=Alignment]
  [vspace=SpaceAboveBelowInPixels]
  [hspace=SpaceBesideInPixels]
  [<param name=Param1 value=Param1Value>]
  [<param name=Param2 value=Param2Value>]
  ...
  [AlternateHTML]
  </applet>
```

The **code** value specifies the name of the applet; technically this also is the applet subclass. Classes and subclasses are explained in Part 2, "The Java language." The class can be something you've created or one of the standard Java classes. Java applet files have the extension .JAVA, but this is not specified in the class name.

The **codebase** attribute is the URL of the Java applet. This is the location of the applet from the perspective of the document that is referring to it. URLs can be relative; they don't need to specify the entire address of the document if that location will always be the same relative to the current location. For example, if the file specified by a URL is in the same directory as the current file, the URL can be omitted entirely, because the URL is the location only, not the actual name of the applet (which is equal to the code attribute plus the extension .CLASS).

The **alt** attribute allows you to indicate which text (enclosed in double quotes) should display if the browser is unable to run the applet. This will happen only if the browser already knows what an applet tag is.

The **name** attribute lets you specify an applet instance name, which can be useful when you want applets on the same page to communicate with each other.

The **width** and **height** attributes specify how large, in pixels, the window that contains the Java applet will be. Every applet runs in a window, even though most of them do not have a window border around them. For example, the animations of Duke, which you see throughout the Java HTML documentation, have borderless windows with backgrounds that are the same color as the document on which they are placed. This gives the illusion of the animation being a seamless part of the HTML document.

The **align** attribute specifies how the applet will be aligned on the page. Valid values are **left**, **right**, **top**, **texttop**, **middle**, **absmiddle**, **baseline**, **bottom**, and **absbottom**.

The **vspace** and **hspace** attributes specify how much buffer space, in pixels, should be placed above and below or to the left and right, respectively, of the applet.

Following these standard attributes are one or more optional, applet-specific attributes. These are startup parameters for the applet, and their number and format is under the control of the applet author. Note that these parameters each are placed within their own set of angle brackets.

Take a look at the following applet tag for the "Simple 3D Model Viewer" applet, which is available on the Sun server from http://java.sun.com/applets/applets/WireFrame/example1.html:

```
<applet code=ThreeD.class width=100 height=100>
<param name=model value=models/cube.obj>
</applet>
```

In this tag, the **code=** attribute points to the ThreeD.class file. Because there is no **codebase** attribute, the class file is located in the same directory as the example1.html file. The **model=** attribute is an attribute that this class file understands, and the value for this attribute is models/cube.obj. The **width** and **height** attributes specify the size of the applet's window in pixels. All other parameters, in this case, are optional, and the appropriate defaults will be used.

Once HotJava knows what the operating parameters of the applet are, it can request the applet from the Web server.

RETRIEVING A JAVA APPLET

Unlike HTML documents, which are interpreted as they arrive, the Java applet is not executed until it has arrived in its entirety. At that time, the browser passes the information obtained from the <applet> tag to the applet as command-line parameters. Because the applet contains actual program code transported over a relatively slow, public, and heterogeneous network, there are three important issues that must be addressed: compactness, portability, and security.

THE NEED FOR COMPACT CODE

All computing technologies have limits that cause their users frustration. In the PC world, the biggest headache, for many years, has been the 640K (actually 1024K, if you want to split hairs) memory limitation that is the result of using only 16 bits for addressing memory. Programs have grown far beyond the small confines of that memory space, and this has necessitated all kinds of tricks and generated millions of dollars in revenue for vendors of memory managers such as QEMM.

The Internet's biggest bottleneck is the speed of the slowest link in your connection to the network. Although the so-called backbones of the Internet might run at extremely high speeds, most mere mortals who connect to the Internet do so via modem, and the maximum modem speed in common usage at present is 28.8 kilobits per second. That's really quite slow. Even a slow local-area network is several hundred times faster.

If not for this speed restriction, it might be possible to use ordinary commercial software over the Internet, once issues of portability and security were addressed. That's not likely to happen anytime soon (although there are some interesting telephone technologies on the horizon that could significantly improve the speed of local access).

Java addresses the speed bottleneck in two ways. First, Java code itself is compact. There's little wasted space in a Java program; instructions are coded in a tight binary format. Second, Java applets are small. That's why they're called applets, not applications.

> If you want users to keep coming back to your Web site, you can't afford to waste their time by making them download huge, monolithic programs. If you do have a large program, think about ways to break it down in smaller applet components. Java applets can call each other, so you don't need to present the entire program to the user right at the beginning. Give your users a starting point, and let them find their own path through your program, just as you would break up a hypertext document into as many subdocuments as is practical. (See Part 4 for more information on Web site planning.

THE NEED FOR PORTABLE CODE

Because the Internet is a collection of quite different kinds of computers, any application shared across the Internet needs to be able to run in the same way on those different computers. This is called *platform independence*, and it's a sort of Holy Grail for the computer industry.

The problem with platform independence is one of standards. At their heart, all computers have a processor of some kind that executes machine-code instructions. Machine code is a pretty arcane language and practically no one programs in it directly; however, at some point, all software must be translated into it. This usually happens through a

layered set of software. At the top level is the program that the user is familiar with. It might be a word processor, a spreadsheet, or perhaps a Web browser like HotJava. This software rarely communicates directly with the processor. Instead, it talks to the operating system, which itself can be divided into a number of levels, each of which becomes more obscure and difficult to understand the closer it gets to machine code.

The purpose of having levels of software is to shield the programmer from unneeded complexity. At a high level, a few instructions accomplish a lot of activity, because they're translated and multiplied as they approach the processor, but the programmer is largely at the mercy of the programmers who wrote the lower-level code. At a low level, it might take many instructions to accomplish very little, but the programmer has complete control over the processor (and the other hardware in the computer).

Because different processors understand different machine code, it's difficult, if not impossible, to have one program that can run on absolutely any computer. Some processors can emulate other processors' instruction sets, but this usually is far from an ideal solution because emulation invariably consumes a lot of resources, and the processor then runs too slow when compared with the native processor.

In any case, simple emulation isn't the answer to platform independence because programs aren't written at such a low level anyway; they're written to run on different operating systems. If you create a program for Windows NT and put it on your Web server, only people who are running Windows NT will get any benefit from downloading that program.

Platform independence requires a translation level to exist at some point in the chain between the end-user's application and the processor. Java's solution is to put the translation code in the Web browser itself. That means that Java itself (or rather, that Java Virtual Engine, which is described later in this chapter) must be ported to every platform that will support Java. However, because this code interprets other program code, you only have to do it once for each platform, rather than once for each application that is to run on that platform.

THE NEED FOR SECURITY

Retrieving data, such as a hypertext document, from an unknown source isn't a particularly risky proposition. At the worst, you might end up retrieving a document that offends your sensibilities. Retrieving program code, which is what happens in a Java session, is fraught with danger. If there were no restrictions on what a Java program could do, you might inadvertently pick up a program somewhere that could do malicious damage to your system.

Java security is handled on several levels. There are the security options in the browser, which are described in appendix A. These options control which computers the browser can safely load applets from and which documents those applets are permitted to retrieve.

Assuming that the browser allows an applet to load, it then must be able to contain that applet within known boundaries. The most obvious danger here is the use of pointers.

SECURITY AND POINTERS

Arguably the standard for application development in the 1990s is the C++ programming language, and the Java language owes much of its structure to C++ as well. One of the most powerful features of C++ (and C, which preceded it) is its use of pointers to memory locations. The big problem with pointers is that they are difficult to control. By using pointers, an application can reference memory beyond its own assigned areas, perhaps reading private information from another running application.

In the interests of security, Java does away with pointers entirely. For C/C++ programmers, this will mean a moderate change in programming style. The most common use of pointers is for processing arrays of data, for which Java supplies true arrays. The removal of pointers from the language specification also means that the potential for bugs is greatly reduced.

Java also embodies a number of security provisions in the language classes themselves. These provisions are discussed in more detail in chapter 25.

Even if Java applications themselves are secure, it's only because they obey the rules set down by the Java compiler. What's to prevent someone from forging a Java program that does not obey the rules? As it turns out, Java programs themselves are designed to be verifiable.

JAVA PROGRAM FORMAT

The Java language is (for the most part) an interpreted language, as opposed to a compiled language. In a compiled language, source code is translated into processor-specific machine code, usually via an intermediate step that allows various precompiled object modules to be incorporated into the final product. In an interpreted language, source code is translated into an intermediate (usually binary) format that is read by an interpreter at run-time.

THE JAVA INTERPRETER

In general, interpreted languages are slower than compiled languages because interpretation of the intermediate code format takes processor resources. The great advantage, and the one that Java realizes, is that the intermediate code can have a single format, and the interpreter can take care of translating to different platforms.

JAVA BYTECODE FORMAT

In Java, the intermediate language is composed of a series of bytes, called *bytecodes*, which always have the same, platform-independent format. Bytecodes consist of a one byte instruction called an *opcode* and optionally one or more *operands*, or parameters to the instruction. Operands can be one or more bytes in length. If an operand is more than one byte long, it is stored in big-endian order, with the high-order byte first. With few exceptions, all instructions in the program are arranged in eight bit, byte-sized chunks. This keeps program code compact, because there's normally no need to ascertain the boundaries of an instruction, as would happen if the byte length were variable.

When the interpreter executes a Java program, it's essentially processing a stream of bytecodes. The code runs quickly, for an interpreted language. However, in cases where speed is all-important, the interpreter can translate the bytecodes into processor-specific

machine instructions on the fly. The bytecodes are designed for easy translation so the overhead is minimal, but this is only practical for code that will execute multiple times and therefore recover the processor cycles lost during the translation. Translated bytecodes run at speeds very nearly that of native C/C++ code.

The bytecode format also makes it relatively easy to incorporate certain rules into the structure of Java programs, and this is done for security reasons. The interpreter cannot assume that it's going to be receiving a valid program rather than a hacked program with malicious purposes.

As compared to a compiled program written in C or C++, a Java program contains a great deal more information on data types and allowed access methods. This makes it possible to ensure that various classes and constructs are used in the way that they are intended to be used and not in some unexpected manner and for unknown purposes.

Java programs, without losing their flexibility, are forced down the straight and narrow path. Information that normally would be available only at compile time to determine whether the program structure was valid are also available at run-time. That way, even if the author attempts to force a program to perform an illegal action (by modifying the program after compilation, by modifying or defeating the Java compiler's safeguards, or by writing a new Java compiler that does not have the safeguards built in), the Java interpreter still can detect attempts to perform illegal actions.

THE JAVA VIRTUAL MACHINE

When a Java applet is loaded, the Java interpreter reads the bytecode stream and parses it into instructions. It then passes these instructions to the Java Virtual Machine (JVM), which is the heart of the Java runtime system.

The JVM is an abstracted front end to the machine-specific back end where program instructions actually get executed. All programs ultimately have to be designed to run on a machine of some kind or other. Because Java is designed to run on various platforms, the only way to design one program for them all is to create a virtual computer

specification, write with that specification in mind, then create the needed translation layers between the virtual computer and the actual machine that Java is running on.

The JVM specification is an open specification. Sun's aim in publishing it is to encourage others to port the JVM to new platforms and to produce enhanced Java compilers and interpreters. This approach isn't without precedent. The IBM Personal Computer, which had an open specification (excluding the ROM BIOS), enjoyed far greater success than its rivals from Apple Computer Corp, which had (until recently) a closed specification. If it can happen for real computers, why not for virtual computers?

As much as possible, the JVM specifies what Java instructions are to accomplish, rather than how they are to work. It's essential that compiled Java code be able to execute on any vendor's JVM.

The key components of the Java program format that must be adhered to are the instruction set syntax and opcode values, the value of identifiers in instructions and structures, the layout of supporting structures, and the Java class file object format.

All of this still leaves considerable room for innovation. There are no restrictions on areas such as the development environment, the compiler's speed and ability to optimize (provided it creates valid Java code), and the speed and optimization of the runtime library (again, provided it can read Java code). As Java makes its way onto the Internet, we are starting to see a groundswell of support for Java by everyone from independent developers with special-purpose development tools to major vendors like Borland and Symantec who are coming out with Java-tailored programming environments. For a more detailed look at industry support for Java at the time of this writing, turn to appendix B.

JVM COMPONENTS

The Java Virtual Machine has five essential components: an instruction set, registers, a stack, a heap (garbage-collected), and a method area.

The implementation of each of these components is not specified in the JVM document. If you think that you can write better garbage-collection routines or slicker instruction implementations than exist in the current implementation, Sun encourages you to do so. All you have to do is adhere to the specification for the inputs and outputs. For the vast majority of Java programmers, however, the remaining part of this chapter is informational only. It's unlikely that you will have any reason to build your own implementation of the JVM.

THE INSTRUCTION SET

The instruction set, as described briefly earlier in this chapter, consists of a byte-sized opcode followed, optionally, by one or more variable-length operands. JVM instructions are very much like a generalized (rather than specialized) assembly-language instruction set, designed to be as nearly aligned as possible to the instruction set of the popular hardware platforms.

REGISTERS

Just like any real physical computer, the Java Virtual Machine has *registers*, or temporary storage areas for "virtual processor" data.

THE STACK

The Java *stack* is 32 bits wide and therefore cannot exceed four gigabytes. Otherwise, it is under no restrictions. Stack memory does not have to be contiguous.

THE GARBAGE-COLLECTED HEAP

The *heap* is where classes and data types are allocated memory. Because the heap is automatically garbage-collected, there is no provision (or need) for programmers to explicitly deallocate memory.

THE METHOD AREA

The *method calling area* is roughly analogous to the program code area in many executable program formats.

GETTING UPDATED DOCUMENTS

As of this writing, the Java Virtual Machine is not yet fully documented. For the complete (indeed, for the latest) specification, go to the Java home page at *http://java.sun.com*.

RUNNING JAVA CODE

The Java virtual machine, for all intents and purposes, takes the place of the physical computer on which the HotJava browser (or any Java-powered browser) is running. That means that, from the perspective of the bytecode stream, all Java-powered browsers look the same. It's fair to say that there's never a need to port Java to a new hardware platform, because all Java runs on the same platform: the Java Virtual Machine. The drawback to all this is that you have to port the JVM to every platform that you want Java to run on.

SUMMARY

The three great issues of delivering software across the Internet are portability, compactness, and security. The key design components of the Java language (and therefore Java applets) that address these issues are the Java bytecode format and the Java Virtual Machine. Java bytecodes are the portable, compact form of program instructions, which also contain additional information for self-validation and secure operation. The Java Virtual Machine interprets these bytecodes in a consistent way across all hardware platforms, and the end result is that the World Wide Web becomes a conduit for interactive programming.

JAVA LANGUAGE CONCEPTS

IN THE PREVIOUS CHAPTERS, you learned some Internet/World Wide Web concepts that are essential to getting the most out of Java. You also learned about Java applets and the means by which the HotJava browser (and other browsers, such as Netscape Navigator) executes those applets.

In this chapter, you'll begin your journey toward mastering the Java programming language. If you have some (or much) C++ programming experience, you'll find your progress quite rapid at first. In any case, the majority of Java programmers still are nearer the start of that journey simply because Java is a relatively new language.

AN UNUSUAL ORIGIN

Although Java appears to have been designed from the ground up as an Internet/Web programming language, that isn't how it started out. Java originally was part of a project at Sun Microsystems called Oak, which was directed first at creating a heterogeneous network of household consumer electronic devices and later at developing software for the intereactive television market.

In recent years, television has begun an evolution from a one-way delivery of information, which the consumer could choose to either view or ignore, to a two-way communication where the user gets some measure of control over the presentation of the information.

One example of this evolution is digital direct broadcast satellite television. In 1994, Hughes Communication launched its DirecTv service in North America. DirecTv, and other similar services under development around the world, takes TV broadcasting to a new level of complexity. The broadcaster must deliver not only the video and audio streams, but a certain amount of data to moderate and control the user's access to the programming. Pay-per-view programs must be shown to the viewer only when an appropriate request has been made by the user (and approved by the system). The system also must black out certain programming, as when a sporting event may not be shown in the city where the event is happening. This control is exercised by the set-top box, which sits between the satellite dish and the television.

Some of the programming required by the set-top box, such as the signal decryption algorithms, the communication protocols used to receive instructions from the hand-held remote control, and so on can be built in at the factory. Other capabilities, such as displaying a grid of available programs, displaying pricing and detailed information for an individual program, or blacking out a program based on the viewer's postal code requires current data from the satellite's data stream.

As of this writing, set-top boxes are largely hardwired or firmwired (the latter typically is done via smart cards that are issued to the user). The set-top boxes can display various kinds of information as received from the satellite, but only in preset ways. In this respect, set-top box technology is a lot like the pre-Java World Wide Web, where the content can be anything, but the presentation of that content is somewhat limited. If, for example, it turns out that the set-top box firmware contains a bug such that it does not properly black out sporting events for a certain set of postal codes, then the only option is to replace the firmware in each box or replace each and every box in its entirety.

There are a large number of functions that the set-top box must perform, and if the "intelligence" behind those functions can be embodied in software rather than in hardware or firmware, then upgrading the box is as easy as delivering a new data stream containing the software. This updating of software via the data stream is exactly what Java was designed to do.

As the Oak project continued to develop the Java language, a number of things occurred along the way that serendipitously created a much larger opportunity for Java than originally envisioned. As Sun continued to position itself as the leader in network-based Unix computing, it also became obvious that the number of Internet service providers and, by inference, the number of Internet consumers was growing at a nearly exponential rate. At some point along the way, with the relative limitations of HTML "programming," it became clear that a programming language for the Internet was needed. This realization became the driving force behind the development of Java as we know it today.

If the Java developers had stayed true to their original purpose, services such as interactive and direct broadcast satellite television might be built around Java, instead of on proprietary firmware

standards. On the other hand, Web-site programming is arguably a whole lot more fun than making a TV black out a Raiders game, so the consumer electronics industry's loss is our gain. However, don't count Java out yet for consumer electronics. There's every reason to believe that Java will come full circle and yet be used for various kinds of embedded systems, or perhaps tomorrow's Java-compatible browser will take the place of today's "dumb" television sets.

SECURITY AND PORTABILITY

It's a helpful coincidence that consumer electronics software faces two of the same issues that Web software faces: security and portability.

For example, vendors of satellite TV sell programming, often on a pay-per-view basis. They can't afford to give that air time away for free. That means that pay-per-view programming (and, in fact, usually all programming) has to be encrypted before transmission to the satellite and decrypted on reception from the satellite. The set-top box has to have some way of tracking which programs the viewer has requested, evaluate whether to grant the request (is the customer paid up, is the program available for the location, etc.), and know how to disable the channel when the program ends so that the viewer doesn't get a free look at the following program. All of this information has to be securely transacted, and the mechanisms used have to be reasonably secure against attempts at signal piracy.

By comparison, if you are a Web site owner or Web site developer trying to earn revenues from the "sales" of your Java applets, applications, and classes, you want some measure of protection. Ensuring that those outside of your customer base cannot receive the product that you have to sell is what copy protection is all about. Java provides protection from the unwanted intrusion, reception, or insertion of trap doors, Trojan horses, or lookalike receivers. Ideally, this means more competitive pricing, better overall service, and greater reliability and investment protection. As well, Java's security options give you a means of protecting your customers from receiving, running, or distributing potentially hazardous software, which increases the value of your product.

Portability is as important in consumer electronics as it is in Web site programming. You probably have a lot more computers in your house than you think. Your VCR, your stereo, your microwave oven, and any number of other gadgets might be controlled by a microprocessor (often a chip such as the Zilog Z80, which was the brains of an earlier generation of computers—and yes, that does mean that someday your microwave oven might have a Pentium inside it).

As home automation becomes more popular, these devices will need to start talking with each other, and it's more likely that a software standard will evolve than that all of the manufacturers of consumer electronics will adopt a common hardware platform. Just as Java was designed to tie together disparate electronic devices, it now is being used to integrate the various hardware platforms that people use to connect to the World Wide Web.

Portability is one of Java's strongest selling points. Because of the "middleware" layer of the Java virtual machine, any Java class can run on any machine that Java has been ported to (excluding, of course, the occasional Java version incompatibilities, such as occurred between the last alpha and version 1.0).

Portability is realized at two levels. Not only are applets portable from machine to machine without recompilation, but the Java interpreter and Java Virtual Machine also have been specifically designed and constructed to be portable across hardware architectures. You do have to recompile the interpreter and virtual machine for new chip sets. However, because the virtual machine specification is public and source code is available, this is a less onerous task than you might think.

If it is your intention to make money porting Java to new platforms, then you need to license Java from Sun. This process includes specific legal rights and restrictions and is best spelled out in sufficient detail by referencing the Java home pages at *http://java.sun.com*. Sun Microsystems is concerned with porting Java to the most popular platforms, including the Mac and the various I386 operating systems (Windows, Windows 95, Windows NT), but other ports (such as one for Linux and another for the Amiga) are being undertaken by other organizations. See appendix B for more information on Java ports.

MOTIVATION FOR CREATING JAVA

As Sun expanded its business interests to include the intelligent set-top box interactive video market, the first order of business was to provide a software infrastructure that would allow service providers to offer truly interactive TV. As well, the software interfaces and objects themselves had to be compact, robust, and easy to update or replace.

The initial work in developing this software, which eventually birthed Java, was done in C++. There's nothing that unusual about using C++ for this kind of work. The problem is that the C++ language doesn't exactly lend itself to bug-free coding.

Today's smallest computing devices are being endowed with ever increasingly complex and numerous lines of embedded code—often real-time C code or C++ code that is rife with bugs. Some experts estimate that there is one bug per 10 lines of code. This level of bugginess, although endemic, is not exactly good for customer relations. Unfortunately, vendors also are faced with market pressure to bring newer, flashier, and so-called better products out in what seems like less time. Nasty people, we consumers.

In trying to solve the vendors' problem of balancing quality control with realistic engineering schedules, the Java developers themselves ran into a number of problems that started with compiler technology limitations and resulted in the realization that what the team needed was a new language. At the risk of over simplification, it is accurate to say that the team took the best features of C++, discarded what they didn't need, and added some needed new capabilities.

During the design process, the developers were guided by the following goals:

- The language had to be easy to develop with, certainly easier to use than C++.
- The language had to be object-oriented.
- The language needed to be multithreaded so that multiple processes could run concurrently within a single program.

- Programs created with this language had to be reasonably crash-proof.
- Programs created with this language should clean up unused memory automatically, using a technique known as *garbage collection*.

EASE OF DEVELOPMENT

Java is designed to be a full-featured, robust programming language without many of the unsafe, complicated, and unused features of the C and C++. It uses a C-like syntax, so it is familiar to many programmers. Comments are similar to C/C++, control structures are formatted comparably, and many of the keywords are identical.

This similarity to an existing, popular language is a passive enabler of rapid applet development (RAD). People familiar with C++ will be able to most rapidly port or develop applications in Java as they will benefit from being in somewhat familiar territory. However, non-C++ programmers might find the concepts rather vague or obscure at first. This book will attempt to impart enough real-world relevance so that almost anyone can implement first without fully understanding what's happening. Comprehension will come with time and most quickly when you realize that you want to modify existing code to accomplish some new functionality.

OBJECT ORIENTED

Java was designed to enable ease of development of object-oriented programming tasks and object-oriented systems. This distinction is important, as some object-oriented programming environments might make it easier to manage or implement a development process that already is too complex, but not necessarily make it easier to design and implement the task itself. What results, in many cases is a system so complex that, without the development tools at hand, code recyclers and code maintainers are as much at a loss to understand the systems that they're building as the legions of BASIC spaghetti-GOTO code writing fiends of the 1970s.

A competent Java programmer is far more likely to deduce what a given Java class or package is doing than an equivalently gifted C++

programmer trying to span all possible code paths and intended or unintended "side effects." All of this means that Java code is highly portable between programmers, which can have a significant benefit when it comes to getting the code out the door. In the world of software development, time to market is everything and is measured in days or weeks. In the marketplace of the Internet, time to market might eventually evolve into hours or (heaven forbid) even minutes.

Most importantly, there are far fewer concepts and features to cope with in Java than there are in C++. It's not what's in Java; perhaps, it's what's *not* in Java. For example, take the total absence of pointers in Java. Beginner and not-so-clever programmers will no longer have to deal with mentally dereferencing data pointers of potentially different sizes—a very common source of significant bugs in C and C++ programs. Also, the all-too-clever programmer is prevented from traipsing through process memory and potentially system memory using pointer arithmetic.

As well, Java does not provide for structs, typedefs, #defines, or explicit memory deallocation. While some might argue that these missing features are what define languages such as C and C++, these features are not required to make a robust, full-featured object-oriented programming language.

> If you really can't live without the "missing" features of C and C++, you still have the option of linking in native code from your favorite C/C++ compiler. Doing so, however, defeats many of the best aspects of Java, including most portability features, security, and robustness. If your users are particularly concerned with security issues, they might not be willing to download your platform-specific callable libraries.

MULTITHREADING

Perhaps the one feature of Java that will create more fans than any other in both the programmer and end-user communities is the native multithreading support in Java

For example, if you're using the HotJava browser, it really is nice to be able to do something else while waiting for your content to be served to you. After all, you might be waiting for a particularly important application and its data, but there are all those other non Java-enabled

sites that you've been meaning to visit, and it's times like these when you can exploit the threaded nature of the HotJava browser.

Multithreading is best described as a much finer-grained version of multicomputing. In the 1970s and 1980s, one of the fundamental paradigm shifts in the commercial computer industry was the use of midrange and mini computer systems as general-purpose work servers that could perform many tasks at the same time. As these features migrated from the system level to the user level, people began to figure out that they too could make the system run a few of their applications concurrently. Even better, in a virtual memory multicomputing environment, many of these applications could execute at the same time by sharing access to the system memory and CPU. Each application had its own internal view of the system and of the memory map and could live and work symbiotically with other processes on the system by swapping internal memory maps and process stacks in and out of memory.

Java takes this multicomputing concept one step farther, offering per-process threads of control. Did you ever get thoroughly frustrated because your spreadsheet or word processor wouldn't run because it was spooling output to the printer? When using an operating system that supports threading, the programmer can create a spooling thread that frees the main application from waiting for the spooling to complete and instead returns control to the user immediately. However, threading methods vary widely between operating systems and generally are treated as extensions to a given programming language, creating discord in the software-development world.

Note: Java also will adapt to a multiprocessing environment, where there are multiple CPUs on the current system. In this manner, Java can execute several threads of control across multiple processors.

When using a language like Java that natively supports threading, writing threaded applications is much easier. Java threads are the same from platform to platform, and that means that Java threads can be debugged consistently from platform to platform. This is a huge win over C or C++, and even more so over Ada, which, despite its parallel and object-oriented origins, has managed to all but disappear from the radar screen of programming languages (except at the DOD).

ROBUST

One of the worst features of applications developed in C and C++ is the dreaded protected-memory access, where an application attempts to use a memory location it has no business using. It's as easy as dereferencing one pointer too many, and in Unix systems, it generally crashes the application and forces a core dump. In Windows, this kind of memory access is the justifiably hated UAE (Unrecoverable Application Error), euphemistically renamed to a General Protection Fault (GPF). The Macintosh will show you a cheery Bomb icon when you get a memory access fault, demonstrating again how important it is to have a sense of humor in this business.

Invalid memory access, by any name, is bad news. Depending on the type of fault and the operating system in use, you might get an application halt, the operating system itself might go on vacation (either of which can result in lost or corrupted data), and at the very worst, you might even catastrophically damage your hard drive (which is very hard to do, but not impossible).

In object-oriented vocabulary, this sort of condition is referred to as an *exception*, and it certainly isn't a graceful end to life. Java's ability to catch and handle exceptions gracefully within the language, as well as the absence of language features such as pointers, makes it inherently more robust. This stability is vital to the acceptance and future development of the language, as the people who start using Java content will not tolerate applets that can render their machines useless and result in lost and/or corrupted data.

AUTOMATIC GARBAGE COLLECTION

Automatic garbage collection is a memory-management feature that is most appreciated by developers but that ultimately benefits end users.

When dynamically allocated memory made its way into commercial programming languages, the resulting software became considerably more complex and powerful. Along with the benefits of dynamic memory allocation, however, came the plague of having to account for all the memory your application used during execution.

If you dynamically allocated memory to store, say, a linked list, and the list shrank considerably or simply wasn't needed anymore, you had to specifically free up that memory so that the same program (or another program) could use that space for other purposes. C and C++ programmers are required to do this or their applications end up using the entire system heap.

The failure to deallocate dynamic memory is also known as a *memory leak*. While the consequences to the program of having lost some small chunks of system memory aren't necessarily disastrous, the more blocks of memory that don't get deallocated, and the larger they are, the quicker they render the most powerful machine and operating system useless to the user. Memory leaks are the vampires of the software world, sucking the life blood out of computers and rendering the silicon soul a zombie until the eve of the next day—or the next reboot, which ever comes first.

Java solves this problem by implementing the concept of automatic garbage collection. Programmers are free to allocate dynamic memory through instantiation of run-time classes or explicit allocation as they always were. Now, however, they don't have to worry about deallocating previously allocated memory. Java does it for you with a garbage collector thread that actually manages the free space pool and reclaims space as it becomes available.

As users exercise the interfaces and classes of Java applets and applications, memory is allocated and automatically deallocated as the current execution thread leaves the scope of control and also leaves behind used data that needs to be reclaimed. By automating this process, Java virtually eliminates any chance of forgotten memory leaks.

The concepts of ease of development, object orientation, multithreading, robustness, and automatic garbage collection, taken individually, are all sensible and useful attributes of any programming language. Taken together, as in Java, they make for an immensely powerful and useful combination of features that makes the development process faster and safer and that improves the quality of the end product.

APPLETS, APPLICATIONS, CONTENT HANDLERS, AND PROTOCOL HANDLERS

At this stage of the game, it is important to make some vital distinctions about the following topics: applets, applications, and handlers. Just as there is a distinct difference between HotJava the browser and Java the language, so too is there a very similar distinction between applets and applications. As we have stated in previous chapters, the HotJava browser is written in Java and is an example of a Java application.

Applets usually are smaller pieces of Java code that can be loaded, interpreted, and run from the HotJava browser or any Java compatible browser.

Applications, such as HotJava, are standalone executable units that do whatever you want them to; however, they do not require a Java-compatible browser to execute, whereas applets do. An applet is a Java program that is run inside a Java-compliant browser, and is in fact an extension of the browser in the case of HotJava. A Java application is a Java program that is run outside of a Java-compliant browser; a perfect example being the HotJava browser itself.

Content handlers allow you a means of extending the capabilities of the Java-compliant browser. *Content* is any information that the browser retrieves from the Web server. An HTML document is one kind of content, an RTF (Rich Text Format) file is another, as is a GIF (Graphics Interchange Format) file. Some of these types are built into HotJava, but others will be added by third-party vendors or possibly by you. The whole point of having content handlers is to be able to extend the Java-compliant browser to handle new, as-yet-unforeseen data types.

When a Java-compliant browser encounters a content type that it doesn't recognize, it can load a class of precompiled content handlers (Java classes) that can process this content. This dynamically adaptive behavior is a strong testament to the extensible nature of Java applications.

Protocol handlers provide a means for a Java program to implement new protocols in a Java-compliant browser. A perfect example is dealing with 3D geometric content such as is used by the Virtual Reality Modeling Language (VRML). While VRML files are processed as new content via the content handler, the interaction and control software for the environment will most likely be implemented as a protocol of control commands. An example of this forms the basis for implementing a Java-based VRML parser and control application.

What's more, a Java protocol handler can not only deal with a standard definition of VRML behaviors and protocols, it also allows others to extend them with new protocols if they desire, which will be mandatory for the successful evolution of VRML or other 3D Web content solutions.

THE VISUALIZATION OF THE INTERNET

Although the Java language is designed to compete with other general-purpose languages and can be use to create large applications just as might be created with C or C++, we believe that the most important aspect of Java is its suitability to developing software for the World Wide Web and the subsequent visual representation, or visualization, of the Internet.

It's a curiosity that, in the computer world, information is increasingly being represented by graphic images. The instruction to save a file is replaced by a picture of a floppy disk, the instruction to print a file by a picture of a printer, and so on. These pictures, or icons, are intended to make the program easier to use. This progression is in sharp contrast to the evolution of written language, which moved from picture writing to more symbolic forms of representation. Whether this change is smartening us up or "dumbing" us down is open for debate, but clearly the Web is one of the forces moving us toward a more visual presentation of information.

Java represents a quantum leap in the Web's capabilities. Before Java, the kinds of information presented to users have been limited largely to the HTML specification, which is a relatively narrow and high-level set of standards for information presentation and formatting. HTML formats

text, displays graphics, and allows for limited kinds of user input, such as data-entry fields, tables, and clickable image maps. All that is well and good; however, when you compare the level of sophistication and complexity in Web documents to that of the vast array of software now available for personal computers, it becomes clear that the Web is, for all its cool graphics and happenin' hypertext, a somewhat primitive work (and play) environment.

In some ways, software development on the Web will parallel software development on non-Web platforms. For one thing, software application interfaces for personal computers already have been through a considerable transformation, from character user interfaces, (CUIs, pronounced "cooeys") to graphical user interfaces (GUIs, pronounced "gooeys"). Likewise, Internet software started out as CUI software, but the advent of the World Wide Web brought about a shift to Web GUIs. Java applet software enters the game at the GUI level, embedding itself in the browser's GUI.

Java brings the Web quite close to the same level of sophistication that the non-Web software industry enjoys by providing similar foundations for application development. While the Web still is limited by bandwidth and the restrictions inherent in multiplatform development, it offers a program setting unlike any other. You now can write software that is instantly available worldwide and that interacts with other Web sites worldwide.

History suggests that it's a mistake to assume that more technology is always better technology, so it's probably not the case that Java automatically will make the Web a better place. We might be in the information age, but as you've probably noticed, that usually means there's just more information around and not that it's necessarily better or more easily found information. As a Java programmer, however, you have the opportunity to use Java to make applications and information on the Web more understandable and easier to find.

THE JAVA DEVELOPMENT ENVIRONMENT

THE JAVA DEVELOPMENT KIT, or JDK for short, was released around the August/September time-frame in 1995. This coincided with the beta release of Java, taking it from alpha 1.3 to a beta release. Despite all of the best intentions, compatibility was broken between the two versions. However, the extent of this incompatibility was not devastating to Java's burgeoning popularity. To address the API breakages, the JDK provides a Unix SED script to convert Java code from alpha 1.3 to beta, which makes for a fairly painless transition, all things considered. If you do not have a version of SED available, sufficient documentation is provided that tells you exactly which things will need to change and gives examples, such as the HTML tags that identify applets. These things were to be expected in the alpha/beta transitions as Sun had said there would be changes in the API.

Although this book covers the 1.0 release of Java, the Java Development Kit on the CD-ROM consists of the beta version of Java. Because the CD-ROM had to be mastered before this book was completed, we were able to update only the manuscript to 1.0 compatibility.

The CD-ROM does not include a beta version of the HotJava browser. Instead, because this is a developers release, an applet viewer has been included as a sort of scratchpad to develop with instead of a full-fledged browser. As of this writing, Netscape is shipping a beta release of Netscape Navigator version 2.0 that allows you to execute Java beta and version 1.0 code (not alpha). A beta version of the HotJava browser is expected to debut before publication of this book and should be released as a supported software product from Sun some time in early spring of 1996.

SETTING UP THE ENVIRONMENT

For the time being, the development environment for Java developers will look very different, depending on the needs of the people and the project. This is another way of saying that you need to plan on finding

development tools that you like, and there are relatively few of them right now. Any development environment for a C-like language requires some basic workshop tools. You need a text editor or source-code generator to create Java source, or you can port existing code. If you don't have any custom code-generating facilities handy, you'll need to edit much of the Java code by hand. To get the latest information on what tools are available, visit the Java home page (at *http://java.sun.com*) on a regular basis and also check out the Java newsgroup, currently *comp.lang.java*. As of this writing, Borland and Sun have each announced plans to market Java code development products. Borland's will be an addition to their existing C++ development product, and Sun's will be the Java Development Environment (JDE) and currently is in beta evaluation with selected sites.

Java is a very new language, and as with the early stages of any language, it's not that uncommon to find yourself working on something that you think you should be able to buy off the shelf. Be patient, keep your electronic eyes and ears open, and you'll most likely find what you need. Every software development tool has to be written by someone, however, and a certain percentage of you will create tools that other will use.

If you have come up with a useful class or package or some other development aid and the quality of your work is good, consider making it available to others, whether on a paid or unpaid basis. Sun is sponsoring the first, possibly only, Java Cup International contest, while that contest might be over by the time you read this book, you will be able to benefit directly from it, as the source code and classes for all winning entries will be made available free of charge to anyone. This means that there will be an enormously rich selection of Java applets, applications, and utilities to pick from.

SOURCE-CODE EDITORS

As a relatively new programming language, Java doesn't yet have a fully integrated development environment, such as most of the popular

C/C++ compilers provide. Happily, Java programmers' needs are relatively simple because the development cycle is so straightforward. One thing that you will have to provide to do Java programming (at this stage, anyway) is a source-code editor.

PROGRAMMERS' EDITORS

The main requirement for any programming editor is that it save files as straight text. Most word processors save formatting information along with the text, which can only cause problems for compilers like javac.

Virtually all operating systems come with a usable text editor (such as NotePad, on the various versions of Windows) but these generally are basic in design and made for writing batch files and the like, not composing software. A good programmer's editor has features like configurable hot keys, macro capability, templates that automate common programming operations, and so on.

Some of the more popular programmers editors are Brief from UnderWare and Microsoft's Write or Word. As for Unix Java developers, it is safe to say that the majority of the Java code in existence was developed using **vi**, the visual text editor. EMACS is another good choice for Unix developers looking for an extensible, full-featured editor. Whichever editor you choose, it should be able to save files with four-character extensions (Java source files end with .java) and filenames should be saved in mixed case, if the operating system supports this feature.

HTML EDITORS

For the HTML authoring, if you aren't editing documents by hand as many still do, you should select an HTML authoring package that will allow you to define Java applet extensions that can be inserted into the HTML text wherever you want to insert applet tags. If this is not possible, it should at least be a trivial matter to search the HTML that it generates and insert the applet tags. Be warned that such modifications might make the document incompatible with the original authoring package when you go back to update it.

If you don't have an authoring tool, you certainly can use your programming editor to create HTML documents

If you're following the exercises in this book, you should have the following basic directories created for development:

- Solaris: /home/wspwj/src/java
  /home/wspwj/jdk
- Windows 95: \wspwj\src\java
  \wspwj\jdk

THE JAVA COMPILER

The Java compiler for Windows 95/NT is javac.exe; for Solaris, it is simply javac. The compiler is found under the \jdk\java\bin directory in Windows 95/NT and under the jdk/java/bin directory for Solaris.

The command-line syntax is:

```
$javac [options] filename.java ...
```

javac compiles Java source code into Java classes (which are described later in this chapter, in the section "The Java interpreter"). You can specify more than one Java source file on the command line.

javac depends on the settings of three environment variables or resources:

- JAVA_HOME—Where Java is installed on the current machine
- CLASSPATH—The directory paths to be searched for other Java classes
- PATH—Your own search path should point to the bin directory of Java, found where JAVA_HOME points to.

If a Java source file references a class, the source for which is not found in any of the Java files passed to the compiler, the compiler looks in the directories (separated by semicolons) specified in the **CLASSPATH** environment variable. At this point, the compiler is looking for compiled class files rather than source, because it's only capable of working on the current source-code module.

> If you want, you can set **CLASSPATH** so that it points to only the classes subdirectory, but you will need to fully qualify the class names according to the directory where they can be found. For example, the Applet class is found in the directory /classes/java/applet, and if you reference the class as simply Applet, the compiler will not find the class file. If, on the other hand, you reference the class as java.applet.Applet, the compiler will look in the **CLASSPATH** directory for the subdirectories that make up the full class specification.

There are two versions of the compiler: javac.exe and javac_g.exe. The latter is a nonoptimized version of the interpreter that is intended for use with the Java debugger. The options listed in the following section apply to both compilers unless otherwise noted.

COMPILER OPTIONS

The Java compiler takes a number of command-line options, the usage string returned with:

```
$ javac -help
```

returns the following:

```
$ javac [-g][-O][-debug][-depend][-nowarn][-verbose] [-classpath path][-
nowrite][-d dir] file.java...
```

The compiler takes the options:

-G The **-g** option adds debugging information including line numbers and, if optimization is turned off, local variable information to the class file.

-O The **-O** option turns on optimizations. Static, final, and private methods will be compiled inline to save time on method calls, this implies that method code can be duplicated and your class files will be larger.

-DEBUG The **-debug** option generates a trace of compiler activity. Unlike **-verbose**, which lists, which classes and source files are being processed, this flag produces a complete dump of methods and declarations. For example, the HelloWebWorld applet discussed in chapter 4 produces the following listing when compiled with **javac HelloWebWorld.java -debug**:

```
public void paint(java.awt.Graphics);
{
  (method g#0 drawString "Hello, WebWorld!" 25 25);
}
[check field HelloWebWorld.paint]
{
  (method g#0 drawString "Hello, WebWorld!" 25 25);
}
{
  (method g#19494568 drawString "Hello, WebWorld!" 25 25);
}
[check field HelloWebWorld.<init>]
{
}
{
  (method super <init>);
  {
  }
}
[inline field HelloWebWorld.paint]
[inlined field HelloWebWorld.paint]
(method g#19494568 drawString "Hello, WebWorld!" 25 25);
[code field HelloWebWorld.paint]
[inline field HelloWebWorld.<init>]
[inlined field HelloWebWorld.<init>]
(method super <init>);
[code field HelloWebWorld.<init>]
```

-NOWARN The **-nowarn** option turns off compiler warnings only.

-VERBOSE The **-verbose** option displays all and any messages about what source and class files are being processed by the compiler, and whatever else the compiler writers decided to spit out with the **-v** flag enabled, such as the amount of time taken to load a class. The verbose listing for HelloWebWorld is as follows:

```
[parsed HelloWebWorld.java in 490ms]
[loaded f:\java\classes\java\applet\Applet.class in 110ms]
[checking class HelloWebWorld]
[loaded f:\java\classes\java\awt\Panel.class in 0ms]
[loaded f:\java\classes\java\awt\Container.class in 160ms]
[loaded f:\java\classes\java\awt\Component.class in 280ms]
[loaded f:\java\classes\java\lang\Object.class in 50ms]
```

```
[loaded f:\java\classes\java\awt\image\ImageObserver.class in 0ms]
[loaded f:\java\classes\java\awt\Graphics.class in 110ms]
[wrote HelloWebWorld.class]
[done in 1710ms]
```

-CLASSPATH *PATH* The **-classpath** option overrides the **CLASSPATH** environment variable. Use **-classpath** to specify a list of directories, separated by semicolons, that java.exe will search for required classes. For example, on Solaris:

```
/cdrom/mcgraw-hill/web/classes:/home/fiske/src/java/classes:
/home/harms/classes
```

On a Windows machine, the slashes will be backslashes, and the colons will be semicolons. If you are using only standard Java classes in their default subdirectories, you probably will find it easiest to just set **CLASSPATH** to java/classes and not bother with the **-classpath** option.

-D *DIRECTORY* The **-d** option specifies a new root directory for the class hierarchy. The compiler begins its search for classes in the root directory and looks in subdirectories as specified in the class names. For instance, in the declaration **java.awt.Graphics**, the compiler will look in the root class directory (usually java/classes) for a subdirectory java, and in that directory a subdirectory called awt, and in awt for a class file called Graphics.class. As with the **-classpath** option, if you're only using the standard Java classes in their default subdirectories and have set **CLASSPATH** to point to the java/classes directory, you don't need to fiddle with this option.

THE JAVA APPLET VIEWER

Although it's possible to run a Java applet with the Java interpreter (which is discussed later in this chapter), for most of your testing, you'll find it to your advantage to set up a Web document that has an HTML Java specific applet tag corresponding to the applet that you are testing and run the document through the applet viewer. Most applets are designed to be run in the context of a Web document, and you'll want to be sure that the applet is correctly positioned and is being fed the correct parameters. The CD that accompanies this book provides a complete test-bed for all the source code examples that we'll be using throughout the text and should help you get it right when you go to use these examples in your own works.

Note: The AppletViewer is offered by Sun in the absence of a beta-or 1.0-capable HotJava browser. In the future, the HotJava 1.0 browser will take precedence, and the AppletViewer will (most likely) disappear altogether.

CREATING A WEB TEST DOCUMENT

A Web test document can be quite simple. The following listing shows one such document, which displays the "Hello, WebWorld" applet when the file is read with a Java enabled browser, as discussed in chapter 6:

```
<html>
<head>
<title>Hello WebWorld Demo</title>
</head>

<body>
<h1>Hello World</h1>
<hr>
A simple application that displays the text "Hello World."
<p>
<applet code=HelloWorld.class Width=100 Height=100>
</applet>
<p>
</body>
</html>
```

That's really all you need for a simple application. The only parts of this HTML document that concern the applet specifically are the **<applet>** tag and the following **</applet>** tag. Note that this example is for version 1.0 of Java; the alpha 3 version used a slightly different format for the **<applet>** tag.

RUNNING THE APPLET VIEWER

To view an applet with the applet viewer, make sure you've created an HTML document with a valid applet tag and use the following command:

```
$ AppletViewer document
```

If you're viewing a document that has a tag for the HelloWebWorld applet, you'll see the applet viewer as shown in Figure 5-1.

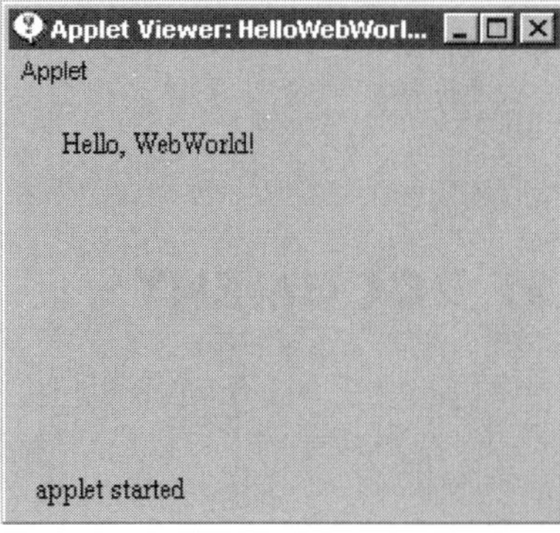

Figure 5-1
The applet viewer running the HelloWebWorld applet.

The following is a list of the AppletViewer debugging options:

- **!!**—Repeat the last command
- **catch <*class id*>**—Break for the specified exception
- **classes**—List the currently known classes
- **cont**—Continue execution from the breakpoint
- **down [*n*] frames**—Move down a thread's stack
- **dump <*id*> [*id(s)*]**—Print all object information
- **exit** (or **quit**)—Exit the debugger
- **help** (or **?**)—List the commands
- **ignore <*class id*>**—Ignore when the specified exception occurs
- **list [*line number*]**—Print the source code
- **load *classname***—Load the Java class to be debugged
- **memory**—Report memory usage
- **methods <*class id*>**—List a class's methods
- **print <*id*> [*id(s)*]**—Print an object or field
- **resume [*thread id(s)*]**—Resume threads (default: all)
- **run <*class*> [*args*]**—Start execution of a loaded Java class
- **step**—Execute the current line
- **stop in <*classid*>.<*method*>**—Set a breakpoint in a method

- **suspend [*thread id(s)*]**—Suspend threads (default: all)
- **thread <*thread id*>**—Set the default thread
- **threadgroups**—List the threadgroups
- **threads [*threadgroup*]**—List the threads
- **up [*n* frames]**—Move up a thread's stack
- **use [*source file path*]**—Display or change the source path
- **where [*thread id*]** ¦ all—Dump a thread's stack

THE JAVA UTILITIES

In addition to the essential compiler and applet viewer/debugger, Java also comes with a set of utilities that can be useful once you get beyond the basic applet programming stage. The utilities include the header/stub utility, the disassembler, the API documentation generator, and the Java interpreter.

THE HEADER/STUB UTILITY

The Java header stub utility for Windows 95/NT is javah.exe; for Solaris, it is simply javah. It is found under the \jdk\java\bin directory in Windows 95/NT and under the jdk/java/bin directory for Solaris.

The javah utility is provided for producing C header (.h) and (optionally) stub files, which are needed if you want to link C code into a Java applet. (See chapter 16 for more on linking in C code.) The header files contain a struct with fields corresponding to the class's instance variables.

The command-line syntax is:

```
javah [options] classes...
```

Usage:

```
javah [-v] [-version] [-l filename] classes...

javah [options] classname ...
```

The ***classname*** specifies which Java classes the utility is to produce headers and/or stubs for.

There are two versions of the header utility: javah.exe and javah_g.exe, which is a nonoptimized version of the interpreter intended for use with debuggers. The options listed in the following paragraphs apply to both versions of the utility.

javah takes the following options:

-O *OUTPUTFILE* The **-o** option concatenates all generated header and/or source files into the file specified by ***outputfile***.

-D *DIRECTORY* The **-d** option specifies the directory where javah is to create the header and/or stub files.

-TD *DIRECTORY* The **-td** option specifies the directory to be used for temporary files. If this option is not specified, javah will create the files in the directory specified by the **%TEMP%** environment variable (or, if that variable does not exist, in **%TMP%**). If no temp directory is found, javah will create the directory \tmp.

-STUBS The **-stubs** option causes stub files to be generated in the Stubs directory or the directory specified by the **-d** option.

-VERBOSE The **-verbose** option causes javah to display messages indicating the status of the files that it is generating.

-CLASSPATH *PATH* The **-classpath** option specifies a list of directories, separated by semicolons, that java.exe will search for the required classes. If this option is not used, javah will look in the directories listed in the **CLASSPATH** environment variable (which was discussed earlier in this chapter).

THE JAVA DISASSEMBLER

The Java disassembler for Windows 95/NT is javap.exe; for Solaris, it is simply javap. It is found under the jdk\java\bin directory in Windows 95/NT and under the jdk/java/bin directory for Solaris.

The command-line syntax is:

```
javap [options] files...
```

Usage:

```
javap [-v] [-c] [-p] [-h] [-verify] [-verify-verbose] files...
```

javap takes the following options:

-C The **-c** option prints out the disassembled code for each of the methods in the class. These instructions are JVM (Java Virtual Machine) code statements.

-L The **-l** option prints out line and local variable tables.

-CLASSPATH *PATH* The **-classpath** option specifies a list of directories, separated by semicolons, that java.exe will search for the required classes. If this option is not used, javah will look in the directories listed in the **CLASSPATH** environment variable (which was discussed earlier in this chapter).

THE API DOCUMENTATION GENERATOR

The Java documentation generator for Windows 95/NT is javadoc.exe; for Solaris, it is simply javadoc. javadoc is a utility that prepares an HTML document from your Java source file that documents the classes defined in that source file.

The command-line syntax is:

```
javadoc [options] package | filename.java
```

javadoc takes the following options:

-CLASSPATH *PATH* The **-classpath** option specifies a list of directories, separated by semicolons, that java.exe will search for the required classes. If this option is not used, javah will look in the directories listed in the **CLASSPATH** environment variable (which was discussed earlier in this chapter).

Javadoc is the utility that Sun used to build the documentation files for the API, and you can use it in just the same way that they did to create your own HTML documents to supplement the standard set.

Some of javadoc's output is entirely dependent on the source code. The class hierarchy diagram, the constructor index, and the method index are all created from the source, but all of the descriptive information is taken from comments. To make your documentation come out looking like the standard documentation, you'll primarily need to add appropriate variable comments in expected format. The following text is from java/src/canvas.java:

```
/**
 * A Canvas component. This is a generic component which
 * needs to be subclassed in order to add some interesting
 * functionality.
 *
 * @version   1.5 08/17/95
 * @author Sami Shaio
 */
```

The first line of the variable comment section is vital; javaprof detects the beginning of a documentation comment section by the slash followed by two asterisks. Place the text before the item that you want to be described. In this example, the text appears just before the Canvas class declaration.

> Because javadoc is creating HTML documents, you can incorporate any HTML tags that you want into your source code comments, and they will be passed along by javadoc. You should avoid using heading tags, however, because the API documentation has its own heading format.

You'll also note several tags in the comment that begin with the @ character. Such tags are given special formatting. As of the time of writing, they include:

SEE *CLASSREFERENCE* The *classreference* parameter can be a class name, such as **Applet** or **String**, or a fully qualified class name, such as **java.applet.Applet**. You also can append a class's method name by separating the class and the method with a pound sign, as in **String#toUpperCase**.

VERSION *TEXT* The *text* parameter is any information that you want to display for the version information.

AUTHOR *NAME* The *name* can be any text that you want to use to describe the author (be nice!). You can have multiple author tags; all of them will be collected under a single heading.

The **@author** and **@version** tags cannot appear inside variable comments, but **@see** tags are allowed.

Once you've created your HTML documentation, you'll want to copy it to the /adidocs directory along with all of the standard documentation. If you want to keep your docs separate, you'll need to make a subdirectory under that directory called images and copy in all of the .GIF files from the /adidocs/images directory, as these are used to create the nice little colored markers for the various sections of the documentation.

THE JAVA INTERPRETER

The Java interpreter for Windows 95/NT is java.exe; for Solaris, it is simply java. It is found under the jdk\java\bin directory in Windows 95/NT and under the jdk/java/bin directory for Solaris.

The command-line syntax is

```
java [-options] class
```

The ***class*** parameter specifies which Java class is to be interpreted. Java classes can take optional arguments. The class name must come after the options so that any arguments can be passed to the class by the interpreter. Because every applet ultimately is a class based on the app class, it's quite accurate to say that an applet is the same thing as a class. An applet actually is an extension of the Applet superclass. However, you also might want to execute a class that is part of the Java class library, in which case it's not accurate to say that a class is the same thing as an applet. For the sake of clarity, then, this discussion of the Java interpreter will use the term *class* to refer to the compiled Java code that is interpreted.

Java classes that the interpreter can use are always in an intermediately compiled, bytecode format. This is different from a purely interpreted language, such as BASIC or Lisp, which actually reads source code and translates at runtime. With intermediate classes, most of the overhead of parsing, syntax, and semantic checking already is done for you, thereby increasing performance significantly over true interpreted languages.

You use javac.exe, the Java compiler, to compile *filename*.java source files into compiled Java classes that are in a Java-specific bytecode format, much like object code from a C or C++ compilation (except as noted in the following discussion on interpreter options).

There are two versions of the interpreter: java.exe and java_g.exe. The latter is a nonoptimized version of the interpreter that is intended for use with debuggers. The options listed in the following paragraphs apply to both interpreters unless otherwise noted.

The java options include:

-HELP The **-help** option prints out a list of available commands.

-V, -VERBOSE The **-v** and **-verbose** options cause the interpreter to display a message (through stdout) each time a class is loaded. When you're encountering some unexpected behavior, it can be quite helpful to see which parts of the library actually are being used. This is a poor man's batch tracing tool. Some bugs are found more quickly when you can run through a long series of classes looking for a pattern.

-DEBUG The **-debug** option enables Java debugging.

-NOASYNCGC The **-noasyncgc** option turns off asynchronous garbage collection. The process that does garbage collection runs on a separate thread, and if you disable it with this option, no garbage collection is done until the thread is invoked manually or the program runs out of memory. See the section in chapter 4, "Automatic garbage collection."

-VERBOSEGC The **-verbosegc** option prints a message when garbage collections occur.

-CS, -CHECKSOURCE The **-cs** and **-checksource** options check the date/time stamps of the Java source file against the class file. If the source file is newer, it compiles the source before loading the class.

-SS *X* The **-ss** option sets the stack size for C code threads. (See chapter 16 for more information on linking C code with Java.) Use the same method for specifying memory amounts as for the **-oss** option. The default value for C threads is 64K. It is not recommended that you try to tweak this, because this draws from the total system pool, which should be substantially larger than the Java heap.

-OSS *X* The **-oss** option sets the stack size for Java code. Every new Java thread created while the class executes will inherit ***x*** bytes of stack memory. As with the **-ms** option, you can use **k** to specify kilobytes and **m** to specify megabytes. The default value is 400K. If you know the size of the largest required stack, you can use this as a tuning parameter to minimize memory usage.

-MS *X* The **-ms** option specifies the number of bytes to be allocated to the garbage-collected heap. Use a simple number to allocate actual bytes, use the number followed by **k** (with no intervening space) to allocate kilobytes, or use the number followed by **m** to allocated megabytes. The default value is 3MB.

-MX<*NUMBER*> The **-mx** option sets the maximum Java heap size.

-D<*NAME*>=<*VALUE*> The **-d** option sets a system property.

-CLASSPATH <*DIRECTORIES SEPARATED BY COLONS*> The **-classpath** option specifies a list of directories, separated by semicolons, that java.exe will search for the required classes.

-PROF The **-prof** option generates profiling data. This tells you how much time your program is spending where, which can be a big help in improving the performance of an applet. It's not unusual for a program that runs very slowly to do so because a small portion of the code is improperly designed or should be translated to native instructions at runtime. The alpha version of Java included javaprof, a profiling "pretty printer," but this utility was not included with the release used at the time of this writing.

-VERIFY The **-verify** option tells the interpreter to apply bytecode verification tests to all classes, not just those loaded by the class loader (i.e., over the network).

-VERIFYREMOTE The **-verifyremote** option tells the interpreter to apply bytecode verification tests to those classes that are loaded by the classloader (i.e., over the network). This is the default setting, on the assumption that those classes that already exist on your computer are known to you and therefore are not likely to contain malicious hacked code.

-NOVERIFY The **-noverify** option turns off all bytecode verification.

-VERBOSEGC The **-verbosegc** option tells the garbage-collection thread to print out a message anytime it throws out some trash (i.e., frees up memory).

-T The **-t** option generates a trace file of virtual machine instructions executed. This option is available only with java_g.exe.

In addition to the **-classpath** option, you also can set the search path for user-defined classes with the **CLASSPATH** environment variable. As with **-classpath**, directories are separated by semicolons. The **-classpath** option overrides the **CLASSPATH** environment variable.

SUMMARY

As a complete program development environment, Java currently is something other than fully integrated, although this is understandable given that the language still is quite young. The only part of the development environment that you, as a programmer, absolutely have to come up with is a source code editor (OLE will be included in the forthcoming JDE), and the only two kinds of files that you have to create with that editor are Java source files and at least one HTML document that you can use, in conjunction with the applet viewer, to try out your applets. If you're writing Java applications rather than applets, you don't need either the HTML document or the applet viewer, and you can use the Java interpreter instead.

For most developers, writing applications will be a cycle of making source-code changes, invoking the javac compiler, then testing the results either via the applet viewer or the Java interpreter.

Java does come with a couple of handy utilities, particularly the javadoc documentation generator, which lets you (almost) automatically create HTML pages that describe your classes. C/C++ programmers who want to link in native methods will want to use the header/stub utility. Java also includes a disassembler, for those who are in the habit of taking things apart.

As Java matures, the development environment will become more integrated and more capable. Sun and other companies are at work on visual design tools, class browsers, and the like. Java programming is only going to get easier and faster from this point on.

ESSENTIAL JAVA APPLET PROGRAMMING

THIS CHAPTER will introduce you to the fundamental issues of Java Web site programming, including the choice between applet and application programming and Java's object orientation, all in the context of Java's version of the standard, not to say predictable, "Hello, World" program (or, in our case, the "Hello WebWorld" program).

APPLET OR APPLICATION PROGRAMMING?

The first choice that you have to make when approaching Java programming is what kind of program you want to produce: an applet or an application. *Applications* are full-fledged Java programs that can be run standalone (via the Java interpreter). When you create Java applications, you are using Java the same way that you would use any other programming language. If you can write a program with Smalltalk or C++, chances are that you can write it with Java. Such programs reside and execute locally on the user's computer. Although applications could be transferred over the Internet, such transfer would happen the same way that you'd obtain any other non-Java software, probably via FTP. You'd then have to install and run the software yourself.

Java applets, on the other hand, are specialized Java programs that are designed to be embedded in Web pages, transmitted over the Web, and executed via a Java-capable browser on the user's computer.

Although Java is one of the most significant application programming languages to come along in recent years, the focus of this book is on Java as a tool for enhancing the World Wide Web. That means starting with applet programming rather than application programming.

It is possible and sometimes necessary to write Java applications that communicate with Java applets (as you'll see in Part 3 of this book). However, as a place to begin learning Java, applets have certain advantages over applications.

Unlike applications, applets have certain preset requirements (they are called via the APP HTML tag, and they conform to certain restrictions imposed by the browser execution environment, such as the need to

automatically shut down when the page that they belong to is no longer being viewed, and so on). Even the simplest of applets contain considerable predetermined functionality. All that code has been fully tested, so you have a reliable base on which to build your own programming.

Enough preliminaries—on to the code!

THE "HELLO, WEBWORLD" APPLET

It's an admittedly questionable ritual, but it seems that all new programming languages have to prove themselves by greeting the world with a small (or sometimes not-so-small) program that displays a cheery "Hello, World" message on the screen. The code in Figure 6-1 is an applet that displays "Hello, WebWorld" (none of the applets in this book are so pretentious as to assume the entire world is watching).

Figure 6-1 The "Hello, WebWorld" Java applet.

```
//
// Sample HelloWebWorld applet
//
import java.applet.Applet;
import java.awt.Graphics;

public class HelloWebWorld extends java.applet.Applet {
        public void paint (Graphics g) {
                g.drawString("Hello, WebWorld!", 25, 25);
        }
}
```

To create this Java applet, you'll need to either type the listing shown in Figure 6-1 into your source editor (being sure to save it as a text-only file) or, if you're in a big rush, copy it from the /cdrom/mcghill/Sparc/Tutorial or \cdrom\mcghill\x86\Tutorial directories on the CD-ROM. Don't worry right now if you don't understand what all of the statements mean; we'll get to the details shortly.

Assuming that you've typed in the source, save the listing that you've just created as HelloWebWorld.java. This is a Java source file that will

become a compiled, self-contained Java applet. If your operating system supports mixed-case filenames, take particular care to type the filename exactly as shown or the compiler will have trouble finding the source file (assuming you're following the tutorial instructions exactly). For the same reason, type the listing exactly as shown, as the resulting .class filename will be taken from the class name.

Compile the HelloWebWorld.java file into a runnable HelloWebWorld.class file by executing the following from the command prompt:

```
javac HelloWebWorld.java
```

If you run into problems compiling the file, be sure that you've typed it in exactly as shown and that your search path and the CLASSPATH environment variable are set up correctly. If the compile is successful, you also will need a short HTML test document with an appropriate **<applet>** tag, such as the one shown in Figure 6-2.

Figure 6-2 A short HTML test document (TESTBED.HTML) suitable for running the HelloWebWorld applet.

```
<title>Hello WebWorld Demo</title>
</head>
<body>
<applet code="HelloWebWorld.class" width=362
height=210>
</applet>
<p>
```

To see the HelloWebWorld applet in action, make sure that the HelloWebWorld.class file exists and is in the current directory. To run the applet, execute the following from the command prompt:

```
AppletViewer TESTBED.HTML
```

You should see the AppletViewer execute the applet from the testbed document, as shown in Figure 6-3.

This small Java applet demonstrates a number of fundamental concepts and techniques in Java programming. If you're familiar with C++, you should find the listing relatively easy to follow. If not, the following notes offer some explanation.

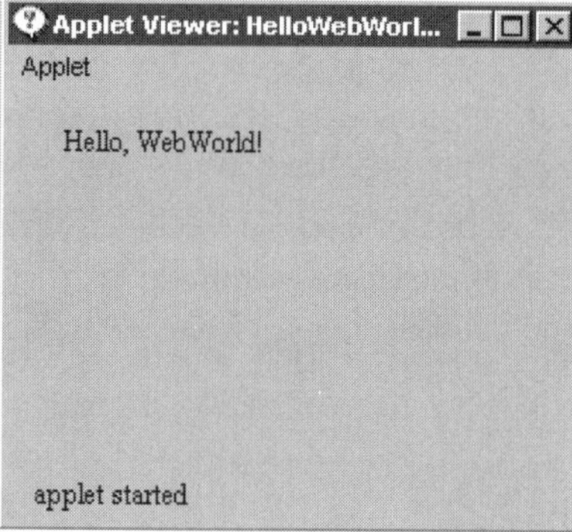

Figure 6-3
The HelloWebWorld applet in action.

ADDING SOURCE COMMENTS

As you might have guessed, the first three lines of the program listing are comments only. Java supports C++-style commenting. Any text following a double-slash is ignored by the compiler, as is all text contained between a slash-asterisk and the following asterisk-slash. Therefore:

```
//
// Sample HelloWebWorld applet
//
```

and

```
/*
 * Sample HelloWebWorld applet
 */
```

both have identical results. In the second example, the asterisk in front of the text is for readability only. Commenting your code is good practice, even if you're not expecting someone else to have to read and understand your code.

THE IMPORT STATEMENT

This applet listing begins with two **import** statements, which let the compiler know that this applet makes use of compiled Java code (also known as a Java class) from another source. The **import** statement really is just there to let the compiler know what class names are available; the actual code within the class is going to be referenced later in the applet's source code listing.

As discussed earlier in this chapter, a basic Java applet (and this one is about as basic as you can get) has to embody quite a bit of functionality, and there's no sense in making you, the programmer, write this code or even forcing you to see what the code does. Instead, all of the Java applet code (and all of the other standard Java functionality) is precompiled into .class files and kept in various subdirectories under the classes subdirectory of your Java directory.

Every applet, therefore, will have at least the following **import** statement:

```
import java.applet.Applet;
```

An unadorned applet does very little other than take up space on your Web document, so you'll need to add some additional code to make it do something useful. In this case, you want the applet to display the text "Hello, WebWorld." As it turns out, the code that places text on an applet is contained in the java.awt.Graphics class, hence the need for the second **import** statement:

```
import java.awt.Graphics;
```

THE CLASS DEFINITION

The **import** statement makes the compiler aware of the existence of the Applet class. However, how do you go about actually making use of that code? In a non-object-oriented programming language, you'd have to make a physical copy of the source code for Applet and modify it to suit your needs. Because Java is an object-oriented programming language, however, you do something quite a bit easier: You create a derived class, or copy of the class, without duplicating the source code:

```
public class HelloWebWorld extends java.applet.Applet {
```

Let's dissect this line. The **public** keyword indicates that the class that you're creating is going to be visible to other classes. (It's possible to restrict a class's visibility, or *scope*, but all applets will have at least one class that is public.)

The **class** keyword defines this class as a new class, and the label that follows (**HelloWebWorld**) is the name of the new class. This label also is used to define the name of the class file. In this case, the compiler will create a file called HelloWebWorld.class (note the mixed-case filename, which exactly follows the class name in the source listing).

The **extends** keyword is followed by the name of the class that HelloWebWorld is going to be based on. **extends** is used because it quite logically indicates that the new class will have all of the capabilities of the Applet class, but will almost certainly add some of its own. This is called *inheritance* and is described in more detail a little later in this chapter. For now, all that you need to know is that you're basing your Java applet on a large quantity of tried and tested code, rather than having to write everything yourself.

THE TEXT OUTPUT CODE

All that remains of this applet is the code that writes out the text "Hello, WebWorld!":

```
public void paint (Graphics g) {
        g.drawString("Hello, WebWorld!," 25, 25);
    }
```

The first line of this code fragment is a paint function (or *method*, to use the proper terminology) that makes use of the graphics library to write out to the screen whatever information you care to put there. This is a very short code block because the applet is only printing out a single text string. Most applets will have somewhat more complex **paint()** methods. The code:

```
g.drawString("Hello, WebWorld!," 25, 25);
```

actually draws the text on the applet, in this case 25 pixels below and to the right of the upper-left-hand corner of the applet window.

That's all there is to a simple applet. Really understanding how the source code becomes the applet, on the other hand, demands at least a passing knowledge of the underlying concepts of Java programming, and that means learning about objects and object-oriented programming (OOP).

AN OBJECT-ORIENTED PROGRAMMING PRIMER

Most OO language tutorials start off at a very basic level. You might learn how to create a very simple object, how to enhance that object,

how to use that object to do quite simple things. In this book, you'll start learning about objects at the Applet level. Applets are one type of object. Applets also are fairly complex objects, but because you don't need to know much about their complexity to use them, they make an excellent example of the benefits of object-oriented programming.

Aside from starting with fairly well-developed objects, this part of the chapter will take you through the basic principles of object-oriented programming (OOP) in what might seem like a very brief period of time. If you've heard a lot about how difficult OOP can be to learn, relax. The basic principles of OOP aren't all that difficult to grasp. As with any other type of programming language, an OOP language like Java can take a long time to master, but you don't have to master Java to be productive. Expertise will come with time and practice. The purpose of this book is to help you get started on the right road in the shortest period of time.

If you've never done any object-oriented programming before, then you're in for a treat, because Java is one of the easiest (and safest) ways to learn about the object model. If you have some OOP experience, you'll find many of Java's concepts quite familiar. Either way Java is a pleasure to work with.

One of the Java design team's goals was to create an object-oriented language that was both easy to use and relatively fail-safe, both for the programmer and the user. As it turns out, these are complementary goals. Many of the features that make some OO languages (particularly C++) very difficult to learn are the same features that cause the nastiest bugs.

Nevertheless, there are a few OO concepts that it will pay you to understand well, and chief among these (naturally enough) is the idea of the object.

SOFTWARE AS OBJECTS

First of all, there really isn't anything that remarkable about the idea of a software "object." If you've done any programming, you've undoubtedly written code that could be defined as an object, whether you knew it or not. What is an object? For purposes of this discussion, think of an *object* as a unique, identifiable, self-contained portion of a program.

There actually are many more facets to objects than that, but it's a good place to start. A more pertinent question is why is an software object a good thing? One way to answer is by contrasting object orientation with another well-known (if not exactly popular) programming concept: spaghetti code.

AVOIDING SPAGHETTI CODE

Spaghetti code, particularly somebody else's spaghetti code, is every programmer's nightmare. This term is applied to code that has no obvious structure beyond a starting point. Once the code starts to execute, just about anything can and will happen, and the only way to find out is to start working your way down a "noodle" of code execution.

Early BASIC programmers often were terrific sources of spaghetti code, because early forms of the language were relatively unstructured. A program, more often than not, was one long unbroken series of instructions. Because almost all programs have portions that get called more than once, BASIC provided the deadly GOTO statement, which let you jump to any line at all, and the RETURN statement that sent you back to the point immediately following the GOTO. Throw in a dozen nested GOTOs, make half of them conditional on code in other "gone to" code, and if you could make it work, you had job security civil servants could only dream of, because no one but you would ever again be able to figure out what that code was supposed to do.

There's really no way you can use the term *object* to describe any part of such a program, unless perhaps you apply it to the entire program, in which case the term doesn't add any new meaning.

STRUCTURED LANGUAGES

Over time, researchers (undoubtedly motivated by having to maintain somebody else's spaghetti code) developed more structured programming languages. These languages (C is a good example) make it possible to put commonly used code into functions or routines. This compartmentalization makes the code more readable and maintainable; however, in many cases, if you look at the program as a whole, you still have a monolithic mass of code. There are individual blocks of code all right, but they all have to be able to communicate with other blocks of code, and too often they do this via shared, global data. The result is

that any given function, called in exactly the same way, can produce wildly different results at different times, depending on what other previously called functions have done with the global data.

What's worse is that, in an application of any size, there will be numerous duplicated blocks of code. While a well-designed program will have many functions that embody the most frequently used code and that could be considered a type of object, it's inevitable that the program will require minor variations on these functions that cannot be accommodated in a single code block. The more code that is duplicated, the harder the application is to maintain, because a bug discovered in one version of a duplicated block will have to be fixed in the others as well.

Structured languages are a great improvement over spaghetti code, but they clearly have their own limitations, most of which the object model addresses with some success.

OBJECTS, ENCAPSULATION, AND INHERITANCE

Object-oriented languages take all of the interconnected code of structured languages and break it down into separate, self-sufficient units called objects. One of the features of an object is its ability to contain both code and data. In and of itself, that's not such a big deal, because just about any language lets you create a self-contained function that incorporates data with the code. An object, however, is more like a collection of functions than a single function and normally is designed to deal with only the data that is contained within the object, rather than with shared global data. This combining of code and data in an object is called encapsulation.If you want an object to do anything, you need to communicate with it via the functions, or methods (as they are properly known) that belong to that object. The object is essentially self-contained; it has all the data it needs and all of the methods necessary to work with that data.

Because the way that the rest of the program interacts with the object is determined by the methods, you can make substantial changes to an object to improve or enhance its performance, without having to change any of the other objects that use it. This simplifies software maintenance (in theory, at least) because individual programmers can develop objects without having to know how they interact with the rest of the system.

Encapsulation addresses the problem of carving an application up into objects of workable size; another mechanism, *inheritance*, deals with the problem of code duplication.

INHERITANCE AND CODE REUSABILITY

In an OO language, objects are described in something called a *class hierarchy*. A *class* is a description of an object and not an object itself, whereas an object is an instance of a class. However, in practice, the distinction isn't all that important, and you'll probably find yourself using the term *class* to refer to the object described by that class.

At the top of the class hierarchy is a single, simple class from which all other classes are descended. Every class except the top-level class is a subclass of the class above it. A class that has subclasses is also known as a *superclass*. The big trick with classes is that they inherit all the features of their superclass. This has enormous consequences for code reusability.

If all classes did was inherit their superclass's definition, they wouldn't be a whole lot of use. Fortunately, they also can add new methods and data to that definition. As an example, if you have a class that contains all of the code required to display a file selection window, but under some circumstances you want to use this window to choose graphics files and display a preview of the selected file, you don't need to make a complete duplicate of the file selection class. Instead, you create a subclass of the file selection class. Because that subclass inherits the capability to select files, you only need to add to it the code required to display graphic images.

This inheritance means that any number of subclasses can share a common code base. If it turns out that there's a bug in one of the high-level classes that affects all of the subclasses, you can fix the bug and have all of the subclasses functioning correctly again. (That's the theory, anyway. In practice, because a subclass inherits the characteristics of all its superclasses all of the way back to the top level, or base class, it's not always obvious where to go looking for the problem code.)

In any OO program, you'll create one or more classes based on one of the classes in the class library, or on a class you created, which itself

might be based on a class in the class library, or on a class you've created, or...well, you get the idea. However, you want to be a bit careful about creating vast new hierarchies of classes, for the reason just mentioned: The bigger your hierarchy, the more difficult it can be to track down bugs.

Some languages support multiple inheritance, where a subclass can inherit properties from more than one superclass. Java allows only single inheritance, although you can achieve a form of multiple inheritance by using interfaces, which are discussed in chapter 11.

In Java, the top-level class is called java.lang.object. All objects in the Java class hierarchy are descended from this one class. As a top-level class, java.lang.object contains a number of methods that any class might at one time or another find useful. Some of these methods are:

- **clone()**, which creates an identical copy of the current class
- **equals()**, which compares the current object to a specified object
- **getClass()**, which returns the class of the current object
- **wait()**, which instructs the object to temporarily suspend whatever it is doing.

You can use these methods with any object in the Java class library.

POLYMORPHISM

Polymorphism is defined generically as the ability of an object to assume different forms. In object-oriented programming, polymorphism refers to the ability of an object to be treated as a member of more than one class depending on the situation. Polymorphism also refers to the mechanism by which a method can, at runtime, determine the class of an object and interact with it accordingly.

For example, suppose that you define a class to represent different types of vehicles. This Vehicle class will define many characteristics that are common to all vehicles: weight, color, length, and so on. In addition, this class also might define methods common to all types of vehicles. For this example, assume that **move** is defined as such a method. The vehicle class is shown in Figure 6-4.

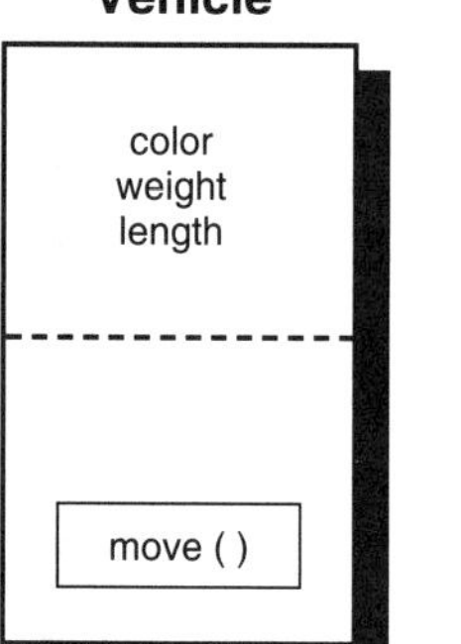

Figure 6-4
A simple Vehicle class.

Because generic vehicles aren't particularly interesting, you might create new classes that extend the basic Vehicle class by inheriting from it; for example, a car class. This new Car class inherits all of the characteristics of a Vehicle: color, weight, etc., as well as any method defined by Vehicle, like the **move** method. However, because cars move differently than other vehicles, the Car class defines a new **move** method that overrides the one that it inherited from Vehicle (see Figure 6-5). *Method overriding* occurs whenever a subclass defines a method that has the same name, return type, and number and types of arguments as the parent class.

> If you only change the return type of a method, the compiler will not recognize this as an override of the existing method and will generate an error. If all you want to do is change the return type, you'll need to either choose a new name for the method or alter the parameter list in some suitably nondamaging way.

Other subclasses of Vehicle can be defined similarly, each with its own way of moving, as shown in Figure 6-6.

The power of polymorphism is that a single method can be defined that can manipulate these related classes without having to define a specific method for each class. For example, a class might be defined that has a method that moves vehicles. This method, perhaps called **moveVehicle**, takes a Vehicle as one of its parameters and calls the vehicle's **move** method somewhere within. Through polymorphism, you can pass **moveVehicle** a Car, a Train, or a Boat, all of which are subclasses of Vehicle. When the object's **move** method is called, it will be the **move** method specific to Car, Train, or Boat that gets invoked. Conceptually, the object gets passed to the method as a Vehicle and "polymorphs" to a car, train, or boat on the fly.

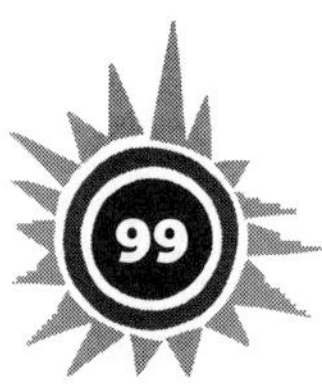

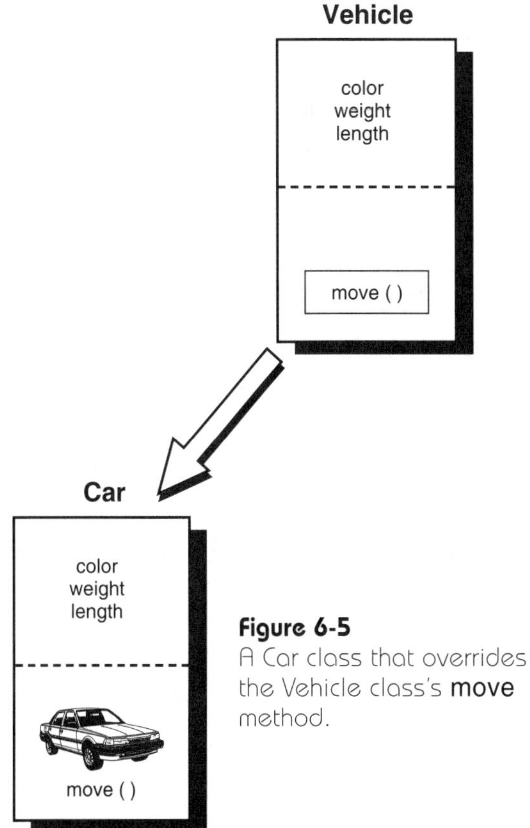

Figure 6-5
A Car class that overrides the Vehicle class's **move** method.

METHOD OVERLOADING

There are times when you might want to call the same method with different arguments. For example, you might want to be able to tell a Car how far you want it to move by passing an integer to the **move** method. We also might want to be able to specify a direction in addition to the distance:

```
aCar.move(2);          // move forward 2 units
aCar.move(5, "left");  // now move 5 units to the left
```

This can be accomplished by defining two different **move** methods in the Car class, each taking a different set of arguments. This concept of defining methods of the same name, but with different arguments or return types, is called *method overloading*. The appropriate "version" of the overloaded method is called, based upon the number and types of arguments.

Figure 6-6 Several subclasses of Vehicle with unique **move** methods.

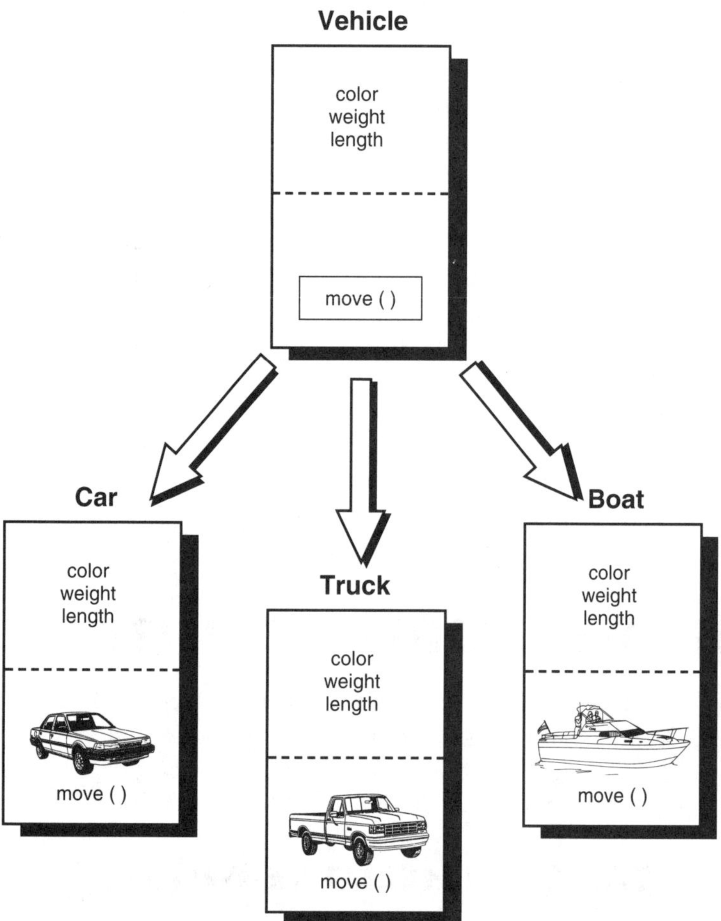

CONSTRUCTING AND DESTROYING OBJECTS

When you use a traditional structured programming language, you deal with exactly the source code that makes up a function. At run time, the compiled code that corresponds to that source is simply loaded into memory and executed. When you use an OO language, however, you are dealing with a code object that is made up of a certain amount of code that belongs to that object, plus a range of properties that are obtained from the classes that class/object is descended from. As a

result, the object has to be assembled at runtime from one or more pieces. Typically, OO languages use a special method, called a *constructor*, to assemble the object so that it can be used and use another method to destroy the object when the program is done with it.

In Java, object creation and destruction sometimes is done automatically, and sometimes you have to do it explicitly (well, we never said that this was going to be a complete cakewalk). Constructor methods are built into the classes, and objects normally are destroyed by the automatic garbage collection that's built into Java. The exceptions to this rule will be discussed as they come up.

There's a lot that goes in a Java application, by virtue of all of this hidden code that's tucked away in all of those superclasses. For the beginning Java programmer, one of the biggest hurdles is building a mental model of what's really going on, because we can guarantee that those few lines of code that make up a basic applet don't come anywhere near to telling you the whole story. With that in mind, let's take another look at the HelloWebWorld applet.

HELLOWEBWORLD REVISITED

If you've managed to read through the previous section of this chapter, you should now have a basic understanding of object-oriented programming concepts. It's time to apply those concepts, particularly inheritance and method overriding, to the HelloWebWorld applet.

INHERITANCE IN HELLOWEBWORLD

Take another look at the code fragment that declares the HelloWebWorld applet:

```
public class HelloWebWorld extends java.applet.Applet {
    public void paint (Graphics g) {
        g.drawString("Hello Web World!," 25, 25);
    }
}
```

As discussed earlier in this chapter, the first line of this fragment actually defines the new class HelloWebWorld as a subclass of the Applet class, which already contains a whole lot of functionality. By virtue of the statement:

```
public class HelloWebWorld extends java.applet.Applet
```

HelloWebWorld will automatically inherit the ability to stake out some space on a Web page as its own, write to the screen when it's on a visible part of the page, cease writing to the screen when it's hidden, and so on. None of that is hinted at in this source code; to know that's what's happening, you have to know about the superclass Applet (and, in fact, about all of the classes above Applet, all of the way to java.lang.object, the topmost object in the hierarchy).

> The period separator is used to indicate the relationship between class and subclass. In the declaration java.awt.Graphics, the Graphics class (which is concerned with drawing functions) is a subclass of the awt class, which is concerned with the broad issues of displaying and maintaining windows. Similarly, java.applet.Applet refers to the Applet class, which is a specialized subclass of the applet class.

All new subclasses add something to the classes that they're descended from, and HelloWebWorld is no exception. All of the modifications and additions to Applet that HelloWebWorld makes are contained in a block of code defined by a pair of braces. There can be other pairs of braces within that block of code; however, when you get to the brace that matches the one after the class declaration, you've come to the end of the code that makes up that class. In a simple applet, there will only be one class declaration, but there's no inherent restriction in the number of classes that can functionally make up an applet.

INSIDE THE CLASS—DATA AND METHODS

Within that class declaration, encompassed by the pair of braces, you'll see only two other kinds of declarations: data and methods. HelloWebWorld has no data and only one declaration, and that's for the **paint()** method:

```
public void paint (Graphics g) {
        g.drawString("Hello Web World!," 25, 25);
    }
```

Methods, like functions in other, non-OO languages, are simply blocks of code that perform some often-used function and that can take parameters and return values. The major difference between functions and methods is that methods belong to a particular class and act on

data that is part of that class, whereas functions can act on any data and don't necessarily have any inherent notion of belonging to a set of functions.

THE POLYMORPHIC PAINT() METHOD

Another difference between methods and traditional functions is that methods are inherited from the class's superclass. Consider the **paint()** method just listed. If you go back to Figure 6-1 and look at the entire code listing, you will not find any place where the **paint()** method actually is called. It looks to be just so much dead weight. The secret is that there is a **paint()** method that HelloWebWorld inherited from Applet. Because you've declared your own **paint()** method, your applet will call your method instead of its own inherited **paint()** method (which does nothing except draw a window background).

The **paint()** method is declared as a public method, meaning it can be called from outside the class itself. This is necessary because, although the HelloWebWorld class is an applet, it is essentially under the control of the HotJava (or other Java-enabled) browser, which will be controlling the applet via other method calls. The **paint()** method also is declared as void, meaning it does not return any value.

COMMONLY USED APPLET METHODS

Among the most important Applet class methods are those, like **paint()**, that are called automatically at certain times during the life of the applet and that serve essentially as placeholders for code that you write. These methods are the same C functions or C++ methods that you've had to write time and time again whenever you needed to initialize, handle errors, or perform housekeeping and process cleanup. In Java, applets automatically have these declared for them. These methods are covered in the following paragraphs.

PUBLIC VOID INIT() The **init()** method is called right after the an object of this class is instantiated or created by the runtime interpreter. The **init()** method is provided as a guaranteed initialization sequence for code that you always want to execute on class startup. **init()** is declared within the Applet class.

PUBLIC VOID START() By default, this method is called every time the applet's page is visited, even if the applet is not on a visible part of the page. It starts program execution or optionally starts a separate thread of execution. You can override the behavior of **start()** with many features that you, the applet programmer, will want to control; for example, rewriting the start method so that the applet begins to run only when the user performs a specified action, instead of immediately upon being visited or becoming visible in the browser. **start()** is declared within the Applet class.

PUBLIC VOID PAINT(GRAPHICS G) The **paint()** method is called whenever the applet becomes visible and draws the application's output on the screen. **paint()** is your opportunity to control first looks and appearances and is where you will want to focus a lot of attention for look and feel issues.

The **paint()** method is a little more complex than the **init()** method. Like **init()**, it is declared as public and void, for the same reasons, but it takes as its parameter the Graphics class.

In Java, parameters are passed as a pair of identifiers; the first part being the parameter type, and the second being parameter name. In the case of the **paint()** method, the type is the Graphics class (which was imported with the **import java.awt.Graphics** statement) and the name of the parameter is g, which is an instance of Graphics.

Unlike **init()** and **start()**, **paint()** is declared not in the Applet class, but two levels above Applet, in the container class. While **init()** and **start()** (and a number of other methods) are appropriate only to applets, **paint()** is useful to anything that has a visual representation. In Java, such things are called *components*.

PUBLIC VOID STOP() The **stop()** method is called when the user leaves the applet's page. It halts applet execution, or threads of execution that belong to this applet, unless otherwise specified (threads are discussed in more detail in chapter 15). **stop()** is declared within the Applet class.

PUBLIC VOID DESTROY() The **destroy()** method is called when the applet is discarded, as when the applet's page is not the current page

and the document cache is flushed, or when the applet is reloaded. **destroy()** is where a majority of the automatic garbage collection is performed and is used to free resources used by applets if they're of a sort that the automatic garbage collection won't take care of. **destroy()** is declared within the Applet class.

WHAT'S MISSING?

If you already have some programming experience, you might think that something's missing from the applet examples in this chapter. After all, there is no explicit starting point, or main() method, that marks the beginning of code execution. Applets actually do have a main() method, but it's another one of those methods that's tucked away and automatically executed when the applet is run. Applets are run when a browser encounters an applet tag in a Web document, and the <applet> tag always specifies a Java class, so there's never any doubt about where the code should start to execute. Even if you have two classes in a single source file, the compiler will create a separate .class file for each of them.

It's quite possible to have a main() method in an applet. In later chapters, you'll see examples of this approach, which does give you a greater measure of control over when and how a particular class (or set of classes) is used. Applets with an explicitly declared main() method actually are applications, but that doesn't prevent you from using them in Web documents, exactly as you would an applet without a main() method.

GETTING TO THE FUN STUFF

There are a lot of aspects to Java programming, and the remaining chapters in this part of the book cover the most commonly used features of the Java language. If you want to get a head start on the fun stuff, have a look at Part 3 of this book, which discusses some real world Java applets. If you find yourself referring back to this part of the book to understand what's going on in Part 3, well, that's just fine. Sometimes a finger on a page is the best hypertext link of all.

7 DECLARING AND EVALUATING DATA

ALL PROGRAMMING LANGUAGES work with data of some sort, and good languages offer a useful variety of data types. Java's data types include various kinds of numerics, strings, booleans (true/false values), and arrays. Often a particular programming problem can be addressed with a number of different data types, but if you consistently choose the best type for the situation, you'll have programs that are more compact, faster, and less prone to bugs caused by overrunning the capacity of the data type.

In this part of the book, you'll learn about the actual data types themselves, how they are declared, how they are implemented, etc. However, to *use* any of the data that you declare, you will use the corresponding Java classes to create and manipulate the data. These classes are rather extensive and are discussed in some detail in chapter 11, "Using Java classes." This chapter introduces the data types themselves and the available methods of evaluating that data.

INTEGER DATA TYPES

All integer data types are signed, meaning that the values can be positive or negative. Keep in mind that, because signed variables devote one bit to the sign, they only have half the positive and negative numeric range of unsigned variables. If you're accustomed to using unsigned data types similar to Java's signed types, be sure to choose a type with a sufficient maximum value. For example, if you wanted to keep an array larger than 255, don't use a byte, which has a minimum value of –128. You would need to declare an array index of type short, whose size is 16 bits, because that is the next larger integer data type available. A 16-bit signed value can take on positive values greater than 255 and negative values less than 255.

Table 7-1 shows Java's integer data types and the amount of storage, in bits, that each type uses (there are typically 8 bits to a byte).

TABLE 7-1 Java's signed integer data types.

Data type	Size	Min value	Max value
byte	8 bits	–128	127
short	16 bits	–32768	32767
int	32 bits	–2147483648	2147483647
long	64 bits	very small	very big

FLOATING POINT DATA TYPES

Java has two floating point data types: float and double. (See Table 7-2.) Both of these data types are implemented as a subset of the IEEE 754 standard. Paraphrasing from the Java Language Specification, the following differences are mentioned with respect to Java's implementation of the IEEE 754 standard:

- Nonstop arithmetic—Java will not throw exceptions on the following conditions: invalid operation, division by zero, overflow, underflow, or inexact.
- Rounding—Java rounds inexact results to the nearest representable value, with ties going to the value with a 0 least significant bit. Java rounds towards zero when converting floats to integer.
- Extended formats: Java does not support extended formats, except that the data type double serves as single-extended.

TABLE 7-2 Java's floating point data types.

Data type	Size	Min value	Max value
float	32 bits	1.401298e-45	3.402823e+38
double	64 bits	4.940656e-324d	1.797693e+308d

The following example allocates two kinds of floating point variables, which we'll call **flt** and **dbl** for single and double precision, and the four integer sizes, which we'll call **byt**, **shrt**, **intgr**, and **lng** for byte, short, integer, and long:

```
float   flt;

double  dbl;

byte    byt;

short   shrt;

long    lng;
```

Note that, because Java is designed as a 32-bit language, the default integer size also is 32 bits.

STRINGS, CHARACTERS, AND LITERALS

Java implements strings with the String classes and uses the Unicode character set, which is designed to accommodate the vast majority of known written languages. Unicode uses 16-bit characters, which allow for a much greater possible number of characters, rather than the 8-bit characters of the ASCII and ANSI character sets, so Java strings are stored as arrays of 16-bit unsigned integers. Strings are null-terminated, the same as C and C++ strings; that is, all strings are terminated with and delimited by the value of 0.

Character literals are single characters and have the type char. They are written enclosed in single quotes. Note that by using escape sequences, it is possible to actually represent a single character as a sequence of two or more characters. At compile time, the Java compiler recognizes the escape sequence and converts the text to a single character representation.

The following are examples of character literals:

- **'0'**—The Unicode character 0.
- **'a'**—The Unicode character *a*.

- **'Z'**—The Unicode character *Z.*
- **'\n'**—The Unicode representation for a "new line" character—used when printing to standard output.

String literals usually are used to assign a value to a Java string class. The format of a literal is zero or more characters enclosed in double quotes.

The following are examples of string literals:

- **"This is an example of string literal"**
- **"This is another"**
- " " (This is an empty string)

Java uses the String and StringBuffer classes to implement character-array functions as you might be familiar with in C or C++. The String class is for objects that you will declare only once and will never change. This is identical to a string constant in C or C++. The StringBuffer class is for strings that will change content and possibly size. Both these classes are discussed in chapter 11, "Using Java classes."

ARRAYS

An *array* is simply a collection of identical data types that can be referenced by an element number, which also is known as a *subscript.* In Java, arrays actually are objects and are descended directly from the base Object class, making them what are called *first class objects.*

Here is a simple example of declaring a 32-character array in Java:

```
int javarray[] = new char[32];
```

(Recall that characters in Java are based on Unicode, so any such string will automatically take up *twice* the space, in this case 64 bytes for a 32-character array. This will take some getting used to.)

All array objects have a variable called .length, which allows you to determine the current size or number of elements in the array. You can

reference this variable by appending .length to the name of the array, as in this example:

```
int mylength;
mylength - javaarray.length;
```

You can create arrays of any data type, as well as arrays of objects that are themselves composed of data type primitives. While Java does not support multidimensional arrays, you can declare an array of an array, as in this example:

```
short Table[][] = new short[5][7];
```

Arrays are a key part of Java's ability to produce secure code. In many languages (notably C and C++), pointers, which are variables that "point" to memory locations, are used to manipulate or access data. The problem with pointers is that the compiler has little, if any, control over the runtime usage of that pointer. For example, the compiler might not be able to determine precisely what memory location a dereferenced and potentially coerced pointer might access.

Java uses arrays instead of pointers and always enforces subscript checking to make sure that only a valid array element is being addressed. An attempt to reference an out-of-range subscript results in the program throwing an exception. Just about the only way that a Java program could reference an out-of-range subscript would be if the bytecode had been hacked. Unless directed otherwise by the person using it, the Java interpreter will validate the bytecode format that all classes obtained from another location (i.e., over the Internet) to make sure that the code itself has not been modified into a format that the Java compiler does not permit.

> Like most modern languages, array subscripts in Java start at 0, so the last element in a 10-element array will have a subscript of 9. The length variable, however, returns the actual number of elements, so if you want to use that variable to ensure that you are referencing a valid subscript, use the value array.length–1 as the maximum subscript.

OPERATORS

There's no point in having data if you can't tell what it is or manipulate its value. The following tables cover the operators available in the Java language. The most commonly used operators are discussed in more detail in the following section.

Table 7-3 lists the binary integer operators. Table 7-4 lists the unary integer operators. Table 7-5 lists the integer relational operators and produce boolean results. Table 7-6 lists other operators that are recognized.

TABLE 7-3 The binary integer operators.

Operator	Description
+	Addition/concatenation—Used to add two numbers or combine two strings
–	Subtraction—Used to subtract one number from another
*	Multiplication—Used to multiply two numbers
/	Division—Used to divide
%	Modulus—Returns the remainder of a division
&	Bitwise AND
|	Bitwise OR
^	Bitwise XOR
<<	Shift bits left
>>	Shift bits right
>>>	Shift bits right and fill empty bits with zero

TABLE 7-4
The unary integer operators.

Operator	Description
–	Integer negation
~	Bitwise complement
++	Increment by one
––	Decrement by one

TABLE 7-5 The integer relational operators and produced boolean results.

Operator	Description
<	Less than
>	Greater than
<=	Less than or equal to
>=	Greater than or equal to
==	Equal to (This is only a test of equality, not an assignment! See the section titled "Assignment versus evaluation.")
!=	Not equal to

TABLE 7-6 Other operators that are recognized.

Operator	Description
|=	Bitwise OR, result assigned to left-hand variable
&=	Bitwise AND, result assigned to left-hand variable
/=	Divided by, result assigned to left-hand variable
*=	Multiplied by, result assigned to left-hand variable
−=	Subtract from, result assigned to left-hand variable
>>=	Bitwise right shift, result assigned to left-hand variable
<<=	Bitwise left shift, result assigned to left-hand variable
%=	Modulus, result assigned to left-hand variable
^=	Bitwise XOR, result assigned to left-hand variable
+=	Addition, result assigned to left-hand variable
>>>=	Shift bits right and fill empty bits with zero, result assigned to left-hand variable
&&	Logical AND
||	Logical OR

ASSIGNMENT VERSUS EVALUATION

The = operator is an assignment operator. The == operator is an evaluation operator. The first one actually changes the value of the memory location associated with the variable on the left side of the operator; the second one simply evaluates whether one side of the operator is equal to the other and returns the boolean result, true of false. These operators are potentially the source of much confusion because, if not used properly, your code will not work quite the way that you might have intended. Simple assignments, such as:

```
a = 7;
```

will work as you'd think; the value 7 is assigned to the variable **a** on the left hand side of the = operator. On the other hand, many programmers continue to assume that the code fragment:

```
if (a = 7) {
```

would only evaluate to true of the variable **a** has the value 7; however, the real result is that the value 7 is being assigned to the variable, so the expression will always be true.

While the syntax of most of the other operators will prevent you from making this kind of mistake, it is worth pointing out this common but crucial oversight.

ADDITION AND SUBTRACTION OPERATORS

The simple addition subtraction operators are + and –, and they work just the way they always have:

```
a = b + c;
a = b - c;
```

Java also supports auto-increment addition and subtraction and supports prefix and postfix usage. The following statements are all valid:

```
++a;
a++;
—b;
b—;
```

The first line, **++a**, implements prefix auto-incrementing and will *first* increment the variable **a** by one, *then* return that value if being evaluated. Incrementing often is used within loops to keep track of the number of iterations of the loop. The second line, **a++**, uses postfix auto-incrementing and will return the current value of **a** first if being evaluated, *then* increment the variable **a**. The third and fourth lines show that the same rules hold for subtraction.

The **+=** (plus equal) and **−=** (minus equal) notation is supported for shorthand increments and decrements. The following examples will result in a being increment by four and b being decremented by 5:

```
a += 4;
b -= 5;
```

instead of having to write:

```
a = a + 4;
b = b - 5;
```

THE MULTIPLICATION AND DIVISION OPERATORS

The basic multiplication operator is *, and the division operator is /. For example:

```
a = b * c;
a = b / c;
```

Like the addition and subtraction operators, both operators implement the ***=** (star equal) and **/=** (div equal) shorthand notation:

```
a *= b;
c /= a;
```

THE MODULUS OPERATOR

The modulus operator is **%** and is pronounced "mod." Although it isn't the most common of operators, it is one of the most useful. The modulus operator returns the *remainder after division* of the specified variable. Essentially this says perform the division but, instead of returning the dividend, return the remainder:

```
b = 23;
a = b % 20;
```

The variable **a** will receive a value of 3. A typical use of the modulus operator is to return a day of the week from a date stored as the number of days since some arbitrary starting point. The code:

```
DayOfWeek = Date % 7;
```

will return a value from 0 to 6, which can be used to obtain a day name from a seven-element string array.

As shown earlier, the modulus operator can be combined with the equal sign to "mod equal" a new value, as in:

```
a %= 20;
```

BITWISE OPERATORS

If you're doing a lot of business application development, it's unlikely that you'll spend much time at the bit level. The one exception is that methods that take parameters (arguments) sometimes are structured to take more than one value per parameter. Because the minimum size of a data element passed to a method is a single byte, there are a minimum of eight options that can be passed within that parameter, if the method's designer stores one meaningful value per bit. You then can pass in just the flags that you want by combining the appropriate constants with bitwise operators.

If you are a "bit twiddler," one of those curious souls with a passion for never using two bits where one will do, Java gives you the tools that you need to carve up the bytes.

The **&** operator is a bitwise AND. The two data items that it operates on are compared bit by bit. If the two bits are both true (value of 1), then the corresponding bit in the resulting data item will be true.

The | operator is a bitwise OR. The two data items that it operates on are compared bit by bit. If either one of the two bits is true (value of 1), then the corresponding bit in the resulting data item will be true.

The **^** operator is an exclusive bitwise OR. Like the bitwise OR, the data items are compared bit by bit, but the resulting bit will be true only if one of the two bits being compared is true. If both bits are false or both bits are true, the resulting bit also will be true.

The **<<** and **>>** operators shift the bits in the variable one bit to the left or right, preserving the sign of the variable (remember that all Java integers are signed). The **>>>** operator shifts bits to the right but fills in the new bit spaces with zeros.

RELATIONAL OPERATORS

Relational operators indicate relative values of tested variables. These are **<**, the less-than operator; **>**, the greater-than operator; **<=**, the less-than-or-equal operator; **>=**, the greater-than-or-equal operator; and **!=**, the not equal operator.

OPERATOR PRECEDENCE

The precedence of operators is very important; it defines the rules of order for how expressions are parsed and what operations are applied when, thereby providing a *deterministic* behavior that the Java compiler writers can implement and the programmer can adhere to.

From the *Java Language Specification, May 1995,* the operators from highest to lowest precedence are:

```
. [] ()
++ — ! ~ instanceof
* / %
+ -
<< >> >>>
< > <= >=
== !=
&
^
|
&&
?:
```

```
=  op=
,
```

If you're in doubt about the order in which operators are evaluated, remember that you can always use parentheses to force a particular order of evaluation. In any given statement, all expressions that are inside parentheses are evaluated before they are used in any other expression. According to operator precedence, the statement:

```
a = 12 + 3 * 3;
```

will evaluate to 17 (12 + 9) because multiplication has a higher precedence than addition. The statement:

```
a = 12 + (3 * 3);
```

will evaluate in exactly the same way but has the advantage of being a little more readable. The statement:

```
a = (12 + 3) * 3;
```

will come out to 45 (15 * 3) because the parentheses have forced a different precedence of operations.

SCOPE

Data declarations can appear anywhere in a Java program where a program statement is allowable, but where they appear determines their scope, or visibility. Unless otherwise tagged, all declarations are valid within the scope of the current block of code, as delimited by braces (code blocks are discussed in more detail in chapter 8). As in C and C++, data declarations also are valid within the head of **for** statements, and there are examples of that kind of declaration in chapter 8 as well.

Consider the following simple (and relatively useless) applet that does nothing but demonstrate what happens when you attempt to use a byte variable to hold a number that it is not designed to hold:

```
import java.applet.Applet;
import java.awt.*;
```

```
public class Test extends Applet {
  public void paint (Graphics g) {
    int j = 0;
    for (byte i=0 ;j < 130;i++) {
     j++;
     System.out.println(i);
    }
  }
}
```

If you compile and run this applet, you'll see that it prints out the value of the byte variable **i**, up to and past the point at which it exceeds the values that it is capable of handling. (Don't worry too much if you don't understand the **for** loop; that's covered in chapter 8, "Statements, expressions, and control flow.") The variable **j** is used so that the **for** loop knows when to exit.

The variable **j** is declared inside the block of code that defines the applet's **paint()** method. That means that you can add code anywhere inside the method that uses **j**, and the compiler will like you. If you attempt to reference **j** outside that method, say by adding the code:

```
System.out.println(j);
```

in the **update()** method, you'll get a compiler error that says:

```
Undefined variable: j
```

because the compiler does not see a declaration for **j**. If you put the declaration for **j** just after the class declaration:

```
public class Test extends Applet {
  int j = 0;
```

the compile will succeed, because **j**'s scope now is the entire class, including both the **update()** and **paint()** methods.

> You should make a practice of restricting the scope of declarations as much as possible. Increasing the scope of a variable increases the likelihood of unexpected interactions between classes and methods.

SUMMARY

Java gives you most of the data declaration tools of an advanced programming language. Most noticeably missing from the language is any kind of pointer declaration. However, as chapter 3 points out, this is a deliberate omission to enhance Java's stability and ensure the secure execution of applets that otherwise might use pointers to go wandering through system memory. Although there are some programming tricks that you won't be able to do with Java, in most cases, this loss will be more than offset by the stability of the applets and applications that you create.

8 STATEMENTS, EXPRESSIONS, AND CONTROL FLOW

IN CHAPTER 7, "Declaring and evaluating data," you learned about the various data types that are available and a means to operate on them in Java programs. Computer programs, however, are made up not just of data, but also of instructions that manipulate that data. All computer languages need some sort of convention for structuring those instructions, and in this chapter, you'll learn about Java's program statements and expressions.

PROGRAM STATEMENTS

In Java, as in C/C++, individual instruction are called *statements* and are the fundamental building blocks that all Java code is built on. Simple statements are delimited by the semicolon character. For example, the code:

```
g.drawString("Hello Web World!", 25, 25);
```

which is part of the HelloWebWorld source code listing from chapter 6, "Essential Java applet programming," is a complete statement that draws the quoted text in an applet's display window. If the terminating semicolon is not present, the compiler will assume that the following line of text is part of the statement just as if it were on the same line as the beginning of the statement. The Java compiler applies the same rules for white space, line continuation, and token delimiters as the C preprocessor for C and C++.

GROUPING STATEMENTS TOGETHER

Few programs are made up of just a series of consecutive statements. More often, statements are grouped together so that they can be easily executed when a certain condition is met or because they are used together to accomplish a particular purpose. Statements grouped together are called a *block*, and blocks of Java code are delineated by a pair of braces.

This is an example of a block of code:

```
{
  Dimension d = size();
  g.setColor(Color.black);
```

```
  int xoff = d.width / 3;
  int yoff = d.height / 3;
  g.drawLine(xoff, 0, xoff, d.height);
  g.drawLine(2*xoff, 0, 2*xoff, d.height);
  g.drawLine(0, yoff, d.width, yoff);
  g.drawLine(0, 2*yoff, d.width, 2*yoff);
}
```

Because Java inherits its source code structure from C/C++, the readability of the source code is in large part up to the programmer. Like C/C++, Java doesn't care about all of the white space (including paragraph marks) that make the code readable to our eyes. From the compiler's perspective, this code:

```
import java.applet.Applet;
import java.awt.*;
public class Test extends Applet {
  public void paint (Graphics g) {
    int j = 0;
    for (byte i=0 ;j < 130;i++) {
     j++;
     System.out.println(i);
    }
  }
}
```

is completely identical to this code:

```
import java.applet.Applet;import java.awt.*;public class Test extends
Applet {public void paint (Graphics g) {int j = 0;for (byte i=0 ;j <
130;i++) {j++;System.out.println(i);}}}
```

Now, which of these source files would you rather work with?

There are some conventions in C/C++ programming (and therefore in Java programming) that make the code a little difficult for beginners to read. One of these is that code blocks are seldom laid out in the form:

```
           {
  a bunch of source code
}
```

More often, the style used is:

```
(if this statement is true, execute the following code){
 a bunch of source code
}
```

For example, you'll see the applet **paint()** method usually declared like this:

```
public void paint (Graphics g) {
  // do something
}
```

The opening brace is at the end of the method declaration, and by convention (in this book, at least), the closing brace lines up with the beginning of the line that contains the opening brace.

If you're new to this coding style, you might find it helpful sometimes to rearrange the braces so that you can easily see where code blocks begin and end. That same code fragment could just as easily be written:

```
public void paint (Graphics g)
{
  // do something
}
```

Remember, just as the compiler will let you take out line breaks, it won't care if you put in some line breaks either (as long as you don't dismember any statements in the process).

Note that, while individual statements within the code block generally terminate with a semicolon, method declarations (which begin a code block) and statements that are used to determine if a code block will execute do not themselves terminate with semicolons. They are terminated by the code block itself.

EXPRESSIONS IN JAVA

Expressions are the application of operators to data and are how you turn one thing into another thing. While chapter 7, "Declaring and evaluating data," didn't discuss expressions, most of the examples in that chapter make use of expressions to get across the purpose of a given operator. If you haven't read chapter 7, you should quickly flip back and take a look at the list of operators supported in Java as well as the precedence of operations. If you have some experience with C or C++, you'll find the treatment of expressions familiar.

This section discusses the application of operators to specific kinds of data, such as integers, booleans, floating point values, arrays, strings, and objects.

INTEGER EXPRESSIONS

Integer expressions simply are the use of whole number data types that are declared as type **int**. There are some special notes regarding expressions involving integers of mixed sizes. By default, the result of any integer expression is of type and size **int**. When an expression involving integers of different sizes is evaluated, the result is always **int**, unless any of the data in the expression is of type **long**, in which case the result of the expression is always returned as a **long**. This implies that operations on bytes and shorts will always return a result of type and size **int**, not **short** or **byte**. The following code segment demonstrates several common integer expressions:

```
byte     byteVal
short    shortVal;
int      intVal;
long     longVal;

intVal = 1;        // Sets 32-bit integer equal to 1.
byteVal = 1;       // Sets 8-bit integer equal to 1.
shortVal = 1;      // Sets 16-bit integer equal to 1.
longVal = 1;       // Sets 64-bit integer equal to 1.

intVal |= intval + 1;        // bitwise or
if (intVal || shortVal)      // logical or
intVal &= intval + 1;        // bitwise and
if (intVal && shortVal)      // logical and
```

BOOLEAN EXPRESSIONS

Boolean expressions return either true or false when evaluated at run time. You should use boolean expressions consistently, and we strongly suggest that you avoid double negative boolean expressions, which are very confusing. By naming your boolean variables consistently, you will avoid creating awkward program statements that can be very difficult to read, as in this example:

```
int   redFlagSet = 1;
int   greenFlagNotSet = 1;
if ( !greenFlagNotSet && redFlagSet)
```

Trying to deduce what "not not set" means can be very confusing. Rewriting the code as:

```
int   redFlagSet = 1;
int   greenFlagSet = 0;
if (greenFlagSet && redFlagSet)
```

yields a more readable result.

Boolean expressions can be combined with other boolean expressions to yield some fairly complex statements, such as:

```
int   done;
int almostDone;
int nearlyDone;
int totallyDone;
if ((almostDone || nearlyDone) && (!totallyDone || !done))
   getItDone();
```

This says that, if you are almost done or nearly done and you are not totally done or not even done, you'd better get it done. This is the algorithm that the authors of this book used to determine whether to go out for pizza or order in and continue working on the manuscript.

FLOATING POINT EXPRESSIONS

Floating point numbers have a number of uses in a general-purpose programming language. However, due to the large number of issues surrounding their proper use and implementation, they are not as straight-forward as simpler data types. That is not to say Java complicates the matter; Java follows the IEEE 754 floating point specification. The real problem with floating point expressions is floating point expressions, which are not as accurate as, say, binary-coded decimal expressions. The much-publicized flaw in early yields of the Pentium chip troubled many people who would no doubt be terrified to learn that floating point math does not give absolute mathematical precision, even if the FPU on the processor is working flawlessly.

The following operations are allowable on floating point numbers of both single and double precision: – (unary negation), +, –, *, and /, as well as the assignment operators, +=, -=, /=, and *=. The ++ and — auto-incrementing operators add and subtract 1.0 respectively. In the

case of mixed precision expressions (single and double), the result and the operation are evaluated as double precision.

Java does not produce floating point exceptions. Instead, in the case of underflow, Java generates *NaN*, which stands for Not a Number and refers to floating point values too small to represent. In the case of overflow and division by 0, Java will yield *Inf*, which stands for infinite or indeterminate result.

For complete details regarding floating point issues, you are recommended to read the IEEE 754 floating point specification, as well as the Java Language Specification 1.0 from Sun Microsystems, which documents implementation specific issues.

ARRAY-BASED EXPRESSIONS

Arrays are operated on using the traditional subscripting method, which will return the value of the nth object in the subscripted array location. Arrays can be accessed only within the bounds of their array size, which is available in the return value of array.length.

Arrays are always allocated memory at runtime and are created with the new operator:

```
int i[] = new int[12];
```

creates an array **i** of 12 elements. A multidimensional array of 3×4 elements would be declared as:

```
int j[][] = new int[3][4];
```

When you reference an array of arrays, you need to specify all of the subscripts. The subscript range is checked at runtime, not compile time. Issuing a statement like:

```
j[12] = 5;
```

where j is an array of less than 13 elements (remember that the first array element is 0, not 1) will generate an array-out-of-bounds exception.

OBJECT EXPRESSIONS

Objects can be used in expressions to test for membership in a specific class or subclass of a given class. The **instanceof** binary operator is used to perform the test, as in the following example:

```
if ((battleShip instanceof Armada) || (battleShip instanceof Fleet))
```

This expression tests to see if the object battleShip is either an instance of the Armada object or an instance of the Fleet object.

CONTROLLING PROGRAM FLOW

One of the most useful features of higher-level programming languages such as Java is the ability to use a reasonably logical, if not natural, vocabulary to control how program flow is to be organized and executed. The constructs that Java uses should be familiar to most programmers and already known to C/C++ programmers. If they're new to you, you should be able to get the idea from a close reading of this section.

THE IF...ELSE STATEMENT

Perhaps the most commonly used program flow construct is the **if** statement, which is optionally paired with one or more **else** statements. A simple **if** statement looks like this:

```
if (a==b) {
  j = 4;
}
```

The expression in parentheses following the **if** is always evaluated to a boolean (true/false) result. If the result is true, the code inside the braces will be executed. The expression can be as complicated as you like and can include method calls.

The simple **if** statement is sufficient if you are just trying to decide whether or not to go down one path of execution. If, however, you want to take an alternate path when the expression evaluates to false, use an **if...else** construct:

```
if (a==b) {
  j = 4;
}
else {
  j = 5;
}
```

If either code block is short enough to be contained on a single line, you can dispense with the braces entirely. The previous code fragment also could be written as:

```
if (a==b) {
  j = 4;
}
else j = 5;
```

A slightly more involved version of **if...else** allows you to test more than one expression:

```
if (a==b) {
 System.out.println("a is equal to b");
}
else if (a==c){
 System.out.println("a is equal to c");
}
else if {a==d){
 System.out.println("a is equal to d");
}
else {
 System.out.println("no match found");
}
```

In this example, all of the **else**s (except the last one) have been replaced with:

```
else if (expression)
```

The **if...else if** construct executes differently from a series of **if** statements. In an **if...else if** construct, as soon as one of the expressions is evaluated as true and the code following that expression has executed, program execution jumps to the end of the **if...else if** chain. If you attempt to build a similar test out of a series of if statements, each **if** statement will execute in turn, whether or not one of the **if** expressions is true.

THE SWITCH STATEMENT

If you have an expression that can evaluate to one of a large number of integer values, it usually is best to use a **switch** statement rather than a lengthy series of **if...else if** statements. A **switch** statement evaluates its argument, which is either an integer or an integer expression, then jumps to the **case** label that has a matching constant integer value. Execution in the **switch** statement continues from that label until a **break** statement is encountered or until the end of the **switch** statement is reached. For example, if an integer variable **x** could take on even values between 2 and 10, you could use a **switch** statement like the following:

```
switch(x) {
  case 2 :
    k = 37;
    break;
  case 4 :
  case 6 :
    k = .0035;
    l = 123;
    break;
  case 8 :
    k = 42;
  case 10 :
    l = 2;
    break;
 default :
    k = 0;
    break;
}
```

Take a look at the **case 4** line in the previous example. If **x** evaluates to 4, execution will continue with the first statement reached after the **case 4** label. In the example, that is the assignment of .0035 to **k** after the **case 6** label. Now look at the **case 8** label. If **x** has the value of 8, execution will proceed with the **k = 42** line, then continue on past the **case 10** label, falling through to the **l = 2** line. The **break** statement will complete the **switch** statement whenever it is encountered. Finally, if **x** evaluates to any number other than 2, 4, 6, 8, or 10, the execution jumps to the **default** label.

Note: The order of the labels in a **switch** statement is arbitrary. The **default** label, if used, typically is put at the end but can legally occur anywhere in the **switch** statement. If you put the **default** label at the end, you might be tempted to forgo the **break** statement because

execution will fall through to the end of the **switch** statement anyway. Avoid this temptation. You never know when someone might add another label after the default, and you probably don't want execution to fall through into their code by "default."

THE WHILE LOOP

Java provides several kinds of loop constructs that let you execute the same code repetitively. One of these constructs is the **while** loop, which continues to execute as long as the expression named in the **while** statement continues to evaluate to true:

```
while (i < 100) {
  i = getNewValue();
}
```

If the expression is false when the program reaches the **while** loop, the loop will not execute at all. If you require the loop to always execute at least once, you'll either need to ensure that the expression will evaluate to true when the loop begins or use the **do...while** loop.

THE DO...WHILE LOOP

The **do...while** loop is another variation on the **while** loop, with the **while** condition test at the end of the loop. This means that the loop always executes at least once:

```
do {
  i = getNewValue();
} while (i < 100);
```

With both the **while** and the **do...while** loop, you should be careful that you ensure that the condition that terminates the loop becomes true. There are few things more embarrassing to a programmer than unintentionally putting a program in an infinite loop. This loop will never terminate because the programmer (okay, it was us) used the assignment operator = instead of the equality operator ==. On each loop, **i** is assigned the value of 100. Integer expressions are converted to boolean according to the following rule: 0 is false; anything else is true. Because 100 is nonzero, it is converted to "true," and the loop repeats forever.

THE FOR LOOP

The **for** loop is the most powerful of the looping constructs. There are three parameters to a typical implementation: the initialization, which sets the initial value for the loop counter; the counter test, which terminates the loop when it evaluates to false; and the action, which often (but not necessarily) involves implementing the loop counter. The layout is like this:

```
for (counter initialization; counter test; action) {
 statement(s);
}
```

A typical implementation looks like this:

```
for (int i = 0; i < 10; i++) {
 System.out.println("loop " + i);
}
```

When you declare variables inside a loop, their scope is restricted to that level of the loop and any loops or other constructs nested inside that loop. The counter variable, when declared as shown previously, has scope for the body of the loop. An alternate implementation can go as follows:

```
int i;
for (i = 0; i < 10; i++) {
```

In this example, i has the scope of the code block outside the **for** loop.

You do not need to use the counter initialization at all, if you don't want to. Just leave the first parameter blank. You might want to do this when setting a loop on a variable that is initialized earlier in the class. In this case, the **for** statement would look something like:

```
for (; i < 10; i++) {
```

You also can leave off the third parameter, but if you do this, you should be careful that you still have a mechanism for incrementing the counter.

The **for** loop commonly is used for stepping through array elements and for any kind of processing where some action has to happen a specified number of times.

THE BREAK, CONTINUE, AND LABEL STATEMENTS

The **break**, **continue**, and label statements provide an additional mechanism for altering the normal behavior of **while**, **do...while**, and **for** loops. You use these statements when you have a specific need to "break" the normal flow of execution of your program, usually to accommodate some special case or awkward logic.

The **break** statement terminates the currently executing loop. In its simplest form, it is used with an expression that determines the break condition. In the following example, the loop will terminate as soon as **i** reaches a value of 5:

```
for (int i = 0; i < 10; i++) {
  System.out.println("loop " + i);
  if (i == 5) break;
}
```

While the **break** statement terminates a loop, the **continue** statement returns execution to the top of the loop, bypassing all subsequent code. The following example prints out all of the numbers between 1 and 30 except those that are divided evenly by 6:

```
for (int i = 1; i < 30; i++) {
  if (i%6 == 0) continue;
  System.out.println("loop " + i);
}
```

The **continue** and **break** statements are very useful, but there are some circumstances where they aren't quite enough. Consider the following code fragment:

```
int a=0,b=5;
for (int i=0; i<50; i++) {
  for (int j=0; j<50; j++) {
    for (int k=0; k<50; k++) {
      if (j == b) {
        // break out of all loops;
      }
    }
  }
}
```

Here are three nested loops, and in the innermost loop, there is a test to find out if code execution should break out of all of the loops at once. If all you have is the standard **break** statement, the only way you can break out of all of the loops is to create a boolean variable that indicates the loop is to terminate, then test each loop to see whether you need to issue a break out of that loop. Things get really messy if there's a lot of code within the nested loops and multiple points where a break would be required.

A much simpler solution to the problem is to combine the use of labels with the **break** statement. The *label* statement is used to identify a specific statement that can be referred to when the **break** and **continue** statements are used. When the Java compiler sees a label statement, it makes an entry in its internal tables to allow control to be transferred from the currently executing **break** or **continue** statement to the statement defined by the label:

```
int a=0,b=5;
for (int i=0; i<50; i++) {
  for (int j=0; j<50; j++) {
    for (int k=0; k<50; k++) {
      if (j == b) {
        break endloop;
      }
    }
  }
}
:endloop
```

In this example, when the **break endloop;** statement is encountered, execution jumps immediately to the **:endloop** label, effectively shortcutting all of the loops.

Labels also can be used with the **continue** statement. In this example, when the expression in the inner loop evaluates to true, execution immediately returns to the top of the second loop:

```
int a=0,b=5;
for (int i=0; i<50; i++) {
  :SecondLoop
  for (int j=0; j<50; j++) {
    for (int k=0; k<50; k++) {
      for (int r=0; r<5; r++) {
        if (j == b) {
          continue SecondLoop;
        }
```

```
            }
        }
    }
}
```

When combined with labels, **continue** and **break** function a little like the **goto** statement common to many programming languages. Although **goto** is a reserved word in the Java language, there currently is no **goto** statement, which is more good than bad. Although there are occasions when a **goto** is useful (as the previous examples demonstrate), the presence of **goto** is an invitation to the kind of spaghetti code that we all like to think that we left behind us years. While labels in the context of loops are very useful, it is best to avoid overuse of these statements as they can cause confusion to others trying to understand your code.

THE RETURN STATEMENT

Lastly, the **return** statement is worth a special mention. The **return** statement will immediately return control to the previous calling method. The return also can return a value to the calling method (which might or might not be in the same class):

```
return [returnvalue];
```

The need for and the type of the value returned are both determined by the method declaration. All methods except constructors have a return type. However, if the return type is void, no value is returned.

If a variable or value is placed after the **return** statement, that value will be put on the stack as the return value of this class. The value or variable type returned must agree with the class type of the current class. If you attempt to return a value from a method that is declared with the **void** return type, the compiler will post an error.

SUMMARY

Java is a full-featured programming language with powerful language constructs much like those found in C/C++. Java's expressions allow you to evaluate just about every kind of data imaginable. Control flow statements like **if**, **if...else**, **do**, **do...while**, and **switch** let you build the kinds of program logic real-world applications require.

The better you understand how Java evaluates data and controls program flow, the more effective and compact your code will be. This chapter is just an introduction to the many facets of code design; mastery is a somewhat longer, but potentially very enjoyable, process.

9

APPLETS

GETTING USER INPUT

IN CHAPTER 6, you learned about the basic structure of Java applets, their object orientation, and a little about how to affect the behavior of an applet by using a few of the standard applet methods. In this chapter, you'll learn about some more standard methods and explore ways of collecting user input.

Although the examples discussed in this chapter are in the context of an applet, rather than a Java application, the basic approach is the same whichever kind of Java program you're writing. Applet programmers currently do have a somewhat easier task than application programmers, because the users' expectations of what applications can do tends to be quite a lot higher than what most people expect out of an applet running on a Web page. After all, before Java, it wasn't practical to embed actual program code in a Web page.

GETTING INPUT FROM THE MOUSE

In addition to the automatically called methods discussed in chapter 6, there are a number of methods that you can use at your discretion to detect mouse movements, keypresses, loss/gain of focus, and so on. Figure 9-1 shows the source for a small applet that traps a variety of mouse actions and displays or prints out messages accordingly.

By now you should be familiar with the overall structure of a Java applet. There are import statements at the top of the listing, followed by the MouseTest class declaration. Within MouseTest are seven method declarations, all enclosed within braces. You're already familiar with the **paint()** method:

```
// paint is called whenever the applet needs to be redisplayed
public void paint (Graphics g) {
  g.drawString("Mouse X " + MouseX + " Mouse Y " + MouseY,10,10);

}
```

Here the **paint()** method will be used to display the mouse coordinates; you'll see how this is invoked a little later on.

The first of the mouse methods listed is the **mouseDown()** method:

```
// mouseDown executes when the mouse button is pressed
public boolean mouseDown(Event evt, int x, int y) {
  System.out.println("The mouse button is down.");
  return true;
}
```

Figure 9-1 The MouseTest applet source code.

```
import java.applet.Applet;
import java.awt.*;

public class MouseTest extends Applet {
   int MouseX;
   int MouseY;

  // paint is called whenever the applet needs to be redisplayed
  public void paint (Graphics g) {
     g.drawString("Mouse X " + MouseX + " Mouse Y " + MouseY,10,10);
  }

  // mouseDown executes when the mouse button is pressed
  public boolean mouseDown(Event evt, int x, int y) {
      System.out.println("The mouse button is down.");
    return true;
  }

  // mouseDrag executes when the mouse is moved with the button held down
  public boolean mouseDrag(Event evt, int x, int y) {
      System.out.println("Someone is dragging the mouse!");
    return true;
  }

  // mouseUp executes when the mouse button is released
  public boolean mouseUp(Event evt, int x, int y) {
      System.out.println("The mouse button is up.");
    return true;
  }

  // mouseMove executes when the mouse is moving
  public boolean mouseMove(Event evt, int x, int y) {
     MouseX = x;
     MouseY = y;
     repaint();
    return true;
  }

  // mouseEnter executes when the mouse enters the applet's window
  public boolean mouseEnter(Event evt, int x, int y) {
      System.out.println("The mouse has entered the applet.");
    return true;
  }

  // mouseExit executes when the mouse leaves the applet's window
  public boolean mouseExit(Event evt, int x, int y) {
      System.out.println("Ladies and Gentlemen, the Mouse has left the applet!");
    return true;
  }
}    // end of class MouseTest
```

In chapter 6, you saw how certain applet methods—like **init()**, **start()**, and **paint()**—are automatically called when an applet loads. Similarly, mouse methods like **mouseDown()** are invoked by the user taking an action, such as pressing a mouse key. The operating system detects the mouse keypress and notifies the applet via a message, or *event*. These events are the primary means of communication between you and the user, and if you know how and why events happen, you'll find Java programming all that much easier to understand.

Note: In this discussion, the term "operating sytem" is inclusive of the window-management code, although, on some platforms, window management really is just an application running on the operating system.

EVENTS MAKE THE GUI WORLD GO 'ROUND

Programming for a graphical user interface (GUI) is a considerably different experience from programming for a character user interface (CUI), and it's not just because GUIs have a prettier face.

In a CUI program, you often can force users down a particular path of data input. You collect data for field A, validate it, then go on to field B, knowing that field A has valid data. GUIs, on the other hand, allow the user to navigate around the screen by means of a pointing device like a mouse or digitizing tablet. This means that there is no set sequence of events that you can rely on your users to follow. They might press the **OK** button before they fill in any of the fields that you have so lovingly prepared for their input, or they might make a choice box selection that's subsequently invalidated by another choice box selection.

In a program that allows you to have multiple windows open at a single time, you don't even know which window the user is going to go to next. In a GUI operating system, you typically can have any number of programs open at one time, so you can't even be sure that, when a user clicks on the region of the screen where you're displaying your program, your program is going to be the topmost one and therefore visible to the user.

It's the responsibility of the GUI-based operating system (be it Windows 95, Solaris, or Macintosh System 7) to make sure that all of these programs cooperate and interact properly with the user. The operating system and the GUI do this through a system of events and messages.

Technically, an *event* is something that happens (a mouse click, a keypress, the system clock counting off the seconds), and a *message* is an internal communication that results from that event. However, it's commonplace to talk of messages and events as if they are the same thing, so don't get too hung up on the terminology.

MESSAGE QUEUES AND EVENT LOOPS

To see events and messages in action, run the MouseTest applet. Either type in the code listing from Figure 9-1, or obtain the MouseTest.java source file from the tutorial\chapter9 directory on the CD-ROM. Compile the source file and create an HTML document with the tag:

```
<applet code="MouseTest.class" width=200 height=200>
</applet>
```

Run the HTML file through the applet viewer to see the MouseTest applet in action. The applet should look something like Figure 9-2.

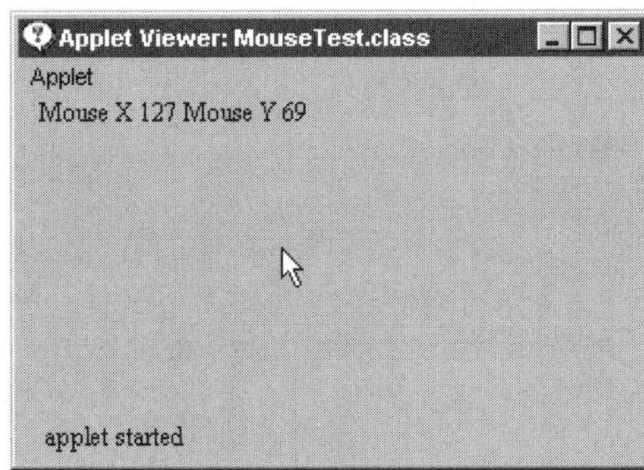

Figure 9-2
The MouseTest applet running in the applet viewer.

Position the applet viewer so that you also can see the text window that you launched the applet viewer from. Experiment with the mouse by moving it over the applet, away from the applet, clicking the mouse button while over the applet, and so on. You'll see output in the text window similar to that shown in Figure 9-3.

As you move the mouse around or click its buttons, the operating system generates a barrage of events (or messages) indicating the fact that the mouse has moved, its new position, the state of its buttons, and so on. These events are fed into one or more queues and doled out as appropriate to the programs running on the operating system.

Figure 9-3 Text output from the MouseTest applet.

```
status: applet loaded
status: applet initialized
status: applet started
The mouse has entered the applet.
The mouse button is down.
Someone is dragging the mouse!
Someone is dragging the mouse!
Someone is dragging the mouse!
Someone is dragging the mouse!
The mouse button is up.
The mouse button is down.
Someone is dragging the mouse!
Someone is dragging the mouse!
The mouse button is up.
The mouse button is down.
Someone is dragging the mouse!
Someone is dragging the mouse!
Someone is dragging the mouse!
Someone is dragging the mouse!
Someone is dragging the mouse!
The mouse button is up.
The mouse button is down.
Someone is dragging the mouse!
Someone is dragging the mouse!
Someone is dragging the mouse!
Someone is dragging the mouse!
The mouse button is up.
Ladies and Gentlemen, the Mouse has left the applet!
status: applet stopped
status: applet destroyed
status: applet disposed
```

It's up to the operating system to know which application ought to get which events. When you move the mouse over the applet, you'll see the text:

```
The mouse has entered the applet.
```

appear in the command window. The code that triggers this message is:

```
public boolean mouseEnter(Event evt, int x, int y) {
  System.out.println("The mouse has entered the applet.");
  return true;
}
```

The **mouseEnter()** method is automatically invoked by the applet when the operating system posts the **MOUSE_ENTER** event to the applet. The **mouseEnter()** method uses the **System.out.println()** method to display an appropriate message to StdOut (in this case, the command window that you launched the applet viewer from). You'll see another message posted by **mouseExit()**, but you can rest assured that, if you move the cursor onto another application as you move it off the applet viewer, that application will receive a **MOUSE_ENTER** message and will respond to it if it sees fit to do so.

Mouse events apply to pointing devices in general, not just mice. You'll notice that there are no mouse methods for left or right mouse button actions. Because Java is a multiplatform programming language, it must accommodate the lowest common denominator, and some systems (such as the Macintosh) only have a single mouse button.

Although there is not a separate **mouseLeftDown()**, etc. method, you *can* figure out which mouse button was pressed on a multibutton mouse by checking the Event object's modifier field. For example, on Solaris, where there are three mouse buttons:

```
public boolean mouseDown (Event e) {
  switch(e.modifiers) {
  case 0: System.out.println("Left mouse button pressed"); break;
  case 1: System.out.println("Middle mouse button pressed"); break;
  case 2: System.out.println("Right mouse button pressed"); break;
  }
return true;
  }
```

DISPLAYING THE MOUSE COORDINATES

Most of the mouse methods in this applet use the **System.out.println()** method to display output, and that's handy for debugging and just seeing what's going on in the applet. The **mouseMove()** method takes a slightly different approach, displaying the mouse X and Y coordinates on the applet window:

```
public boolean mouseMove(Event evt, int x, int y) {
  MouseX = x;
  MouseY = y;
  repaint();
  return true;
}
```

As you probably can guess from the listing, the **x** and **y** parameters hold the X and Y coordinates (in pixels, relative to the top-left corner of the applet) of the current mouse position. The **mouseMove()** method is automatically executed whenever the operating system detects a mouse movement. However, there's a little problem in displaying this value on the applet, because the **x** and **y** parameters are local to the **mouseMove()** method, whereas you'll need to put your display code in the **paint()** method. The solution is to declare two int variables at the start of the class (**MouseX** and **MouseY**) so that they'll be visible to all of the methods within the class. In the **mouseMove()** method, you copy the **x** and **y** values to **MouseX** and **MouseY** and call the **repaint()** method, which invokes **paint()** and causes a redisplay.

BUTTONS

Adding buttons to an applet involves several steps. First, you'll need to declare a button in the data section of your applet, right after the applet class declaration:

```
Button button1;
```

This declares **button1** as a Button "type," but the button that will be referred to by **button1** doesn't itself yet exist. To create the button, put the following code in the applet's **init()** method:

```
button1 = new Button("Button 1");
add(Button1);
```

The first line of that code fragment creates a new instance of a button object with the text "Button 1" and assigns that instance to the identifier **button1**, declared as a Button type. You need to take one more step before the button actually will appear on the applet's window, and that's to **add()** the button object.

The complete code for the ButtonTest applet is shown in Figure 9-4. Compile the ButtonTest applet and run it via the AppletViewer. You should see the applet shown in Figure 9-5.

When you use the **add()** statement to add a button to an applet (or a frame or a panel), you're actually invoking a layout manager, which is a Java class that arranges objects like buttons and entry fields on the window. If you don't specify a layout manager, the applet uses

Figure 9-4 The ButtonTest applet.

```
import java.applet.Applet;
import java.awt.*;

public class ButtonTest extends Applet {
  Button btn1;
  Button btn2;

    // init is called when the applet first loads
    public void init() {
      btn1 = new Button("Button 1");
      add(btn1);
      btn2 = new Button("Button 2");
      add(btn2);
    }

}    // end of class ButtonTest
```

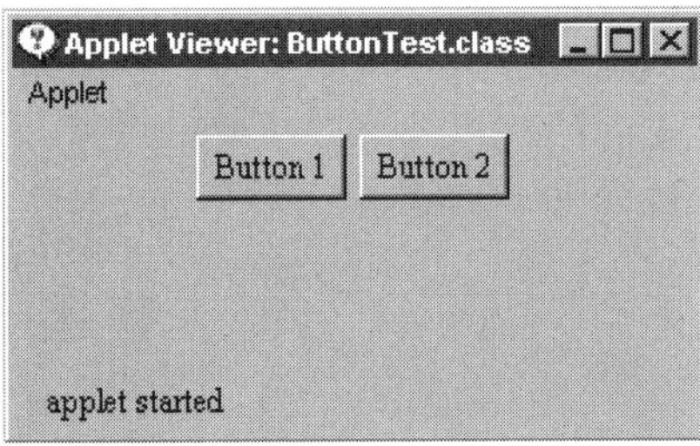

Figure 9-5
The ButtonTest applet.

FlowLayout, which just arranges the specified objects on the applet from left to right, starting at the top and working down. There's more on layout managers in chapter 10, "Applets: Frames, panels, and canvases."

> It is possible to specify exact X and Y coordinates for objects like buttons, using the **object.reshape()** method, but there's a danger in doing this. The X and Y coordinates are always specified in pixels. For objects that don't display text (such as lines, boxes, ellipses, and images), pixels make suitable units of measurements; however, when an object displays text, things get more complicated. For example, buttons have to be large enough to contain their text. You might design a button that looks just fine on your screen, but someone else has a higher resolution screen with a larger default font, and the text that fits nicely on your button looks cramped or doesn't fit at all on the user's screen. The only way around this is to determine ratio of pixels to average character font width/height, and scale the button size

accordingly. If you have to do this for all the objects on your window, it can get a bit tedious, which is why Java comes with layout managers that are designed to do a "best fit."

PROCESSING BUTTON MESSAGES

OK, so you can put a button on a window—big deal. What you really want is to do something following a button press, and that means that you have to be able to trap the event that is generated when the button is pressed. Happily, there is a method called **action()** that—like **init()**, **paint()**, and a number of other methods—already is part of the applet. To use **action()**, you simply create your own method declaration that overrides the built-in method, just as you do with **init()**, **paint()**, and the others:

```
public boolean action (Event e, Object o) {
  if (e.target instanceof Button) {
    String label = (String)o;
    if (label=="Button 2") {
      System.out.println("Pressed Button2!");
    }
    if (label=="Button 1") {
      System.out.println("Pressed Button1!");
    }
  }
  return true;
}
```

The action() method receives an event, called **e** in the code, and an object, called **o**. Events are instances of the class event, and if you look at the API documentation for **java.awt.event**, you'll see that events have a number of associated values that can be referenced, among them **target**. There can be any number and type of events received by the **action()** method. So to narrow the field, you use the code:

```
if (e.target instanceof Button) {
```

which translates as "if the target of this event is an object that is an instance of the Button class."

That gets you down to buttons. However, if you have more than one button, you also need to know which one was pressed, and you can do that via the text displayed on the button. The code:

```
String label = (String)o;
```

creates a string variable called **label** and assigns to it the string cast, or conversion to a string, of the object **o**. You then can test the value in the label against the value expected for a given button:

```
if (label=="Button 2") {
```

In the event that the text for the buttons can change while the applet is running, or if your buttons don't have unique labels, you might want to use another approach. The statement:

```
if (e.target.equals(button1)
```

tests for the target being the same as the button declaration. By using a combination of these techniques, you can determine if the text of a button has changed.

Figure 9-6 shows a code listing for the ButtonTest applet, which uses **System.out.println()** to display a message when a particular button is pressed.

Figure 9-6 An enhanced ButtonTest applet which displays messages when its buttons are pressed.

```
import java.applet.Applet;
import java.awt.*;

public class ButtonTest extends Applet {
  Button btn1;
  Button btn2;

    // init is called when the applet first loads
    public void init() {
      btn1 = new Button("Button 1");
      add(btn1);
      btn2 = new Button("Button 2");
      add(btn2);
    }

    // action processes window events
    public boolean action (Event e, Object o){
      if (e.target instanceof Button) {
        String label = (String)o;
        if(label == "Button 1") {
          System.out.println("Pressed Button 1!");
        } else if(label == "Button 2") {
          System.out.println("Pressed Button 2!");
        }
      }
      return true;
    }
}    // end of class ButtonTest
```

CHOICE BUTTONS (DROP-DOWN LISTS)

The *choice button*, also called a *drop-down list* box, is a commonly used component in GUI programming environments. Choice buttons are created in much the same way as ordinary buttons. However, as they will contain a list of choices rather than a single text string, you need to add a bit of code in those choices. You start with creating a new instance of the Choice class:

```
PizzaSize = new Choice();
```

then add the items that will be displayed in the choice button:

```
PizzaSize.addItem("Small");
PizzaSize.addItem("Medium");
PizzaSize.addItem("Large");
PizzaSize.addItem("Hard To Carry");
```

and finally add the choice button to the applet:

```
add(PizzaSize);
```

The result is a choice button that looks like one of those in Figure 9-7. The full source for the ChoiceTest applet in Figure 9-7 is shown in Figure 9-8.

The ChoiceTest applet uses a slightly different **action()** method declaration than was used for the button event, where the text of the button was used as the identifying feature. Generally, when a component is selected, you want to know which one it is. With choice buttons, there is a greater likelihood that two buttons will return the same text.

The **action()** method in ChoiceTest.java determines which choice box was used by comparing the event target with each of the choice objects. The code:

```
if (e.target instanceof Choice) {
```

filters out only the events that belong to Choice buttons, and the code:

```
if (e.target.equals(ExtraTopping)) {
```

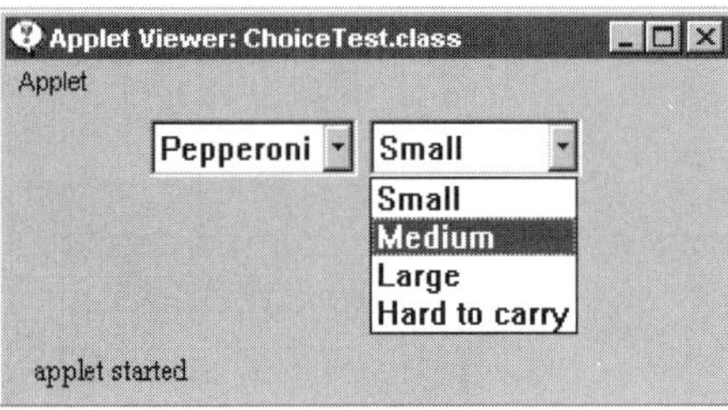

Figure 9-7 Two ChoiceTest applet, showing two choice buttons, one of which is currently selected for input.

uses the method **equals()** to test to see if the target of this event is the Choice called **ExtraTopping**. If it is, the **System.out.println()** method displays the selected value. Actually, this second option is the only one that you really need to test for the choice button being completed, because **e.target.equals(ExtraTopping)** will always refer only to the choice button **ExtraTopping**.

Run the ChoiceTest applet, and choose options from each of the choice buttons. As you make a choice, you'll see the value of that choice displayed in the command window from which you ran the applet viewer.

Figure 9-8 The code listing for the ChoiceTest applet.

```
import java.applet.Applet;
import java.awt.*;

public class ChoiceTest extends Applet {
  Choice ExtraTopping;
  Choice PizzaSize;

    // init is called when the applet first loads
    public void init() {
      ExtraTopping = new Choice();
      ExtraTopping.addItem("Pepperoni");
      ExtraTopping.addItem("Anchovies");
      ExtraTopping.addItem("Extra Cheese");
      add(ExtraTopping);
      PizzaSize = new Choice();
      PizzaSize.addItem("Small");
      PizzaSize.addItem("Medium");
      PizzaSize.addItem("Large");
      PizzaSize.addItem("Hard to carry");
      add(PizzaSize);
    }
}    // end of class ChoiceTest
```

CHECKBOXES

Another common type of component is the *checkbox*, which displays a label and a box that is either filled or empty, indicating a true or false condition. As with other components, you'll need to declare a button in the data section of your applet, right after the applet class declaration:

```
Checkbox cbh;
```

This declares **cbh** as a Checkbox type. To create the checkbox, you put the following code in the applet's **init()** method:

```
cbh = new Checkbox("Hungry");
add(cbh);
```

You specify the text that you want the checkbox to have in the parameter to the Checkbox constructor.

Figure 9-9 shows the CheckboxTest applet with several checkboxes.

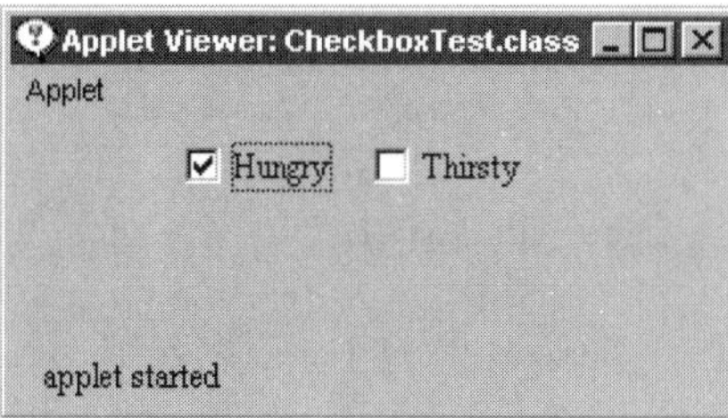

Figure 9-9
The CheckboxTest applet with several checkboxes.

As with many other components, you can use the **action()** method to trap the **ACTION_EVENT** event that is generated whenever the user selects or deselects the checkbox. Just knowing that the user has selected a checkbox doesn't do you a whole lot of good; you also need to know the value of that event. To do this, you need to convert the argument associated with **ACTION_EVENT** to a string value. You do that with the code shown inside the **System.out.println** statement:

```
if (e.target.equals(cbh)) {
  System.out.println("Hungry = " + e.arg.toString());
}
```

If you run this applet and click on the check boxes, you'll see a series of true/false statements:

```
Hungry = true
Thirsty = true
Thirsty = false
Hungry = false
```

Figure 9-10 shows the complete code listing for the Checkbox applet.

Figure 9-10 The complete code listing for the Checkbox applet.

```
import java.applet.Applet;
import java.awt.*;

public class CheckboxTest extends Applet {
  Checkbox cbh;
  Checkbox cht;

    // init is called when the applet first loads
    public void init() {
      cbh = new Checkbox("Hungry");
      add(cbh);
      cht = new Checkbox("Thirsty");
      add(cht);
    }

    // action processes window events
    public boolean action (Event e, Object o){
      if (e.target.equals(cbh)){
        System.out.println("Hungry = " +
e.arg.toString());
      }
      if (e.target.equals(cht)){
        System.out.println("Thirsty = " +
e.arg.toString());
      }
      return true;
```

GROUPCHECKBOXES (RADIO BUTTONS)

Grouped checkboxes are checkboxes that are combined into a single logical unit, such that only one of the checkboxes can be true at any given time. On many systems, these components are called *radio buttons* because they function much like the mechanical tuner buttons on an old-style car radio. The individual checkboxes also are usually round rather than square, as single checkboxes are.

You declare and create GroupCheckboxes much the way that you do single checkboxes, except that, when you get to the component creation code in the **init()** method, you first create the GroupCheckbox that will contain all the checkboxes:

```
cbgnr = new CheckboxGroup();
add(cbgnr = new Checkbox("Not Ready," cbg, false));
add(cbgr = new Checkbox("Ready," cbg, false));
```

Note that you create a new CheckboxGroup, but you do not at any point **add()** it. However, you do create new Checkboxes and **add()** them as well. There is a slightly different syntax used in this example, as compared to earlier examples, which combines the **new()** and **add()** methods, but the effect is identical to writing:

```
new Checkbox("Not Ready", cbg, false);
add(cbgnr);
```

When you're checking for the result of a selection, you check the individual checkboxes, not the CheckboxGroup, which is just a container for the checkboxes (and which ensures that only one check box is active at a time).

Figure 9-11 shows the CheckboxGroupTest applet in action. Figure 9-12 contains the source code for the CheckboxGroupTest applet.

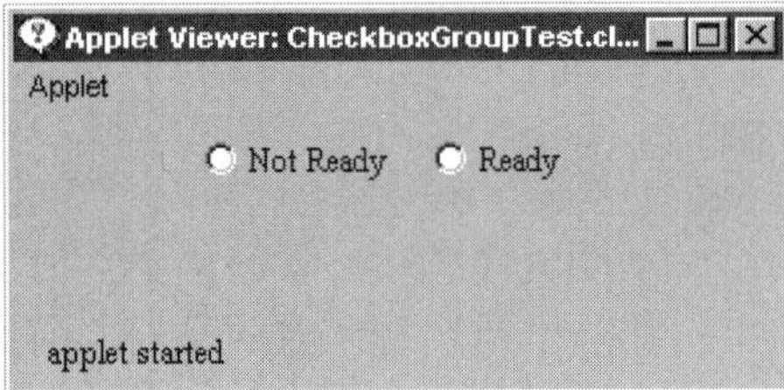

Figure 9-11 The CheckboxGroupTest applet in action.

Figure 9-12 The source code for the CheckboxGroupTest applet.

```
import java.applet.Applet;
import java.awt.*;

public class CheckboxGroupTest extends Applet {
  CheckboxGroup cbg;
  Checkbox cbgnr;
  Checkbox cbgr;

    // init is called when the applet first loads
    public void init() {
      cbg = new CheckboxGroup();
      add(cbgnr = new Checkbox("Not Ready", cbg, false));
      add(cbgr = new Checkbox("Ready", cbg, false));
    }

    // action processes window events
    public boolean action (Event e, Object o){
      if (e.target.equals(cbgnr)){
        System.out.println("Not ready!");
      }
      if (e.target.equals(cbgr)){
        System.out.println("Ready!");
      }
      return true;
    }
}    // end of class CheckboxGroupTest
```

LABELS

Labels are one of the most straightforward components to add to an applet, because they just sit there on the screen and don't collect any

data or receive input (at least not until the library allows some way of adding hot keys to labels so that they can function as prompts). So why use labels instead of **g.drawString()**? If you simply draw your text on screen, it will appear exactly at the pixel location that you give. However, because you really know nothing about the relationship between pixel size and component size on your user's machine, it's quite likely that what looks fine on your machine will look like garbage on somebody else's machine.

Labels are objects, just as other components are, and that means that they can be moved around the applet's window, have their alignment changed, and so on, just like other components. You'll find that it's much better to let the applet manage lining your labels up with the things that they label than actually writing the string out to the window. Just how this automatic component positioning works is covered in chapter 10, "Applets: Frames, panels, and canvases."

The code for labels is mercifully short:

```
public class LabelTest extends Applet {

  Label lbl;

  public void init() {

    lbl = new Label("Nothing but a label");

    add(lbl);

  }

}
```

Figure 9-13 shows the LabelTest applet in action. Exciting, isn't it?

Note: You can dynamically get and set label text with the **getText()** and **setText()** methods. However, if you reset the label's string to a longer string, you must **resize()** the label. Otherwise, the new label will be truncated.

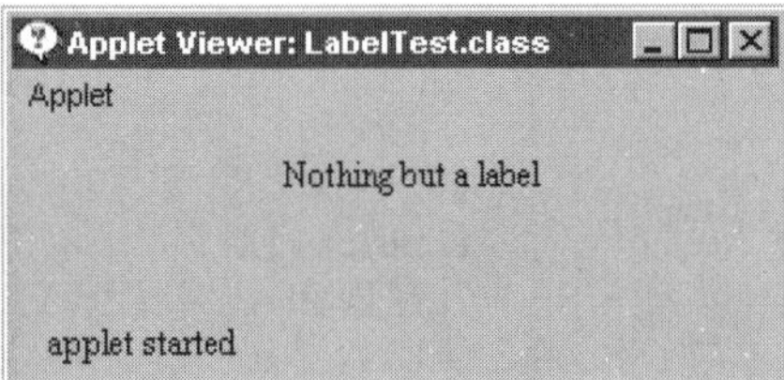

Figure 9-13
The LabelTest applet in action.

TEXTFIELDS

Java has two kinds of text-entry components: one for single line text entry and the other for multiple-line text entry. TextFields are of the former variety and are the most common way of getting free-form text input from the user.

TextField implementation pretty much follows the pattern of the other components, but there are several options for how you define the component.

If you don't specify any parameters to the new TextField, you'll get a single-character sized field, with no text in the field:

```
tf1 = new TextField();
```

If you want there to be some text already in the field, just pass it in:

```
tf2 = new TextField("A");
```

You also can pass in the width of the TextField in characters. If the TextField is to have default text, make the text the first parameter and the number of columns the second parameter:

```
tf3 = new TextField(30);
tf4 = new TextField("This is a read-only TextField" ,20);
```

TextFields have a number of methods relating to their size and behavior. One of the most useful of these is the method to make the TextField read-only:

```
tf4.setEditable(false);
```

Figure 9-14 shows the TextFieldTest applet in action.

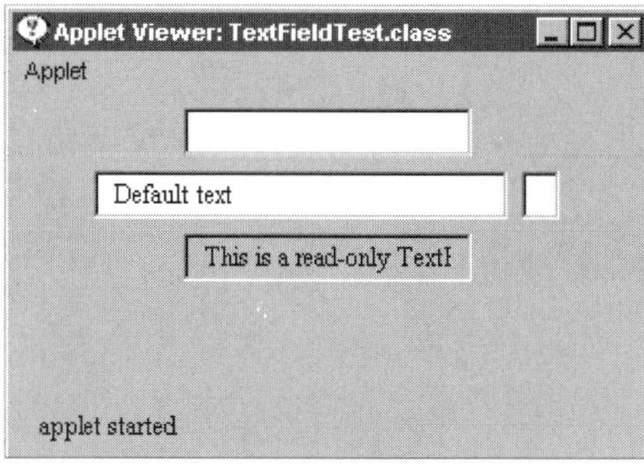

Figure 9-14
The TextFieldTest applet in action.

If the applet looks different on your computer, it's probably because the applet size is not the same. The applet will automatically position controls according to the available space and any other constraints put on placement, but that's a subject for the following chapter. For right now, it's enough to see that, if you change the width of the applet, the TextFields will move around to be as near the top of the applet as possible.

When you press Enter in a TextField, an action event is generated. You can test for this event with the following code:

```
public boolean action (Event e, Object o) {
  if (e.target.equals(tf1)) {
    System.out.println("TextField 1 completed!");
  }
  return true;
}
```

Figure 9-15 contains the TextFieldTest source code.

TEXTAREAS

TextArea components are much like TextField components, except that they are used for multiple-line text entry, so they do not produce an action event when the Enter key is pressed, because Enter is a valid way to begin a new line of text. If you want to do something with the text entered, you should provide a button or other component that can be used as a trigger for the text processing action.

Figure 9-15 The TextFieldTest source code.

```
import java.applet.Applet;
import java.awt.*;

public class TextFieldTest extends Applet {
  TextField tf1;
  TextField tf2;
  TextField tf3;
  TextField tf4;

    // init is called when the applet first loads
    public void init() {
      tf1 = new TextField(20);
      add(tf1);
      tf2 = new TextField("Default text",30);
      add(tf2);
      tf3 = new TextField();
      add(tf3);
      tf4 = new TextField("This is a read-only TextField",20);
      add(tf4);
      tf4.setEditable(false);
    }

    // action processes window events
    public boolean action (Event e, Object o){
      if (e.target.equals(tf1)){
        System.out.println("TextField 1 completed!");
      }
      return true;
    }
}     // end of class TextFieldTest
```

TextAreas also require you to specify the lines and columns of text, rather than just the columns. For example, to declare a TextArea of 4 lines and 40 columns, use the statement:

```
ta3 = new TextArea(4,40);
```

If you want this text area to have some default text, you can make that the first parameter instead:

```
ta3 = new TextArea("This text area is set to be read-only.", 40, 40);
```

As with TextFields, you can make a TextArea read-only (or read/write) with the **setEditable()** function:

```
ta1.setEditable(false);
```

Figure 9-16 shows the TextAreaTest applet. Figure 9-17 contains the source code for the TextAreaTest applet.

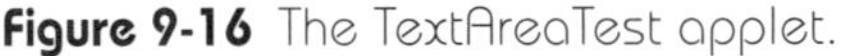

Figure 9-16 The TextAreaTest applet.

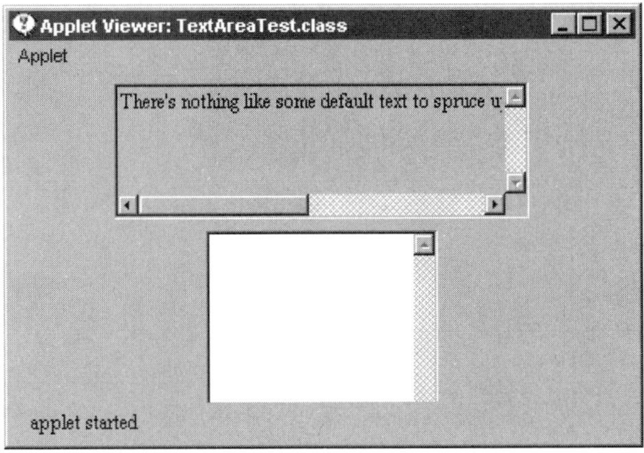

Figure 9-17 The source code for the TextAreaTest applet.

```
import java.applet.Applet;
import java.awt.*;

public class TextAreaTest extends Applet {
  TextArea ta1;
  TextArea ta2;
  TextArea ta3;

    // init is called when the applet first loads
    public void init() {
      ta1 = new TextArea("There's nothing like some default text to spruce up an
otherwise barren text area, wouldn't you say?",4,40);
      add(ta1);
      ta1.setEditable(false);
      ta2 = new TextArea(15,21);
      add(ta2);
      ta3 = new TextArea("This text area is set to be read-only.",4,40);
      add(ta3);
    }
}    // end of class TextAreaTest
```

SCROLLBARS

Scrollbars are another commonly used component, but they're handled a little differently from the other components. You create the scrollbar in the familiar way, with a few additional parameters:

```
sb = new Scrollbar(Scrollbar.HORIZONTAL,50,10,0,100);
add(sb);
```

The first parameter of the constructor will be **Scrollbar.HORIZONTAL** or **Scrollbar.VERTICAL**. The second parameter is the value that you want the control to have when it's initialized. This, together with the minimum and maximum values (the last two parameters in the list), will determine where on the scrollbar the "thumb" will appear.

The third parameter is, in effect, the page size. If you have a minimum value of 0 and a maximum value of 100, and the page size (called *visible* in the Java documentation) is 25, clicking in the area between the thumb and the end of the scrollbar will increase or decrease the position by 25. If you are using the scrollbar to manage a text or graphic that will fit on the window, then make the size equal to the percentage of the text or graphic that is visible, times the total range of the scrollbar. If you are using the scrollbar simply to choose a value, then you can make the page size a suitable step value.

Scrollbar event handling is a little different from other components. Buttons, text fields, and the like generally use the **action()** method (which executes whenever an **ACTION_EVENT** occurs) to trigger any component-related code. Scrollbars, however, post a number of events, so rather than have a series of methods, each of which responds to a separate event, you just use the **handleEvent()** method:

```
public boolean handleEvent(Event e) {
  if (e.target.equals(sb)) {
    System.out.println(e.toString());
  }
  return super.handleEvent(e);
}
```

Actually, this code will respond to any event at all that's posted to the scrollbar, which will be one of those listed in Table 9-1.

TABLE 9-1 The events that are posted to the scrollbar.

Event	Description
SCROLL_LINE_UP	The user has clicked on the arrow at the top or left button of the scrollbar.
SCROLL_LINE_DOWN	The user has clicked on the arrow at the bottom or right of the scrollbar.
SCROLL_PAGE_UP	The user has clicked in the region between the thumb and the top or left of the scrollbar.
SCROLL_PAGE_DOWN	The user has clicked in the region between the thumb and the bottom or right of the scrollbar.
SCROLL_ABSOLUTE	The user dragged the thumb to a new location.

Usually, all that you care about is the new position of the thumb, which you can print out with the code:

```
System.out.println(((Scrollbar)e.target).getValue());
```

If you want to trap individual events, you can use code similar to the following:

```
public boolean handleEvent(Event e) {
  if (e.target.equals(sb)) {
    if (e.id == e.SCROLL_LINE_UP) {
```

If you'd like to see what kinds of events are going on inside your program, try inserting the code:

```
System.out.println(e.toString());
```

as the first line in the handleEvent method. As you move the mouse around and click on various components, you'll see something like the following:

```
java.awt.Event[id=503,x=190,y=16,target=Main[0,0,378x218,layout=java.awt.
FlowLayout]]
java.awt.Event[id=601,x=184,y=9,target=java.awt.Scrollbar[184,9,50x15,val
=25,vis=true,min=0,max=100,horz],arg=25]
java.awt.Event[id=503,x=193,y=5,target=Main[0,0,378x218,layout=java.awt.F
lowLayout]]
java.awt.Event[id=505,x=211,y=71,target=Main[0,0,378x218,layout=java.awt.
FlowLayout]]
```

To translate the event numbers to the constants that you see in code, have a look at src/java/awt/Event.java. You'll see that 503 translates to **MOUSE_MOVE**, 505 to **MOUSE_EXIT**, and 601 to **SCROLL_LINE_UP**.

As you've probably gathered, there are a number of ways to respond to component events. Although most of the examples in this chapter use the **action()** method, they could just as easily all use **handleEvent()**, provided that the code within **handleEvent()** tested for **ACTION_EVENT**. For example, the code:

```
public boolean handleEvent(Event e) {
  if (e.id == e.ACTION_EVENT) {
    if (e.target.equals(sb)) {
```

is identical in function to the code:

```
public boolean action (Event e, Object o) {
  if (e.target.equals(sb)) {
```

Clearly, if all you need to do is trap the **ACTION** event, it's a lot less trouble to use the **action()** method than **handleEvent()**.

Figure 9-18 shows the ScrollbarTest applet. Figure 9-19 contains the source code for the ScrollbarTest applet.

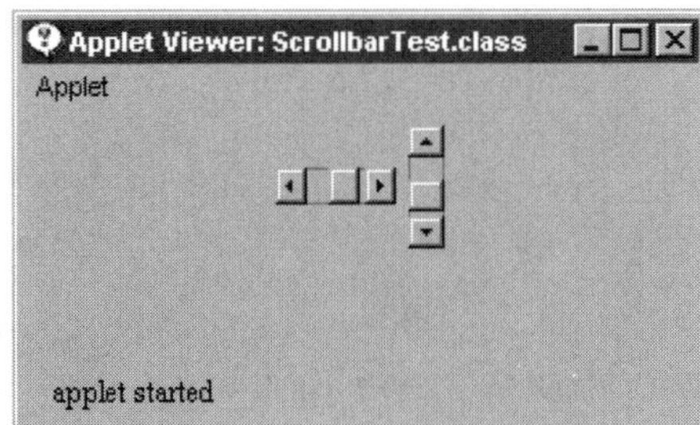

Figure 9-18
The ScrollbarTest applet.

Figure 9-19 The source code for the ScrollbarTest applet.

```
import java.applet.Applet;
import java.awt.*;

public class ScrollbarTest extends Applet {
  Scrollbar sbh;
  Scrollbar sbv;

    // init is called when the applet first loads
    public void init() {
      sbh = new Scrollbar(Scrollbar.HORIZONTAL,50,10,0,100);
      add(sbh);
      sbv = new Scrollbar(Scrollbar.VERTICAL,12,2,1,40);
      add(sbv);
    }

    // handleEvent processes all window events
    public boolean handleEvent(Event e){
      if (e.target.equals(sbh)){
        System.out.println(e.toString());
        System.out.println(((Scrollbar)e.target).getValue());
      }
      return super.handleEvent(e);
    }
}    // end of class ScrollbarTest
```

SUMMARY

Java comes with a number of stock components that you can use to build a full-featured interface for your programs. However, creating the components is only the first step; you also need to tie all of those pieces together in a cohesive, functioning whole. That's the subject of the next chapter: "Writing Java applets: Panels, layouts, and canvases."

10

WRITING JAVA APPLETS

PANELS, LAYOUTS, AND CANVASES

IN CHAPTER 9, "Writing Java applets: Getting user input," you learned how to create components and put those components on an applet window. In this chapter, you'll learn how to arrange items on a window through the use of panels and how to use canvases as drawing areas. It's quite possible to create applets without using panels or canvases; however, as you'll see, both these classes can be immensely useful, especially when applets (or applications, for that matter) begin to get complex.

PANELS

As Figure 10-1 shows, *panels* are a subclass of the Container class, which is simply a AWT class that can contain other AWT components, such as buttons, lists, text fields, and so on. In fact, Panel is almost identical to Container, except that it has a slightly different **addNotify()** method.

```
java.lang.Object
  └──┬java.awt.Component
     └───┬java.awt.Container
         └───java.awt.Panel
```

Figure 10-1
The Panel class hierarchy.

To give you a better idea of what Panel is good for, consider the Applet class, which is a subclass of Panel. (See Figure 10-2.)

```
──java.awt.Panel
   └───java.applet.applet
```

Figure 10-2
The Applet class.

The Applet class supplements Panel with the methods that related to Applet-only functionality, such as **getAudioClip()**, **getCodeBase()**, **getDocumentBase()**, **getImage(*URL*)**, **getParameter(*String*)**, **init()**, **play(*URL*)**, **start()**, and **stop()**. All of the rest of the functionality in applets comes from the Panel class. If you've written an applet, you've already used a panel.

Although panels are AWT components, you don't really "see" them on the screen. Panels are borderless, invisible containers; their most common use is to group components together on the screen. Panels

don't exist on their own but are used in the context of a Frame or Window (or in the context of an HTML document, in the case of applets).

USING PANELS FOR PLATFORM INDEPENDENCE

If you write simple applets that have few components, you might never need to use panels explicitly. The one panel that is the applet will suffice. One you get more than a few components in an applet, however, you'll probably want to be specific about where those components are located. That's where panels come in.

In a GUI program, if a component has any attached text, the amount of space (vertical and horizontal) that component requires will depend on the font in use. In a platform-specific application, you usually can specify exactly where, on the screen, you want a particular component to appear, because you can have some reasonable confidence in how your system handles any given font.

Once you start designing programs for cross-platform use, things get a little trickier. Your Java applet might run on Windows 95 in your office, but it could equally well be running on a Sparcstation or even something like a Personal Digital Assistant (PDA). The applet might look fairly similar on the Windows 95 box and the Sparcstation, but the PDA might have quite different constraints on how wide the page is, what shape buttons will be, and so on.

The solution to the problem of varying screen constraints is to group components that have to appear next to each other onto a panel and use as many panels as are necessary. You can fine-tune the relative location of components using layout managers, as will be discussed later in this chapter, but the basic idea is to lump related controls together and let Java work out how to display them at runtime. (See Figure 10-3.)

Figure 10-3 A simple applet with buttons in two panels.

```
import java.applet.Applet;
import java.awt.*;

public class TwoPanelTest extends Applet {
  FirstPanel pnl1;
  SecondPanel pnl2;

    // init is called when the applet first loads
    public void init() {
      pnl1 = new FirstPanel();
      add(pnl1);
      pnl2 = new SecondPanel();
      add(pnl2);
    }
}    // end of class TwoPanelTest

class FirstPanel extends Panel {
  Button btn1;

    // init is called when the applet first loads
    public FirstPanel() {
      btn1 = new Button("Panel 1 Button");
      add(btn1);
    }

    // action processes window events
    public boolean action (Event e, Object o){
      if (e.target.equals(btn1)){
        System.out.println("Button 1 pressed!");
      }
      return true;
    }
}

class SecondPanel extends Panel {
  Button btn2;

    // init is called when the applet first loads
    public SecondPanel() {
      btn2 = new Button("Panel 2 Button");
      add(btn2);
    }
```

```
    // action processes window events
    public boolean action (Event e, Object o){
      if (e.target.equals(btn2)){
        System.out.println("Button 2 pressed!");
      }
      return true;
    }
}
```

You create panels the same way that you create other components. First, declare the panel:

```
FirstPanel pnl1;
```

There's one noticeable difference between this code and that used to declare, say, a Button component; the class type is not Panel, but a class that you declare, which is derived from Panel:

```
class FirstPanel extends Panel {
  Button btn1;

  public FirstPanel() {
    btn1 = new Button("Panel 1 Button");
    add(btn1);
  }
}
```

You subclass Panel to create your own panel class because, as a container, the panel will use its own constructor to create the components that will be a part of the panel. In this example, the **FirstPanel()** method is the constructor method, and it always has the same name as the class. When you create an instance of the FirstPanel class with the code:

```
pnl1 = new FirstPanel();
```

you're really calling the **FirstPanel()** constructor method. Constructors are discussed in more detail in chapter 11, "Using Java classes." For now, you can think of the panel constructor method as being similar in function to the applet's **init()** method.

Although Java's approach to laying out components might seem restrictive, especially if you invest a lot of design work in your application interface, it does have one important benefit: it makes localization of programs considerably easier. When designing a

program for use with multiple languages, programmers working in the English language usually have to allow for considerable extra space on components, because most languages require more characters to express the same information. With Java, you can let the runtime system worry about giving components sufficient space, whatever the translation of the text.

USING PANELS TO ISOLATE EVENTS

Contrast the code for the TwoPanelTest applet in Figure 10-3 with the code for the TwoButtonTest applet in Figure 10-4.

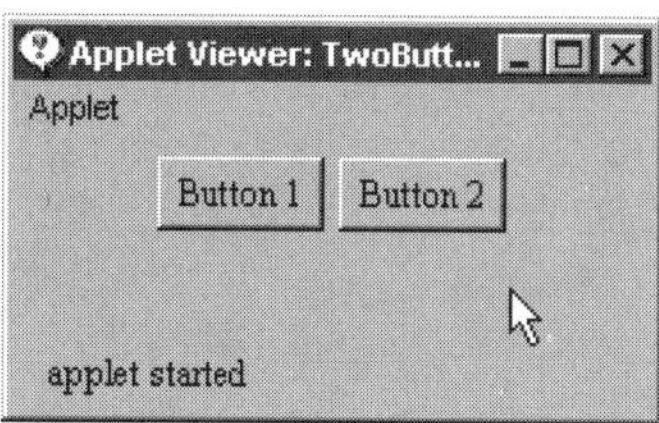

Figure 10-4
The TwoButtonTest applet.

In TwoButtonTest, the buttons are created in the **init()** method, while in TwoPanelTest the two panels are created in the applet **init()** method, and the buttons are created in the constructors of the panels. Furthermore, the code to display a message when a button is pressed now is associated with each panel respectively, rather than with the applet itself. That's because container-type components, such as panels, receive the window manager messages about the components that they contain.

Because the applet is a subclass of panel, what you really have in the TwoPanelTest applet is two panels that are sitting inside another (applet) panel. You can process the messages for components from within the panel to which they were added (via the **add()** method).

Because panels each have their own event handling, you can use panels not just to organize components visually, but to give different areas of your applet different kinds of behavior. For example, you could set up a panel that only displays an image, and any time the mouse is moved over the image (detected via the **mouseEnter()** method, as described in chapter 9, "Writing Java applets: Getting user input"), the

applet plays a sound file. This sound file, for example, could describe what will happen if the user clicks on the image (detected via the **mouseDown()** method.

So far this discussion has covered what panels are and how panels manage events for the components that they contain. You'll also want to have some control over just how components are laid out in a panel, and that's the job of the layout manager.

LAYOUT MANAGERS

As discussed earlier in this chapter, the problem with platform-independent software is that you have no assurance of how much space any given component will require when your applet/application is run on the client's system. Java comes with a set of predefined classes, called *layout managers*, that use several approaches to allow you to create a layout for your components, without restricting the components to a particular size and location.

FLOWLAYOUT

Anytime you add components to a container (such as a panel or applet), Java uses some kind of layout manager to determine where these components should appear. The simplest of the layout managers is called FlowLayout, and it's also the one that Java uses if you don't specify a layout manager.

FlowLayout simply lays out the components from left to right, starting at the top of the window and working down. Once a row is filled, the components in the row are centered. You can see FlowLayout in action if you run either TwoPanelTest or TwoButtonTest. If the AppletViewer window is large enough, both buttons appear side by side, as shown in Figure 10-5. If you narrow the window enough, the buttons will not fit side by side and FlowLayout will automatically reposition them, as shown in Figure 10-6.

It probably won't take you long to exhaust the possibilities offered by FlowLayout, in which case you'll need to explicitly invoke one of the other layout managers.

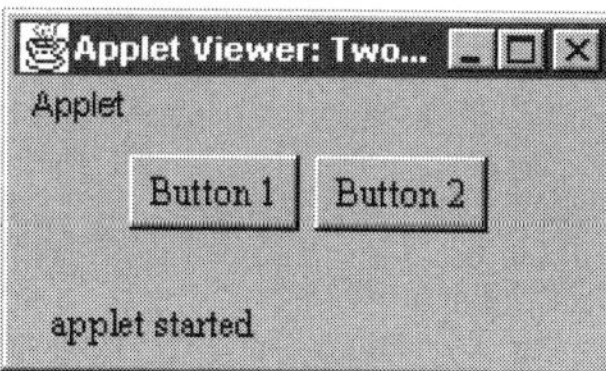

Figure 10-5
FlowLayout displaying buttons side by side in TwoButtonTest.

Figure 10-6
FlowLayout displaying buttons one above the other in TwoButtonTest.

BORDERLAYOUT

BorderLayout divides the current container up into five regions, labeled North, South, East, West, and Center. To use this layout manager, put the following code in the applet's **init()** method or the panel's constructor method:

```
setLayout(new BorderLayout());
```

Then, when you add the components to the applet or panel, specify the component's placement:

```
nb = new Button("N");
   add("North,"nb);
   sb = new Button("S");
   add("South,"sb);
   eb = new Button("E");
   add("East,"eb);
   wb = new Button("W");
   add("West,"wb);
   ta = new TextArea(10,27);
   add("Center,"ta);
```

The result will be a window that looks like Figure 10-7. (Figure 10-8 contains the source code for BorderLayoutTest.)

Figure 10-7 The BorderLayoutTest applet.

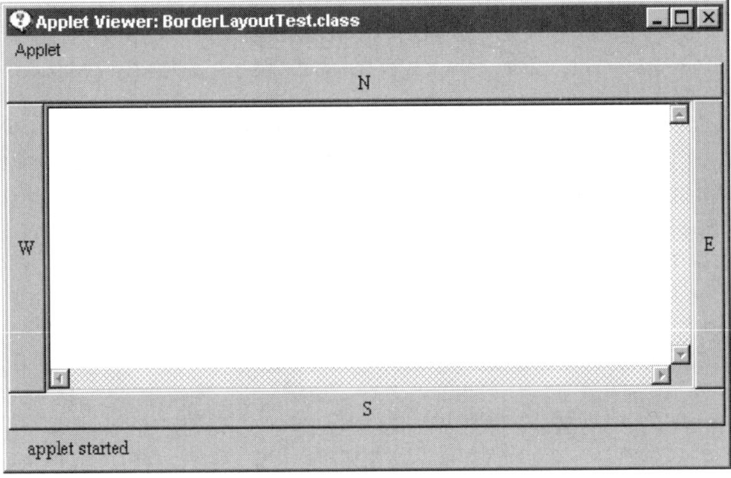

Figure 10-8 The BorderLayoutTest source code.

```
import java.applet.Applet;
import java.awt.*;

public class BorderLayoutTest extends Applet {
  Button nb;
  Button sb;
  Button eb;
  Button wb;
  TextArea ta;

    // init is called when the applet first loads
    public void init() {
      setLayout(new BorderLayout());
      nb = new Button("N");
      add("North",nb);
      sb = new Button("S");
      add("South",sb);
      eb = new Button("E");
      add("East",eb);
      wb = new Button("W");
      add("West",wb);
      ta = new TextArea(10,27);
      add("Center",ta);
    }
}    // end of class BorderLayoutTest
```

If you resize this applet, you'll see that the layout manager adjusts the amount of space allocated to each component accordingly. The biggest winner/loser in the reorganization is the center region, which gets whatever is left over after the outside regions have been resized.

BorderLayoutTest is used more often for panels (which will contain layouts of other components) than for buttons and text components, but panels aren't visible, so there's not much point in showing you those. A typical use for a BorderLayout is to set up North, Center, and South panels for forms. The center area is where you'll put all of the fields for the form (you'll need another layout manager to handle the display of fields on the panel). You can use the North and South panels for form controls (**Save** and **Cancel** buttons, and so forth).

BorderLayout is not good for laying out individual noncontainer components because you can't have more than one component in each of the five regions (actually, you can, but only the last one added will be visible).

GRIDLAYOUT

GridLayout is a layout manager that lets you arrange components in an X/Y grid. All components in the grid will be exactly the same size, so this manager is useful when you want to create something like a grid of images, or a keypad, or some other regular arrangement.

GridLayout is particularly easy to use. Consider the following applet that displays six buttons:

```
import java.applet.Applet;
import java.awt.*;
public class GridLayoutTest extends Applet {
  Button b1, b2, b3, b4, b5, b6;
  public void init() {
    add(b1 = new Button("1"));
    add(b2 = new Button("2"));
    add(b3 = new Button("3"));
    add(b4 = new Button("4"));
    add(b5 = new Button("5"));
    add(b6 = new Button("6"));
  }
} // end of class GridLayoutTest
```

As is, this applet displays six buttons, as shown in Figure 10-9.

Figure 10-9 The GridLayoutTest applet using a FlowLayout.

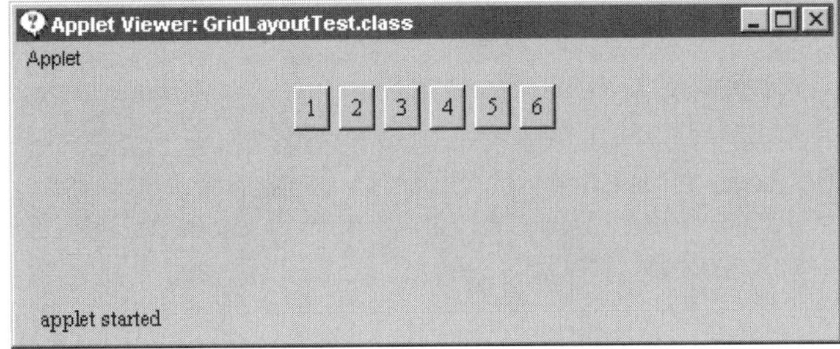

Add this single line of code to the top of the **init()** method:

```
setLayout(new GridLayout(2,3));
```

The applet now displays the buttons in a grid that fills up the applet window, as shown in Figure 10-10.

Figure 10-10 The GridLayoutTest applet using a GridLayout.

GRIDBAGLAYOUT

Of all the layout managers that come with Java, GridBagLayout is the most likely candidate for day-to-day placement of components. Unfortunately, it's also the most difficult of the layout managers to use.

GridBagLayout is useful when you want to put a variable number of components on each row.

GridBagLayout is paired with another class, called GridBagConstraints, which determines just how the components are going to be laid out. To use GridBagLayout, you first set the base constraints, then add a component, then, if necessary, modify the constraints before you add each successive component.

To create a new GridBag layout, first create an instance of the GridBagLayout class, then an instance of the GridBagConstraints class. Finally, set the current layout to the instance of the GridBagLayout class:

```
GridBagLayout gridbag = new GridBagLayout();
GridBagConstraints c = new GridBagConstraints();
setLayout(gridbag);
```

From this point on, you'll use the instance of GridBagConstraints (called **c** in this example) to position each of the components within the grid.

THE GRIDBAGLAYOUT GRID

At the heart of how GridBagLayout works is the grid that it uses to lay out components. This grid has a variable number of rows and, within each row, a variable number of columns. Just how many columns there are is determined (usually) by how many components are added to that row. For example, if you use the following code to create a line of buttons:

```
c.fill = GridBagConstraints.BOTH;
b1 = new Button("Button 1");
gb.setConstraints(b1,c);
add(b1);
b2 = new Button("Button 2");
gb.setConstraints(b2,c);
add(b2);
b3 = new Button("Button 3");
c.gridwidth = GridBagConstraints.REMAINDER;
gb.setConstraints(b3,c);
add(b3);
```

you'll end up with a horizontal row of three equally sized buttons. By using the **REMAINDER** constant for the width of the third button, you're

telling the layout manager that this button is to be the last button in the row. That sets the grid size at 1x3. If you repeat this code for three more buttons, you'll have a 2x3 grid of buttons.

> The code **c.fill = GridBagConstraints.BOTH** specifies that the following components should be expanded to fill the available space in the cell. The reason that this code is used in the example is to give you a visual idea of the actual size of the cell.

You can easily vary both the size of the individual columns and the number of columns in a row. Figure 10-11 shows an applet with two panels of controls; the panel on the left displays a varying number of columns and column sizes.

Figure 10-11 The GBLTestB applet.

The source code for the GLBTestB applet is shown in Figure 10-12. This applet displays two panels; however, at the moment, we're only concerned with the left-hand panel. Look in the source for the class called DisplayPanel.

Figure 10-12 The GBLTestB applet source code.

```
import java.applet.Applet;
import java.awt.*;
import java.io.*;
import java.net.*;
import java.util.*;
import java.io.InputStream;

public class GBLTestB extends Applet {

    public void init() {
      setLayout(new BorderLayout());
      DisplayPanel displayPanel = new DisplayPanel();
```

Figure 10-12 Continued.

```
      add("Center",displayPanel);
      ControlPanel controlPanel = new ControlPanel();
      add("East",controlPanel);
    }

}

class ControlPanel extends Panel {
    Button save,cancel,help;

    public ControlPanel() {
      GridBagLayout gb = new GridBagLayout();
      GridBagConstraints c = new GridBagConstraints();
      setLayout(gb);
      c.weightx = 1;
      c.weighty = 1;
      c.gridwidth = GridBagConstraints.REMAINDER;
      save = new Button("Save");
      gb.setConstraints(save,c);
      add(save);
      cancel = new Button("Cancel");
      gb.setConstraints(cancel,c);
      add(cancel);
      help = new Button("Help");
      gb.setConstraints(help,c);
      add(help);
    }

    public boolean action (Event e, Object o){
      return true;
    }

}

class DisplayPanel extends Panel {
    Button b1, b2, b3, b4;

    public DisplayPanel() {
      GridBagLayout gb = new GridBagLayout();
      GridBagConstraints c = new GridBagConstraints();
      setLayout(gb);
      c.weightx = 1;
      c.weighty = 1;
```

```
        c.gridwidth = 1;
        c.fill = GridBagConstraints.BOTH;
        b1 = new Button("Button 1");
        gb.setConstraints(b1,c);
        add(b1);
        c.weightx = 3;
        b2 = new Button("Button 2");
        gb.setConstraints(b2,c);
        add(b2);
        c.weightx = 1;
        b3 = new Button("Button 3");
        c.gridwidth = GridBagConstraints.REMAINDER;
        gb.setConstraints(b3,c);
        add(b3);
        b4 = new Button("Button 4");
        c.gridwidth = GridBagConstraints.REMAINDER;
        gb.setConstraints(b4,c);
        add(b4);
    }

}
```

In addition to setting up the GridBagLayout manager, the DisplayPanel constructor introduces several new constraints. The **weightx** and **weighty** constraints tell GridBagLayout how much of any given column or row to assign to a particular component. The default value is one, and if all components have the same value, then all cells (with one component per cell) will be the same size.

In **DisplayPanel()**, the second cell, which has a **weightx** of 3, takes up proportionally more of the row than the buttons on either side, which have a **weightx** of 1. The second button, which takes up the entire row, simply has a **gridwidth** of GridBagConstrains.REMAINDER, so it takes up the entire row.

This approach to variable-sized cells is discussed in more detail in the Java documentation for GridBagLayout and demonstrates some other nifty tricks (including a button-making method that reduces the amount of coding required). When all you want to do is lay out some fields for a form, however, there is a simpler approach.

FORM LAYOUT WITH GRIDBAGLAYOUT

The number of cells in a GridBagLayout can be implicitly specified by adding a number of components to a layout or explicitly specified with the use of the **gridx** and **gridy** constraints. This is a useful approach to take when laying out a form where you have rows of label/component pairs. Such a form is shown in Figure 10-13. (Figure 10-14 contains the source code for the GBLTest applet.)

Figure 10-13 The GBLTest applet.

Figure 10-14 The GBLTest applet source code.

```
import java.applet.Applet;
import java.awt.*;
import java.io.*;
import java.net.*;
import java.util.*;
import java.io.InputStream;

public class GBLTest extends Applet {

    public void init() {
      setLayout(new BorderLayout());
      DisplayPanel displayPanel = new DisplayPanel();
      add("Center",displayPanel);
      ControlPanel controlPanel = new ControlPanel();
      add("East",controlPanel);
    }

}

class ControlPanel extends Panel {
    Button save,cancel,help;
```

```
    public ControlPanel() {
      GridBagLayout gb = new GridBagLayout();
      GridBagConstraints c = new GridBagConstraints();
      setLayout(gb);
      c.weightx = 1;
      c.weighty = 1;
      c.gridwidth = GridBagConstraints.REMAINDER;
      save = new Button("Save");
      gb.setConstraints(save,c);
      add(save);
      cancel = new Button("Cancel");
      gb.setConstraints(cancel,c);
      add(cancel);
      help = new Button("Help");
      gb.setConstraints(help,c);
      add(help);
    }

    public boolean action (Event e, Object o){
      return true;
    }

}

class DisplayPanel extends Panel {
    Label la, lb, lc;
    TextField tfa, tfb, tfc, tfd;

    public DisplayPanel() {
      int colAwidth = 1;
      int colBwidth = 5;
      GridBagLayout gb = new GridBagLayout();
      GridBagConstraints c = new GridBagConstraints();
      setLayout(gb);
//      c.weightx = colAwidth;
      c.weighty = 1;
      c.gridx = 0;
      c.gridy = 0;
      c.anchor = GridBagConstraints.WEST;
      /*  add first label/field pair  */
      la = new Label("Very Long Label 1");
      gb.setConstraints(la,c);
      add(la);
      tfa = new TextField("Text Field 1",20);
      c.gridx = 1;
```

Figure 10-14 Continued.

```
//        c.weightx = colBwidth;
        gb.setConstraints(tfa,c);
        add(tfa);
        /*  add second label/field pair  */
        lb = new Label("Label 2");
        c.gridy = 1;
        c.gridx = 0;
//        c.weightx = colAwidth;
        gb.setConstraints(lb,c);
        add(lb);
        tfb = new TextField("Text Field 2",40);
        c.gridx = 1;
//        c.weightx = colBwidth;
        gb.setConstraints(tfb,c);
        add(tfb);
        /*  add second label/field pair  */
        lc = new Label("Label 3");
        c.gridy = 2;
        c.gridx = 0;
        c.weightx = colAwidth;
        gb.setConstraints(lc,c);
        add(lc);
        tfc = new TextField("Text Field 3",30);
        c.gridx = 1;
        c.weightx = colBwidth;
        gb.setConstraints(tfc,c);
        add(tfc);
    }

}
```

The difference between this applet and the previous GBLTestB applet is in the approach to setting out the columns. This applet uses the **gridx** and **gridy** constraints to define the dimensions of the grid. The constraints used for the first component are:

```
c.gridx = 0;
c.gridy = 0;
```

This code tells the layout manager to put the component, a label, in the first row. The second component, an entry field, is assigned to the second column with the code:

```
c.gridx = 1;
```

When the second cell is specified, the grid "grows" to two columns. Now you continue with the same approach for the next two label/text field pairs, except that **c.gridy** is incremented each time.

It's likely that you'll need more space for the entry fields than for the labels, and you can adjust the column widths as before by using the **weightx** constraint. When you use the **gridx/gridy** method, the last weighting applied to a cell is the one that holds. Accordingly, only the last label/text field pair has a weighting specified.

CARDLAYOUT

The CardLayout manager is what you use when you want to create a set of components (usually panels) that occupy the same space but only one of which is visible at any one time. This approach is analogous to Windows' wizards, which guide the user through a series of steps via **Next** and **Previous** buttons (usually augmented by **Cancel** and **Finish**). Each click of **Next** or **Previous** displays the next or previous page, or card, of the wizard. If you lay out a series of panels with the CardLayout manager, you can put whatever components that you want on each of those panels.

Figure 10-15 shows the SimpleCardTest applet, with the third of four cards visible. (Figure 10-16 contains the source code for the SimpleCardTest applet.)

Figure 10-15 The SimpleCardTest applet.

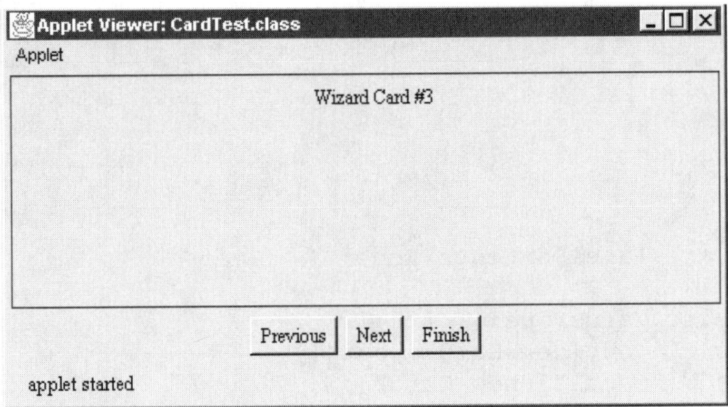

Figure 10-16 The source code for the SimpleCardTest applet.

```
import java.applet.Applet;
import java.awt.*;
import java.io.*;
import java.net.*;
import java.util.*;
import java.io.InputStream;

public class SimpleCardTest extends Applet {
    CardsPanel cardsPanel;

    public void init() {
      setLayout(new BorderLayout());
      add("Center",cardsPanel = new CardsPanel());
      Panel controlPanel = new Panel();
      controlPanel.add(new Button("Previous"));
      controlPanel.add(new Button("Next"));
      controlPanel.add(new Button("Finish"));
      add("South",controlPanel);
    }
    public boolean action(Event e, Object o){
      if ("Previous".equals(o)) {
        ((CardLayout)
cardsPanel.getLayout()).previous(cardsPanel);
      }
      else if ("Next".equals(o)) {
        ((CardLayout)
cardsPanel.getLayout()).next(cardsPanel);
      }
      else if ("Finish".equals(o)) {
         System.out.println("Finished with wizard!");
      }
      return true;
    }

}


class CardsPanel extends Panel {

    public CardsPanel() {
      setLayout(new CardLayout());
      add("Card1", new Card1());
      add("Card2", new Card2());
```

```
      add("Card3", new Card3());
      add("Card4", new Card4());
    }

}

class Card1 extends Panel{

  public Card1() {
    add(new Label("Wizard Card #1"));
  }
  public void paint(Graphics g){
      Rectangle r = this.bounds();
      g.setColor(Color.black);
      g.drawRect(2,2,r.width-4,r.height-4);
  }
}

class Card2 extends Panel{

  public Card2() {
    add(new Label("Wizard Card #2"));
  }
  public void paint(Graphics g){
      Rectangle r = this.bounds();
      g.setColor(Color.red);
      g.drawRect(2,2,r.width-4,r.height-4);
  }
}

class Card3 extends Panel{

  public Card3() {
    add(new Label("Wizard Card #3"));
  }
  public void paint(Graphics g){
      Rectangle r = this.bounds();
      g.setColor(Color.blue);
      g.drawRect(2,2,r.width-4,r.height-4);
  }
}

class Card4 extends Panel{
```

Figure 10-16 Continued.

```
  public Card4() {
    add(new Label("Wizard Card #4"));
  }
  public void paint(Graphics g){
       Rectangle r = this.bounds();
       g.setColor(Color.green);
       g.drawRect(2,2,r.width-4,r.height-4);
  }
}
```

The SimpleCardTest applet does just two things: It displays a card layout of panels, and it gives you several buttons with which to navigate the panels. All the code for the buttons, including the panel that they reside on, is declared inside the applet. This way, the button handling code doesn't have to navigate back up the class hierarchy and then back down again to gain access to the panel with the card layout.

The panel that will contain the "cards" is declared like any other panel:

```
add("Center",cardsPanel = new CardsPanel());
```

and added in the center position on the applet's BorderLayout. The CardsPanel constructor adds the panels that will each make up one card in the card layout:

```
public CardsPanel() {
  setLayout(new CardLayout());
  add("Card1," new Card1());
  add("Card2," new Card2());
  add("Card3," new Card3());
  add("Card4," new Card4());
}
```

In this example, the individual card panels are quite simple; they just display a label and a colored box around the panel. You'll want to add something more substantial to your own card panels.

There are two examples of card layouts in the JDK. One is called CardTest and is a demonstration of the different layout managers. As you choose the various cards, you get different layouts, so you might not exactly get the point that you're flipping through the cards as well. The other, much easier to understand example, is the GraphicsTest applet, which displays various panels of graphic objects.

OTHER LAYOUT MANAGERS

There's no reason you have to feel limited to the layout managers that come with Java. There already are a number of other layout managers in circulation, and if you can't find what you want, you can always write your own.

CANVASES

Unlike panels, canvases are a direct subclass of the Component class, rather than a subclass of Container. Canvases usually are used as components on which to draw graphics objects. You still can do graphics on a panel, so if you have a need for graphics mixed with other controls, you should use a panel instead of a canvas.

For just graphics, however, canvases are ideal because they provide a boundary for drawing operations. All the drawing done by the canvas's **paint()** method will happen inside the borders of the canvas.

Figure 10-17 shows an applet that demonstrates the use of a canvas. All this applet does is leave a trail of dots (mouse droppings, if you like) whenever the user presses the mouse button and drags the mouse. (Figure 10-18 contains the source code for the CanvasTest applet.)

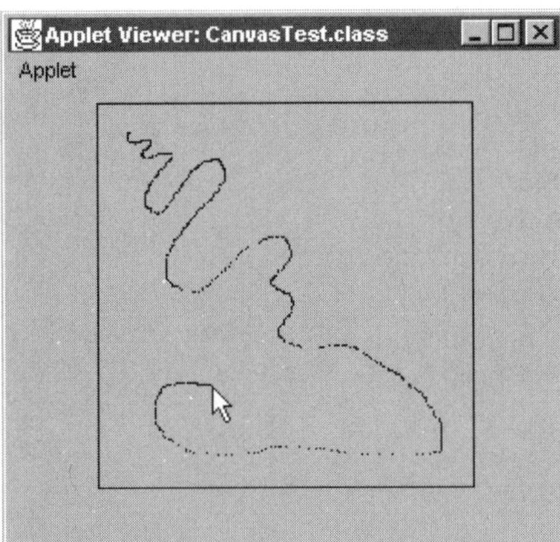

Figure 10-17
The CanvasTest applet.

Figure 10-18 The source code for the CanvasTest applet.

```
import java.applet.Applet;
import java.awt.*;
import java.util.Vector;

public class CanvasTest extends Applet {

  DrawCanvas c;

  public void init() {
    DrawCanvas dc = new DrawCanvas();
    dc.reshape(0,0,200,200);
    add(dc);
  }
}

class DrawCanvas extends Canvas {

  Vector points = new Vector();

  public boolean handleEvent(Event e) {
    if (e.id == Event.MOUSE_DRAG) {
      points.addElement(new Rectangle(e.x, e.y, -1, -1));
      repaint();
    }
    return super.handleEvent(e);
  }

  public void update(Graphics g) {
    paint(g);
  }

  public void paint(Graphics g) {
    int np = points.size();
    Rectangle r = bounds();
    g.drawRect(1,1,r.width-2,r.height-2);
    for (int i=0; i < np; i++) {
       Rectangle p = (Rectangle)points.elementAt(i);
       g.drawLine(p.x, p.y, p.x, p.y);
    }
  }
}
```

As you can see from the source code, canvases are declared and instantiated much like any other component. The canvas itself has two methods declared: **handleEvent()**, to trap the mouse-drag event, and **paint()**, to display the dots drawn by the mouse.

Everything here should look familiar to you by now, except perhaps for the Vector **class()**. Vectors are like a growable array, or a linked list, if you prefer. Each time the canvas receives a **MOUSE_DRAG** event, the Vector method **addelement()** is used to add a rectangle object to the points instance of Vector. (Using rectangle is overkill here as it has four elements—**x**, **y**, **width**, and **height**—whereas dimension has only two, so a point object would be a suitable replacement. Rectangle is used as an aid to the reader wanting to connect the dots with lines.)

Within the canvas's **paint()** method, the code:

```
int np = points.size();
```

simply determines the number of elements in the points object, so you know how many times to loop through points. Within the **for** loop, the code:

```
Rectangle p = (Rectangle)points.elementAt(i);
```

retrieves the element and casts it back to a locally declared rectangle object so that you can reference the elements of the rectangle again.

SUMMARY

Panels and layout managers are immensely useful tools, whether you're writing applets or applications. Because of Java's portability, the standard techniques of placing components at exact screen locations is a dangerous practice and, more likely than not, will result in components appearing in sizes and places that you did not expect.

Panels begin to address this problem by allowing you to organize controls into functional groups. Layout managers finish the picture by giving you a variety of ways to organize components (including other panels) within a panel.

Just as panels let you contain components, canvases give you a way to contain graphics operations in a given area. You also can use layout managers to organize the location of canvases, just as you use them for other components.

Panels, canvases, and layout managers are all tools that help you organize your applets and applications so that their functionality remains unimpaired, whatever platform your code ends up running on.

11 USING JAVA CLASSES

THE BEST OBJECT-ORIENTED LANGUAGE is essentially useless without a substantial library of support code. In Java, this support code is all found in the Java class libraries. So far in this book, we've concentrated on the basic constructs of the language itself and really have only broken the surface of the class library. This chapter will give you an overview of the libraries that not only includes much of the functionality that you'd expect of a general purpose language, but also includes a number of classes specifically tailored to programming on and for the Internet.

Keep in mind that the class descriptions that follow apply no matter which platform you are designing your code to run on (provided, of course, the Java interpreter has been ported to that platform). Think about it; compile once, run many! This concept virtually breaks the "OS lock" of traditional hardware-specific operating system binary application compatibility requirements. You don't have to compile your programs in Java for Microsoft Windows, then in Java for Sparc, and then in Java for Macintosh. Instead, you compile your Java sources once, and they will run on any platform that supports Java.

Even if you don't think that you'll use most of the classes in the library, it will almost certainly be worth your while to study them all. Chances are that you'll come across a situation where the perfect solution is a class that you haven't tried out yet, or perhaps one class or another will suggest an entirely new applet or application to you.

DEFINING TERMS: CLASSES, METHODS, PACKAGES, AND INTERFACES

Primarily, the Java class library is made up of classes and their associated methods; however, because the class library is quite vast, it's organized into packages of classes and interfaces that classes can implement. This first part of the chapter takes you through some of the basic terminology used in describing the class library.

DEFINING CLASSES

Although Java is an object-oriented programming language, a Java program does not itself contain objects, only classes, which are descriptions of objects. To use an object in a program, you have to create it (and the object must be destroyed when it is no longer needed, although this normally is done automatically). Most of your work with the class library will involve creating new instances (objects) of library classes or defining new subclasses based on the library classes, then creating new instances of those subclasses.

Classes are defined with the **class** keyword. Consider the following simple definition of a class called Ship:

```
class Ship {
  int  presentSpeed;
}
```

This class is made up of a single variable called **presentSpeed**, of type int. This class can have an elegant simplicity about it, but it's pretty much useless unless we can find some way of getting at the data in the class. That's where methods come in.

DEFINING METHODS

Almost all of the classes in the library have one or more methods. Methods are the equivalent of functions in C or what are referred to as procedures and functions in Pascal. In other words, a method is a means to an end; the end being some access to or change in an object. Objects are static entities that in and of themselves don't really do anything more interesting than provide a storage place for their data. Methods are the operations that you perform on or with other objects. Without methods, you could allocate lots of data, but you wouldn't be able to do anything with the data.

If you added a method to the Ship class to determine the value of the **presentSpeed** variable, it might look something like the following (ignoring for the moment that there isn't yet any means of actually *setting* the speed of the ship):

```
class Ship {
  int presentSpeed;
```

```
  int GetKnots() {
    return presentSpeed;
  }
}
```

CREATING AN INSTANCE OF A CLASS

You've created a class that has the ability to provide information about its insides—good! However, a class is just the definition of an object; to actually get an object to work with, you have to create an instance of the class. Somewhere outside this class, there will be a line of code (hypothetical, for purposes of this discussion) something like:

```
Ship myship = new Ship();
```

which just says create an object called **myship**, of type Ship, and make it a new instance of Ship. The **Ship()** method is what's called a *constructor method*, and all classes have constructors. This code also could be written, somewhat less compactly, as:

```
Ship myship;
myship = new Ship();
```

> If you're writing an applet, then the code that calls the class constructor actually is executing inside the browser. This is why applets have an **init()** method, in which you can place startup code, but do not need to have an explicitly declared constructor.

You've probably noticed something missing here. We have some code that calls a class's constructor, and we have a class, but there's no actual constructor method declared yet. In Java, *constructors have the same name as the class*. In this example, the constructor looks like this:

```
Ship (int a) {
  presentSpeed = a;
}
```

Constructors don't have to have parameters, but this one does. The purpose is that, when you create a new object of type Ship, you can, at the same time, set the speed at which that ship is traveling. So we need to step back in the code and update the hypothetical constructor call to:

```
Ship myship = new Ship(12);
```

The constructor now creates a new instance of Ship, called **myship**.

If you'd like to know more about this ship, you can add a couple of methods within the class body to set and read the ship's speed:

```
protected int SetKnots(int b) {
  presentSpeed = b;
  return 1;
}
int GetKnots() {
 return presentSpeed;
}
```

Add one more method for giving the maximum speed of a ship:

```
int MaxKnots() {
  return 100;
}
```

and the class is pretty much done. Figure 11-1 contains the complete code listing for the Ship class.

Figure 11-1 The complete code listing for the Ship class.

```
class Ship {
  int presentSpeed;
  Ship ( int a ) {
    presentSpeed = a;
  }
  protected int SetKnots(int b) {
    presentSpeed = b;
    return 1;
  }
  int GetKnots() {
    return presentSpeed;
  }
  int MaxKnots() {
    return 100;
  }
}
```

CREATING SUBCLASSES

The Ship class is an example of a base class; it isn't descended from any other class. While you certainly can use a base class, you want to

keep them to a minimum. Wherever possible, you should base any new class on a suitable existing class by using the **extends** keyword. Figure 11-2 shows a subclass of the Ship class, called Battleship.

Figure 11-2 The Battleship class, a subclass of the Ship class.

```
class Battleship extends Ship {
// Use the constructor method of the parent,
// or superclass.
  Battleship ( int a ) {
    super(a);
  }

// Set the max speed of this class of ship to 28 knots.
  int MaxKnots() {
    return 28;
  }

// Add 5 knots to the speed.
  int SetKnots() {
    presentSpeed = presentSpeed + 5;
    return 1;
  }
}
```

The constructor method **Battleship()** doesn't want to do anything different construction-wise from what the Ship class does, so it simply calls the Ship class's constructor with the code:

```
super(a);
```

However, the **MaxKnots()** and **SetKnots()** methods do implement different code in their bodies. This is called *method overriding* and is discussed a little later in this chapter.

You now have a Ship class and a modified subclass of ship called Battleship. Get out the champagne, and send them on their way. In Figure 11-3, the class DemoShip is a base class that launches (pun unintended) the application and that creates an instance of Ship and an instance of Battleship. (The Ship and Battleship classes are assumed to have been separately compiled and their .class files are in a directory specified in the **CLASSPATH** environment variable.)

Figure 11-3 The DemoShip Java application.

```
import Ship;
import Battleship;
class DemoShip {
public static void main ( String args[]) {
  System.out.println("This is the DemoShip application!");

  // Instantiate an object called Titanic of the Ship class
  // and set its current speed to 15 knots.
  Ship Titanic = new Ship(15);

  // Instantiate an object called s1 of the integer class
  // and assign it the maximum possible speed of the new
  // ship Titanic.
  int s1 = Titanic.MaxKnots();

  // Instantiate an object called Enterprise of the
  // Battleship class and set it's speed to 18 knots.

  Battleship Enterprise = new Battleship(18);

  // Instantiate an object called s2 of the integer class
  // and assign it the maximum possible speed of a Battleship.
  int s2 = Enterprise.MaxKnots(); // s2 = 28;

  System.out.println("The Titanic's speed is..." + Titanic.presentSpeed);
  System.out.println("The Titanic's max speed is..." + s1);
  System.out.println("The Enterprise's speed is..." + Enterprise.presentSpeed);
  System.out.println("The Enterprise's max speed is..." + s2);
  }
}
```

Running this application yields the following output:

```
This is the DemoShip application!
The Titanic's speed is...15
The Titanic's max speed is...100
The Enterprise's speed is...18
The Enterprise's max speed is...28
```

OVERRIDING METHODS

Because a subclass by default inherits the methods of its superclass, you don't need to redeclare those methods; you can just call them.

Redeclaring existing methods is called *overriding* and is an extremely useful capability.

Both the Ship and Battleship classes have a **MaxKnots()** method. Ship's **MaxKnots()** looks like this:

```
int MaxKnots() {
  return 100;
}
```

and Battleship's MaxKnots looks like this:

```
int MaxKnots() {
  return 28;
}
```

Overriding the **MaxKnots()** method of the parent class makes Battleship (and any of its subclasses that do not override **MaxKnots**) separate and distinct from just any kind of ship. This is a ship that can go only 28 knots.

DATA HIDING

Almost every modern object-oriented language provides some mechanism to hide data in one part of the program from other parts of the program. If you've ever programmed in the most basic of BASICs, you'll recall that everything in the program was global to the rest of the program. In very large programs with lots of variables, this made variable naming a rather nasty chore. Worse than that, an inadvertent use of the wrong variable could easily bring a program to its knees. This kind of globally shared data might make for good "war stories," but that's its only charm.

In large programming systems, where thousands of lines of code from multiple developers are being integrated, there has to be a way of protecting your methods and their data from being unintentionally (or intentionally, if your code is being hacked) modified or misread. This protection is known as *data hiding*.

Java provides three levels of data classification: **public**, **protected**, and **private**.

The **public** directive tells compiler that any class, method, or variable is available to any other class, method, or variable.

The most restrictive directive is the **private** directive. When applied to methods or variables, the compiler will generate a compile-time error when an attempt is made to override that method or variable or if you try to apply the private directive to data that has previously been declared as **public** or **protected**.

When applying the **protected** directive, the method or variable is available only to the methods or variables in the current class or in any derived subclasses. Sibling classes, which are classes that share the same superclass, are prevented from accessing data or methods marked as protected. Note the use of the protected directive in the **SetKnots()** method in the Ship class:

```
// Define a method for setting the current speed of the ship.
  protected int SetKnots(int b) {
    presentSpeed = b;
    return 1;
  }
```

If another subclass of Ship were to be defined, such as a Raft class, it would be considered to be a sibling class and could not access the **SetSpeed()** method, thereby forcing the raft to never have it's speed altered.

In the previous example, also note that, in the subclass Battleship, the **SetKnots()** method is overridden to add 5 more knots to the speed of the Enterprise. This is possible because the Battleship class is a subclass of the Ship class, and the speed variable **presentSpeed** is only marked as protected, making it available for access by subclasses of the class Ship.

ABSTRACT METHODS

Abstract methods simply are methods with no code in them. They are placeholders for methods that subclasses of the class must implement. Abstract methods do not have a method body but end in a semicolon.

INTERFACES

Interfaces are Java's alternative to multiple inheritance. An interface specifies a number of classes and their methods but does not attach any code to those methods. For instance, the Runnable interface declares a single method **run()**, which must be implemented by any

class that uses (via the **implements** keyword) the Runnable interface. A class can implement more than one interface.

THE JAVA API PACKAGES

The Java API packages (API stands for *application programming interface*) contain the core Java language classes, including those for handling numeric and string data, a graphical user interface and window system, classes for using system resources on the client computer, managing threads of execution, and handling exceptions and errors.

Table 11-1 lists the packages that make up the Java class library.

TABLE 11-1 The packages that make up the Java class library.

Package	Purpose
java.applet	Basic applet functionality
java.awt	Creation and use of all GUI components, including frames, windows, menus, and various data-display and data-entry components. Every applet, and any application that uses a window, makes some use of java.awt.
java.awt.image	Specialized image-handling classes. You can display images without using this class; however, if you want to manipulate those images in any way, you should look here.
java.awt.peer	These classes are part of the multiplatform support in Java; most programmers will not need to be concerned with these classes at all.
java.io	These classes implement all sorts of keyboard and file input and output. Most applet viewers don't allow direct file I/O by applets for security reasons. If you're writing applets, you ordinarily will be using GUI components to get input from the user. For both these reasons, this package is mainly the province of application programmers.
java.lang	These are the basic constructs of the java language, including the "object" object, wrappers for the standard data types, math and string handling functions, and multithreading support. All applets and applications make some use of classes in this package.
java.net	This is all of the Internet/Web-specific stuff; you'll use these classes to initiate and manage a communication link between a Java applet and a Java (or other) Web server application.
java.util	This package contains a number of useful programmers' utilities such as a hash table class, a vector class (for managing linked lists), a string parser, and the like.

The remainder of this chapter contains annotated listings of the Java class library's packages.

THE JAVA LANGUAGE PACKAGE: JAVA.LANG

This package and its constituent classes—exceptions, interfaces, and errors—literally define the implementation of the Java language. This is Java instantiated from a paper specification and defines the very core of what anyone porting Java to new platforms must conform to for compliance with the standard Java API. As such, this actually is pretty basic stuff. You will see that almost all of the components we've been talking about in previous chapters are now collected into one complete set. Note that the **java.lang** package is the only Java package that is included by default by the Java compiler, implying that it's not necessary for you to write an **import** statement for this class.

JAVA.LANG CLASSES

The **java.lang** classes are listed in Table 11-2.

JAVA.LANG INTERFACES

There is only one interface for the **java.lang** package, the *Runnable* interface. This interface is designed to provide a common protocol for objects that want to execute code while they are active. For example, Runnable is implemented by class Thread. Being active simply means that a thread has been started and has not yet been stopped.

In addition, Runnable provides the means for a class to be active while not subclassing Thread. A class that implements Runnable can run without subclassing Thread by instantiating a Thread instance and passing itself in as the target. In most cases, the Runnable interface should be used if you are planning to override only the **run()** method and no other Thread methods. This is important because classes should not be subclassed unless the programmer intends on modifying or enhancing the fundamental behavior of the class.

TABLE 11-2 The java.lang classes.

Class	Description
Boolean	An object wrapper for Boolean data values.
Character	An object wrapper for Character data values. Methods include case conversion and testing.
Class	Every object is an instance of some class, and this class includes methods for determining the name of the class, the name of the class loader, the name of the superclass, and more.
ClassLoader	This is an abstract class used to determine how classes are loaded in the runtime environment. It is not needed if you explicitly declare all your classes but is very useful if you don't.
Double	An object wrapper for Double data values. Variables for max and min values, methods to convert to other data types, and more.
Float	An object wrapper for Float data values. Variables for max and min values, methods to convert to other data types, and more.
Integer	An object wrapper for Integer data values. Variables for max and min values, methods to convert to other data types, and more.
Long	An object wrapper for Long data values. Variables for max and min values, methods to convert to other data types, and more.
Math	An extensive class with methods for most math functions. This class cannot be subclassed.
Number	An abstract superclass for numeric scalar types.
Object	This is the root of the class hierarchy. The methods **clone()**, **copy()**, **equals()**, **getClass()**, **hashCode()**, **notify()**, **notifyAll()**, **toString()**, and **wait()** are available for *all* Java objects.
Process	This class defines subprocesses; referenced by System classes.
Runtime	Library loading, memory status, and localized input/output streams.
Security Manager	An abstract class that allows for inspection of classloaders.
String	A general class of string objects. Methods include character comparisons, concatenation, byte copying, complex string searching, and much more.
StringBuffer	Used to create dynamically resizable strings. The compiler uses this when concatenating strings.
System	A variety of utility methods, including array copying, setting system security, running garbage collection (manually), and more.
Thread	Manages the creation of new threads of execution. Various methods for initiating, examining, and controlling threads.
ThreadGroup	A group of threads, with various methods of managing the thread group.
Throwable	An object that signals that an exception has occurred.

The Runnable interface implements a single method, called **run()**. This method is executed when a Runnable object is activated. The **run()** method is the "soul" of a Thread. It is in this method that all of the action of a Thread takes place.

JAVA.LANG EXCEPTIONS

The java.lang exceptions are:

- ArithmeticException
- ArrayIndexOutOfBoundsException
- ArrayStoreException
- ClassCastException
- ClassNotFoundException
- Exception
- IllegalAccessException
- IllegalArgumentException
- IllegalThreadStateException
- IndexOutOfBoundsException
- InstantiationException
- InterruptedException
- NegativeArraySizeException
- NoSuchMethodException
- NullPointerException
- NumberFormatException
- RuntimeException
- SecurityException
- StringIndexOutOfBoundsException

JAVA.LANG ERRORS

The java.lang errors are:

- AbstractMethodError
- ClassCircularityError
- ClassFormatError
- Error
- IllegalAccessError
- IncompatibleClassChangeError
- InstantiationError
- InternalError
- LinkageError
- NoClassDefFoundError
- NoSuchFieldError
- NoSuchMethodError
- OutOfMemoryError
- StackOverflowError
- ThreadDeath
- UnknownError
- UnsatisfiedLinkError
- VerifyError
- VirtualMachineError

THE JAVA APPLET PACKAGE: JAVA.APPLET

The applet package contains three interfaces and a single applet class, which is required to write Java applets. This will likely be the most widely used class for the majority of Java developers. Even people who are writing Java applications still will want and need to write supporting

applets. The thing to keep in mind about the applet class is that it is an extension of the Panel class of the Java language. As such, you could write your own extension to the Panel class (i.e., your own version of the applet class). For most people, it won't make sense to do this, but it is worth knowing that it can be done. The applet methods are:

- **destroy()**—Cleans up whatever resources are being held, if they are not likely to be cleaned up with automatic garbage collection.
- **getAppletContext()**—Gets a handle to the applet context.
- **getAppletInfo()**—Returns a string that contains information about the author, version, and copyright of the applet.
- **getAudioClip(*URL*)**, **getAudioClip(*URL*, *String*)**—Gets an audio clip from the specified URL.
- **getCodeBase()**—Gets the base URL for the currently executing class.
- **getDocumentBase()**—Gets the base URL for the Web document that the class is called from.
- **getImage(*URL*)**, **getImage(*URL*, *String*)**—Gets an image from a given URL.
- **getParameter(*String*)**—Gets the specified applet parameter.
- **getParameterInfo()**—Returns an array of strings that describe the parameters that are understood by this applet.
- **init()**—Called automatically when the applet initializes.
- **isActive()**—Returns true if the applet is active.
- **play(*URL*)**, **play(*URL*, *String*)**—Plays an audio clip.
- **resize(*int*, *int*)**—Resizes the applet to the new width/height.
- **showStatus(*String*)**—Shows a status message in the applet's context.
- **start()**—Called when the applet starts.
- **stop()**—Called when the applet stops.

The following three interfaces also are available for the applet programmer:

- AppletContext
- AppletStub
- AudioClip

The next two sections will describe the AppletContext and the AudioClip interfaces and their methods. The AppletStub generally is not used by applet programmers, so we will not discuss it further.

APPLETCONTEXT

This interface corresponds to an applet's environment. It can be used by an applet to obtain information from the applet's environment, which usually is the browser or the applet viewer.

The AppletContext interface offers the following methods:

- **getApplet(*String*)**—Gets an applet by name.
- **getApplets()**—Enumerates the applets in the current context (typically the Web page).
- **getAudioClip(*URL*)**—Gets an audio clip from the specified URL.
- **getImage(*URL*)**—Gets an image from the specified URL.
- **showDocument(*URL*)**—Shows the document specified in the URL.
- **showStatus(*String*)**—Shows a status string.

AUDIOCLIP

The AudioClip interface provides a very simplistic but useful set of methods for playing audio within applets:

- **play()**—Starts playing the clip instantiated in AudioClip. Each time this is called, the clip is restarted from the beginning.
- **loop()**—Starts playing the clip instantiated in AudioClip, and repeats continuously until **stop()** is called.
- **stop()**—Stops playing the clip.

THE JAVA INPUT/OUTPUT PACKAGE: JAVA.IO

The input/output (I/O) package contains classes for reading data into, and sending data out of, a Java program. Most commonly, these classes are used for reading and writing files. The package includes several classes specifically for sequential and random file access, but you also can use other types of data streams. These data streams are local to the site where the Java program is executing. If you want to move data over an Internet connection, you will want to study the Java networking package.

JAVA.IO CLASSES

The java.io classes are listed in Table 11-3.

TABLE 11-3 The java.io classes.

Class	Description
BufferedInputStream	Buffered input grabs a lot of characters at once to reduce the number of reads.
BufferedOutputStream	Buffered output; data is only written out when the stream is flushed or the buffer is full.
ByteArrayInputStream	Sets up an array as an input stream.
ByteArrayOutputStream	Sets up an array as an output stream.
DataInputStream	A data input stream that reads primitive data types identically across all platforms.
DataOutputStream	A data output stream that reads primitive data types identically across all platforms.
File	Declares a file name; most system-dependent factors, such as path and file separators, are handled by this class.
FileInputStream	Set up a file input stream, read/write data.
FileOutputStream	Set up a file output stream, read/write data.
FilterInputStream	Set up an byte-filtered file input stream, read/write data.
FilterOutputStream	Set up a byte-filtered file output stream, read/write data.

TABLE 11-3 Continued.

Class	Description
InputStream	The base class for all input streams.
LineNumberInputStream	An input stream that keeps track of line numbers.
OutputStream	The base class for all output streams.
PipedInputStream	Used with PipedOutputStream to create a piped stream between two threads.
PipedOutputStream	Used with PipedInputStream to create a piped stream between two threads.
PrintStream	An output stream with added methods to control printing of objects, strings, arrays, and more.
PushbackInputStream	An input stream with a one-byte pushback buffer.
RandomAccessFile	Create/manipulate a random-access file in read-only or read-write mode.
SequenceInputStream	Converts a sequence of input streams into a single input stream.
StreamTokenizer	A particularly useful class that lets you build various kinds of stream parsers.
StringBufferInputStream	An input stream implemented as a growable string buffer.

JAVA.IO EXCEPTIONS

The java.io exceptions are:

- EOFException
- FileNotFoundException
- IOException
- InterruptedIOException
- UTFDataFormatException

JAVA.IO INTERFACES

The java.io interfaces are listed in Table 11-4.

TABLE 11-4 The java.io interfaces.

Interface	Description
DataInput	Describes streams that can read input in a machine-independent format.
DataOutput	Describes streams that can write output in a machine-independent format.
FilenameFilter	Allows you to set up a filter for which files should be included in a file list.

THE JAVA UTILITY PACKAGE: JAVA.UTIL

The utility package contains a number of classes that embody commonly used programming structures and methods. Included are a date class (which gives you a system-independent way of dealing with calendar dates), a random-number generator, a string tokenizer, a hash table, and more.

JAVA.UTIL CLASSES

The java.util classes are listed in Table 11-5.

JAVA.UTIL EXCEPTIONS

The java.util exception is EmptyStackException.

JAVA.UTIL INTERFACES

The java.util interfaces are listed in Table 11-6.

TABLE 11-5 The java.util classes.

Class	Description
BitSet	A growable set of bits.
Date	System-independent date/time representations. Includes methods to get/create/compare dates and times.
Dictionary	The abstract parent of Hashtable, which maps key values and therefore affects collating sequences.
Hashtable	A hashtable class.
Observable	A class that provides for event notification between objects.
Properties	A hashtable that can be saved/loaded from a stream.
Random	A pseudo-random number generator. You can specify a seed or have the system calculate one from the current time.
Stack	A Last-In-First-Out stack.
StringTokenizer	A class to build string parsers.
Vector	A linked list, or "growable" array class. Space can be allocated manually, but needed space will always be obtained automatically.

TABLE 11-6 The java.util interfaces.

Interface	Description
Enumeration	Specifies a set of methods for enumerating a set of values. Used with Vector, Hashtable.
Observer	When implemented, allows all classes to be observable by instances of the Observer class.

THE JAVA NETWORKING PACKAGE: JAVA.NET

The networking package contains classes used to create and manipulate network connections. Included are classes to implement socket operations, connect to a URL, manage a content stream from the URL, obtain Internet addresses, and so on. You'll find this package useful if you want to do any kind of communication between a Java program and another entity (e.g., a Web server or another Java program) at a different Internet location.

JAVA.NET CLASSES

The java.net classes are listed in Table 11-7.

TABLE 11-7 The java.net classes.

Class	Description
ContentHandler	This class reads data from a URLConnection and makes that data into an object of a specified type. Standard MIME types are implemented. Content handlers should be called indirectly, via URL.getContent() or URLConnection.getContent().
InetAddress	An Internet address class; includes methods for getting all addresses for a host, getting raw IP addresses by host name, and more.
ServerSocket	A server socket; uses SocketImpl to do the actual operations.
Socket	A client socket; uses SocketImpl to do the actual operations.
SocketImpl	An abstract socket implementation class.
URL	A Uniform Reference Locator object.
URLConnection	An active connection to a URL; this is an abstract class.
URLStreamHandler	An abstract class for handling the data stream from the URL.

JAVA.NET EXCEPTIONS

The java.net exceptions are:

- MalformedURLException
- ProtocolException
- SocketException
- UnknownHostException
- UnknownServiceException

JAVA.NET INTERFACES

The java.net interfaces are listed in Table 11-8.

TABLE 11-8 The java.net interfaces.

Interface	Description
ContentHandlerFactory	Used by the URLStreamHandler class to create ContentHandlers for various MIME data types.
SocketImplFactory	Used by the SocketImpl class to create suitable socket implementations.
URLStreamHandlerFactory	Used by the URLStreamHandler class to create URLStreamHandlers for various MIME data types.

THE JAVA ABSTRACT WINDOW TOOLKIT PACKAGE: JAVA.AWT

The Abstract Window Toolkit (AWT) is the collection of classes that you will use if you want to present any kind of dialog to the user. Included are classes to create and manage various kinds of windows and menus, display graphics, get user input, and more. AWT consists of a base package, as well as two related packages. The image package specializes in handling various kinds of images. If you're writing applications, as opposed to applets, this package will be the foundation of much of your work. If you're writing applets, you can start with the applet package, which already embodies many AWT capabilities.

JAVA.AWT CLASSES

The java.awt classes are listed in Table 11-9.

JAVA.AWT EXCEPTIONS

The java.awt exception is AWTException.

JAVA.AWT ERRORS

The java.awt error is AWTError.

JAVA.AWT INTERFACES

The java.awt interfaces are listed in Table 11-10.

TABLE 11-9 The java.awt classes.

Class	Description
BorderLayout	A type of layout manager that lays out five regions: North, South, East, West, and Center.
Button	A labeled button component.
Canvas	A component usually used to create a region on the window where graphics primitives are used.
CardLayout	A layout manager for a container that contains several "cards." This is analogous to "wizards" in Windows.
Checkbox	A true/false checkbox component.
CheckboxGroup	A group of checkbox components, also called radio buttons in some systems.
CheckboxMenuItem	A menu item that can be checked on/off.
Choice	A multiple-choice button component (also called a drop-down list box in some systems).
Color	A class that incorporates RGB colors. Includes standard colors and the capability to create new colors.
Component	An abstract AWT component that can be used as a basis for custom components.
Container	An abstract AWT component that can be used as a basis for custom containers.
Dialog	A dialog-style window. The default layout is BorderLayout.
Dimension	A class that encapsulates width and height.
Event	A class for the standard events, including mouse events, keyboard events, and focus events.
FileDialog	Displays a standard file selection dialog. Includes methods for specifying default directories, filename filter, and more.
FlowLayout	A layout manager that lays out buttons left to right, starting at the top of the window. Each line is centered.
Font	A class for specifying fonts.
FontMetrics	A class for getting a font's metrics, including character width, height, leading, ascent, descent, and more.
Frame	Creates a top-level window with a title and a border. Optionally the window can be resizable, iconizable, and have a menu bar.

TABLE 11-9 Continued.

Class	Description
Graphics	The abstract class for all graphics components. This class contains an extensive list of methods for drawing and manipulating graphics components.
GridBagConstraints	Used with GridBagLayout. Specifies the constraints for how GridBagLayout will display components.
GridBagLayout	A layout manager that allows for components to be laid out in complex grid patterns.
GridLayout	A layout manager that lays out components in an array of rows and columns.
Image	An image component. The most common image format used is GIF.
Insets	A class used to specify insets for a container.
Label	A label component. Alignment can be specified.
List	A list box component. Includes methods for adding/deleting items from the list. Multiple selection is optional.
MediaTracker	A utility class for keeping track of and prioritizing media objects, such as images and audio clips.
Menu	A menu that is composed of a menu bar. These can be fixed or tear-off menus.
MenuBar	A menu bar that is bound to a frame.
MenuComponent	This is the superclass of all menu-related components.
MenuItem	Creates a new menu item.
Panel	A general-purpose container class. Because panels have their own layout managers, complex window layouts can be constructed by placing a number of panels, each containing a layout of components, on a window.
Point	An X-Y coordinate class.
Polygon	A list of X and Y coordinates.
Rectangle	A rectangle defined by X, Y, width, and height.
Scrollbar	A vertical or horizontal scrollbar component.
TextArea	A scrollable multiple-line text field component. Default text can be specified.

TABLE 11-9 Continued.

Class	Description
TextComponent	A component that allows editing of text. This is the superclass for TextArea and TextField.
TextField	A singe-line text field component. Default text can be specified.
Toolkit	This class is used to bind the abstract AWT classes to a particular native toolkit implementation. Not an issue for most programmers.
Window	A top-level window with no borders and no menubar.

TABLE 11-10 The java.awt interfaces.

Interface	Description
LayoutManager	Defines the interface for classes (typically panels) that know how to lay out Containers. Includes methods for adding/removing components and determining optimal layout size.
MenuContainer	This is the superclass of all menu-related containers. Includes methods for getting the font, posting an event, and removing the menu component.

THE JAVA ABSTRACT WINDOW TOOLKIT IMAGE PACKAGE: JAVA.AWT.IMAGE

The java.awt.image is an extension of the window toolkit and provides a number of commonly used image-manipulation functions available for use in native Java by developers.

JAVA.AWT.IMAGE CLASSES

The java.awt.image classes are listed in Table 11-11.

TABLE 11-11 The java.awt.image classes.

Class	Description
ColorModel	An abstract class for the methods of translating from pixel values to the color components for an image.
CropImageFilter	Used for producing cropped versions of existing images.
DirectColorModel	A color model similar to an X11 TrueColor visual.
FilteredImageSource	A class for creating a color-filtered version of an original image.
ImageFilter	Intended for use in conjunction with FilteredImageSource to produce filtered versions of existing objects. Defines the methods used to deliver data from an ImageProducer to an ImageConsumer.
IndexColorModel	An abstract class for the methods of translating from pixel values to the color components for an image via indices into a fixed colormap.
MemoryImageSource	A class that uses an array to produce pixel values for an Image.
RGBImageFilter	Intended for use in conjunction with FilteredImageSource to produce filtered versions of existing objects in the default RGB ColorModel. Defines the methods used to deliver data from an ImageProducer to an ImageConsumer.

JAVA.AWT.IMAGE INTERFACES

The java.awt.image interfaces are listed in Table 11-12.

TABLE 11-12 The java.awt.image interfaces.

Interface	Description
ImageConsumer	ImageConsumers are the data input for ImageProducers. There normally will be some sort of filtering going on between the two.
ImageObserver	An interface for tracking information about the transformation of an image between a producer and a consumer.
ImageProducer	ImageProducers are the data output from ImageConsumers. There normally will be some sort of filtering going on between the two.

THE JAVA ABSTRACT WINDOW TOOLKIT PEER PACKAGE

The AWT Peer package implements classes used by the developers of Java when porting the language to different platforms. It's unlikely that you will need to use any of these classes.

BEYOND THE STANDARD PACKAGES

As you create your own classes to augment the standard Java classes, you might find it useful to group these classes into packages as well. As the market for Java tools develops, you also might find yourself purchasing additional class packages from third-party vendors. This brings up an interesting aspect of the current crisis in software licensing, software upgrading, maintenance, and distribution.

By now, it is hard to imagine that most, if not all of you reading this book have been affected by software version incompatibilities. This book was written using a common text-processing application that suffers from these very issues. Over the course of time, software vendors change the way their applications work and usually add new features and functionality (as well as bugs). Vendors that do not change or update their applications quickly find themselves behind the times and behind their competitors in sales. Market share, time to market, and installed base are everything in the for-profit software world.

However, with multiple versions of applications that have to be supported, in multiple versions of a given operating system, or in the worst case, on multiple operating systems across several hardware platforms, the support matrix gets impossible to successfully test against, usually leading to a raft of bugs in any new major release of software. The very force that demands these new features, paying customers, usually ends up suffering for these mistakes. And so it goes, until now.

In a world of Java-based applications, one of the most formidable barriers to widely usable software has been smashed: the hardware-specific and operating-system-specific requirements that have to be met before using an application. Java programs need to be compiled only once. As well, because Java programs are created, live, and work in a network-centric world, they are inherently portable and transportable. Why go to the store to buy the latest version of JavaDoom when you can simply click on a hyperlink on the ID Software home page and *rent* the latest version of the game for the short time that you want to use it?

In the future, software licensing and software prices will totally reinvent themselves, and Java might be one of the first tools to pave the way. In one possible future, you won't buy software, you'll rent it and be charged only for the time that you use it. All documentation will be online and available for your use, not clogging up your hard drive. In this future, software vendors will begin to look more and more like software *integrators* that provide a core function or functions, then outsource a plug-in like architecture to other software vendors around the world.

When you go to run your application *du jour*, you will never know what machines it came from or who put it together. In fact, you will never really run the same application twice, as it will only consist of the various classes and methods that you needed that day. The rest of the code stays at home on some Internet server somewhere, waiting for you to access it and pay for it when you need it.

By using a temporally based licensing and purchasing scheme, you will potentially reap the benefits of vastly reduced software costs (cost reduction is ultimately up to the vendors but will be driven by consumer demand) at significantly greater ease of use. You will *always* have the latest version, as the application is no longer stored on your hard drive as a permanent fixture but instead lives on the Internet where the application vendor assumes the responsibility for maintaining the most current and stable release. Take a look at the best example of this today, Netscape. People beat down their network door to get the latest versions. Netscape embeds hyperlinks and methods for downloading the latest version of their browser, all in a deceivingly simple effort to avoid shipping software through the "normal" channels: retail, wholesale, and snail mail.

ERROR AND EXCEPTION HANDLING

IN JUST ABOUT any Java program, something can go unexpectedly wrong. Code that compiles fine might attempt an illegal operation, such as attempting to open a connection to an invalid URL or referencing a nonexistent object. When something does go wrong at runtime, the seriousness of the problem depends both on what happens and where it happens.

WHAT HAPPENS: ERRORS VERSUS EXCEPTIONS

There is a loosely defined distinction between defining a problem in code as an error or as an exception. *Errors* generally are considered as any condition that the program (or in the case of Java, the Java interpreter) considers invalid. Such conditions usually are the result of some bug in the code, and if you examine the code carefully you probably will be able to predict the occurrence of the error.

In contrast, exceptions are considered "exceptional" errors, which are not really predictable. An exception could be the program running out of memory or a needed file not being found on the system.

WHERE IT HAPPENS: CLIMBING OUT OF THE CLASS WELL

Where a problem occurs can be as important as the problem itself. Consider for a moment a moderately large object-oriented program that is well underway. The current point of program execution will be nested several, or perhaps many, levels of classes deep. The notion of object orientation is well and good when everything is working as expected, but what happens when, deep in the bowels of that Java application, something goes wrong? Should your program just give up and head for the command line with exit(-1)? Or should it attempt to gracefully handle the condition? If the program does try to handle the problem, how does the class tell the calling class what's happened? How does the class get access to data structures and methods that it might need? All of these issues suddenly become painfully important.

In nonobject-oriented languages such as C and Pascal, it was almost always up to the programmer to decide what to do. In most cases, programmers invented specific, consistent ways of dealing with errors. In the case of many programmers integrating their code with that of other people who invented their own error handling procedures, the result was more often than not a tower of Babel.

With each programmer trying to handle their own errors, both messages to the user and the resulting behavior of the code were inconsistent across the merged application. Usually a global error or condition handler was the result, cobbled together by the master system integrators. Most often, the error handler required detailed knowledge of almost every major data structure of every large part of the system, making it unwieldy, invasive of the code, and very difficult to maintain. What's more, although these global error-handling approaches provided some consistency in handling errors, the implementation was almost always awkward and arbitrary when viewed in the greater context of large programming systems in general.

THROW, CATCH, AND TRY

In C++ and more recently in Java, the notion of exception handling has been standardized into native language features that can be implemented and maintained in a consistent manner. In true object-oriented fashion, these new descriptive terms define how exceptions are dealt with: **catch** and **throw**. Java adds the **try** directive to signify that a piece of code is able to throw an exception in the first place.

Assume that you have a block of code that can detect the fact that the parameters being passed in are out of range. For example, we'll revisit the example in chapter 10 that implements the Ship class. Recall that, by default, the basic ship's maximum speed was 100 knots. Suppose someone decided to try to set the ship's speed beyond this already absurd limit. As a programmer, how would you handle it?

By modifying the basic ship class to handle an exception of setting the speed too fast, here's how you can solve the problem in Java. First, you create an exception called **TooFast()**:

```
class TooFast extends Exception {
}
```

You'll notice that TooFast doesn't have any methods or variables. Exceptions can have constructors that take parameters, such as an error message, but they don't need to.

The second step is to enclose the code that might encounter the exception within a try block:

```
try {
  if (b >= 100) {
    throw new TooFast();
  }
```

If you look at Figure 12-1, you'll see that this block of code goes inside the **SetKnots()** method. If the maximum speed of the ship is set to more than 100, the **TooFast()** exception is thrown. The following code comes right after the try block, and catches the exception:

```
} catch (TooFast e) {
   System.out.println("\n Going too fast!");
}
```

This is a somewhat trivial example, in that you could more easily just write the code to print out an error message if the result exceeds 100. The point is that the code inside the try block can go many class levels deep, and if an exception occurs within that nesting, the program will back all of the way out and exit the try block, where the catch block will pick up the error condition.

The example in Figure 12-1 covers the most basic example of how to define your own exception handler. Exception handlers always force the currently executing method to resume execution after the **catch** statement that matched the specified exception. You cannot force control to resume after the **throw**; therefore, if you need to tidy things up, you will most likely need to do this in the handler itself. Exceptions can be nested, allowing exception handling to happen in more than one place. This is a useful technique when especially disastrous errors force you to transfer control of error handling from the most deeply nested method to the handler for the previous method. By doing this, you preserve code integrity by not forcing the creation of one huge error handler to clean up everything. Instead, you have a built-in language feature that will roll back exceptions as far as you want them to.

Figure 12-1 An example of exception handling in Java.

```
//
// A simple example of declaring an exception
// handler, throwing the exception and handling
// it..
// First we'll declare the exception as an extension
// of the basic Exception class
//
class TooFast extends Exception {
}

class Ship {
    int         presentSpeed;
// use the constructor to define the speed of the ship.
    Ship ( int a ) {
        presentSpeed = a;
    }
// Define a method for determining how fast the ship is going.
    int GetKnots() {
        return presentSpeed;
    }
// Provide a method for giving the maximum speed of a ship.
    int MaxKnots() {
        return 100;
        }
// Define a method for setting the current speed of the ship.
    int SetKnots(int b) {
// Enclose the code that throws the exception with a "try"
// Look in the if-then statement to find the throw...
        try {
            if (b >= 100) {
                throw new TooFast();
            }
        presentSpeed = b;
// Now close the try with a catch condition that will
// transfer control to the TooFast exception.
//
        } catch (TooFast e) {
            System.out.println("\n Going too fast!");
        }
        return 1;
    }
}
class DemoException {
```

Figure 12-1 Continued.

```
public static void main ( String args[]) {
    // Say hello to the user...
    System.out.println("DemoException");
    // Instantiate an object called Bismarck of the Ship
    // class and set its current speed to 0 knots.
    Ship Bismarck = new Ship(0);
    // Now try to set its speed to 150 knots, forcing
    // the exception to be thrown
    //
    Bismarck.SetKnots(150);
    }
}
```

As you might expect, the Java runtime interpreter can and does throw exceptions of its own. These are known as Java *runtime exceptions*. The following runtime exceptions have been defined in Java:

- ArithmeticException
- NullPointerException
- IncompatibleClassChangeException
- ClassCastException
- OutOfMemoryException
- NoClassDefFoundException
- IncompatibleTypeException
- ArrayIndexOutOfBoundsException
- UnsatisfiedLinkException
- InternalExceptions (should never be thrown!)

FINALLY, FINALLY

One last note on exceptions is on the use of the **finally** directive. **Finally** is essentially a way of allowing you to say to the compiler, "Expect everything to go correctly, but if it doesn't, then when I throw this exception and handle it, *finally*, do these things"

Here's the previous example modified to show how you can use the **finally** statement to set the ship's speed to 0. Seeing as how anything over 100 knots is unreasonable, we might as well set the speed to 0:

```
try {
  if (b >= 100) {
    throw new TooFast();
    }
  presentSpeed = b;
  // Now close the try with a catch condition
  // which will transfer control to the
  // TooFast exception.
  //
  } catch (TooFast e) {
    System.out.println("\n Going too fast!");
  } finally {
    presentSpeed = 0;
  }
```

SUMMARY

Error and exception handling in any object-oriented language is almost always worthy of an entire book devoted solely to the ins and outs of dealing with abnormal execution conditions. For more detailed references on exceptions, the place to go is the source: *http://java.sun.com.*

WRITING JAVA APPLICATIONS

SO FAR IN PART 2, we've been discussing Java applets, which are Java programs based on the applet class and designed to run in the context of Web pages. You also can use Java to write standalone applications that run via the Java interpreter. Standalone applications usually are larger than applets in size and scope, and because they don't execute in the context of a browser, they cannot rely on outside instructions as to when they should start up, shut down, or do any of the other things that browsers tell applets to do. While applets run in the context of a browser, applications run in the wider context of the operating system and accordingly have a somewhat wider range of uses.

This chapter describes the unique features of Java applications and application programming, from the **main()** starting point to the use of AWT to build a full-featured GUI interface.

THE MAIN() FUNCTION

The starting point for any Java application is the class file that starts program execution, and that class file's starting point is the **main()** function. The following is a Java "Hello World" application that demonstrates **main()**:

```
class HelloWorld{
  public static void main(String args[]) {
    System.out.println ("Hello World!")
  }
}
```

Although applications require a **main()** method, this does not by itself distinguish applets from applications. All applets have a **main()** method that you can override if you want, but you don't need to because the browser invokes the **main()** method automatically whenever it loads an applet class. If **main()** has not been overridden, control immediately passes to the **init()** method.

You'll often find that, when you're developing a class, you test it by running it from the command line, perhaps with various parameters to simulate the class's use in a production environment. Once the class is working properly, you might be tempted to take out unneeded **main()** methods, because only the class that launches the application really needs to be there. Resist the temptation! As long as you can leave

those **main()** methods in without any ill effects on your application, you might find them useful at some future time, or they might come in handy for other developers who end up using your classes.

READING MAIN() ARGUMENTS

The **main()** method has one parameter, a string array that contains all of the command-line arguments (if any) that were passed to the program. Where the array has the label **args**, the code:

```
argcount = args.length
```

will return the number of command-line arguments, and you can use that value to determine how many elements of the array to read. Do keep in mind that the first element in an array has an index of 0. If you use a loop to read the array, you'll want to start at 0, increment by one, and stop after the array element that you've read is one less than the number of arguments:

```
int j, argcount;

if (argcount > 0) {
  for (j = 0, j < count; j++) {
    System.out.println("Argument " + (j+1) + " " args[j]);
  }
}
```

Unlike C and C++, Java does not pass in the name of the program as the first command-line argument, so you have to use another means to get the name of the program (i.e., the class name) at runtime. You can extract the class name of any object at runtime using something like:

```
object.getClass().getName();
```

So, you might think that, in a Java application, you could do something like:

```
class MyClass {
  public static void main(String args[]) {
  System.out.println("Class name is " + this.getClass().getName());
}
...
```

but you can't, because **getClass()** operates on an *object*. Because **main()** is static, it is a class method. There is no **this** for it to operate on.

Instead, if you want, you can create a new instance of the current class, then use the **.getClass().getName()** methods to return the name of the class:

```
class MyClass {
  static void main(String args[]) {
    System.out.println("Class name is "
        + (new MyClass()).getClass().getName());
  }
```

Effectively, you've just created an object for the methods to work with.

Now, you might initially wonder why you would do this rather than just type:

```
System.out.println("Class name is MyClass");
```

If you never change the name of your classes, then this code will work, but then there's also no need to determine the class name because you already know what it is. Getting a class name is only done if you're not sure at runtime what it is. The new **MyClass().getClass().getName()** code will always return a correct value valid regardless of the class name.

As compared to the "Hello WebWorld" applet in chapter 8, the HelloWorld application has very little functionality. Unlike HelloWebWorld, HelloWorld does not extend any existing class; it merely creates a new class out of whole cloth, which prints out the string "Hello World!" On the other hand, HelloWebWorld extends the applet class and so inherits the code that loads the applet, pauses it when the applet's location on the Web page isn't visible, terminates it when the page is unloaded, and so on.

All applets run in the context of a browser, so they each are allocated a window (on the Web page) in which they can display text and other components and collect input. To create a window in which an application can display information, you need to create a frame.

CREATING A FRAME

To create a frame in an application, you base the class on the Frame class. The Frame class incorporates much of the functionality that you're used to seeing in applets, except for the browser-specific code. There

also is one major difference in how the application is instantiated. An applet is automatically instantiated; you don't see the code that creates a new instance of the applet class (unless the applet writer has chosen to override **main()** and do this explicitly). In an application, you have to create a new instance of the class, and you do that by calling a constructor method from in the **main()** method.

CONSTRUCTOR METHODS

A *constructor method* is a method that actually creates the object, which in this case is a frame. Constructor methods have the same name as the class, which can be a little confusing if you're not used to this terminology.

If you have a class called MyFrame, declared as follows:

```
class MyFrame extends Frame {
```

you'll also have at least one method within that class, also called MyFrame, such as:

```
public MyFrame() {
  // do any needed initialization
}
```

Although this method will have the same name as the class, it can have any number of parameters. This example just doesn't happen to have any. You can have more than one constructor if you like and call one or another constructor based on command-line arguments.

Now that you have a constructor method, you need to call it, and you do that from the **main()** method. Creating new instances of class objects is much like creating other new instances:

```
MyFrame ibf;
ibf = new MyFrame();
```

Finally, after calling the constructor, call the **start()** method:

```
ibf.start();
```

The complete code for a minimal application with frame is shown in Figure 13-1.

Figure 13-1 The MyFrame Java application.

```
import java.awt.*;
class MyFrame extends Frame {
  public MyFrame(){
    resize(300,300);
  }
  public void start(){
    show();
  }
  public boolean mouseDown(Event e, int x, int y){
    hide();
    dispose();
    System.exit(0);
    return false;
  }
  public static void main(String args[]) {
    MyFrame ibf;
    ibf = new MyFrame();
    ibf.start();
  }
}
```

MULTIPLE CONSTRUCTORS

As I mentioned earlier, you can have more than one constructor. For example, if you optionally want to be able to tell your frame to resize itself to dimensions other than 300×300, you could add a second constructor as follows:

```
public MyFrame(int w, int h){
  resize(w, h);
}
```

Now, if you create the new instance of MyFrame as:

```
ibf = new MyFrame(200,100);
```

the second constructor will be called, because it has a matching prototype. If you create the new instance of MyFrame as:

```
ibf = new MyFrame();
```

the first constructor will be called.

CALLING OTHER CONSTRUCTORS

You also can call constructors from other constructors. For example, because both constructors resize the frame, the code is somewhat repetitious. It's cleaner to just have one method (the one with the **w** and **h** parameters) do the resizing. Rewrite the first constructor as follows:

```
public MyFrame() {
  this(300, 300);
}
```

The syntax for calling another constructor is to use the **this** keyword, which identifies the current object. Because the current object is MyFrame, the code:

```
this(300,300);
```

is identical to:

```
MyFrame(300,300);
```

which is effectively the method that gets called when you instantiate a new MyFrame with the code:

```
ibf = new MyFrame(300,300);
```

That syntax works for calling constructors in the current class. What about when you want to call the constructor in the superclass? MyFrame is a subclass of the AWT Frame class, and if you look at the documentation for Frame, you'll see that it has two constructors: **Frame()** and **Frame(*String*)**. The second form of the constructor puts the text passed to it in the title of the frame window.

You can use superclass constructors, but the call has to be the first code in the constructor, because all superclass constructor code has to execute before any of the current class constructor code executes. The **super** keyword identifies the superclass of the current class:

```
public MyFrame (int width, int height, String title) {
  super(title);
  resize(width, height);
}
```

Because you've added the capability to set a title, you'll probably want to be able to optionally specify a title, a width, and a height. That makes for four constructors, which could look like this:

```
public MyFrame() {
  resize(300,300);
}
public MyFrame(String Title) {
  super(title);
  resize(300,300);
}
public MyFrame(int w, int h) {
  resize(w, h);
}
public MyFrame(int w, int h, String title) {
  super(title);
  resize(w, h);
}
```

The duplicated code is starting to pile up now. **resize()** is there four times, and the **super** class constructor is there twice. Aside from creating code bloat, the more complicated constructors become, the more likelihood there is that you'll forget to update some of that duplicated code, such as if you decide to change the default window size. It's always better to keep as few copies (ideally only one) of any block of code that accomplishes some distinct purpose.

These constructors can be rewritten as follows:

```
public MyFrame() {
  this("");
}
public MyFrame(String title) {
  this(300,300,title);
}
public MyFrame(int w, int h) {
  this(w, h,"");
}
public MyFrame(int w, int h, String title) {
 super(title);
  resize(w, h);
}
```

Notice that the constructor that incorporates all of the possible parameters is the one that is finally called. All of the other constructors either call this constructor or call a constructor that calls this constructor.

SHUTTING DOWN THE FRAME

We've discussed creating and instantiating the frame, but there's one other detail to take care of, and that's shutting down the frame politely. There are any number of ways of triggering this; however, in this example, a simple mouse click anywhere in the application frame does the trick and calls three important lines of code:

```
hide();
dispose();
System.exit(0);
```

The **hide()** method makes the window invisible, just as **show()** made it visible in the **start()** method. **dispose()** frees up used system resources, and **System.exit()** shuts down the Java virtual machine (that is, the Java interpreter) and tells the interpreter to exit with the provided exit code. An exit code of zero indicates that the shutdown proceeded without error.

THE WINDOW_DESTROY EVENT

Because Java applications run in a window system, they are under the control of a window manager like Windows or X Window. That window manager provides the frame surrounding the application, the resize handles, the title bar, and the menu and iconify buttons at the top of the window. When a user chooses the **Close**, **Quit**, or **Exit** options from the window menu, they are interacting with the window manager, *not* with the application directly. The window manager takes the request and forwards it to the application in the form of a **WINDOW_DESTROY** event. It is up to the application to take appropriate action. If your application does not handle this event, the only way that the user will be able to shut down the application is if you've provided an **Exit** or **Close** button of your own. Even if you have such a means available, you should always respond to the **WINDOW_DESTROY** event in an appropriate manner, or your users will think there's something wrong with your application. The code to do so is quite simple:

```
public boolean handleEvent(Event e) {
  if (e.id == Event.WINDOW_DESTROY) {
    hide();
    dispose();
    System.exit(0);
    return true;
```

```
  }
  else
    return super.handleEvent(e);
}
```

You already should be familiar with the **handleEvent()** method from the chapters on applet programming. Here the code does a simple test to determine if the event is the **WINDOW_DESTROY** event. If it is, the application executes the code to hide the window, free resources, and terminate the Java virtual machine.

If the event is not a **WINDOW_DESTROY** event, then the application passes the event back to the superclass's event-handling method using:

```
return super.handleEvent(e);
```

If you do not use this code, all window events other than **WINDOW_DESTROY** will be gobbled up by this method, which processes events before any other method (such as **mouseDown()**). Passing the event back to the superclass ensures that all of the other methods that rely on events will get their chance.

Any Frame should trap this event and take appropriate action. For base Frames of an application, this probably means quitting gracefully, perhaps asking the user first if they would like to save the last 20 hours of work. For subframes, it might mean disposing of the frame, if you plan on recreating it each time before displaying it. (Figure 13-2 shows a frame that pops up in a subframe.) Otherwise, it probably is best just to hide the frame and **show()** it later as needed. In any case, you might want to set up a class method, such as **okToClose()**, and call it when the **WINDOW_DESTROY** event arrives to determine whether or not to go ahead with the shutdown code.

OTHER WINDOW EVENTS

There are several other window manager events that a conscientious Java programmer should trap, including events to iconify and deiconify and the resize event. (For a full list of window events see java.awt.Event.)

Figure 13-2 A version of MyFrame that pops up a subframe.

```
import java.awt.*;

class SubFrame extends Frame {
  public boolean handleEvent(Event e) {
    if (e.id == Event.WINDOW_DESTROY) {
      hide();
      return true;
    }
    else
      return super.handleEvent(e);
  }
}

class MyFrame extends Frame {

  static SubFrame fr;

  public static void main(String args[]) {
      MyFrame f = new MyFrame();
      fr = new SubFrame();
      f.resize(100,100);
      f.show();
      fr.resize(50,50);
      fr.show();
  }
  public boolean handleEvent(Event e) {
      if (e.id == Event.WINDOW_DESTROY) {
        fr.dispose();
        dispose();
        System.exit(0);
        return true;
      }
      else
        return super.handleEvent(e);
      }
}
```

The **WINDOW_ICONIFY** event indicates that the window manager has detected a mouse click on the iconify button (or an appropriate keyboard shortcut) and has iconified your application accordingly. The window management is done automatically for you, but your program continues to run, even though it has no displayed window. You'll want to stop any threads that shouldn't be eating up CPU time, halt redisplay of graphic objects, and stop any other program behavior that isn't appropriate while the program is iconified. Your program does continue to run normally when iconified unless you tell it otherwise.

The IconTest example in Figure 13-3 is the MyFrame example but with code added to trap iconify/deiconify messages and have the base frame hide and show the child when it gets the appropriate messages.

Figure 13-3 The IconTest application.

```
import java.awt.*;

class SubFrame extends Frame {
  public boolean handleEvent(Event e) {
    switch (e.id) {
    case Event.WINDOW_DESTROY:
      hide();
      return true;
    case Event.WINDOW_ICONIFY:
      System.out.println("SubFrame Got Iconify");
      return true;
    default:
      return super.handleEvent(e);
    }
  }
}

class IconTest extends Frame {

  static SubFrame fr;

  public static void main(String args[]) {
    IconTest f = new IconTest();
    fr = new SubFrame();
    f.resize(100,100);
    f.show();
    fr.resize(50,50);
    fr.show();
  }
  public boolean handleEvent(Event e) {
    switch (e.id) {
    case Event.WINDOW_DESTROY:
      fr.dispose();
```

```
        dispose();
        System.exit(0);
        return true;
      case Event.WINDOW_ICONIFY:
        fr.hide();
        System.out.println("Frame Got Iconify");
        return true;
      case Event.WINDOW_DEICONIFY:
        fr.show();
        System.out.println("Frame Got Deiconify");
        return true;
      default:
        return super.handleEvent(e);
      }
    }
  }
```

ADDING A MENU TO THE FRAME

All but the simplest applications have a number of functions available to the user, and the usual way of organizing these is through a menu. In Java, there are menus, menu components, and menu bars.

Creating menus is a straightforward process. First, a clarification: A *menu* is a single list of items from which the user can choose. An application has a *menu bar*, which will contain one or more menus that drop down from the menu bar. In this discussion, a menu is one list of menu items (components), and a menu bar is the collection of all the menus.

The first step in adding a menu to a frame then is to create a new MenuBar:

```
MenuBar mb = new MenuBar();
```

Next, create at least one menu. You'll add it to the menu bar later:

```
Menu mf = new Menu("File");
```

Add several items to the new menu:

```
mf.add(new MenuItem("Print");
mf.addSeparator();
mf.add(new MenuItem("Exit");
```

Note the use of the **addSeparator()** method to put a separator line between the **Print** and **Exit** menu items. Now add the menu to the menu bar:

```
mb.add(mf);
```

Finally, make the menu bar the frame's active menu bar:

```
setMenuBar(mb);
```

The menu created by this code is shown in Figure 13-4. (Figure 13-5 contains the complete source code for a small application that displays the File menu.)

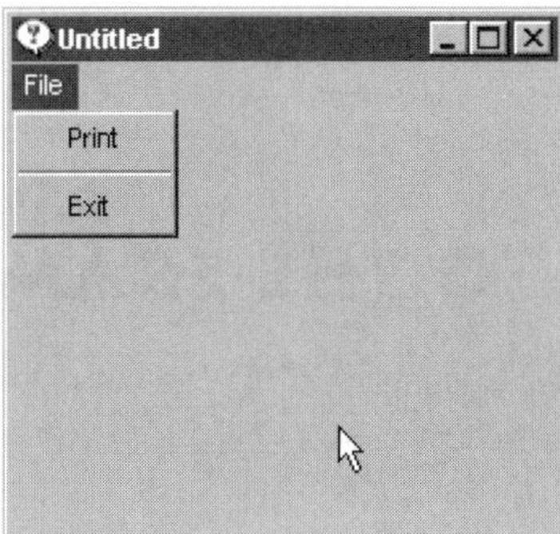

Figure 13-4 A small application with a File menu.

Figure 13-5 The complete source code for a small application that displays the File menu.

```
import java.awt.*;

class MenuTest extends Frame {

  public MenuTest(){
    resize(300,300);
    MenuBar mb = new MenuBar();
    Menu mf = new Menu("File");
    mf.add(new MenuItem("Print"));
    mf.addSeparator();
    mf.add(new MenuItem("Exit"));
    mb.add(mf);
    setMenuBar(mb);
  }
```

```
  public void start(){
    show();
  }

  public boolean handleEvent(Event e) {
    if (e.id == Event.WINDOW_DESTROY){
      dispose();
      System.exit(0);
      return true;
    }
    else
       return super.handleEvent(e);
  }
  public static void main(String args[]) {
    MenuTest mt;
    mt = new MenuTest();
    mt.start();
  }
}
```

You check for a menu item being chosen much the way that you test for a button press: either by matching the text of the chosen item or by matching the object (which requires an extra step in declaring the menu item, as discussed later). The following code matches menu items based on text and, because this is the **Exit** menu item, calls the code to terminate the application:

```
public boolean handleEvent(Event e) {
  if (e.target instanceof MenuItem) {
    if ("Exit."equals(((MenuItem)e.target).getLabel())) {
      dispose();
      System.exit(0);
      return true;
    }
 return true;
  }
  else
    return super.handleEvent(e);
}
```

The event in question actually is **ACTION_EVENT**; however, because that's the only event that menu items get, all you really have to do is test for a match on any event.

As mentioned earlier, you also can determine which menu item is chosen by the menu item object. Declare a MenuItem type with class scope (if

you declare it within the constructor, it won't be visible to **handleEvent()**):

```
MenuItem exitItem;
```

Create the new menu item:

```
exitItem = new MenuItem("Exit");
mf.add(exitItem);
```

The event-checking code becomes a little shorter:

```
public boolean handleEvent(Event e) {
  if (e.target.equals(exitItem)) {
    // process the exit menu item
```

MENU CHECKBOXES

Aside from standard menu items and separators, menus also can have checkboxes. Such menu items typically have a check mark or other indicator that appears when the checkbox is set to true.

To create a menu checkbox, you can use code something like:

```
m.add(newCheckboxMenuItem("This is a checkbox");
```

To find out what the value of that checkbox is, you'll need to add the following code inside the **handleEvent()** method:

```
if (e.target instanceof CheckboxMenuItem) {
  if ("A Checkbox."equals(((CheckboxMenuItem)e.target).getLabel())) {
    System.out.println("Checkbox is "+
(((CheckboxMenuItem)e.target)).getState());
  }
  return true;
}
```

You also can use the **setState()** method to preset the checkbox's state.

ADDING PANELS, CANVASES, AND OTHER GUI COMPONENTS

The rest of the GUI components are all handled pretty much the same way that they are for applets, and that subject was covered in chapter

10, "Writing Java applets: Panels, layouts, and canvases," so there's no need to repeat that information here. The only difference between how applets handle these components and how applications do is that your applets probably won't have any menus (unless you create a frame from within your applet, which is certainly possible) to use to interact with the various components.

APPLICATION-ONLY LANGUAGE FEATURES

There are a number of features available to applications that are not available to applets or that applets can have restricted access to. An example of the latter is the use of platform-specific code, also called *native methods* because they are native to a particular platform. Because native methods are written in other programming languages that do not share Java's security features, they are not permitted in Java applets. This doesn't mean that you can't write Internet/World Wide Web applications that use native methods; it just means that you can't deliver them to your users as applets.

Applications also have no restrictions on their file I/O, whereas applets can be prevented from reading/writing files on clients machines. (Part 4 of this book discusses security issues in more detail.) If you do a lot of applet programming, you'll sooner or later come up against this restriction. The solution, in many cases, is to set up an application on the Web server that does the file I/O (perhaps using native methods) and to establish a client-server relationship between the applet and the application. For details on creating this kind of application, turn to Part 3.

SUMMARY

Although applications usually take a little more work to write than applets, they also suffer from fewer constraints. You're not designing something that has to be retrieved over the Internet, so you don't need to be concerned about keeping applications small. If you have some legacy code, you have the option of linking that into your Java applications, whereas applets do not allow C code for security reasons.

However, most of Java's language features are available equally to applets and applications, and most coding techniques are likewise applicable to both types of programs. It's probably a little easier to start with applet programming, but the difficulty of the programming task at hand will have a lot more to do with what you're trying to accomplish than whether you're writing an applet or an application.

THE JAVA DEBUGGER

UNLESS YOU'VE FALLEN into the habit of writing flawless code, there will come a time when your applet or application doesn't behave as expected. Sometimes a few well-placed **System.out.println** statements will be enough to put you on the trail of the problem. Other times, however, you'll need to use the Java debugger.

In its present form, the Java debugger (jdb) is a command-line tool. To use it, you'll need to compile the classes to be debugged by using the **-g** flag when calling javac, which causes the compiler to include symbolic information that will make debugging much easier.

To run the debugger on an application, you type:

```
$ jdb classname
```

where ***classname*** is the name of the class file that begins the application.

To run the debugger on an applet, you use the **-debug** parameter with the applet viewer:

```
$ appletviewer -debug appletdocument.html
```

where ***appletdocument*** is the name of the HTML file that contains the applet's tag. In either case, you'll see the same debugger window. Although the following discussion focuses on applets, you can apply the same principles and techniques to debugging applications.

DEBUGGING THE LISTDISPLAY APPLET

Before you begin debugging, take a moment to become familiar with the ListDisplay applet, as shown in Figure 14-1. (Figure 14-2 contains the source code for the ListDisplay applet.) ListDisplay will be the "debuggee" and is a demonstration of a linked list, if you're not familiar with them. Linked lists commonly are used when you want to store information about a series of items, where the items are related to each other. In ListDisplay, the linked list is used to store the locations of each point marked by the user clicking the mouse button and to draw connecting lines between those points. To see how ListDisplay works, run the applet from the applet viewer, without the debugger.

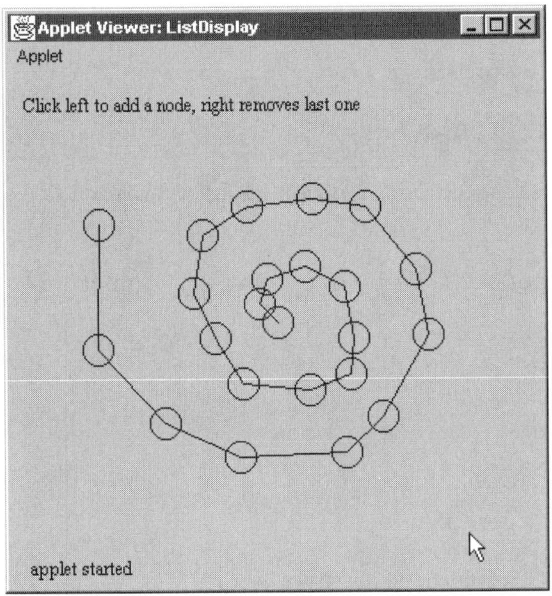

Figure 14-1
The ListDisplay applet.

Figure 14-2 The source code for the ListDisplay applet.

```
import java.awt.*;
import java.applet.Applet;
import LinkedList;

public class ListDisplay extends Applet implements ForEach {
  Image buffer;
  Graphics gc;
  boolean drawn = false;
  LinkedList theList = new LinkedList();
  int lastX, lastY;

  public void init() {
    buffer = createImage(400, 400);
    gc = buffer.getGraphics();
    clearGraphics(gc);
  }

  void clearGraphics(Graphics g) {
    gc.setColor(Color.lightGray);
    gc.fillRect(0, 0, 400, 400);
    gc.setColor(Color.black);
  }
```

Figure 14-2 Continued.

```
  public void paint(Graphics g) {
    if (drawn) {
      g.drawImage(buffer,0,0,this);
    }
    g.drawString("Click left to add a node, right removes last one", 10, 25);
  }

  public boolean mouseDown(Event evt, int x, int y) {
    try {
      if (evt.modifiers == 0) { // left - add a node
        theList.insert(new Point(x, y));
      }
      else { // right -  delete a node
        theList.remove();
      }
    } catch (OffListException e) {}

    // Traverse the list and draw the nodes...
    clearGraphics(gc);

    lastX = -1;
    lastY = -1;
    theList.iterate(this);

    drawn = true;
    repaint();
    return true;
  }

  public void update(Graphics g) {
    paint(g);
  }

  public boolean forEach(Object obj) {
    Point p = (Point)obj;
    gc.drawOval(p.x-10, p.y-10, 20, 20);
    if (lastX != -1 || lastY != -1)
      gc.drawLine(lastX, lastY, p.x, p.y);
    lastX = p.x;
    lastY = p.y;
    return true;
  }
}
```

Because the ListDisplay applet uses a number of additional classes (see Figure 14-2), you'll probably find it easiest to copy the files from the Tutorial\Chapter_14 directory on the CD-ROM to a working directory on your hard disk, rather than creating and compiling the source yourself.

Before you start debugging, run the ListDisplay applet in AppletViewer without the debugger. ListDisplay has a simple user interface. When you click in the applet with the left mouse button, the applet draws a circle representing a node on a linked list at the location of the mouse click. Each subsequent left mouse click will add a circle (Node) and draw a line between the new node and the previous node. If you click the right mouse button, the last node on the linked list will be removed.

STARTING THE DEBUGGER

The overall objective of this debugging session is to set a breakpoint that will allow you to observe the LinkedList class in action. The mouse clicks are received by the applet via the **mouseDown()** and **mouseUp()** methods (these methods were discussed in chapter 9, "Writing Java applets: Getting user input"). The ListDisplay applet uses the **mouseDown()** method as the trigger for creating new nodes. When **mouseDown()** is called, the applet creates a Point object (see java.awt.Point) to store the X and Y coordinates of the mouse event and adds the Point to the linked list. Because **mouseDown()** is where all the action is, you'll eventually set a breakpoint there so that you can stop the applet and examine its state.

First, start up AppletViewer in debug mode. This is done by using the **-debug** switch on the command line. In debug mode, AppletViewer will return to you a debugger prompt without actually starting the applet or displaying the AppletViewer window:

```
$ appletviewer -debug example.html
Initializing jdb...
0xee30c460:class(sun.applet.AppletViewer)
>
```

> Before starting AppletViewer in debug mode, be sure that the **CLASSPATH** environment variable is set to include the ListDisplay applet's directory, or you'll get a number of exceptions from the Class Loader. While it is possible to ignore these exceptions in the debugger by continuing past them, you probably will encounter other problems later on.

The Java debugger actually has loaded the AppletViewer class but has suspended the class before displaying its window.

EXAMINING THREADS

As you'll see in chapter 15, "Threads for applications and applets," all applets have at least one thread of execution. To examine the threads running when the applet starts up, you can use the **threads** command:

```
> threads
Group system:
 1. (java.lang.Thread)0xee3001f8         clock handler
cond.
 2. (java.lang.Thread)0xee3002a0         Idle thread
runni
 3. (java.lang.Thread)0xee300318         Async Garbage Collector
cond.
 4. (java.lang.Thread)0xee300370         Finalizer thread
cond.
 5. (java.lang.Thread)0xee300a18         Debugger agent
runni
 6. (sun.tools.debug.BreakpointHandler)0xee30a918 Breakpoint handler
cond.
Group main:
 7. (java.lang.Thread)0xee3000a0 main suspended
>
```

It might surprise you to discover that there are seven threads running before your applet has even been started. Of these seven threads, six are in the system threadgroup. These are all threads associated with either the Java runtime or the debugger. AppletViewer is in the main threadgroup and is suspended at this point.

> You might see a slightly different display, including a different number of threads, depending on revisions to the debugger and operating system differences. On Windows 95, for example, the previous thread listing might be skipped entirely, with the four running threads discussed next being the only threads visible.

The numbers prefixing each thread are the threads' ID for the purposes of the debugger. For example, this ID is used when switching between threads while debugging.

Now, start the applet running and see what threads are running once the applet is up and running:

```
> run
run sun.applet.AppletViewer example.html
running ...
```

Once you run the applet, execution proceeds normally, and the AppletViewer window appears and begins to run the applet. Use the **threads** command again to see what's changed:

```
main[1] threads
Group sun.applet.AppletViewer.main:
 1. (sun.awt.motif.InputThread)0xee30e5d0 AWT-Input        running
 2. (java.lang.Thread)0xee30e5f8          AWT-Motif        cond. waiting
 3. (sun.awt.ScreenUpdater)0xee30e968     Screen Updater   cond. waiting
Group group applet-ListDisplay:
 4. (java.lang.Thread)0xee30e480 thread applet-ListDisplay cond. waiting
main[1]
```

After the **run** command, the prompt changes to **main[1]**, indicating that the current thread is the first thread in the AppletViewer.main threadgroup. While the applet is running and you have not hit a breakpoint, you are in the context of the thread called **main** (which you saw in the previous output from the **threads** command.) AppletViewer has created 4 more threads (you're up to 11 for those keeping score!) in two threadgroups. The **threads** command will display all of the threads defined in the context of the current threadgroup. So what happened to the other 7 threads? If you switch contexts to the system threadgroup, you can see them all:

```
main[1] threadgroup system
main[1] threads
Group system:
 1. (java.lang.Thread)0xee3001f8          clock handler
cond.
 2. (java.lang.Thread)0xee3002a0          Idle thread
runni
 3. (java.lang.Thread)0xee300318          Async Garbage Collector
cond.
 4. (java.lang.Thread)0xee300370          Finalizer thread
cond.
 5. (java.lang.Thread)0xee300a18          Debugger agent
runni
 6. (sun.tools.debug.BreakpointHandler)0xee30a918 Breakpoint handler
cond.
Group main:
 7. (java.lang.Thread)0xee3000a0          main                    cond.
waiting
Group sun.applet.AppletViewer.main:
 8. (sun.awt.motif.InputThread)0xee30e668 AWT-Input               running
```

```
 9. (java.lang.Thread)0xee30e690          AWT-Motif          cond.
waiting
10. (sun.awt.ScreenUpdater)0xee30ea00     Screen Updater     cond.
waiting
Group group applet-ListDisplay:
11. (java.lang.Thread)0xee30e518 thread applet-ListDisplay    cond.
waiting
main[1]
```

Now switch back to the previous threadgroup:

```
main[1] threadgroup sun.applet.AppletViewer.main
main[1]
```

SETTING BREAKPOINTS

Before you get around to actually setting the breakpoint and examining the linked list, it bears mentioning that, of the 11 threads that have been created, only three actually are running. Two of these, the Idle thread and the Debugger Agent thread, are in the system threadgroup, and one is AWT-Input, which is in the AppletViewer threadgroup.

The two threads in the system threadgroup are not important to you in debugging the applet, but the AWT-Input thread is what is watching the applet for input. Let's not keep it waiting any longer. Go to the applet and click a few times to build up the linked list. This will give you some data to look at.

Next, set a breakpoint in the **mouseDown()** method:

```
main[1] stop in ListDisplay.mouseDown
Breakpoint set in ListDisplay.mouseDown
main[1]
```

Now when you go to the applet and click the left mouse button, you will hit the breakpoint (actually, you can click any mouse button; they all generate events that get passed to **mouseDown()**):

```
main[1]
Breakpoint hit: ListDisplay.mouseDown (ListDisplay:35)
AWT-Motif[1]
```

If you now examine the threads, you'll see that the state of the threads has changed. The prompt also has changed to indicate that the current thread is now AWT-Motif (or, if you're running under another operating system, say Windows 95, it will be called AWT-Callback-Win32):

```
AWT-Motif[1] threads
Group sun.applet.AppletViewer.main:
 1. (sun.awt.motif.InputThread)0xee30e668 AWT-Input        suspended
 2. (java.lang.Thread)0xee30e690          AWT-Motif        at
breakpoint
 3. (sun.awt.ScreenUpdater)0xee30ea00     Screen Updater   suspended
Group group applet-ListDisplay:
 4. (java.lang.Thread)0xee30e518 thread applet-ListDisplay  suspended
AWT-Motif[1]
```

The **where** command will tell you what the stack of the current thread looks like:

```
AWT-Motif[1] where
 [1] ListDisplay.mouseDown (ListDisplay:35)
 [2] java.awt.Component.handleEvent (Component:883)
 [3] java.awt.Component.postEvent (Component:838)
 [4] sun.awt.motif.MComponentPeer.handleMouseDown (MComponentPeer:221)
AWT-Motif[1]
```

Line [1] indicates that you are in the **mouseDown()** method of a ListDisplay object and are on line 35 of the corresponding source code. Line [2] tells you that **mouseDown()** was called by the **handleEvent()** method on line 883 in the Component class, and so on down the list.

The stack can tell you how you got where you are. The **list** command tells you exactly where you are in the source code:

```
AWT-Motif[1] list
31    }
32
33    public boolean mouseDown(Event evt, int x, int y) {
34      try {
35 =>     if (evt.modifiers == 0) { // left—add a node
36          theList.insert(new Point(x, y));
37        }
38        else { // right— delete a node
39          theList.remove();
AWT-Motif[1]
```

You now know that you are in the **mouseDown()** method, about to check the modifiers flag on the Event object. (The modifiers flag will tell you which mouse button was pressed.) Because you "preloaded" the linked list by clicking several times before setting the breakpoint, you can do some meaningful exploration. First, take a look at the LinkedList object, theList:

```
AWT-Motif[1] dump theList
this.theList = (LinkedList)0xee30ec40 {
  public Node first = (Node)0xee30f148
```

```
  public Node cursor = (Node)0xee30f5a0
}
AWT-Motif[1]
```

EXAMINING INSTANCE VARIABLES

The **dump** command will show the instance variables and their current values. Here the linked list has a Node object in each of the two instance variables. Because they each have unique values (addresses), they refer to two distinct Node objects. Let's look at the Node referred to by first:

```
AWT-Motif[1] dump this.theList.first
this.theList.first = (Node)0xee30f148 {
  Node next = (Node)0xee30f2b0
  Object value = (java.awt.Point)0xee30f130
}
AWT-Motif[1]
```

Notice that it was necessary to fully qualify **first** as **this.theList.first**. Note also that this Node has a handle to the next Node on the list and that its address is different than the address of the Node in theList.cursor. You have at least three unique Nodes on the list. Depending on how many times you clicked the mouse in the applet, your mileage might vary!

You can also display the values of any local variables:

```
AWT-Motif[1] locals
Local variables and arguments:
 this = ListDisplay[0,0,400x400,layout=java.awt.FlowLayout]
 evt =
java.awt.Event[id=501,x=237,y=94,target=ListDisplay[0,0,400x400,layout=ja
va.awt.FlowLayout]]
 x = 237
 y = 94
AWT-Motif[1]
```

In **mouseDown()**, **this**, **evt**, **x**, and **y** are all the local variables that are defined.

You might want to single-step through the mouseDown method:

```
AWT-Motif[1] step
AWT-Motif[1]
Breakpoint hit: ListDisplay.mouseDown (ListDisplay:36)
AWT-Motif[1] list
32
33    public boolean mouseDown(Event evt, int x, int y) {
34      try {
```

```
35        if (evt.modifiers == 0) { // left-add a node
36 =>       theList.insert(new Point(x, y));
37        }
38        else { // right- delete a node
39          theList.remove();
40        }
AWT-Motif[1] step
AWT-Motif[1]
Breakpoint hit: java.awt.Point.<init> (Point:44)
```

This time, use the **!!** shortcut instead of the **step** command (**!!** is used to repeat the last command and is a syntax borrowed from the UNIX C shell):

```
AWT-Motif[1] !!
AWT-Motif[1]
Breakpoint hit: java.lang.Object.<init> (pc 0)
AWT-Motif[1] where
 [1] java.lang.Object.<init> (pc 0)
 [2] java.awt.Point.<init> (Point:44)
 [3] ListDisplay.mouseDown (ListDisplay:36)
 [4] java.awt.Component.handleEvent (Component:883)
 [5] java.awt.Component.postEvent (Component:838)
 [6] sun.awt.motif.MComponentPeer.handleMouseDown (MComponentPeer:221)
AWT-Motif[1]
```

Notice that, as you issued the **step** command while on line 36, you actually stepped into the initialization of the Point object. The second **step** command took you into the initialization of the parent of Point, Object. If you issue several more **step** commands, you eventually will get back out of creation of the Point object and get to the point where you call **insert()**:

```
<several !!'s ommitted...>
AWT-Motif[1] !!
step
AWT-Motif[1]
Breakpoint hit: LinkedList.insert (LinkedList:52)
AWT-Motif[1] list
48    */
49
50    void insert(Object obj) throws OffListException {
51
52 =>   Node newNode = new Node(obj);
53
54      // first see if this is an empty list
55      if ( first == null ){
56        first = newNode;
AWT-Motif[1] locals
Local variables and arguments:
 this = LinkedList@6e30eba8
 obj = java.awt.Point[x=183,y=90]
 newNode is not in scope.
AWT-Motif[1]
```

In the local variables, you can see that **newNode** is not in scope. Until you step past the declaration of **newNode**, you can't legally refer to **newNode**.

To allow the applet to continue without stopping each time that you click the mouse, you need to clear the breakpoint. To do this, you must recall the method and line number of the breakpoint that you set. Because there currently is no way in jdb to list the breakpoints, the easiest way to recall that information is to allow the applet to continue running and clear the breakpoint the next time it is encountered. Use the **cont** command to tell the applet to run until the next breakpoint:

```
AWT-Motif[1] cont
<click the mouse in the applet>
Breakpoint hit: ListDisplay.mouseDown (ListDisplay:35)
AWT-Motif[1] clear ListDisplay:35
Breakpoint cleared at ListDisplay: 35
AWT-Motif[1] cont
<the applet continues until you select quit from the AppletViewer menu or
type the quit command to the debugger.>
AWT-Motif[1]
The application has exited
$
```

THE LINKED-LIST CLASSES

The ListDisplay class uses a set of classes that together make up an implementation of a linked list. (See Figures 14-3 through 14-6.) You are free to use these classes in your own programming.

Figure 14-3 The LinkedList class source code.

```
/**
 * A LinkedList class.
 *
 * @author Irving Salisbury III
 * @author Jeffrey C. Rice
 * @version %I%
 */
class LinkedList {
  /**
   * The first item on the list.
   */
  public Node first;
```

```
/**
 * The current item.
 */
public Node cursor;

/**
 * Create the list.
 */
LinkedList() {
  first = null;
  cursor = null;
}

/**
 * Insert an element into the first spot in the list
 * and set cursor to the new element.
 *
 * @param obj the object to be installed.
 */

void insertFirst(Object obj) {
  Node newNode = new Node(obj);

  newNode.next = first;
  first = newNode;
  cursor = newNode;
}

/**
 * Add an item to the list after item at cursor and advance
 * the cursor.
 *
 * @param obj The object to be installed.
 * @exception OffListException If cursor is not on a valid node.
 */

void insert(Object obj) throws OffListException {

  Node newNode = new Node(obj);

  // first see if this is an empty list
  if ( first == null ){
    first = newNode;
    cursor = newNode;
  }
```

Figure 14-3 Continued.

```
    else if (!off()) { // otherwise put this after the cursor
      newNode.next = cursor.next;
      cursor.next = newNode;
      cursor = newNode;
    }
    else {
      throw new OffListException();
    }
  }

  /**
   * Remove the current item at cursor if possible
   * and reset cursor to the previous item in list
   *
   * @exception OffListException If cursor is off list.
   */
  void remove() throws OffListException {
    Node originalCursor = cursor;
    Node previous = null;

    if (off())
      throw new OffListException();

    // Scan through the list to find the previous Node.
    start();

    while (!off() && !cursor.equals(originalCursor)) {
      previous=cursor;
      next();
    }

    // Now let's see what happened from the loop
    if (previous == null) {
      // We must be at the first node in the list
      first = cursor.next;
      cursor = first;
    }
    else {
      previous.next = cursor.next;
      cursor = (cursor.next == null)? previous : cursor.next;
    }
  }
```

```
/**
 * Gives the item at the current cursor in the list.
 *
 * @return current object.
 * @exception OffListException If cursor is off the list.
 */
Object item() throws OffListException {
  if (off())
    throw new OffListException();

  return cursor.value;
}

/**
 * See if the cursor is not valid
 *
 * @return true if cursor is off the list
 *
 */
boolean off() {
  return (cursor == null);
}

/**
 * See if the list is empty or not
 * @return true if the list is empty.
 */
boolean isEmpty(){
  return (first == null);
}

/**
 * Sets cursor to first item in list
 */
void start(){
  cursor = first;
}

/**
 * Moves cursor one item forward in the list.
 *
 * @exception OffListException If cursor is off the list.
 */
void next() throws OffListException {
```

Figure 14-3 Continued.

```
    if(off())
      throw new OffListException();
    cursor = cursor.next;
  }

  public void iterate(ForEach f) {
    Node i;

    for (i = first; i != null; i = i.next) {
      if (f.forEach(i.value) == false)
        break;
    }
  }
}
```

Figure 14-4 The Node class source code.

```
/**
 * A Node object is the building block for linked lists,
 * doubly-linked lists, etc.  It is used to store an Object
 *
 * @author Irving Salisbury III
 * @author Jeffrey C. Rice
 * @version %I%
 */

class Node {

  /**
   * The next Node in the chain.
   */
  Node next;

  /**
   * The object this node stores.
   */
  Object value;

  /**
   * Create the Node
   *
   * @param obj the object to be stored at this node.
   */
  Node(Object obj) {
    value = obj;
    next = null;
  }
}
```

Figure 14-5 The ForEach class source code.

```
public interface ForEach {
  public boolean forEach(Object obj);
}
```

Figure 14-6 The OffListException class source code.

```
/**
 * Thrown when the cursor of a linked list is null.
 *
 * @see java.lang.Exception
 * @version     %I%
 * @author      Irv Salisbury III
 * @author      Jeffrey C. Rice
 */
class OffListException extends Exception {
  /**
   * Constructs an OffListException with the specified detail message.
   * A detail message is a String that describes this particular exception.
   * @param s the detail message
   */
  public OffListException(String s) {
    super(s);
  }

  /**
   * Constructs an OffListException with no detail message.
   * A detail message is a String that describes this particular exception.
   */
  public OffListException() {
    super();
  }
}
```

SUMMARY

The Java debugger can be a valuable tool in locating and correcting problems in applets and applications. However, there are several things to keep in mind. First, jdb is a read-only debugger. You might have noticed that you didn't change the values of any instance variables. This was not an oversight. At present, there is no way to change program values from within jdb. Second, jdb, like all of the Java software, is still in its infancy at present. Expect changes, improvements, and bug fixes as the debugger matures.

15 THREADS FOR APPLICATIONS AND APPLETS

AS DESCRIBED IN CHAPTER 4, "Java language concepts," Java is a fully multithreaded programming language. If you're not familiar with the concept of threading, then it might take a little bit of getting used to. Essentially, *threading* is a means of dividing up a program into subprograms, much as an operating system like Windows NT can be viewed both as a single entity and as a set of applications each of which runs concurrently with the others.

No two programs ever really run concurrently (at least on any single-processor platform) because the processor must give each program a successive slice of time. Each application takes its turn, and if the turns are small enough and come often enough, the applications give the illusion of running concurrently.

Threads operate the same way; you can have multiple threads of execution in your program, but no two threads can execute instructions at exactly the same time (unless you are executing on a multiprocessor machine, such as a Sparcstation 10 512 MP, but then few of us have that luxury). Just as applications each get a time slice, so do threads. The difference, typically, is that, in a multitasking operating system (in good ones, anyway), the operating system kernel manages which applications get how much time. In a Java applet, the Java runtime library allocates processor time to each thread.

The advantage of multithreading isn't just that you can do (or appear to do) multiple things at once. There are any number of schemes that you can use to do this with just about any language. The big payoff is that you can do it easily, and let Java worry about allocating the resources.

In Java, you can put a class on a thread of execution, and there are two ways of threading classes. You either can use the Runnable interface to add threading to an existing class, or you can create a subclass of the Thread class (which implements the Runnable interface, without you having to). If you are writing a class from scratch, then you're free to use the Thread class; otherwise, you'll need to implement Runnable.

MULTITHREADING WITH THE THREAD CLASS

The following code is a simple Thread subclass that prints out successive numbers at random intervals:

```
class RandomCounter extends Thread {

  int count;


  public void run() {
    while (count < 5000){
      count++;

      Thread.sleep( (int)(Math.random() * 500));
      System.out.println(count);
    }
  }
}
```

This thread has only one method declared, and that is the essential **run()** method, which contains the body of the code that the thread will execute. In the case of the RandomCounter class, the **run()** method executes a **while** loop that prints out a series of numbers. The **Thread.sleep()** method introduces a random delay of up to 500 milliseconds between **while** loop iterations.

> Because **Math.random()** returns a float value between 0 and 1.0, it is necessary to cast it to an int value that is what **Thread.sleep()** expects, but only *after* multiplying the value by 500. Casting **Math.random()** to an int will return a result of 0, except on those rare occasions when it returns a value of 1.0.

To see this threading example in action, you'll need to create a small application that launches two copies of the RandomCount thread:

```
import java.lang.Thread;
import java.lang.Math;

public class ThreadTest {
  public static void main(String args[]) throws java.io.IOException {
    RandomCounter rc1 = new RandomCounter();
    rc1.start();
    RandomCounter rc2 = new RandomCounter();
```

```
    rc2.start();
 char ch;
    ch = (char)System.in.read(); // wait for a keypress
    rc1.stop();
    rc2.stop();
    System.exit(0);
  }
}
```

Note that the **main()** method in this application is declared as throwing the **java.io.IOException**. You should throw this exception (or catch it and deal with it) any time you're using **System.in.read()** to get input from the keyboard (which shouldn't be often, if you're creating GUI applications).

The rest of the **main()** method is pretty ordinary. The code:

```
RandomCounter rc1 = new RandomCounter();
```

declares a new instance of the RandomCounter thread, and the code:

```
rc2.start();
```

starts the thread running. At this point, you really have two threads of execution running in the application, because all applications (and all applets) are always made up of at least one main thread of execution.

In the case of this example, there will be three threads launched: two instances of RandomCounter and the main application thread. The RandomCounter threads will continue to run until either their **run()** methods terminate or they are explicitly instructed to terminate with the **stop()** method. That means that the thread **run()** methods usually incorporate some kind of looping structure or are made up of long processes that are best run concurrently with other processes. The main application thread actually will stop running when it reaches the code that waits for a keypress, but it still is in a "runnable" state. See the next section, "Thread states," for an explanation of the runnable state.

If you look back at RandomCounter, you'll see that the **while** loop executes a maximum of 5000 times, although the end to the application is more likely to come when the following code detects a keypress (unless you're an inordinately patient sort):

```
ch = (char)System.in.read();
```

There are a couple of things that it would be nice to do with this application. For one, it would be helpful to identify which thread is printing out which value. For another, there's a compiler warning that keeps cropping up that warns that **Thread.sleep()** should catch **InterruptedException**. Figure 15-1 shows an amended application that implementns these changes.

Figure 15-1 The ThreadTestB application.

```
import java.lang.Thread;
import java.lang.Math;

public class ThreadTestB{
  public static void main(String args[]) throws java.io.IOException {
    RandomCounter rc1 = new RandomCounter("Thread One");
    rc1.start();
    RandomCounter rc2 = new RandomCounter("Thread Two");
    rc2.start();
    rc1.setPriority(10);
    rc2.setPriority(5);

    char ch;
    ch = (char)System.in.read();
    rc1.stop();
    rc2.stop();
    System.exit(0);
  }

}

class RandomCounter extends Thread {

  String tn;
  int count;

  public RandomCounter(String str){
    super(str);
  }
  public void run() {
    while (count < 5000){
      count++;
//      try{
//          Thread.sleep( (int)(Math.random() * 500));
//      } catch (InterruptedException e) {}
      yield();
      System.out.println(getName() + " - " + count);
    }
  }

}
```

The ThreadTestB application adds a constructor to the RandomClass thread, which takes a single string parameter. This string is passed along to the Thread class constructor with the code:

```
super(str);
```

where it's assigned to the thread's name. Later, the thread retrieves this value with the **getName()** method.

THREAD STATES

What you can do with a thread depends on what state the thread is in. The possible states are *new thread*, *runnable*, *not runnable*, and *dead*.

NEW THREADS

When you first create a thread with the **new** operator, that thread does not have any resources allocated to it. The only permissible thread methods that you can call at this time are **start()**, **stop()**, and **isAlive()**. Calling any other method will result in an **IllegalThreadStateException** being thrown. If you're not in the habit of starting your threads in the same place in the code as they're instantiated or if you repeatedly start and stop threads, you'll need to be sure that your code is aware of the thread state before any other methods are called. You can get some (if not all) information about thread states with the **isAlive()** method, which will return false if the thread is either a new thread or stopped and will return true of the thread is either runnable or not runnable.

RUNNABLE THREADS

After a thread has been started (with the **start()** method), it's considered runnable. The **start()** method allocates resources and calls the **run()** method.

Runnable and running aren't necessarily the same thing. In a single-processor architecture, multiple threads don't actually run at the same time, rather they're time-sliced by the Java runtime system so that each thread gets a certain portion of processor time. How this time is allocated is determined by the thread's priority, which can be in a range of 1 (minimum priority) to 10 (maximum priority). The constants **MIN_PRIORITY**, **NORM_PRIORITY**, and **MAX_PRIORITY** also can be used.

Threads get the same priority as the thread that created them, but you can alter priority with the **setPriority()** method. You also can read a thread's current priority with **getPriority()**. Time slicing and thread priorities are discussed in more detail later in this chapter in the section, "Thread scheduling and management."

NOT RUNNABLE STATE

There are four conditions that cause a thread to be not runnable. If the **suspend()** method is called, the thread suspends operation until the **resume()** method is called. If the **sleep(*time*)** method is called, the thread suspends operation for the time duration (in milliseconds) specified in the ***time*** parameter. If the thread uses the **wait()** method to wait for some condition to be fulfilled, the thread is not runnable, and likewise if it is waiting for I/O.

DEAD STATE

A thread is considered dead if either its **stop()** method has been called or the thread's run method has terminated normally.

THREAD SCHEDULING AND MANAGEMENT

Thread management is one of the biggest challenges that programmers face when moving from a single-threaded to a multithreaded environment. In many cases, they meet the challenge by ignoring it, and they create what are essentially single-threaded applications.

Making the move to multithreaded applications takes a change of mindset. Think about the components of your application and whether there are any processes that can be spun off on their own thread. You might want to do this with a printed report, a file transfer, or anything else that can happen unattended and where the user can continue to work without first getting a response back from that process.

DAEMON THREADS

If you don't come from a UNIX background, you might not have heard the term *daemon thread* before. It doesn't mean your thread is in the

service of Beelzebub (although, depending on your coding skills and how good a day you're having, it might seem that way sometimes). A *daemon* is a thread that's always running in the background, waiting for input. For example, you might create a daemon to handle file transfers. You start the file-transfer daemon when the program starts, and whenever you have a file ready to send off, you notify the daemon of the job. (In this case, because TCP/IP allows for multiple communications processes to execute concurrently, you probably wouldn't expect the file-transfer daemon to actually transfer the file. Instead, you'd have it start a thread to transfer that specific file.)

Daemon threads aren't structurally different from other threads, except that they're marked with a flag as being daemons (via the setDaemon() method). The reason that they're marked is that, when the program shuts down, you don't want to have to shut down all of the daemons manually. The Java runtime knows that, if a thread is a daemon thread, it can be terminated automatically and the program can exit.

THREAD PRIORITIES

When there is more than one thread running in a Java application (or applet), the runtime thread-scheduling system kicks in and decides which thread should get processor time. As discussed earlier, threads have a priority, currently in the range 1 to 10 (although it's wiser to use the constants MIN_PRIORITY, NORM_PRIORITY, and MAX_PRIORITY, as defined in java/src/lang/Thread.java, because the numeric values could change). If one of the threads has a higher priority than all of the other threads, then it and it alone will be executed.

If there are two or more threads with the same high priority, the approach taken by the thread scheduling system will follow the approach taken by the operating system Java is running on.

If the operating system supports only *cooperative multitasking*, where individual programs have to yield control of the system to allow other programs to execute, the first Java thread to get control will run until it's finished, then the second thread will get its chance. If the operating system supports time slicing, where the OS, and not the application, determines how much processor time it gets, the thread-scheduling system will time slice the threads, giving each thread a certain number of milliseconds in turn.

To find out which kind of system you have, take the ThreadTestB application and comment out the **sleep()** code so that the **run()** method looks like this:

```
while (count < 5000) {
  count++;
//   try {
//     Thread.sleep( (int)(Math.random() * 500));
//   } catch (InterruptedException e) {}
  System.out.println(getName() + "-" + count);
}
```

Now run ThreadTestB. If you have a cooperative multitasking system, only one thread will run at a time; however, if you have a time-slicing (or preemptive) multitasking system, the threads will each print out one or more statements before control switches to the other thread.

Note that, even in a cooperative multitasking environment, the two threads do execute in turn if the **sleep()** method is called. That's because, during **sleep()** time, the thread is not runnable. The rule of thumb with Java threads, direct from Sun's documentation, is as follows:

> **Rule:** At any given time, the highest priority runnable thread is running.

If you want to arbitrarily make a thread give up control, even if it has the highest priority of all threads, you can use the **yield()** method. **yield()** tells the thread scheduler to go to the next available thread and give it control.

Go back to the version of ThreadTestB in which you commented out the **sleep()** code. If you're working in a cooperative multitasking environment, you can force the threads to share processor time by replacing the **sleep()** code with a **yield()** method call. You're really duplicating the kind of cooperative behavior required of all programs in a cooperative multitasking operating system.

> Even in a cooperative multitasking environment, Java applets and applications are quite well-behaved in that they yield at reasonable intervals to other programs. Even if you put your Java code into a tight loop, the user still will be able to switch between your Java application and other applications.

SYNCHRONIZATION

When threads share data, problems can arise. The classic example of this is the producer/consumer model, where one thread supplies data to another thread. An example of this code can be found at *http://java.sun.com/tutorial/java/threads/synchronization.html*.

The problem is that you want the data to move between threads in an orderly manner, which roughly translates as a state problem. The data will be moved from one thread to another via a common data holding area. If the producer thread is set up to churn out data and the consumer thread is set up to grab the data that comes in, everything will work well only as long as both threads run at exactly the same speed and, by good fortune, interlock such that the producer places data in the common holding area before the consumer looks for it, and the consumer retrieves the data before the producer attempts to place new data in the common area.

Not even Bill Gates has that kind of luck. Inevitably, the producer will replace the data before the consumer gets a change to read it, or the consumer will read data more than once, thinking the producer still is on the job.

Java addresses this synchronization problem through the user of monitors

SYNCHRONIZING WITH MONITORS

Anytime you create a method with the **synchronized** keyword, the object to which that method belongs gets a special internal flag called a *monitor*. Anytime another object makes a call to that method, the runtime system checks to see if the monitor is in use. If it isn't, the runtime system gives the monitor to the object that is making the call, and the method call goes ahead. When the method finishes executing, the monitor is released. While an object has the monitor, no other object can make a call to that method.

In the case of the producer/consumer model, the common data area class will get the **synchronized** keyword on its data-delivery and retrieval methods. The only additional step is to set up a flag in the

common data area class that indicates when new data has been put in the buffer and when that data has been retrieved.

DEADLOCKED THREADS

Deadlocking sometimes is called "the deadly embrace." This occurs when two threads (or, for that matter, two applications) are competing for access to the same data but are blocked by the actions of the other thread.

Consider a communication system where (for whatever reason, insanity perhaps) a communication thread needs to have continuous access to one of 100 communications ports. The way that it negotiates a port change is to secure access to the second port, before releasing the first port. Anytime the thread changes ports, if the new port is not available, it simply stays hooked up to its current port until the new port is free.

Let's say Comm Thread A is hooked up to Port 12 and Comm Thread B is hooked up to Port 25. Thread A decides to move to Port 25, finds it busy, and begins waiting for Port 25 to free up. Thread B, meanwhile, decides it wants Port 12, finds it busy, and begins waiting for Port 12 to free up. The threads now are deadlocked, because neither can proceed until the other proceeds.

One obvious way to avoid this problem is to not have the thread enter into any kind of waiting condition; if the desired port is not available, move on to another one. This is not always practical, however, because the program's design might require a specific port connection at a specific time or in a given sequence. It might be better to terminate the thread with an exception.

If you do want the thread to wait for the required condition, you should put some sort of time limit on the waiting period. In this example, if the wait exceeds a preset period of time, you could consider that an indication of a deadlocked condition (or execute a specific test for a deadlocked condition) and take corrective action, perhaps by momentarily breaking the rule that all threads have to be connected to a port at all times.

THE RUNNABLE INTERFACE: AN APPLET EXAMPLE

Although you can create many useful kinds of threads based on the Thread class, there is little basic functionality there other than threading. There will be many times when you'd like to thread a panel, a frame, or some other class. To do this, use the Runnable interface.

Figure 15-2 shows the classic NervousText applet from the JDK, modified to display text in a rippling sine wave. This applet demonstrates the use of the Runnable interface.

Figure 15-2 The WaveText applet.

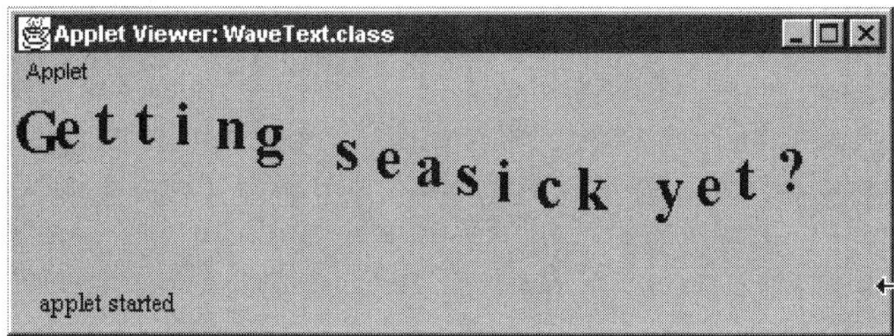

An applet that runs its own thread is distinguished from a standard applet by several features. First, you must specify that the class implements the Runnable interface:

```
public class WaveText extends java.applet.Applet implements Runnable {
```

Next, declare a Thread. Set the thread to null so that you can be sure of starting the thread only one time:

```
Thread appletThread = null;
```

In the applet's **start()** method, create a new instance of appletThread, if none exists, and **start()** it:

```
if(appletThread == null) {
  appletThread = new Thread(this);
  appletThread.start();
}
```

Finally, in the **stop()** method, add the code to shut down the thread:

```
appletThread.stop();
```

You also can use the code **appletThread = null** if you like; setting the thread to null has the same effect as calling the thread's **stop()** method.

Finally, put all of the code that you want to run in the thread into your **run()** method. You also might want to set the thread's priority, or any other thread attributes, at the start of this method.

That's all there is to creating threaded applets. Easy, isn't it?

HOW MANY THREADS?

You've just added the runnable interface to your favorite applet, and you've used it to load your images and sound clips and whatnot in the background, while still giving the user control over what's happening in the foreground. Because every applet already is one thread of execution, launching a thread via the ***threadname*.start()** method means you now have two threads running.

Any time that you have more than one thread running, you need to be aware of the thread-scheduling issues discussed earlier in this chapter. If you want to be sure that your users always have control over your applets, you can set the priority of any threads the applet spawns to a value lower than the applet's priority (which is **NORM_PRIORITY** by default). You can do this by adding the code:

```
Thread.currentThread().setPriority(MIN_PRIORITY)
```

or perhaps:

```
Thread.currentThread().setPriority(NORM_PRIORITY-1)
```

at the start of the **run()** method.

SUMMARY

Java's ability to create multiple threads of execution within applications and applets is one of the language's most useful and powerful features.

It takes most programmers who are unfamiliar with multithreading a long time to adjust their thinking away from the idea of programs as sequences of processes to programs as collections of interacting processes.

Fortunately, threads are easy to implement in Java, whether you're creating daemon threads using the Thread class, adding a thread to your favorite applet, or anything in between.

LINKING NATIVE C CODE

THERE MIGHT BE OCCASIONS when your Java applet needs to access some system resources or functions that are not built into the Java runtime library or Java classes. If that happens, you have the option of linking in native C code. In an ordinary programming language, if you needed to link in code from another language, you'd do this by compiling the C code and statically linking in the resulting binary code.

However, static linking has several problems. For starters, it makes the Java applet system-dependent because the C code must conform to the conventions of the operating system on which it's executing. If you link in a system function compiled on a Sun Sparcstation, and a Web user retrieves your applet and executes it on a computer running Windows 95, the code at best will not run and at worst will run in some unpredictable and possibly harmful way.

The other problem with static linking is it increases the size of the applet/application itself because the actual code in use is linked to it. You might be using only a single system call; however, if that call requires considerable resources, you might end up with a Java applet/application that's simply too big.

It is possible to statically link C code into a Java applet/application, as demonstrated in the make and build scripts for Java itself. In general, however, a far better solution is to link in the needed code dynamically.

DYNAMIC LINKING

In a dynamic linking scheme, the Java application (which is platform-independent) tells the Java interpreter (which is platform-dependent) that it (the applet/application) wants to use a particular system library. The interpreter actually produces the interface to the system library at runtime, rather than at compile time.

The process of dynamically linking native methods into a Java applet/application includes the following steps:

1. Write and compile the Java code that defines the native method in the applet/application.
2. Create a C header file.

❸ Create a stubs file.

❹ Write the C function and compile into a dynamically loadable library (DLL).

CREATING THE JAVA CODE

The Java code involved in using native methods is in three parts: the code that loads the native method's library, the code that declares the method, and the code that executes the method call. Native method calls work like Java method calls, but the first two aspects to using native methods need special treatment.

You'll start by creating a Java class that contains the native method calls. The first code block in this class is the static initializer, which uses the **System.loadLibrary()** method to load the native library (called db.so in this example):

System.loadLibrary() contains the code that builds the platform-dependent runtime interface to the system library. On Solaris, the library file would have the name db.so, while on Windows 95 the file would be called db.dll. This allows you to write one Java application that runs on multiple platforms. Equally important, if **System.loadLibrary()** fails, the class itself will fail to load, giving the Java runtime system a predictable point at which to handle errors.

The actual native methods in the class are distinguished by the use of the **native** keyword. For example, the **search()** native method will perform a search based on an SQL expression passed in as the argument and will return a String object that contains the result of the search:

```
public native String search(String sql);
```

The class file (shown in its entirely in Figure 16-1) is all of the Java source that you need to declare the interface (although you'll want another Java class to make the actual native method calls). This source also gives the header and stub utilities (both discussed shortly) the information that they need to build the rest of the interface between the Java class and the native method.

Figure 16-1 A Java Database class that implements native method calls.

```
package db;

/**
 * A class for demonstrating hooking Java up to a native database.
 * This class only supports three database operations: connect,
 * disconnect, and search.
 */
public class Database {
  static {
    System.loadLibrary("db");
  }
  /**
   * Session ID for this connection
   */
  protected public int sid;

  /**
   * Flag indicating whether this connection is open
   */
  protected boolean connected;

  /**
   * The db username
   */
  protected String userName;

  /**
   * The password
   */
  protected String password;

  public Database() {
    this("unknown", "unknown");
    connected = false;
    sid = -1;
  }

  public Database(String uname, String passwd) {
    userName = uname;
    password = passwd;
    connected = false;
    sid = -1;
  }
```

```
  public void setPassword(String pwd) {
    this.password = pwd;
  }

  public void setUsername(String uname) {
    this.userName = uname;
  }

  public int getSID() {
    return(this.sid);
  }

  public boolean isConnected() {
    return(this.connected);
  }

  public synchronized native boolean connect();

  public synchronized native void disconnect();

  public native String search(String b);
}
```

CREATING THE HEADER FILE

Before you create your C code, run the javah utility on the class file to create a C header file, which will contain the C version of the class definition in the Java class:

```
$ javah class
```

The generated header file (which will have the class name, but ending in .h) contains a struct that corresponds to the class definition, as well as a function signature (or prototype). You'll use this signature when you create the C code that the Java class calls.

The header file created from the java source in Figure 16-1 is shown in Figure 16-2. Note that function signatures have the package name and the class name prefixed, separated by underscores.

Figure 16-2 db_Database.h

```
/* DO NOT EDIT THIS FILE - it is machine generated */
#include <native.h>
/* Header for class db_Database */

#ifndef _Included_db_Database
#define _Included_db_Database
struct Hjava_lang_String;

typedef struct Classdb_Database {
    long sid;
    /*boolean*/ long connected;
    struct Hjava_lang_String *userName;
    struct Hjava_lang_String *password;
} Classdb_Database;
HandleTo(db_Database);

extern /*boolean*/ long db_Database_connect(struct Hdb_Database *);
extern void db_Database_disconnect(struct Hdb_Database *);
extern struct Hjava_lang_String *db_Database_search(struct
Hdb_Database *,struct Hjava_lang_String *);
#endif
```

CREATING THE STUBS FILE

In addition to the header file, you'll also need a C source file that contains code to connect the Java class and the C method. You can create this stub file by using javah again, but this time with the **-stubs** option:

```
$ javah -stubs class
```

This file will come into play when you create the C DLL. (See Figure 16-3.)

CREATING THE C DLL

You create the C DLL in much the same way that you create any other C DLL. Use the function signature created by javah as your starting point for the method, write whatever code you need, then link the C source code, the header file, and the stub file into the DLL. Figure 16-4 shows the C source code for a small Solaris DLL that queries a database.

Figure 16-3 db_Database.c

```
/* DO NOT EDIT THIS FILE - it is machine generated */
#include <StubPreamble.h>

/* Stubs for class db_Database */
/* SYMBOL: "db_Database/connect()Z",
/*          Java_db_Database_connect_stub */
stack_item *Java_db_Database_connect_stub(stack_item
/*          *_P_,struct execenv *_EE_) {
        extern long db_Database_connect(void *);
        _P_[0].i = (db_Database_connect(_P_[0].p) ? TRUE : FALSE);
        return _P_ + 1;
}
/* SYMBOL: "db_Database/disconnect()V",
/*          Java_db_Database_disconnect_stub */
stack_item *Java_db_Database_disconnect_stub(stack_item
/*          *_P_,struct execenv *_EE_) {
        extern void db_Database_disconnect(void *);
        (void) db_Database_disconnect(_P_[0].p);
        return _P_;
}
/* SYMBOL:
"db_Database/search(Ljava/lang/String;)Ljava/lang/String;",
Java_db_Database_search_stub */
stack_item *Java_db_Database_search_stub(stack_item *_P_,struct execenv *_EE_) {
        extern void* db_Database_search(void *,void *);
        _P_[0].p = db_Database_search(_P_[0].p,((_P_[1].p)));
        return _P_ + 1;
}
```

Figure 16-4 Query.c

```
#ifndef lint
#pragma ident  "@(#)query.c  1.1 31 May 1995 SMCC"
#endif /* lint */
/*
 * First off, we need to include the JAVA internal header files
 * for macros and function prototypes required to manipulate JAVA
 * data structures and functions.
 *
 * SubPreamble.h includes the structure and macro definitions needed
 * to convert JAVA data structures into C data structures.  For
 * example, macros such as "unhand" are defined in StubPreamble.h.
```

Figure 16-4 Continued.

```
 *
 * javaString.h defines the JAVA string maniuplation macros and
 * routines needed to convert between JAVA and C strings.
 *
 */
#include "StubPreamble.h"
#include "javaString.h"

/*
 * These headers are special in that they are generated by JAVAH.
 * These include the C structure definitions for the JAVA classes.
 *
 */
#include "db_Database.h"

#include <stdio.h>
#include "connection.h"

long
db_Database_connect(struct Hdb_Database *this)
{
  int n;
  static int connection = 1234;

#ifdef DEBUG
  fputs("Entered Native connect.\n", stdout);
  fprintf(stdout, "\tUsername= %s\n", makeCString(unhand(this)
          ->userName));
  fprintf(stdout, "\tPassword= %s\n", makeCString(unhand(this)
          ->password));
  fflush(stdout);
#endif

  unhand(this)->sid = connection++;
  n = add_connection(unhand(this)->sid);
#ifdef DEBUG
  fprintf(stdout,"\t%d Connections active.\n", n);
  fflush(stdout);
#endif
  return(TRUE);
}

void
```

```
db_Database_disconnect(struct Hdb_Database *this)
{
  int n;
#ifdef DEBUG
  fputs("Entered Native disconnect.\n", stdout);
  fflush(stdout);
#endif
  unhand(this)->connected = FALSE;
  n = remove_connection(unhand(this)->sid);
  unhand(this)->sid = -1;
#ifdef DEBUG
  fprintf(stdout,"\t%d Connections remaining.\n", n);
  fflush(stdout);
#endif

}

Hjava_lang_String *
db_Database_search(struct Hdb_Database *this,
                   Hjava_lang_String *str)
{
  char *tmp = "Search completed.";
#ifdef DEBUG
  fputs("Entered Native search.\n", stdout);
  fprintf(stdout, "\tSearching Session %d\n", unhand(this)->sid);
  fprintf(stdout, "\tSearch string= %s\n", makeCString(str));

  fflush(stdout);
#endif

  return(makeJavaString(tmp, strlen(tmp)));
}
```

If you're creating DLLs for Windows 95/NT, you'll need to use Microsoft's Visual C++ 2.0. You'll also need to link in javai.lib (or javai_g.lib, if you want to include debug information) as the last argument to the compiler.

Build the DLL using whatever make utility you're accustomed to using. Figure 16-5 shows a Solaris makefile.

Figure 16-5 Makefile

```
# NOTE: Change JAVAHOME to indicate the top level of your JAVA top
#       level directory before building
#
#

all              : library

JAVAC            = $(JAVAHOME)/bin/javac
JAVAH            = $(JAVAHOME)/bin/javah
#
# Default JAVAHOME
#
DEFAULT_JAVAHOME=/share/java
JAVAHOME         = $(DEFAULT_JAVAHOME$(ALT_JAVAHOME))$(ALT_JAVAHOME)
JAVASHAREINC     = $(JAVAHOME)/include
JAVASOLARISINC   = $(JAVAHOME)/include/solaris
JAVASOLARISBLD   = $(JAVAHOME)/include/CClassHeaders
LIBRARY          = libdb
CLASSSTUBDIR     = stubs
CHEADERDIR       = CClassHeaders
PACKAGEDIR       = db
STUBPREAMBLE     = $(JAVASHAREINC)/StubPreamble.h
#CLASS_SWITCH    = -classpath $(CLASSPATH)

CC               = cc
LD               = /usr/ccs/bin/ld
INCLUDES         = -I. -I$(CHEADERDIR) -I$(JAVASHAREINC) -I$(JAVASOLARISINC) \
                   -I$(JAVASOLARISBLD)
DEFINES          = -DDEBUG
CFLAGS           = $(DEFINES) $(INCLUDES) -c

FILES.c          = libstubs.c        \
                   connection.c      \
                   query.c

FILES.o          = $(FILES.c:%.c=%.o)

FILES.java       = Database.java \
                   DatabaseException.java

FILES.class      = $(FILES.java:%.java=$(PACKAGEDIR)/%.class)

EXPORTEDCLASSES = $(PACKAGEDIR).Database $(PACKAGEDIR).DatabaseException
```

```
$(PACKAGEDIR)/%.class : $(PACKAGEDIR)/%.java
                        $(JAVAC) $<

%.o                   : %.c
                        $(CC) $(CFLAGS) $<

library               : classheaders $(FILES.o)
                        $(LD) -G -o $(LIBRARY).so $(FILES.o)

classheaders          : $(FILES.class)
                        @for i in $(EXPORTEDCLASSES) ;        \
                          do                                  \
                            echo $(JAVAH) $(CLASS_SWITCH) -d $(CHEADERDIR)/ $$i ;\
                            $(JAVAH) $(CLASS_SWITCH) -d $(CHEADERDIR)/ $$i ;\
                        done

libstubs.c            : classheaders $(STUBPREAMBLE)
                        $(JAVAH) $(CLASS_SWITCH) -d $(CLASSSTUBDIR)/      \
                          -stubs $(EXPORTEDCLASSES)
                        @ cat $(STUBPREAMBLE) $(CLASSSTUBDIR)/*.c > $@

clobber               :
                        rm -rf $(CHEADERDIR) $(CLASSSTUBDIR) *.so *.class *.o \
                        $(PACKAGEDIR)/*.class libstubs.c
```

CALLING NATIVE METHODS

With your DLL built, all you need to do is import the class/package that contains the native method declarations and call those methods. Java will take care of the rest:

```
Database db = new Database("rice," "xyzzy");
db.connect();
s = db.search("Hello World");
db.disconnect();
```

SECURITY AND NATIVE METHODS

This ability to use C code in a system's own library does raise security concerns. The Java language is designed to prevent security breaches

by strictly controlling how the applet uses memory and other system resources. C code is not under the same constraints. Accordingly, Java-powered browsers, such as Netscape, currently do not allow for applets to load native methods across the Internet. Applets and other classes that are resident on the computer can load native methods that already are resident on the client computer, which means that, if you want your users to be able to use native methods, you'll need to deliver both the appropriate native method libraries and the applets (or the classes they call) to your users in a traditional manner (such as by arranging for a separate download or by shipping disks).

DESIGNING JAVA APPLETS AND APPLICATIONS

APPLET and application design tends to be of two kinds: conscious and unconscious. Most small applets come about as a result of unconscious design; you want a widget that does one function, and you sit down to write the code. With small projects, that's an acceptable and useful approach.

If your applets/applications become a little more complex, some forethought, or conscious design, can save you a lot of grief in the long run. In this chapter, we suggest some starting points for your design efforts.

DEFINING YOUR OBJECTIVES

Ask yourself what you want this applet to accomplish. Should the applet attract users to your page? Collect information? Present information? Process information? Are you designing this applet to perform one, fixed function, or do you want it to be adaptable to a range of functions? If the latter, you will have to decide just how configurable you want the applet to be and what kinds of applet tag parameters will be required.

Like most programming projects, applets might start small but can grow rapidly in scope and function. You might start out to create an applet that does simple animation of a hardcoded series of images. As soon as you want another animation applet, however, you have to create yet another version of that applet. It's much better to design an applet that accommodates a user-specified set of images. That's what the Animator applet, included with the JDK, does. (Animator is discussed in detail in chapter 20, "Animation with Java.")

You want to avoid a too restrictive design in the early stages, yet you also want to avoid rampant featuritis, where you design in a raft of features that you can't possibly implement in the time available. There's a balance of designing in flexibility, while keeping a project manageable, that you learn with experience.

DEFINING YOUR AUDIENCE

Ask yourself who will be using this Java applet. The wider your audience, the more generalized and uncomplicated your applet will need to be. The simplest Java applets run automatically when the user loads the applet's Web document. The next simplest applets run when the user clicks on the applet itself (or interacts with the applet in some other way), and even that simple requirement will often require explicit instruction. Never assume that the user knows what is required to run the applet. It's an axiom that programmers tend to write programs that are more complicated and less documented than users would like them to be.

Keep in mind that you are the programmer, so you naturally know what your applet is intended to do and why it does what it does. Someone who sees your applet for the first (or second or third) time doesn't have all that information. The best way to ensure that your application is understandable is to test it on a group of people who are representative of the less experienced members of your intended audience. Let them kick it around for a while, and above all listen to what they have to say. You'll almost certainly be surprised to discover that some of your favorite little widgets and features either escape their notice completely or simply leave them confused. You'll also find that, because you wrote the program, you tend to take the safe paths through it. Often an inexperienced user will perform a series of actions that you would never try, sometimes with disastrous results.

DEFINING INPUTS AND OUTPUTS

One useful way to think of your applet is in terms of what the inputs and outputs are. What information are you collecting from the user, and what information are you presenting back to the user?

In a simple applet, which executes when the Web document is retrieved, there are no inputs at all, and the output might be an entertaining (or perhaps annoying, depending on whether your intended audience shares your tastes) animation. If you're using an

applet to retrieve database information, the inputs and outputs can become quite complex.

In that case, it's often best to start with the outputs. What kind of information will your users be expecting back from the database? Will a simple text listing do? Should you be creating a custom Web document with links to other information? Are you going to present the information graphically, via yet another Java applet? Once you know the type and format of the information to output, you can work backwards to determine the minimum amount of information to collect from your users to achieve that end.

OUTPUT OPTIONS

A Java applet can have two kinds of output; information that's generated within the applet and information that comes from the server. On the other hand, non-Java Web programs typically get all their output from the server.

Because Java comes with a fairly capable windows library (the Abstract Windows Toolkit, or AWT), you're free to represent output, whether generated locally or on the server, in just about any way you like. You can use graphs, images, various standard GUI components, your own custom GUI components, and so on. As the third-party market for Java tools grows, you'll increasingly have 3D and other multimedia options to choose from.

You also can opt for a more traditional approach. These days, most non-Java Web programs that provide output from the server to the user (such as the results of a search) do so in the form of HTML documents. The most common way to do this is via a Common Gateway Interface, or CGI, script. The user fills out a form on the HTML document and presses a send button, and the browser collects and formats the form information and passes it to the server as a CGI request. The server executes the script specified by the CGI request, which creates an HTML document (either directly or by invoking another program or programs on the server), and that document is massaged a little by the server and then sent off to the user, where the browser formats the data.

You still can take this approach with Java, in which case you really haven't gained anything, as far as the output goes. Nonetheless there will be times when an HTML document is as good a way to represent output as any.

Chapter 18, "Client/server, Java style," covers many aspects of exchanging data between a Java applet and the Web server.

INPUT OPTIONS

The Java class library includes most of the common interface components, such as buttons, checkboxes, text fields, and list boxes. Try to keep your use of these components as standard as possible. For example, buttons are used for completing windows, for bringing up another window, or for executing some other specific action. Use button labels that accurately reflect what the button does.

Use checkboxes for true/false states, even if you're not storing that information in a numeric format. For example, if you have an online pizza parlor and you want the user to specify whether they want the pizza delivered or will pick it up, consider using a checkbox labeled "Hold for pickup" rather than a checkbox group with separate "Hold for pickup" and "Deliver" options. Set the checkbox's default value to whichever is the most common choice (or the one that will cause you the least trouble if left unaltered).

Similarly, if you have more than three options within a checkbox group, use a choice button (a drop-down list). A large number of checkboxes in a group just clutters up the screen.

As with other kinds of software development, your watchword in creating Java applets should be *simplicity*. Don't clutter up your windows with any more checkboxes, entry fields, cutesy widgets, or drop lists than are necessary. When you do create a complex window, group the various window elements by function within a panel. That way, all those components will stay together, even if the applet is drastically resized by the user.

If you have some information that most users will not need to see, consider making it optional, perhaps via another button. You also can use the CardLayout manager (discussed in chapter 10, "Applets: Frames, panels, and canvases," to create "pages" of components, much like tabbed dialogs.

MODULAR DESIGN

Applets impose special constraints on developers because of the relatively slow speed of the average Internet connection. If your applet is a large, complex one, it will take that much longer for it to be delivered over the wire (although to be fair, you can get a lot of functionality into relatively few bytes with Java).

On the other hand, Java loads classes across the Net only as they're required. So, if you break up a fairly large applet into a small applet that calls a number of other classes, only the required classes will be loaded. This is particularly helpful if you have an applet that contains areas most users will never enter. Once the class is loaded, it's available for the duration of the session, so there's only a one-time penalty for loading the class.

Modular design has another important benefit: reusability. Java is a dynamic language; when you create a class that's used by other classes, it's always available for use, whether or not that class changes or the classes that call it change (provided, of course, that all of the methods are correctly invoked). In many languages, program components have to be statically linked together, and if you change one component, you have to relink all of the other components.

Java, on the other hand, is truly a "plug and play" language. Where possible, design your classes to be generically useful. Also learn as much as you can about the third-party market for Java classes and applets. There already are a number of useful freeware classes available, and shareware and commercial classes are coming along as well. See appendix B for more on Java resources, including third-party products.

MODAL VERSUS MODELESS DESIGN

The modality of an application can be loosely defined as the extent to which it forces a user through a predetermined sequence of actions. For example, almost all DOS software is modal. When you choose an option from a typical DOS program's menu, say to bring up a data-entry form, you will be unable to access any other part of the program until you return from that form and choose another option from the menu. Furthermore, you might have to fill out all of the fields on that data-entry form in order. There's often no way to go from the first field to the last without going through all of the intervening fields and along the way executing any field editing code that might exist.

In modal software design, by the organization of the code in the program, the programmer decides what the sequence of events will be. In modeless software, just about any sequence of events can occur. The user can open more than one data-entry form, or any combination of *windows*, as they are more commonly called in modeless languages. The user also can choose fields in any order, usually with the aid of hotkeys or a pointing device, such as a mouse.

Operating systems that have a graphical user interface (GUI)—such as Solaris, the various brands of Windows, and the Macintosh OS—are designed to accommodate modeless software, where the user has more control over what happens in the application. Modal programs dictate to the user the course of action; modeless programs respond to the user's choices.

From a programmer's perspective, modal programs are simpler to write because you can control the order in which the user completes various actions. Modeless programs must respond to any one of a vast number of possible conditions, all of which are communicated to the program through a system of events and messages.

EVENTS AND MESSAGES

Whenever anything happens (that is, an event occurs) in a modeless program, such as the user clicking on a button or pressing a hotkey, the

operating system and/or the window manager, which manages the interface between the user and the program, notifies the program with some sort of message. This means that the program, whatever else it is doing, must be constantly checking for messages so that it can take the proper course of action. In the case of the button press, the program might invoke a procedure call, instantiate a new class, or do whatever is appropriate for its particular operating paradigm. The point is that the program only knows about what's going on via messages it receives.

> In theory, you could write a modeless program that processed all user input directly, but that wouldn't be a good idea for two reasons. First, you'd have to include all of that mouse management and keyboard handling code in every application (for GUI systems, that can be a lot of code). Second, that code would apply to only that one program. You'd still have no mechanism for switching between programs or for ensuring that the various programs used common conventions.

Modeless, GUI environments then typically spend a lot of their time processing messages. From a user perspective, almost all of this message traffic is invisible (except when the system wants to notify you of something that it deems worthy of your attention, such as the fact that your printer is out of paper or the network has just gone down).

Just as whole programs communicate with the system (and with each other) via events, the components of your programs also communicate. From a visual point of view, any program, specifically any Java applet or application, is made up of one or more windows, each of which can contain various types of window elements or controls (such as buttons, entry fields, list boxes, etc.). These windows and controls are loosely tied together by their ability to process messages and perhaps by a more direct kind of relationship, such as a control's dependence on the existence of the window.

For the programmer, this relatively loose organization of program components means additional programming challenges. Because the user can select controls in any order, you cannot afford to base your programs functionality on a particular series of events. Modeless programs force you to think about program design in terms of blocks of behavior (much as object-oriented programming, which is closely allied to GUI operating systems, forces you to think about programs

themselves in terms of blocks of code). What happens when you take a totally random path through your program? You're the programmer, so you know exactly what path to take for maximum effect, but your users don't have the benefit of that knowledge.

Become a student of other programs. Look at your favorite software and analyze its level of modality. Can you jump from menu item to menu item without the program losing its usefulness? Or does it get cluttered and confusing?

A word of caution: Although modeless programs have many advantages for users, you should not assume that modelessness is simply good for its own sake. Even the most modeless programs occasionally find it useful to force the user into a relatively modal state. One way to do this is to disable certain controls under conditions when the use of those controls is unimportant or inappropriate. While such a window might not be fully modal, it's restricted enough to ensure that the user accomplishes the desired aim with a minimum of confusion.

THREADING

As described in chapter 15, "Multithreaded applets and applications," Java programs allow you to run multiple threads of execution within a single applet or application. Threading is a close ally of modeless design. With a threaded program, not only can the user freely switch between different parts of the program, but those different parts can have concurrently executing code.

What happens if the user runs two threads, or two instances of the same thread, at the same time? Does the program still make sense? Is it still obvious to the user how to accomplish the desired goals? Do you need to prevent the user from running multiple instances of certain threads? Although, in many ways, the user is in control over what the program does, you still have to set the constraints within which the user operates.

SECURITY ISSUES

There are several aspects to the whole issue of security, some of which are the province of the Web site administrator and/or related to your browser's security settings. In general, these issues revolve around firewalls and who has access to what Internet domains. Some of these issues are discussed in appendix A, "The HotJava browsers," and some are discussed in Part 4 of this book, which deals with setting up a Java Web server.

There is yet another facet to security, and that is maintaining control over the various parts of your applet. In these early stages of Java applet development, few programmers bother with this kind of security, because most applets do not have any off-limits areas.

However, if you're using Java to create front ends for various kinds of private data, then you might well want to build some security functions into the applet itself. This kind of security has nothing to do with any of Java's built-in security features; it's simply a set of classes that you design and write (or perhaps buy) to restrict access to various parts of your applet (or the classes that the applet calls).

Security systems often are designed to be multiple-level so that different users get access to different parts of the system based on their security clearance. There are a number of ways to implement such a system; however, in general, the easiest way is to use a generalized security function at each access point. That function receives the user ID (obtained through a logon window) and the name of the access point (often the name of the class) and looks in a database of access points and user IDs for a security-clearance level. If that security-clearance level matches, or is lower than, the security-clearance level stored in the user record, the function returns a value indicating that access is granted.

In a more elaborate organization, you might have security classes (in the abstract sense, not the programming sense) so that any given class of users has access to certain parts of the system. In that case, the

function looks up the user's class, then looks up the record that describes the security clearance required.

With any security system, simple or complex, you need some means of maintaining the security database, and that maintenance system also must be secure. Do not keep your security database in an area on the Web server that is accessible to users, or someone might download the database and use it to gain access. Don't assume that just because you've encrypted the security database it's secure. It might be, but some people see encrypted data as a challenge, not a deterrent. On the Web, paranoia pays off. The best security is ensuring that your critical data is kept out of reach.

While we're on the subject of paranoia, you also should limit the number of unsuccessful logon attempts. If you let users keep trying to get into the system, there's nothing to stop a hacker from using an automated logon program to try every possible combination of characters (or, more likely, a list of commonly used passwords like "password") until the door opens. After three unsuccessful attempts, don't just log the user off, show a window that instructs them who to contact about getting access.

It's a good idea to keep track of unsuccessful attempts to log on and post a message to an error log (or have the program e-mail you). If a user makes more than a certain number of logon attempts, you might want to force a delay of some seconds between tries, to prevent a rapid series of break-in attempts. You might even consider locking down the applet if a number of failed logins occur during a set period of time.

Security systems can be a pain to write. Because this is a common enough need, look for third-party vendors to start providing solutions. No such systems were available for review at the time of this writing, but a trip to the Java home page (at *java.sun.com*) will put you on to additional Java resources. You also might want to post a request for information in the *comp.lang.java* newsgroup or browse some of the other resources discussed in appendix B.

SUMMARY

Design work is one of those things that pays off in proportion to the size of the applet or application that you're creating. Small applets and applications might take relatively little design work and not suffer for the lack of it. As your programs grow in complexity, however, you need to take into consideration typical programming issues of GUI interface design, modeless programs, and security issues, as well as the more Java-specific issues of multithreading and program component size and structure.

CLIENT/SERVER, JAVA STYLE

THE MAJORITY of Java applets either contain all of the data that they need to operate or retrieve files (such as images or audio clips) from the Web server. These applets can grab files from the server, but they don't send any information (either entered by the user or created during the applet's operation) back to the server.

Many kinds of applets can benefit from a two-way communication with the server. You might use this kind of connection to set up a server-based database search engine, a local discussion group similar to a USENET newsgroup, or an order-entry system for an online store.

Ultimately, such a system will require the ability to do file input/output (I/O) on the server. Theoretically, applets do have the ability to I/O using one of the classes of the java.io package, such as FileInputStream or FileOutputStream. Unfortunately, these classes will do I/O only on the computer where the Java applet is running (and practically, most browsers restrict Java applets from doing I/O on the client machine for security reasons), while what you really want is for the Java applet to read and write data from the Web server. Finally, even if you could get the applet to do I/O across the Internet, you'd still be faced with the problem of making Java's I/O calls work with your data's format.

THE CLIENT/SERVER MODEL

While the applet can't do direct I/O on the server, a program running on the server doesn't have that restriction. The practical solution to the problem is first to create a data link between the Java applet running on the Web user's computer and a program (a Java application) running on the server. When the applet needs information from the server, it passes a request to the application running on the server. Because the application is an application and not an applet, it's not under the same security restrictions and can employ any one of a number of methods to obtain the required information and then pass that information back to the applet via that same data link.

This approach is just another variation on the client/server theme, with the Java applet as the client and the Java application, which is running on the Web server, as the server.

Most Web applications that do any kind of client/server work do so by using Common Gateway Interface (CGI) scripts to build HTML documents from queries, and they return those documents to the user. This approach suffers from the same limitations as standard HTML documents do: Because the Web is basically sessionless, each query to the database requires reconnecting and reauthenticating the database user. Depending on the database, this process can be quite time-consuming. With Java-based clients, however, it's possible to set up a data link between the applet and the server and to keep that connection open, requiring only a single login and authentication.

SOCKET COMMUNICATIONS

The data link between the client applet and the server application is called a *socket*, which is defined as the combination of an IP address and a port number. Any time that you connect to another computer via TCP/IP, you do so through a port at that computer's IP address. As a user, you ordinarily don't have to specify which port you're using, because certain ports already are assigned to particular purposes. For example, ports 20 and 21 are used for FTP, port 23 is used for TELNET, 79 is the FINGER port, 119 is reserved for NNTP, and so on.

When you set up your own socket communications, you will have to specify one or more port numbers of your own choosing. To avoid conflicts with the standard ports, use port numbers in a relatively unused range, such as 4000 to 8000. You can use numbers all the way to 65K, but port numbers above 8000 might not be subject to the same security restrictions as those below 8000.

Socket communication, as discussed in this chapter, is somewhat different from the kind of communication used to transfer HTML documents, applets, and the files that applets use. When a Web browser or applet requests a file, the connection is established only for the length of time that it takes to deliver the request for the file or to deliver the file itself. When you establish socket communication, however, you're opening a sustained channel between the client and the server. Because sockets stay open, the response time is faster, and you don't have to worry about whether or not you'll get access to the server when you need to.

CREATING A JAVA SERVER APPLICATION

The MTServer application consists primarily of three objects: a MTServer, a ConnectionThread, and a TimerThread. The MTServer is the top-level object in the application. Its sole purpose is to listen for new connections on a predefined port and, when they arrive, create a new ConnectionThread object to deal with it.

The ConnectionThread object represents a separate thread of execution in the application, one per active connection to the server. Connection Threads read incoming data from clients, hand the data off to a DataHandler object for processing, and send the result back to the client. For each ConnectionThread object, there is a TimerThread object. Each TimerThread is yet another thread of execution in the server application. TimerThreads monitor the connections to the clients. When they become "stale" (i.e., have been idle for too long), they stop the ConnectionThread from running and close down the connection to the client.

Figure 18-1 is the source code listing for an application that sits on the Web server and waits for an applet to make a socket connection.

Figure 18-1 The MTServer application.

```
/*
 */
import java.net.*;
import java.io.*;
import ConnectionThread;
import StringReverse;

/**
 * A MTServer class is used to manage multiple connections from
 * Java clients.  Client connections come in, MTServer accepts
 * the connection and hands it off to a ConnectionThread that
 * manages the connection.
 *
 * @see ConnectionThread
 * @see java.net.ServerSocket
 * @author Jeffrey C. Rice
```

```
 * @version 1.5
 */

public class MTServer {
  public static void main(String args[]) {
    ServerSocket serverSock = null;
    Socket sock = null;
    boolean dbg = false;
    int port = 5678;
    int timeout = 150;

    if (args.length > 0) {
      port = Integer.parseInt(args[0]);
      if (args.length > 1)
        dbg = (Integer.parseInt(args[1]) == 1) ? true : false;
    }

    try {
      if (dbg)
        System.out.println("Starting server on port " + port);
      serverSock = new ServerSocket(port, timeout);
      System.out.println("Local address " + serverSock.getInetAddress());
    } catch (IOException e) { }

    while (true) {
      try {
        sock=serverSock.accept();
      } catch (IOException e) { }

      ConnectionThread thr = new ConnectionThread(sock,
                                 new StringReverse(), dbg);
      thr.start();
    }
  }
}
```

MTServer is short and sweet, with only three code blocks. The first block checks for port number passed on the command line. If the parameter is omitted, the port defaults to 5678 (an arbitrarily chosen number).

Next comes a **try{}** block that attempts to establish the server socket that will listen for incoming socket connections:

```
serverSock = new ServerSocket(port, timeout);
```

The ServerSocket constructor takes a port number and a timeout value, in milliseconds. If the constructor fails, you don't have a socket.

However, hopefully all will go well, and you'll be ready for the final block of code, which is a **while** loop that executes forever, or until the user presses Ctrl-C. This is just a command-line program running on the Web server, so it has the simplest of interfaces; however, without too much difficulty, you could modify the program to display a GUI control panel with visual indicators of socket activity.

The **while** loop continually calls the serverSocket's **accept()** method, inside a **try{}** block. The **accept()** method blocks the thread from running until an incoming socket connection request is detected, so the following code, which creates a thread to monitor the connection, doesn't execute until there's a connection to monitor:

```
try {
  sock=serverSock.accept();
} catch (IOException e) { }

ConnectionThread thr = new ConnectionThread(sock,
                       new StringReverse(),
                       dbg);
thr.start();
```

There's one other feature of note in this code. The ConnectionThread constructor takes three parameters: the sock object, sock (which was instantiated by serverSock.accept), a data handler, and a debug flag. The data handler is a class that will be used to process the incoming data from the socket connection. The examples in this chapter use the StringReverse data handler (see Figure 18-2), which simply reverses the incoming data. Your real-world server application will undoubtedly use a more complex data handler, possibly employing native methods to do some sort of database access.

> Because the connection process is threaded, it's safe to assume that this server is designed to handle multiple socket connections at once, yet only one port has been specified. As it turns out, sockets can have more than one connection active, and TCP/IP will keep the data streams separate by connection.

CREATING A NEW CONNECTION THREAD

The ConnectionThread class is rather more substantial than the MTServer class, but then it does the lion's share of the work in managing the

Figure 18-2 The StringReverse data handler.

```
import DataHandler;

/**
 * A Sample Class implementing the DataHandler interface.
 * In practice, process might interface to a
 * database via a native implementation of process().
 *
 * @author Jeffrey C. Rice
 * @version 1.4
 */

public class StringReverse implements DataHandler {

  public String process(String str) {
    int length = str.length();
    int i, j;
    StringBuffer reply = new StringBuffer(length);;

    for(i = (length - 1), j = 0; i >= 0; i--, j++)
      reply.insert(j, str.charAt(i));
    return reply.toString();
  }
}
```

socket communication. Figure 18-3 shows the source for ConnectionThread.

THE CONNECTIONTHREAD CONSTRUCTOR

The ConnectionThread constructor does a couple of interesting things. First, it assigns the passed socket and data handler to its own socket and data handler (there is only one instance of each of these in MTServer that will be reassigned on the next socket connection). Next, the constructor creates an instance of the TimeStamp class, which contains a long integer that stores the last time that the thread saw any activity on the socket:

```
timeStamp = new TimeStamp();
```

Figure 18-3 The ConnectionThread class.

```
/*
 */
import java.net.*;
import java.io.*;
import java.util.Date;
import DataHandler;

/**
 * A TimeStamp class. Used by Connection and TimerThreads to
 * determine when a connection has expired. Stores the time in
 * milliseconds since epoch
 *
 * @see Connection
 * @see TimerThread
 * @see java.util.Date
 * @author Jeffrey C. Rice
 * @version 1.4
 */
class TimeStamp {
  private long lastTouched = 0L;

  /**
   * Refreshes the timestamp.
   */
  public synchronized void update() {
    lastTouched = (new Date()).getTime();
  }

  /**
   * Returns time last updated in milliseconds since epoch.
   *
   * @returns time last touched
   */
  public synchronized long getValue() {
    return lastTouched;
  }
}


/**
 * A class for timing actions by threads.  A TimerThread is
 * given a TimeStamp that is shared with the thread it is
 * timing.  Once started, the TimerThread will sleep for a
```

```
 * specified interval.  If the TimeStamp has not been updated since
 * it went to sleep, the TimerThread will kill the other thread.
 *
 * @see Connection
 * @see TimeStamp
 * @see Thread
 * @author Jeffrey C. Rice
 * @version 1.4
 */
class TimerThread extends Thread {
  private int timeout;  // in seconds
  private TimeStamp timeStamp;
  private ConnectionThread parent;
  private boolean debug;

  /**
   * Create the TimerThread
   *
   * @param t the shared TimeStamp object
   * @param seconds the interval to sleep before checking the
   * TimeStamp @param th the thread to kill if the TimeStamp
   * is not updated (this thread must share the TimeStamp!)
   * @param dbg if true, print debugging information
   */
  public TimerThread(TimeStamp t, int seconds, ConnectionThread th, boolean dbg) {
    super();
    debug = dbg;
    timeStamp = t;
    timeout = seconds;
    parent = th;
  }

  /**
   * Create the TimerThread
   *
   * @param t the shared TimeStamp object
   * @param seconds the interval to sleep before checking the
   * TimeStamp @param th the thread to kill if the TimeStamp
   * is not updated (this thread must share the TimeStamp!)
   */
  public TimerThread(TimeStamp t, int seconds, ConnectionThread th) {
    this(t, seconds, th, false);
  }
```

Figure 18-3 Continued.

```
/**
 * Reset the timeout interval
 *
 * @param seconds the new value
 */
public void setTimeout(int seconds) {
  timeout = seconds;
}

public void run () {
  /*
   * Run forever as long as the other thread keeps updating
   * the TimeStamp object.
   */
  while (true) {
    long t;

    t = timeStamp.getValue();

    if (t > 0 && (((new Date()).getTime() - t) > timeout*1000)) {
      // Time's up! Kill parent thread.
      if (debug)
        System.out.println("Closing parent threads connection...");
        try {
          parent.dataIn.close();
          parent.dataOut.close();
          parent.sock.close();
        }
        catch (IOException e) {}
        /*
         * Break out of loop, exit run(). This will terminate
         * this thread as well...
         */
        break;
    }

    // The TimeStamp was okay... sleep, then check it again.
    try {
      sleep(timeout*1000);
    }
    catch (InterruptedException e) { }
  }
```

```
  }

}

/**
 * A ConnectioThread class is used to handle 2-way data transfers
 * across a socket connection.  It uses DataInputStream and
 * DataOutputStream for the communication.  The data transfer
 * protocol is simple here... first data transfer is an int,
 * indicating how many elements in the byte array that follow.
 *
 * @see TimerThread
 * @see TimeStamp
 * @see Thread
 * @see java.io.DataInputStream
 * @see java.io.DataOutputStream
 * @author Jeffrey C. Rice
 * @version 1.4
 */
class ConnectionThread extends Thread {
  static int thrCount = 0;
  int thrID;
  protected TimerThread tThread;
  protected TimeStamp timeStamp;
  protected Socket sock;
  protected DataOutputStream dataOut;
  protected DataInputStream  dataIn;
  protected DataHandler dataBase;
  protected boolean debug;
  protected byte [] arr = null;

  /**
   * Create the ConnectionThread
   *
   * @param s the socket we are communicating across
   * @param db the DataHandler object that will get us a reply.
   */
  public ConnectionThread(Socket s, DataHandler db) {
    this(s, db, false);
  }

  /**
   * Create the ConnectionThread
   *
   * @param s the socket we are communicating across
```

Figure 18-3 Continued.

```
   * @param db the DataHandler object that will get us a reply.
   * @param dbg if true, debug messages will be printed
   */
  public ConnectionThread(Socket s, DataHandler db, boolean dbg) {
    super();
    debug = dbg;
    sock = s;
    dataBase = db;
    thrID = thrCount++;
    timeStamp = new TimeStamp();

    timeStamp.update();

    // Timer thread will expire connections after 300 seconds.
    tThread = new TimerThread(timeStamp, 300, this, debug);

    try {
      dataOut = new DataOutputStream(sock.getOutputStream());
      dataIn  = new DataInputStream(sock.getInputStream());
    }
    catch (IOException e) { }
  }

  public void run() {
    if (debug)
      System.out.println(this.activeCount() +" threads running");
    // Start timer thread...
    tThread.start();
    String reply = null;

    /*
     * Run forever unless stopped by timer thread or
     * unless client goes away, causing an IOException
     */
    while (true) {

      // Read the <length, string> message from the client
      try {
        int len = dataIn.readInt();  // length
        arr = new byte[len];
        dataIn.readFully(arr);       // the string
      }
      catch (IOException e) {
        if (debug)
          System.out.println("Exception during read...");
        break;
      }
```

```
      // Successful read... update the TimeStamp
      synchronized(timeStamp) {
        timeStamp.update();
      }

      // convert the data to a string
      String str = new String(arr, 0);
      if (debug)
        System.out.println("T[" + thrID + "] "+ str);

      // Now ask our DataHandler object for a reply
      try {
        reply = dataBase.process(str);
      }
      catch (Exception e) {
        System.err.println("Exception in processing...");
      }

      try {
        // if reply is not null send it
        if (reply != null) {
          dataOut.writeInt(reply.length());
          dataOut.writeBytes(reply);
        }
        // otherwise send -1
        else {
          dataOut.writeInt(-1);
        }
        dataOut.flush();

      }
      catch (IOException e) { }
    }
    if (tThread.isAlive())
      tThread.stop();  // if we break out of the while loop...
    try {
      if (debug)
        System.out.println("Closing down socket.");
      dataOut.close();
      dataIn.close();
      sock.close();
    }
    catch (IOException e) { }
  }
}
```

The timestamp will be updated each time that there is a request from a client on this connection. Two objects will use the timestamp. The connection thread will update the timestamp each time that it gets a request, and the TimerThread will look at the timestamp each time it wakes up. The key here is the TimerThread. It monitors the connection, and if the construction has been inactive too long, it will kill the ConnectionThread by closing the connection. This is important because you want to make sure that the connection isn't being held open for some client who has surfed on to some other page.

The TimeStamp class contains methods to read and update the time of last activity. To ensure that the update method gets a lock when updating the time, the **synchronized** keyword is used to mark the **update()** method as the code within the timeStamp object that is to be protected from simultaneous access:

```
synchronized(timeStamp) {
  timeStamp.update();
}
```

Note: This synchronization could have been accomplished by declaring the **update()** method as synchronized and actually would probably better guarantee synchronous access across classes that use TimeStamp objects.

The code for setting and reading the time of last activity is in place; now you need to start a thread that will do the actual monitoring. This thread takes the timeStamp object as one of its parameters:

```
tThread = new TimerThread(timeStamp, 300, this, debug);
```

Finally, the constructor sets up input and output streams for the socket:

```
dataOut = new DataOutputStream(sock.getOutputStream());
dataIn  = new DataInputStream(sock.getInputStream());
```

Keep in mind that, although there might be multiple connections on the same socket, TCP/IP will manage these connections separately, so each of these streams represents the communication only between the server and the particular connection that launched this thread.

THE CONNECTIONTHREAD RUN() METHOD

The **run()** method mainly sits in a loop and waits for data to appear on the input data stream. The **readInt()** method blocks the thread until

something appears for it to read, which, if the message is formatted properly, will be a 32- bit int describing the length of the message. The **readFully()** method loads the string into an array arr, which has been sized to the length of the message.

The ConnectThread's **run()** method catches an IOException. The TimerThread associated with the ConnectionThread will close the connection if the timestamp expires. When this happens, an IOException is generated in the **readInt()** or **readFully()** methods. When the ConnectionThread catches this exception, it breaks out of the loop, stops the TimerThread, and exits.

If the data's read in properly (no exceptions), the timestamp gets updated, the array is cast to a String, and you're ready to process the data!

PROCESSING THE DATA

The data received by the server is processed with a call to the data handler that was passed in to the SocketConnection constructor:

```
String reply = dataBase.process(str);
```

As you'll recall, this data handler simply reverses the string and returns it, but you could make your data handler do anything at all, such as make a native method call to an SQL database and return formatted rows of data or retrieve an image file from a library.

Assuming the process returns some data, the **run()** method writes out an int with the length of the message, then uses the **writeBytes()** method to fire the data back to the client.

When, for whatever reason, the **while** loop terminates (thread death or an IOException), the socket is closed down with **sock.close()**.

That's all you need to set up a socket server on the Web server (plus the server and the rights to run such a process, of course). To launch the socket server, just execute:

```
java MTServer
```

at the command prompt.

CREATING A JAVA CLIENT APPLET

The client applet, the source code for which is shown in Figure 18-4, is mostly taken up with user interface concerns.

Figure 18-4 The PopUp client applet.

```
/*
 */
import java.applet.Applet;
import java.awt.*;

import ClientConnection;
import ConnectionException;

/**
 * A Popup window for doing network queries.
 *
 * @author Jeffrey C. Rice
 * @version     1.2
 */

class ShowButton extends Button {
  Frame frame;
  public ShowButton(Frame f) {
    super("Show");
    frame = f;
  }
  public boolean action(Event e, Object arg) {
    frame.show();
    return true;
  }
}

class HideButton extends Button {
  Frame frame;
  public HideButton(Frame f) {
    super("Hide");
    frame = f;
  }
  public boolean action(Event e, Object arg) {
    frame.hide();
    return true;
  }
}
```

```
class QueryFrame extends Frame {
  Panel topPanel, bottomPanel;
  TextField hostName;
  String hostString;
  TextField portNumber;
  String portString;
  TextField query;
  TextField reply;
  Button sendButton;
  Label statusLabel;
  ClientConnection connection;

  public QueryFrame(String str, String host, String port, int w, int h) {
    super(str);
    hostString = host;
    portString = port;
    setResizable(true);
    populate();
    resize(w, h);
    connection = null;
  }

  protected TextField addLabeledTextField(String labelString,
                                          int width, String initString,
                                          Panel panel,
                                          GridBagLayout gb,
                                          GridBagConstraints gbc) {
    TextField t;
    Label l = new Label(labelString, Label.RIGHT);
    if (initString != null)
      t = new TextField(initString, width);
    else
      t = new TextField(width);
    gbc.gridwidth = 1;
    gbc.weightx = 1.0;
    gbc.anchor = GridBagConstraints.EAST;
    gb.setConstraints(l, gbc);
    panel.add(l);

    gbc.gridwidth = GridBagConstraints.REMAINDER;
    gbc.weightx=4;
    gbc.anchor = GridBagConstraints.WEST;
    gb.setConstraints(t, gbc);
    panel.add(t);
    return t;
  }
```

Figure 18-4 Continued.

```
protected TextField addLabeledTextField(String labelString,
                                        int width,
                                        Panel panel,
                                        GridBagLayout gb,
                                        GridBagConstraints gbc) {
  return addLabeledTextField(labelString, width, null, panel, gb, gbc);
}

void populate() {

  GridBagLayout gridBag = new GridBagLayout();
  GridBagConstraints constraints = new GridBagConstraints();

  setLayout(new GridLayout(2,1));
  topPanel = new Panel();
  topPanel.setLayout(gridBag);
  bottomPanel = new Panel();

  hostName = addLabeledTextField("Host Name:", 20, hostString,
                                 topPanel, gridBag, constraints);
  portNumber = addLabeledTextField("Port Number:", 12, portString,
                                 topPanel, gridBag, constraints);
  query = addLabeledTextField("Query:", 32, topPanel,
                              gridBag, constraints);
  reply = addLabeledTextField("Reply:", 32, topPanel,
                              gridBag, constraints);
  constraints.gridwidth = GridBagConstraints.REMAINDER;
  constraints.weightx = 0.0;
  statusLabel = new Label("Status:", Label.LEFT);
  topPanel.add(statusLabel);

  bottomPanel.add(sendButton = new Button("Send"));

  add(topPanel);
  add(bottomPanel);
}

public void setStatus(String str) {
  statusLabel.resize(topPanel.size().width, statusLabel.size().height);
  statusLabel.setText("Status: " + str);
}

public boolean action(Event e, Object arg) {

  if (e.target.equals(sendButton)) {
    try {
      String msg = query.getText();
      String host = hostName.getText();
```

```
        String port = portNumber.getText();

        /* Check to see if these are new values...
         * if so, make a new connection
         */
        if (connection == null || !connection.isPort(port) ||
          !connection.isHost(host)) {
          if (connection != null)
            connection.closeConnection();
          connection = new ClientConnection(host, port);
        }
        if (msg != null) {
          System.out.println("Sending msg = " + msg);
          connection.send(msg);
          reply.setText(connection.getReply());
        }
        else
          setStatus("Please specify a message...");

      }
      catch (ConnectionException ex) {
        setStatus(ex.getMessage());
      }
    }
    return true;
  }

  // Handle the Close/Exit from window manager.
  public boolean handleEvent(Event e) {
    if (e.id == Event.WINDOW_DESTROY) {
      if (connection != null)
        connection.closeConnection();
      dispose();
      System.exit(1);
      return true;
    }
    else
      return super.handleEvent(e);
  }
}

public class PopUp extends Applet {
  QueryFrame frame;
  HideButton hideButton;
  ShowButton showButton;

  public void init() {
```

Figure 18-4 Continued.

```
    frame = new QueryFrame("DataBase Query",
                           getParameter("host"),
                           getParameter("port"),
                           size().width,
                           size().height);

    hideButton = new HideButton(frame);
    showButton = new ShowButton(frame);
    add(hideButton);
    add(showButton);
    resize(200,30);
  }

  public static void main(String args[]) {
    QueryFrame f = new QueryFrame("DataBase Query", "", "", 400, 350);
    f.show();
  }

}
```

The applet's tag specifies the host computer's name and port number. When the user specifies some text to send to the server and clicks on the **Send** button, the following code executes:

```
String msg = query.getText();
String host = hostName.getText();
String port = portNumber.getText();
if (connection == null || !connection.isPort(port) ||
   !connection.isHost(host)) {
  if (connection != null)
    connection.closeConnection();
  connection = new ClientConnection(host, port);
}
```

Note: Due to security restrictions in most browsers, applets are only allowed to make connections back to the host that they came from. The hostname that the applet uses must exactly match the one in its URL. While passing the hostname of your Web server to the applet via the **param** tag will work most of the time, a more general way is to use the following code:

```
String host = getCodeBase().getHost().getName():
```

in your applet. This will return the hostname as it was given in the URL that got you the applet.

If there is no current connection, the applet attempts to establish one with the call to the ClientConnection constructor.

THE CLIENTCONNECTION CLASS

The ClientConnection class is the partner to the ConnectionThread class that is part of the server application. Figure 18-5 shows the code for ClientConnection, which not only establishes a socket connection with the server but also sends and receives data.

Figure 18-5 The ClientConnection class.

```
/*
 * Add standard disclaimers...
 */

import java.net.*;
import java.io.*;
import ConnectionException;

/**
 * The ClientConnection class establishes a connection with a remote
 * server over a 2-way socket connection.  It uses DataInputStream
 * and DataOutputStream for the communication.  The data transfer
 * protocol is simple here... first data transfer is an int,
 * indicating how many elements in the byte array that follow.
 * Then wait for the reply.
 *
 * @see java.io.DataInputStream
 * @see java.io.DataOutputStream
 * @see java.lang.Exception
 * @see ConnectionException
 *
 * @author      Jeff Rice
 * @version     %I%
 */
class ClientConnection {
  protected byte data[];
  protected Socket socket;
  protected DataInputStream socketIn;
  protected DataOutputStream socketOut;
```

Figure 18-5 Continued.

```
  protected boolean dataReady;
  protected boolean debug;

  /**
   * Create the ClientConnection
   *
   * @param host the name of the host we are talking to
   * @param port the port host is listening for connections at.
   * @param dbg if true, then debug messages will be printed.
   * @exception ConnectionException if host or port are null or if it is
   *            unable to make the connection.
   */
  public ClientConnection(String host, String port, boolean dbg)
         throws ConnectionException {
    debug = dbg;
    if (host == null)
      throw new ConnectionException("No host specified...");
    if (port == null)
      throw new ConnectionException("No port specified...");

       // Open the connection, set flag indicating it is open.
       try {
         socket = new Socket(host, Integer.parseInt(port));
         socketOut = new DataOutputStream(socket.getOutputStream());
         socketIn = new DataInputStream(socket.getInputStream());
       }
       catch (Exception e) {
         throw new ConnectionException("Error opening socket. Check host and
port names.");
       }
  }

  /**
   * Create the ClientConnection
   *
   * @param host the name of the host we are talking to
   * @param port the port host is listening for connections at.
   * @exception ConnectionException if host or port are null or if it is
   *            unable to make the connection.
   */
  public ClientConnection(String host, String port)
         throws ConnectionException {
    this(host, port, false);
```

```
}
/**
 * Get a reply from the server. Synchronized with send() to
 * ensure replys are not retrieved while new data is being received.
 */
public synchronized String getReply() {
  String reply = null;
  if (dataReady) {
    reply = new String(data, 0);
    dataReady = false;
  }
  return reply;
}

/**
 * Send the data to the remote host.
 *
 * @param str the message/query being sent to the server.
 * @exception ConnectionException when the connection is lost.
 */
synchronized public void send(String str) throws ConnectionException {
  // Send the message...
  try {
    socketOut.writeInt(str.length());
    socketOut.writeBytes(str);
    socketOut.flush();
  }
  catch (IOException e) {
    if (debug)
      System.out.println("IO Exception during write...");
    throw new ConnectionException("Error writing data to socket.");
  }

  // Get the reply...
  try {
    int nbytes = socketIn.readInt();
    if (nbytes > 0) {
      data = new byte[nbytes];
      socketIn.readFully(data);
      dataReady = true;
    }
  }
  catch (Exception e) {  // either IO or EOF...
    if (debug)
      System.out.println("IO Exception during read...");
    throw new ConnectionException("Error reading data from socket.");
```

Figure 18-5 Continued.

```
    }
  }
  public boolean isPort(String pt) {
    return(pt.equals(String.valueOf(socket.getPort())));
  }

  public boolean isHost(String h) {
    return(h.equals(socket.getInetAddress().getHostName()));
  }

  public void closeConnection() {
    try {
      socket.close();
    }
    catch (IOException e) {}
  }

  protected void finalize() {
    closeConnection();
  }
}
```

The ClientConnection constructor first attempts to open a new socket and create input and output data streams:

```
socket = new Socket(host, Integer.parseInt(port));
socketOut = new DataOutputStream(socket.getOutputStream());
socketIn = new DataInputStream(socket.getInputStream());
```

If the Socket constructor fails, the data stream constructors will fail, too. An error anywhere here will result in the constructor throwing a ConnectionException.

The **send()** and **getReply()** methods are straightforward and similar in function to their counterparts in ConnectionThread. These methods are synchronized to prevent a reply from being read while data still is being sent.

ESTABLISHING JAVA SERVER/ DATABASE COMMUNICATION

The client/server communication model that is demonstrated in this chapter has numerous applications, but perhaps the most common is as a means of querying databases on the server. This task has two parts: getting access to the data and formatting the data stream.

ACCESSING THE DATABASE

Pending the release of third-party Java classes for existing database systems, your choices for reading the database are most likely limited to using Java's I/O classes to read flat files, linking in native C or C++ methods to read the database directly, or linking in native C or C++ methods that incorporate some other interface to the database (such as DDE or OLE).

See chapter 19, "More client/server: The commodity trading game," for an example of reading flat files.

Java's file I/O capabilities are pretty basic; you can get information about the file read data at offsets or line by line, and so forth. If you want any kind of keyed access, you'll have to build your own keys, which definitely falls into the category of reinventing the wheel. You'll be much better off looking for third-party support for your file format or using native methods to link in the required code. Native methods are discussed in detail in chapter 16, "Linking native C code."

STRATEGIES FOR DESIGNING DATA STREAMS

Establishing the means of communicating with your database is one thing; creating the request for data and formatting the resulting data set is another. Ideally, you'll be able to pick up a third-party solution that will take care of the nasty bits; however, if one isn't forthcoming, you might want to proceed along the following lines.

FORMATTING THE DATA REQUEST

The format of the request for data can be just about anything, from an arbitrary code word to a full-fledged SQL statement. What you use will be dependent on the database system that you're working with. When your code gets the data request, it either retrieves the specified records according to logic that you've built into your data handler class, or it passes the request along to the native method, if that's the approach that you're taking.

In most cases, there also will be a translation step between what the user understands as a request for data and what your database understands as a request for data. It's unwise to expect that the users of your applet are going to know how to properly format a data request for your database system. For example, if you want to give your business customers the opportunity of seeing the status of their account with you, you shouldn't ask them to type in **SELECT * FROM AR WHERE COMPANY_CODE = 12343 AND PAID='N'**. Much better, they should see a button on the screen labeled **Account Status** and have the applet format the appropriate request out of data that it has on hand (such as the company code, which you can collect from your users via a login window that's part of the applet's own security).

FORMATTING THE RETURNED DATA

Formatting and displaying the result of the database query is a task that you might want to divide between the server and the applet. If you want to keep things simple, have the server make a string of each row returned by the query, and concatenate the strings with a suitable separator. On the applet side, parse the received data back into strings, and add each string to a list box with the **addItem()** method.

In a more complex arrangement, you might want to code individual fields within the data stream and display this data selectively. You'll need to take this approach if you want your users to be updating records within the database.

SUMMARY

Socket communication between applet clients and application servers is relatively easy to accomplish with Java, and it opens up a whole new world of possibilities for applet design. One of the most common reasons for doing client/server communications is to enable applets to do I/O on the server, particularly for database access. Depending on your needs, client/server arrangements can be straightforward, as demonstrated in this chapter, or mindbogglingly complex. Particularly with database access, look for third-party toolkits to help your development along.

MORE CLIENT/SERVER

THE COMMODITY TRADING GAME

MUCH HAS BEEN MADE of Java's potential to perform business transactions over the Web. In chapter 18, "Client/server, Java style," you learned how a Java server application can be used to set up a communication link between an applet and the Web server for purposes such as delivering information from a database. In this chapter, you'll learn how to implement security and real-time transactions in the context of the Java Commodity Trading game.

THE GAME

The commodity trading game discussed in this chapter is based loosely on the Milton Bradley card game Pit. In Pit, the objective is to acquire all of the cards of a particular commodity. Each player is dealt a random selection of cards. Then players execute blind trades with each other, offering matching sets of cards in trades of a specific size. For example, if I have two barley cards that I don't want, I can offer a trade of "two." Anyone who wants to trade for my two cards can give me two cards of a matching suite. The two cards that I get might or might not match other cards in my hand. The game continues until one player gets a full hand of matching cards, "cornering the market" on that commodity.

THE OBJECTIVE

The Java Commodity Trading game adds several twists on the Pit card game. First, the objective is to accumulate money, rather than to corner the market on a particular commodity. Players acquire money through the judicious buying, selling, and trading of commodities. Each commodity's market price will fluctuate randomly over time, with a slight upward trend. Players can monitor the prices and trends through the graph applet.

Players also can sell shares only in lot sizes greater than 25 shares. To get 25 or more shares, players can buy shares at market price or execute blind trades with other players, in the spirit of the Pit card game.

ROLES

There are two basic roles associated with the Java Commodity Trading game: Broker and Trader. Each game centers around a single Broker, hosted on a Web server somewhere. The Broker is an automated, unattended process (a Java server application).

Each player participates in the game via a Trader applet. Traders relay their buy, sell, and trade requests to the Broker via an encrypted message. The Broker executes the trade requests (taking a small commission on buy and sell transactions) and sends back an encrypted reply.

> *Disclaimer:* It should be emphasized that the commodity trader *is just a game.* While we use this game to attempt to show several means for doing useful things on the Web (like encrypting transmissions), it is *not* a business- ready implementation. In particular, the encryption scheme implemented here should not be considered secure by any stretch of the imagination! Furthermore, the Broker is not connected to any sort of a database, and no attempt has been made to protect all transactions in the case of a server crash or other catastrophe. It's just a game, folks!

THE IMPLEMENTATION

The game is made up of two logical pieces: the Broker and Trader. Each of these consists of a number of supporting classes, all of which are included on the CD-ROM, even if they're not listed here in their entirety. First, let's look at the Trader, which is what the game players will see.

THE TRADER

The Trader consists of the two applets (trader user interface and commodity price graphing) that will be placed in the HTML file and the supporting classes used by those applets.

THE TRADERUI CLASS

The TraderUI class is the user interface applet. This applet contains a panel that uses the TraderCardLayout layout manager, which is a

subclass of the CardLayout layout manager. As you'll recall from chapter 10, "Applets: Frames, panels, and canvases," the CardLayout layout manager creates a "stack" of panels, only one of which is visible at a time. In TraderUI, TraderCardLayout enables the applet to switch between panels based on the users interaction with the UI.

Most of the TraderUI.java source code is taken up with the mechanics of displaying data and getting user input. Because similar code has been discussed earlier in the book and the TraderUI.java file is rather lengthy, only the highlights will be discussed here. You can find the source for the TraderUI and the related Java files in the Trader directory on the CD-ROM.

Generally speaking, TraderUI.java lists the various panel classes first and the applet class last. Figure 19-1 contains the applet code for TraderUI.

Figure 19-1 The applet portion of TraderUI.java.

```
/**
 * The GUI for the Trader in the Java Commodity Trading Game.
 *
 * @author Jeffrey C. Rice
 * @version     1.4
 */
public class TraderUI extends Applet {
  CardPanel cards;
  Transaction trans;
  Connection connection;

  public void init() {
    String host;
    String port;

    cards = new CardPanel();
    add(cards);
    resize(cards.minimumSize().width, cards.minimumSize().height + 10);
    host = getParameter("host");
     if (host ==null) {
          host = getCodeBase ().getHost((;
     }
    port = getParameter("port");

    connection = new Connection(host, port);
  }
```

```
boolean submit() {
  String reply;
  boolean ret = false;

  // send the transaction... get the reply, update as needed.
  if ((reply = connection.send(trans)) != null) {
    switch(trans.getType()) {
    case Transaction.BUY:
    case Transaction.SELL:
      ret = cards.updateAccountInfo(reply);
      break;
    case Transaction.TRADE:
      if (!reply.equals("PENDING"))
        ret = cards.updateAccountInfo(reply);
      break;
    }
  }
  return ret;
}

void updateInfo() {
  String reply;

  reply = connection.send(new Transaction(Transaction.BALANCE));
  cards.updateAccountInfo(reply);

}

void showError(String err) {
  cards.setErrorMsg(err);
  ((TraderCardLayout)cards.getLayout()).show(cards, "Error",
    false);
}

boolean login(String name, String passwd) {
  String reply;
  String error;
  boolean ret = false;

  if (name.length() == 0 || passwd.length() == 0) {
    showError("Please give a login name and password.");
  }
  else if (connection.connect()) { // make connection
    // login
    reply = connection.send(new Transaction(Transaction.LOGIN,
                            name, passwd));
```

Figure 19-1 Continued.

```
      if (reply == null) {  // error contacting host
        showError(connection.getError());
        connection.disconnect();
      }
      else if (reply.equals(name))  // okay!
        ret = true;
      else {  // login refused...
        showError(reply);
        connection.disconnect();
      }
    }
    else {
      showError(connection.getError());
    }
    return ret;
  }

  public boolean action(Event evt, Object arg) {
    boolean ret = true;
    if (evt.target instanceof List)
      ret =  listAction(evt, arg);
    else if (evt.target instanceof Button)
      ret =  buttonAction(evt, arg);

    return ret;
  }

  /**
   * We are overriding the handleEvent method so that we can get
   * the behavior out of the scrolling list we want.  Specifically,
   * we want single clicks of the mouse to do the same thing as
   * double-clicks. We catch the single-click (LIST_SELECT) and pass it
   * to our listAction() method.
   */
  public boolean handleEvent(Event e) {
    if (e.target instanceof List) {
      List l = (List)e.target;
      if (e.id == Event.LIST_SELECT)
        return listAction(e, l.getItem(((Integer)e.arg).intValue()));
    }
    return super.handleEvent(e);
  }
  public boolean listAction(Event evt, Object arg) {
```

```
  cards.updateTradePanel((String)arg);
  return true;
}

public boolean buttonAction(Event evt, Object arg) {

  if ("Login".equals(arg)) {
    if (login(cards.getLogin(), cards.getPasswd())) {
      // update Trade panel with acct info
      updateInfo();
      // show trade panel
      ((TraderCardLayout)cards.getLayout()).show(cards, "Trade");
    }
  }
  else if ("Submit".equals(arg)) {
    String str = new String();

    // Create the transaction and display it.
    trans = cards.getTransaction();
    if (trans == null) {
      str = "Invalid transaction. Check Quantity... Press Cancel now.";
    }
    else {
      str = "Please confirm: ";
      switch(trans.getType()) {
      case Transaction.BUY:
        str = str + "Buy ";
        break;
      case Transaction.SELL:
        str = str + "Sell ";
        break;
      case Transaction.TRADE:
        str = str + "Trade ";
        break;
      default:
        trans = null;
        str = "Internal error... press Cancel.";
        break;
      }
      if (trans != null)
        str = str + trans.getSize() + " shares of " +
              trans.getCommodity() +".";
    }
    cards.updateConfirm(str);
    ((TraderCardLayout)cards.getLayout()).show(cards, "Confirm");
  }
```

Figure 19-1 Continued.

```
    else if ("Update".equals(arg)) {
      updateInfo();
    }
    else if ("Confirm".equals(arg)) {
      boolean submitted = true;
      // send off the confirmed transaction string.
      if (trans != null)
        submitted = submit();

      if (submitted)
        ((TraderCardLayout)cards.getLayout()).show(cards, "Trade");
      else if (connection.connected) {
        // submit failed, but connection is still up...
        ((TraderCardLayout)cards.getLayout()).setCurrent("Trade");
        showError("Transaction FAILED... check balance and shares and try
again.");
      }
      else {
        // submit failed and connection is down...
        ((TraderCardLayout)cards.getLayout()).setCurrent("Login");
        showError("Connection FAILED... Login again.");
      }
    }
    else if ("Cancel".equals(arg)) {
      ((TraderCardLayout)cards.getLayout()).show(cards, "Trade");
    }
    else if ("OK".equals(arg)) {
      ((TraderCardLayout)cards.getLayout()).showCurrent(cards);
    }
    return true;
  }
```

THE LOGIN PANEL

The CardPanel that contains the login, trading, and error panels is created in TraderUI's **init()** method with the code:

```
cards = new CardPanel();
add(cards);
resize(cards.minimumSize().width, cards.minimumSize().height + 10);
```

The last line of this code fragment resizes the card layout to its minimum size, plus ten pixels height. All of the code that creates the card layout, and sets LoginPanel as the first panel, is contained the declaration for the CardPanel class, earlier in the source file.

CONNECTING TO THE SERVER

After creating the applet's GUI components, the applet next gets the IP address and port number of the server from the **<param>** tag in the HTML, then creates a new socket connection to the host (the process of creating, maintaining, and closing socket connections is discussed in detail in chapter 18):

```
host = getCodeBase().getHost().getName();
port = getParameter("port");
connection = new Connection(host, port);
```

After the connection has been established, the applet is in "wait" mode. The interface has been built and displayed. Of the available panels, the one currently displayed is the LoginPanel.

> To run more than one game at a time, just set up multiple applet tags, each with a different port number.

Because the panels have been created by the applet, it's possible (and convenient) to use the applet's **handleEvent()** and **action()** methods to process all of the messages received by the panels. The panels get the events first, and if they don't do anything with them, the events are passed through to the underlying objects.

LOGGING IN

The LoginPanel asks for the user's User ID and password. Because password-entry fields should not display the characters being typed, after the password field is created, the login panel code uses **setEchoCharacter('*')** to display asterisks instead:

```
passwd.getTextField().setEchoCharacter('*');
```

When the user presses the **Login** button, that action is trapped by the applet's **action()** method, which calls the applet's **login()** method with the

user's ID and password, which it collects via the login panel's **getLogin()** and **getPasswd()** methods.

```
if (login(cards.getLogin(), cards.getPasswd())) {
```

(These last two methods simply retrieve the text values from the entry fields on the panel)

The **login()** method establishes a connection with the Broker (a Java application running on the Web server) and sends the encrypted data:

```
reply = connection.send(new transaction(Transaction.LOGIN,name, passwd));
```

Both the Trader and the Broker format and parse data through a Transaction object. The Transaction class has an instance variable "type" that indicates what kind of transaction this is (Buy, Sell, Trade, Login, etc.). Encapsulating the transaction protocol in a separate class allows the Broker and Trader to easily share the protocol. In addition, if you later decide to add to the protocol, you can do so in one place with minimal impact on other classes.

It's the connection class's **send()** method that invokes encryption. If you look at **send()**'s definition, you'll see the following code:

```
try {
  connection.send(Crypt.crypt(trans.toString()));
  reply = connection.getReply();
  reply = Crypt.crypt(reply);
}
```

The information passed between the trader and broker will be of various kinds; in this case, the reply will contain information retrieved from a text file on the server, which contains User IDs, passwords, and startup parameters for the game (see the accounts file in the trader/broker directory). A string tokenizer is used to break up the string data into separate fields.

The Crypt class (see crypt/Crypt.java) really is just a shell for your own encryption code, because all it does is XOR the string with a default string or one optionally passed in to the crypt() method:

```
for(int i=0; i<len; i++) {
  dst.insert(i, (char)(src.charAt(i) ^ pswd.charAt(i%pswdLen)));
}
```

You *definitely* will want to make your own encryption a little more robust than this; all this class does is demonstrate where and how to call the encryption code.

> If you're particularly security-conscious, you might want to change your security algorithm on a regular basis. One of the beauties of Java applet programming is that the software is automatically distributed to the user each time they view the applet, so you know they'll always have the most current security implementation.

Once login is complete, the applet updates the panel with account information and displays the trading panel of the card layout:

```
updateInfo();
((TraderCardLayout)cards.getLayout()).show(cards, "Trade");
}
```

THE TRADER PANEL

The TradePanel, shown in Figure 19-2, displays a summary of the participant's account status and the number of shares of each commodity.

From the TradePanel, the user will interact with the Broker, buying, selling, and trading. When the user submits a transaction, the transaction is checked (e.g., to see if they have enough shares in their account to do the transaction). If a problem is found, an ErrorPanel is displayed. If the

Figure 19-2 The Trader applet with the trading card displayed.

transaction looks okay, a ConfirmPanel is displayed that describes the transaction and asks for confirmation of the transaction.

The mechanics of the transaction are similar to the process of logging on. The applet's **action()** method traps the button press and, if the request is a confirmation of a trade, sends the appropriate data to the server and waits for a response.

THE COMMODITYGRAPHER APPLET

To play the market with some intelligence (well, we can always hope), you need information about market trends and prices. In the Commodity Trading game, price information is displayed by the CommodityGrapher applet, which creates an instance of a general-purpose graphing class called Grapher.

THE COMMODITYGRAPHER APPLET

The CommodityGrapher applet (Figure 19-3) displays information about the prices of the different commodities, which it obtains from the Broker. Because CommodityGrapher runs independently of the Trader applet, it must set up its own socket communication. CommodityGrapher simply sets up a socket connection and, at regular intervals, polls the Broker for current commodity prices.

Figure 19-3 The CommodityGrapher applet source code

```
import java.awt.*;
import java.applet.Applet;
import java.util.StringTokenizer;
import Crypt;

/**
 * A graphical representation of commodity prices.  This graph applet
 * displays the commodity prices along the y axis as a function of
 * time (x axis).  As the graph fills, the data will scroll off the left
 * side of the graph as new data arrives.

 * @author Jeffrey C. Rice
 * @version     1.4
 */
public class CommodityGrapher extends Applet implements Runnable {
  Grapher grapher;
```

```
HideButton hideButton;
ShowButton showButton;
ClientConnection connection = null;
static final int nPoints = 6;
Thread updateThread;
String host;
String port;
int updateInterval = 60;

/**
 * Init the applet, parse out any params in the html.
 */
public void init() {
  host = getParameter("host");
   if (host == null) {
        host = getCodeBase ().getHost((;
   }
  port = getParameter("port");
  String str = getParameter("interval");
  if (str != null)
    updateInterval = Integer.parseInt(str);

  grapher = new Grapher(this, nPoints);

  resize(size().width, size().height);
  updateThread = new Thread(this, "Update Thread");
  updateThread.start();

}

/**
 * The updateThread will execute this method. Each updateInterval
 * seconds it will send an UPDATE Transaction to the Broker, then
 * it will read the reply and parse out the commodity prices.  The
 * prices are then passed to a Grapher for display.
 */
public void run() {
  Transaction trans = new Transaction(Transaction.UPDATE);
  String reply = null;
  float newPoints[] = new float[nPoints];
  String labels[] = new String[nPoints];

  while (true) {
    try {
      if (connection == null || !connection.isPort(port) ||
        !connection.isHost(host)) {
        if (connection != null)
          connection.closeConnection();
        connection = new ClientConnection(host, port);
```

Figure 19-3 Continued.

```
        }
        //System.out.println("Sending msg = " + trans.toString());
        connection.send(Crypt.crypt(trans.toString()));
        reply = Crypt.crypt(connection.getReply());
        //System.out.println("Reply = " + reply);
      }
      catch (ConnectionException ex) {
        System.out.println("Connection Error:" + ex.getMessage());
        connection.closeConnection();
        connection = null;
      }

      // Parse the reply string
      StringTokenizer st = new StringTokenizer(reply, ":");
      int i = 0;

      while(st.hasMoreTokens()) {
        labels[i] = st.nextToken();
        String tmp = st.nextToken();
        newPoints[i] = Float.valueOf(tmp).floatValue();
        i++;
      }

      // Now graph the data.
      grapher.clear();
      grapher.drawPoints(newPoints);
      grapher.drawAxis(labels, newPoints);
      repaint();
      // Sleep until the next update.
      try {
        Thread.sleep(1000*updateInterval);
      }
      catch (InterruptedException e) {
      }
    }
  }

  public void paint(Graphics g) {
    grapher.paint(g);
  }

  /**
   * Overloaded to eliminate flicker.
   */
  public void update(Graphics g) {
    paint(g);
```

```
  }

  public void start() {
    updateThread.resume();
  }

  /**
   * Suspend the updater Thread when we are off the page.
   */
  public void stop() {
    updateThread.suspend();
  }
}
```

The CommodityGrapher applet itself does not display a graph. While you could put all of the graphing code in the applet, graphing is a common enough function that you'll probably want to make it a separate class so that it can be used elsewhere. That's just what the Grapher class is (Grapher is discussed in the next section).

The CommodityGrapher creates an instance of Grapher and, after each inquiry for new data from the Broker, calls methods in Grapher to display the new data:

```
grapher.clear();
grapher.drawPoints(newPoints);
grapher.drawAxis(labels, newPoints);
repaint();
```

Note that CommodityGrapher's update method has been overridden to avoid the flicker associated with a complete redisplay of the applet:

```
public void update( Graphics g) {
  paint(g);
}
```

THE GRAPHER CLASS

Grapher (Figure 19-4) is a general-purpose graphing class that you can use for a variety of purposes, not just within the Commodity Trading game.

Figure 19-4 The Grapher applet source code.

```
/*
 */
import java.applet.Applet;
import java.awt.*;
import java.util.Random;

/**
 * A class to do strip-chart type graphing.  This class creates a
 * graph of multiple lines as a funtion of time.  When the lines
 * reach the right side of the graph, everything scrolls one pixel to
 * the left with each subsequent point. The graph displays the min and
 * max values on the y axis.  The graph also auto-scales as new min and
 * max values are encountered.
 *
 * @author Jeffrey C. Rice
 * @version     1.2
 */
class Grapher {
  Applet parent;
  int width, height;
  private Image buffer = null;
  private Graphics gc = null;
  private Font labelFont;
  private float minY, maxY;
  float graphPoints[][];
  private int axisX, axisY, axisHeight, axisWidth;
  private int nPoints, nLines;

  private Color colors[] = {
    Color.blue, Color.green, Color.magenta, Color.yellow,
    Color.cyan, Color.red, Color.orange, Color.pink
  };

  /**
   * Create the Grapher.
   *
   * @param applet The applet providing the data to the grapher.
   * @param lines The number of data points provided with each update.
   */
  public Grapher(Applet applet, int lines) {
    parent = applet;
    width = parent.size().width;
    height = parent.size().height;
```

```
  // Init the X-Y axis position.
  axisX = 100;
  axisY = height-20;
  axisWidth = width-axisX-20;
  axisHeight = axisY-20;

  // Number of lines we'll be tracking.
  nLines = lines;

  // Init variables that deal with the data points
  nPoints = 0;
  minY = Float.MAX_VALUE;
  maxY = Float.MIN_VALUE;
  graphPoints = new float[nLines][axisWidth];

  buffer = parent.createImage(width, height);
  gc = buffer.getGraphics();
  labelFont = new Font("TimesRoman", Font.PLAIN, 14);
  clearGraphics(gc);

}

/**
 * Draw the x and y axis and label them.
 *
 * @param labels The array of labels corresponding to the lines.
 * @param newPoints The points to be added to the graph this update.
 */
void drawAxis(String labels[], float newPoints[]) {
  FontMetrics fm =  gc.getFontMetrics(labelFont);
  String min = String.valueOf(minY);
  String max = String.valueOf(maxY);
  int x, w, h;

  gc.setFont(labelFont);
  gc.setColor(Color.black);
  // Draw the X and Y axis
  gc.drawLine(axisX, axisY, axisX + axisWidth, axisY);
  gc.drawLine(axisX, axisY, axisX, axisY - axisHeight);
  // Label them
  w = fm.stringWidth(min);
  x = axisX - w - 5;
  gc.drawString(min, (x<0)? 0 : x, axisY);
  w = fm.stringWidth(max);
  x = axisX - w - 5;
```

Figure 19-4 Continued.

```
  gc.drawString(max, (x<0)? 0 : x, axisY-axisHeight+fm.getHeight());
  // Now draw the graph labels in appropriate colors
  for(int i=0; i<nLines; i++) {
    gc.setColor(colors[i%colors.length]);
    String lab = labels[i] + "(" + newPoints[i] + ")";

    w = fm.stringWidth(lab);
    x = axisX - w - 5;
    gc.drawString(lab, (x<0)? 0 : x, axisY-60-i*30);
  }
}

/**
 * Clear the off screen image.
 */
void clear() {
  clearGraphics(gc);
}

/**
 * Clear the image associated with the Graphics object.
 *
 * @param g The Graphics object to clear..
 */
void clearGraphics(Graphics g) {
  gc.setColor(Color.lightGray);
  gc.fillRect(0, 0, width, height);
}

/**
 * Add the next array of points to the graph. Scroll the
 * graph as necessary.
 *
 * @param newPoints The data points to add.
 */
void drawPoints(float newPoints[]) {

  int i, j;

  for (i=0; i<nLines; i++) {
    // correct axis min/max
    minY = (newPoints[i] < minY)? newPoints[i] : minY;
    maxY = (newPoints[i] > maxY)? newPoints[i] : maxY;
  }
  float rangeY = (float)(maxY - minY);
  float scale = (float)axisHeight / (float)rangeY;
```

```
    for(i=0; i<nLines; i++) {
      gc.setColor(colors[i%colors.length]);

      if (nPoints < axisWidth) {
        // We haven't hit the right margin of the graph yet.
        for (j=0; j<nPoints; j++) {
          if (j > 0) {
            gc.drawLine(axisX-1+j,
                        axisY-(int)((graphPoints[i][j-1]-minY)*scale),
                        axisX+j,
                        axisY-(int)((graphPoints[i][j]-minY)*scale));
          }
        }
        graphPoints[i][j] = newPoints[i];
      }
      else {
        /* We've hit the right margin.  Shift the points over one
         * in the array.
         */
        for (j=0; j<nPoints-1; j++) {
          graphPoints[i][j] = graphPoints[i][j+1];
          if (j > 0) {
            gc.drawLine(axisX-1+j,
                        axisY-(int)((graphPoints[i][j-1]-minY)*scale),
                        axisX+j,
                        axisY-(int)((graphPoints[i][j]-minY)*scale));
          }
        }
        graphPoints[i][j] = newPoints[i];
        gc.drawLine(axisX-1+j,
                    axisY-(int)((graphPoints[i][j-1]-minY)*scale),
                    axisX+j,
                    axisY-(int)((graphPoints[i][j]-minY)*scale));
      }
    }
    nPoints = (nPoints < axisWidth) ? nPoints + 1 : nPoints;
    gc.setColor(Color.lightGray);
  }

  /**
   * Simply copy the off-screen image to the on-screen
   * Graphics object.
   */
  public void paint(Graphics g) {
    g.drawImage(buffer,0,0,parent);
  }

}
```

Notice that Grapher's constructor takes an applet as one of its parameters:

```
public Grapher(Applet applet, int lines) {
```

The parent applet is needed primarily to determine the height and width of the applet's display area.

As with any good graphing tool, Grapher includes methods for drawing labels, plotting points, clearing the image, and so forth. Grapher also uses double-buffering to assemble the image off-screen, then display it all at once in the class's **paint()** method:

```
public void paint(Graphics g) {
  g.drawImage(buffer,0,0,parent);
}
```

TRADER SUPPORT CLASSES

In addition to the previously mentioned classes, Trader also uses the LabeledTextField class (Figure 19-5). LabeledTextField is a panel class that creates a label and a text field from the passed parameters. This is a convenient way to keep text field and label positioned together, whatever else happens to the applet's layout.

Figure 19-5 The LabeledTextField class.

```
import java.awt.*;

/**
 * A labeled TextField.  This class extends Panel to create a
 * panel with a labeled text item on it.  The labeled TextField
 * is centered on the panel.
 *
 * @author Jeffrey C. Rice
 * @version     1.1
 */
public class LabeledTextField extends Panel {
  /**
   * The TextField.
   * @see #getTextField
   */
  protected TextField t;
  /**
```

```
     * The label
     */
    protected Label l;
    /**
     * The layout manager.
     */
    protected GridBagLayout gb;
    protected GridBagConstraints gbc;

    /**
     * Create the LabeledTextField.
     *
     * @param labelString The text for the label.
     * @param width The number of columns in the TextField.
     * @param initString The initial string in the TextField.
     * @param readOnly If true, the Text field is read-only.
     */
    public LabeledTextField(String labelString, int width,
                            String initString, boolean readOnly) {
      super();
      Panel subPanel = new Panel();
      gb = new GridBagLayout();
      gbc = new GridBagConstraints();

      l = new Label(labelString, Label.RIGHT);
      subPanel.setLayout(gb);
      if (initString != null)
        t = new TextField(initString, width);
      else
        t = new TextField(width);
      if (readOnly)
        t.setEditable(false);
      gbc.gridwidth = 1;
      gbc.weightx = 1.0;
      gbc.anchor = GridBagConstraints.EAST;
      gb.setConstraints(l, gbc);
      subPanel.add(l);

      gbc.gridwidth = GridBagConstraints.REMAINDER;
      gbc.weightx=4;
      gbc.anchor = GridBagConstraints.WEST;
      gb.setConstraints(t, gbc);
      subPanel.add(t);
      add(subPanel);
    }
```

Figure 19-5 Continued.

```
  /**
   * Create the LabeledTextField.
   *
   * @param labelString The text for the label.
   * @param width The number of columns in the TextField.
   * @param readOnly If true, the Text field is read-only.
   */
  public LabeledTextField(String labelString, int width,
                          boolean readOnly) {
    this(labelString, width, null, readOnly);
  }

  /**
   * Create the LabeledTextField.
   *
   * @param labelString The text for the label.
   * @param width The number of columns in the TextField.
   * @param initString The initial string in the TextField.
   */
  public LabeledTextField(String labelString, int width,
                          String initString) {
    this(labelString, width, initString, false);
  }

  /**
   * Create the LabeledTextField.
   *
   * @param labelString The text for the label.
   * @param width The number of columns in the TextField.
   */
  public LabeledTextField(String labelString, int width) {
    this(labelString, width, null, false);
  }

  /**
   * Returns a handle to the TextField for direct manipulation.
   */
  public TextField getTextField() {
    return t;
  }
}
```

THE BROKER

The Broker application (Figure 19-6) shares many of the characteristics of, and several classes from, the MTServer application discussed in chapter 18. Like MTServer, Broker waits for clients (Traders and CommodityGraphers) to make connections, and processes the various requests those clients make. As with MTServer, the code for Broker is short and to the point.

Figure 19-6 The Broker application.

```
//

import java.net.ServerSocket;
import java.net.Socket;
import java.io.IOException;

/**
 * The top level of the Broker application portion of the Java Commodity
 * Trading Game.  The Broker is the server end of the game.  Each server
 * represents a single game.  All Traders connected to this Broker
 * participate in the same game.
 *
 * @author Jeffrey C. Rice
 * @version 1.2
 */
public class Broker {
  public static void main(String args[]) {
    // Create the TransactionManager, pass the account filename in.
    TransactionManager tm = new TransactionManager("accounts");
    ServerSocket serverSock = null;
    boolean dbg = false;
    int port = 5678;  // default port.
    int timeout = 300;

    // Parse the command line args.
    if (args.length > 0) {
      port = Integer.parseInt(args[0]);
      if (args.length > 1)
        dbg = (Integer.parseInt(args[1]) == 1) ? true : false;
    }
```

Figure 19-6 Continued.

```
    // Establish this end of the socket connection.
    try {
      if (dbg)
        System.out.println("Starting server on port " + port);
      serverSock = new ServerSocket(port, timeout);
    } catch (IOException e) {
      System.err.println("Error establishing socket on port " + port);
      System.exit(1);
    }

    tm.run(serverSock);
  }
}
```

THE TRANSACTIONMANAGER

Broker differs from MTServer in that, before launching any socket connections, it creates an instance of the TransactionManager. There is one TransactionManager per game, and its job is to maintain data on all of the players and broker transactions between players. The TransactionManager also creates an AccountManager, which maintains a linked list of accounts, and a CommodityManager, which runs the Commodity price simulation and gets commodity information for the TransactionManager.

When a player joins the game, Broker creates a new socket and passes that socket to the TransactionManager's **run()** method, as follows:

```
try {
   serverSock = new ServerSocket(port, timeout);
} catch (IOException e) {
   System.err.println("Error establishing socket on port " + port);
   System.exit(1);
}

tm.run(serverSock);
```

THE TRANSACTIONHANDLER

The TransactionManager will create a new instance of the ConnectionThread class (to manage the connection) with an accompanying instance of the TransactionHandler class (to manage the

data). The TransactionHandler invokes one of five requests from the Trader: login, buy, sell, trade, and update. Most importantly, the constructor for the TransactionHandler passes in the TransactionManager (don't get confused by the names), because it's the TransactionManager that contains the actual buy/sell/trade code:

```
void run(ServerSocket serverSock) {
  Socket sock = null;
  while (true) {
    try {
      sock=serverSock.accept();
    } catch (IOException e) { }

    ConnectionThread thr = new ConnectionThread(sock, new
TransactionHandler(this));
    thr.start();
    }
  }
}
```

BROKER OPERATION: A REVIEW

To review, every Trader (and CommodityGrapher), on making a connection to the Broker, gets spun off into a ConnectionThread. The ConnectionThread class is discussed in detail in chapter 18, but it essentially monitors socket activity, sends and receives data, and kills the socket after a predefined period of inactivity (or when the socket is terminated by the client). The ConnectionThread, as you'll recall, takes a data handler as its second parameter so that it knows what to do with the data it gets. In this case, the data handler is the TransactionHandler class. All clear? Figure 19-7 shows the code for the TransactionHandler.

Figure 19-7 The TransactionHandler class.

```
import java.util.StringTokenizer;
import DataHandler;
import Crypt;
import TransactionManager;
import InvalidTransactionException;

/**
 * The Transaction Handler is looking for five types of requests:
 * login, buy, sell, trade and update.  The formats are:
 * <pre>
 *   login:name:password
```

Figure 19-7 Continued.

```
 *    buy:commodity:quantity
 *    sell:commodity:quantity
 *    trade:commodity:quantity
 *    update:null
 * </pre>
 *
 * For buy, sell and trade the Broker responds with an updated
 * portfolio message:
 * <pre>
 *    balance[:commodity:quantity]...
 * </pre>
 *
 * To an update request, the Broker responds with the current
 * commodity prices:
 * <pre>
 *    commodity:price[:commodity:price]...
 * </pre>
 *
 * @author Jeffrey C. Rice
 * @version 1.5
 */
public class TransactionHandler implements DataHandler {
  /**
   * The Account associated with this TransactionHandler.
   * This variable is null until initialized via a login
   * request from the connected client.
   *
   * @see Account
   */
  private Account account = null;
  /**
   * Print diagnostic messages if true.
   */
  private boolean debug = false;
  /**
   * The parent TransactionManager.
   *
   * @see TransactionManager
   */
  TransactionManager tm;

  /**
   * Create the TransactionHandler.
   *
```

```
 * @param t The parent TransactionManager.
 */
public TransactionHandler(TransactionManager t) {
  if (t != null)
    tm = t;
  else
    debug = true;
}

/**
 * The business end of the TransactionHandler. This method takes the
 * incoming string, decrypts it, converts it to a Transaction object,
 * then process it.
 *
 * @param str The incoming String.
 * @exception InvalidTransactionException If the Transaction object
 *            returned is invalid.
 * @see Crypt
 * @see Transaction
 */
public String process(String str) throws InvalidTransactionException {
  // The decrypted message.
  String clearText = Crypt.crypt(str);
  // The message converted to a Transaction.
  Transaction trans = new Transaction(clearText);

  // Process the Transaction based on its type.
  switch(trans.getType()) {
  case Transaction.LOGIN:
    if (debug)
      System.out.println("Got a login.");
    else {
      account = tm.loginUser(trans.getAccount(), trans.getPasswd());
      if (account != null)
        str = account.name;
      else
        str = "LOGIN REFUSED";
    }
    break;
  case Transaction.BUY:
    if (debug)
      System.out.println("Got a buy.");
    else {
      if (tm.buyShares(account, trans.getCommodity(),
                       trans.getSize()))
```

Figure 19-7 Continued.

```
        str = account.print();
      else
        str = "FAIL";
    }
    break;
  case Transaction.SELL:
    if (debug)
      System.out.println("Got a sell.");
    else {
      if(tm.sellShares(account, trans.getCommodity(),
                       trans.getSize()))
        str = account.print();
      else
        str = "FAIL";
    }
    break;
  case Transaction.TRADE:
    if (debug)
      System.out.println("Got a trade.");
    else {
      if (tm.tradeShares(account, trans.getCommodity(),
                         trans.getSize()))
        str = account.print();
      else
        str = "PENDING";
    }
    break;
  case Transaction.UPDATE:
    if (debug)
      System.out.println("Got a update.");
    else
      str = tm.update();
    break;
  case Transaction.BALANCE:
    if (debug)
      System.out.println("Got a balance.");
    else {
      if (account != null)
        str = account.print();
      else
        str = "FAIL";
    }
    break;
```

```
    default:
      // Tear down the connection...
      if (debug)
        System.err.println("Invalid Transaction received.");
      throw new InvalidTransactionException();
    }
    return Crypt.crypt(str);
  }
}

// A class to test the TransactionHandler class.
class TransTest {
  public static void main(String args[]) {
    Account account = new Account("rice", "xyzzy", 12345.25f);
    TransactionHandler tr = new TransactionHandler(null);
    Transaction trans;
    try {
      trans = new Transaction(Transaction.LOGIN, "rice", "abcdefg");
      tr.process(Crypt.crypt(trans.toString()));

      trans = new Transaction(Transaction.UPDATE);
      tr.process(Crypt.crypt(trans.toString()));

      trans = new Transaction(Transaction.BALANCE);
      tr.process(Crypt.crypt(trans.toString()));

      trans = new Transaction(Transaction.BUY, "barley", 25);
      tr.process(Crypt.crypt(trans.toString()));

      trans = new Transaction(Transaction.SELL, "oats", 5);
      tr.process(Crypt.crypt(trans.toString()));

      trans = new Transaction(Transaction.TRADE, "wheat", 5);
      tr.process(Crypt.crypt(trans.toString()));

    }
    catch (InvalidTransactionException e) {}
  }

}
```

TransactionHandler makes calls back into the TransactionManager to do the actual transactions. Consider the code for a trade:

```
case Transaction.TRADE:
  if (debug)
    System.out.println("Got a trade.");
  else {
    if (tm.tradeShares(account, trans.getCommodity(),
        trans.getSize()))
      str = account.print();
 else
      str = "PENDING";
  }
  break;
```

Note: Both the Broker and Trades utilize the Transaction class. This class encapsulates the protocol used between to Broker and Traders. These are positive results from collecting the protocol into a single class. First, the Broker and Trader can share the class (we are getting software reuse). Second, if we want to add to or change the protocol's implementation, it can be done in one place.

All of the actual transactions are made inside TransactionManager, rather than TransactionHandler, for two reasons. First, all of the data needs to be in one central location. Second, it's vital that only one transaction occur on one block of data at a time; otherwise, the trading data will get corrupted. To keep things simple, this game uses synchronized methods in TransactionManager, which effectively means that only one transaction can occur anywhere in the database at one time. In a real-world, file-based system, you'd probably want to just lock the records involved in the transaction, rather than lock the entire database.

BROKER SUPPORT CLASSES

The Broker application uses a number of classes, and tracking them can be a bit confusing at times. Figure 19-8 shows the relationships between the Broker's objects.

Classes that were not discussed previously are covered briefly in the following sections.

Figure 19-8 The relationships between the Broker's objects.

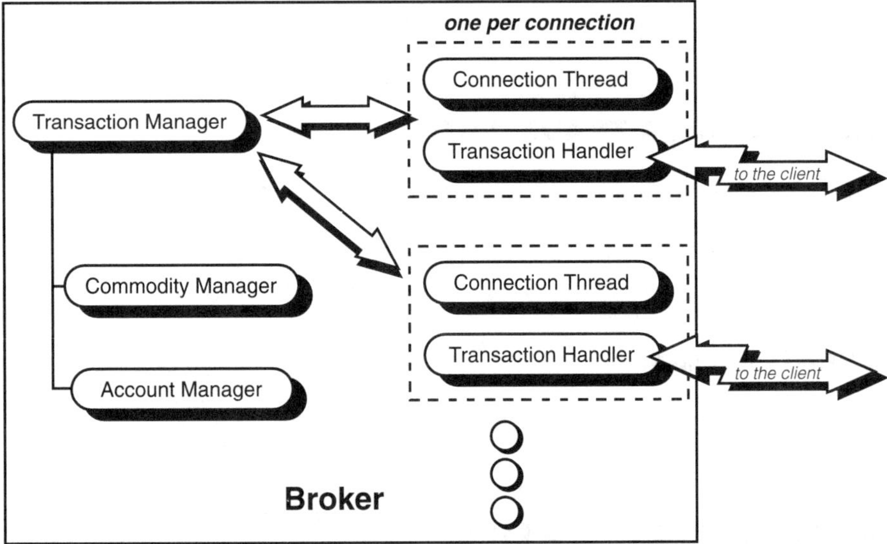

ACCOUNTMANAGER.CLASS

The AccountManager manages the linked list of accounts and includes methods for creating accounts, saving accounts to a file, and finding accounts using various methods.

ACCOUNT.CLASS

The account class is the basic account object, including the login name, password, current balance, and the hashtable that stores account shares.

COMMODITY.CLASS

The Commodity class is the basic commodity object, including the current price, the change since the last price update, the commodity name, the random number generator, and the update thread.

COMMODITYMANAGER.CLASS

The CommodityManager class creates the various commodities (wheat, rice, barley, oats, corn, and soy) and provides methods for looking up their prices.

SHARE.CLASS: A SHARE IN AN ACCOUNT

The share class is the basic share object, including the commodity name and the number of shares owned.

TRADE.CLASS: A TRADE OBJECT

The Trade class is the basic trade object, created for each requested trade. A Trade object includes the account that is making the trade, the commodity, the number of shares, and the trade status. The TransactionManager makes trades by matching like trade objects.

UPDATER.CLASS

The updater class updates commodity prices once per minute. There is one updater for each commodity.

ADDITIONAL CLASSES

Several classes are shared by Broker, Trader and possibly the Client. They are described briefly in the following sections.

FOREACH.CLASS

ForEach is an interface for iterating across lists.

LINKEDLIST.CLASS

The LinkedList class is a general-purpose class for managing linked lists. In the simulation, it is used to store commodities, accounts, etc.

SUMMARY

As the Commodity Trading game demonstrates, Java is an ideal language for developing transaction-oriented business applications that run on multiple platforms across the World Wide Web. Although this commodity trader is only a game, the basic principles of security, client-server operation, and transaction synchronization apply equally well to real-world business applications.

20 ANIMATION WITH JAVA

ANIMATION is quite a complex subject, encompassing many different animation methods and types of software. As Java is a suitable tool for a number of animation techniques, covering all of the possibilities in any kind of detail could easily take an entire book. This chapter discusses one of the most commonly used approaches.

Most Java applets that you now see doing animation do so by reading in a series of images that represent "frames" of the animation, then displaying these images one over the other, repeating the sequence if desired. This kind of animation is fairly straightforward in Java; the JDK comes with an applet called Animator, which, if you like, will do all the work for you. All you have to do is feed Animator a list of images and, optionally, sound files, then let it play your animation.

In this chapter, you'll learn how the Animator applet works and how you can adapt it to suit your own needs. As with most programming, much of the work in this applet is in the details. The fundamental issues are straightforward, but the implementation requires you to think not only about what the applet will do, but about what the user is likely to want the applet to do.

USING THE ANIMATOR APPLET

The Animator applet is located in the demo/Animator subdirectory and is comprised of a single Java file of around 900 lines of code, which compiles to three class files (one applet class and two exception classes).

Animator's behavior is determined largely by the information passed to it in the applet tag. The following is the tag used in EXAMPLE3.HTML, which displays a series of images of Duke, the Java mascot, waving:

```
<applet code=Animator.class width=200 height=200>
<param name=imagesource value="images/Duke">
<param name=endimage value=10>
<param name=soundsource value="audio">
<param name=soundtrack value=spacemusic.au>
<param name=sounds
value="1.au|2.au|3.au|4.au|5.au|6.au|7.au|8.au|9.au|0.au">
<param name=pause value=200>
</applet>
```

In EXAMPLE3.HTML, the Animator is told to look in the images/duke subdirectory for the GIF files that it will display (even if you're running on a Windows machine, you'll need to use the forward slash rather than the backslash in the applet tag). Animator assumes that these images will have a name beginning with *T*, followed by a sequential number starting with 1, and with the extension .GIF. If you have files with other names, you'll need to change them to meet this convention.

The **soundsource** parameter is the name of the subdirectory, if any, where the audio files will be found. The **soundtrack** parameter is the name of a sound file to be played during the entire animation, and the **sounds** parameter is a list of sound files that are to be played for each frame. These files will be matched up one to one with the numbered images, so the number of these files should match the number endimage value. There are several more optional parameters, which are discussed later in this chapter. If you'd like more information on applet tags in general, see chapter 3, "Behind the scenes at a Java session."

Figure 20-1 shows the Animator applet running from the EXAMPLE3.HTML document.

> All of the directories specified in the previous tag are relative to the location of the document that contains this applet tag.

Figure 20-1
The Animator applet running the "waving Duke" animation.

ANIMATOR APPLET CODE OVERVIEW

The animator applet is one of the larger applets that comes with the JDK. If you're not used to reading Java code, it might seem a little

intimidating. However, once you break the applet down into its functional areas, it's not really that complex. To help you follow what's happening in this discussion, we've created a line-numbered listing of the version of Animator that shipped with the 1.0 release of the JDK (Figure 20-2). All of the code fragments from Animator that are discussed in this chapter will have line numbers so that you can quickly locate that code in the main listing. Do *not* attempt to compile the line-numbered code (unless you have a lot of time to waste).

Figure 20-2 The line-numbered code listing for Animator.

```
001 /*
002  * %W% %E% Herb Jellinek
003  *
004  * Copyright (c) 1994-1995 Sun Microsystems, Inc. All Rights Reserved.
005  *
006  * Permission to use, copy, modify, and distribute this software
007  * and its documentation for NON-COMMERCIAL or COMMERCIAL purposes and
008  * without fee is hereby granted.
009  * Please refer to the file http://java.sun.com/copy_trademarks.html
010  * for further important copyright and trademark information and to
011  * http://java.sun.com/licensing.html for further important licensing
012  * information for the Java (tm) Technology.
013  *
014  * SUN MAKES NO REPRESENTATIONS OR WARRANTIES ABOUT THE SUITABILITY OF
015  * THE SOFTWARE, EITHER EXPRESS OR IMPLIED, INCLUDING BUT NOT LIMITED
016  * TO THE IMPLIED WARRANTIES OF MERCHANTABILITY, FITNESS FOR A
017  * PARTICULAR PURPOSE, OR NON-INFRINGEMENT. SUN SHALL NOT BE LIABLE FOR
018  * ANY DAMAGES SUFFERED BY LICENSEE AS A RESULT OF USING, MODIFYING OR
019  * DISTRIBUTING THIS SOFTWARE OR ITS DERIVATIVES.
020  *
021  * THIS SOFTWARE IS NOT DESIGNED OR INTENDED FOR USE OR RESALE AS ON-LINE
022  * CONTROL EQUIPMENT IN HAZARDOUS ENVIRONMENTS REQUIRING FAIL-SAFE
023  * PERFORMANCE, SUCH AS IN THE OPERATION OF NUCLEAR FACILITIES, AIRCRAFT
024  * NAVIGATION OR COMMUNICATION SYSTEMS, AIR TRAFFIC CONTROL, DIRECT LIFE
025  * SUPPORT MACHINES, OR WEAPONS SYSTEMS, IN WHICH THE FAILURE OF THE
026  * SOFTWARE COULD LEAD DIRECTLY TO DEATH, PERSONAL INJURY, OR SEVERE
027  * PHYSICAL OR ENVIRONMENTAL DAMAGE ("HIGH RISK ACTIVITIES"). SUN
028  * SPECIFICALLY DISCLAIMS ANY EXPRESS OR IMPLIED WARRANTY OF FITNESS FOR
029  * HIGH RISK ACTIVITIES.
030  */
031
032 import java.io.InputStream;
033 import java.awt.*;
```

```
import java.awt.image.ImageProducer;
import java.applet.Applet;
import java.applet.AudioClip;
import java.util.Vector;
import java.util.Hashtable;
import java.util.Enumeration;
import java.io.File;
import java.net.URL;
import java.net.MalformedURLException;

/**
 * An applet that plays a sequence of images, as a loop or a one-shot.
 * Can have a soundtrack and/or sound effects tied to individual frames.
 *
 * @author Herb Jellinek
 * @version %I%, %G%
 */

public class Animator extends Applet implements Runnable {

    /**
     * The images, in display order (Images).
     */
    Vector images = null;

    /**
     * Duration of each image (Integers, in milliseconds).
     */
    Hashtable durations = null;

    /**
     * Sound effects for each image (AudioClips).
     */
    Hashtable sounds = null;

    /**
     * Position of each image (Points).
     */
    Hashtable positions = null;

    /**
     * Background image URL, if any.
     */
    URL backgroundImageURL = null;

    /**
```

Figure 20-2 Continued.

```
     * Background image, if any.
     */
    Image backgroundImage = null;

    /**
     * Start-up image URL, if any.
     */
    URL startUpImageURL = null;

    /**
     * Start-up image, if any.
     */
    Image startUpImage = null;

    /**
     * The soundtrack's URL.
     */
    URL soundtrackURL = null;

    /**
     * The soundtrack.
     */
    AudioClip soundtrack;

    /**
     * Largest width.
     */
    int maxWidth = 0;

    /**
     * Largest height.
     */
    int maxHeight = 0;

    /**
     * Was there a problem loading the current image?
     */
    boolean imageLoadError = false;

    /**
     * The directory or URL from which the images are loaded
     */
    URL imageSource = null;
```

```

    /**
     * The directory or URL from which the sounds are loaded
     */
    URL soundSource = null;

    /**
     * The thread animating the images.
     */
    Thread engine = null;

    /**
     * The current loop slot - index into 'images.'
     */
    int frameNum;

    /**
     * frameNum as an Object - suitable for use as a Hashtable key.
     */
    Integer frameNumKey;

    /**
     * The current X position (for painting).
     */
    int xPos = 0;

    /**
     * The current Y position (for painting).
     */
    int yPos = 0;

    /**
     * The default number of milliseconds to wait between frames.
     */
    public static final int defaultPause = 3900;

    /**
     * The global delay between images, which can be overridden by
     * the PAUSE parameter.
     */
    int globalPause = defaultPause;

    /**
     * Whether or not the thread has been paused by the user.
     */
```

Figure 20-2 Continued.

```
    boolean userPause = false;

    /**
     * Repeat the animation?  If false, just play it once.
     */
    boolean repeat;

    /**
     * Load all images before starting display, or do it asynchronously?
     */
    boolean loadFirst;

    /**
     * The offscreen image, used in double buffering
     */
    Image offScrImage;

    /**
     * The offscreen graphics context, used in double buffering
     */
    Graphics offScrGC;

    /**
     * Can we paint yet?
     */
    boolean loaded = false;

    /**
     * Was there an initialization error?
     */
    boolean error = false;

    /**
     * What we call an image file in messages.
     */
    final static String imageLabel = "image";

    /**
     * What we call a sound file in messages.
     */
    final static String soundLabel = "sound";

    /**
     * Print silly debugging info?
```

```
     */
    boolean debug = false;

    /**
     * Info.
     */
    public String getAppletInfo() {
        return "Animator by Herb Jellinek";
    }

    /**
     * Parameter Info
     */
    public String[][] getParameterInfo() {
        String[][] info = {
            {"imagesource", "url",          "a directory"},
            {"startup",     "url",          "displayed at startup"},
            {"background",  "url",          "displayed as background"},
            {"startimage",  "int",          "start index"},
            {"endimage",    "int",          "end index"},
            {"pause",       "int",          "milliseconds"},
            {"pauses",      "ints",         "milliseconds"},
            {"repeat",      "boolean",      "repeat or not"},
            {"positions",   "coordinates", "path"},
            {"soundsource", "url",          "audio directory"},
            {"soundtrack",  "url",          "background music"},
            {"sounds",      "urls",         "audio samples"},
        };
        return info;
    }

    /**
     * Print silly debugging info.
     */
    void dbg(String s) {
        if (debug) {
            System.out.println(s);
        }
    }

    final int setFrameNum(int newFrameNum) {
        frameNumKey = new Integer(frameNum = newFrameNum);
        return frameNum;
```

Figure 20-2 Continued.

```
    }

    public synchronized boolean imageUpdate(Image img, int infoFlags,
                                             int x, int y,
                                             int width, int height) {
        if ((infoFlags & ERROR) != 0) {
            imageLoadError = true;
        }

        notifyAll();
        return true;
    }

    void updateMaxDims(Dimension dim) {
        maxWidth = Math.max(dim.width, maxWidth);
        maxHeight = Math.max(dim.height, maxHeight);
    }

    /**
     * Parse the IMAGES parameter.  It looks like
     * 1|2|3|4|5, etc., where each number (item) names a source image.
     *
     * Returns a Vector of image file names.
     */
    Vector parseImages(String attr) {
        Vector result = new Vector(10);
        for (int i = 0; i < attr.length(); ) {
            int next = attr.indexOf('|', i);
            if (next == -1) next = attr.length();
            String file = attr.substring(i, next);
            result.addElement(file);
            i = next + 1;
        }
        return result;
    }

    /**
     * Fetch the images named in the argument, updating
     * maxWidth and maxHeight as we go.
     * Is restartable.
     *
     * @return URL of the first bogus file we hit, null if OK.
     */
    URL fetchImages(Vector images) {
```

```
        for (int i = 0; i < images.size(); i++) {
            Object o = images.elementAt(i);
            if (o instanceof URL) {
                URL url = (URL)o;
                tellLoadingMsg(url, imageLabel);
                Image im = getImage(url);
                try {
                    updateMaxDims(getImageDimensions(im));
                } catch (Exception e) {
                    return url;
                }
                images.setElementAt(im, i);
            }
        }
        return null;
    }

    /**
     * Parse the SOUNDS parameter.  It looks like
     * train.au||hello.au||stop.au, etc., where each item refers to a
     * source image.  Empty items mean that the corresponding image
     * has no associated sound.
     *
     * @return a Hashtable of SoundClips keyed to Integer frame numbers.
     */
    Hashtable parseSounds(String attr, Vector images)
    throws MalformedURLException {
        Hashtable result = new Hashtable();

        int imageNum = 0;
        int numImages = images.size();
        for (int i = 0; i < attr.length(); ) {
            if (imageNum >= numImages) break;

            int next = attr.indexOf('|', i);
            if (next == -1) next = attr.length();

            String sound = attr.substring(i, next);
            if (sound.length() != 0) {
                result.put(new Integer(imageNum),
                           new URL(soundSource, sound));
            }
            i = next + 1;
            imageNum++;
        }
```

Figure 20-2 Continued.

```

        return result;
    }

    /**
     * Fetch the sounds named in the argument.
     * Is restartable.
     *
     * @return URL of the first bogus file we hit, null if OK.
     */
    URL fetchSounds(Hashtable sounds) {
        for (Enumeration e = sounds.keys() ; e.hasMoreElements() ;) {
            Integer num = (Integer)e.nextElement();
            Object o = sounds.get(num);
            if (o instanceof URL) {
                URL file = (URL)o;
                tellLoadingMsg(file, soundLabel);
                try {
                    sounds.put(num, getAudioClip(file));
                } catch (Exception ex) {
                    return file;
                }
            }
        }
        return null;
    }

    /**
     * Parse the PAUSES parameter.  It looks like
     * 1000|500|||750, etc., where each item corresponds to a
     * source image. Empty items mean that the corresponding image
     * has no special duration, and should use the global one.
     *
     * @return a Hashtable of Integer pauses keyed to Integer
     * frame numbers.
     */
    Hashtable parseDurations(String attr, Vector images) {
        Hashtable result = new Hashtable();

        int imageNum = 0;
        int numImages = images.size();
        for (int i = 0; i < attr.length(); ) {
            if (imageNum >= numImages) break;

```

```
            int next = attr.indexOf('|', i);
            if (next == -1) next = attr.length();

            if (i != next - 1) {
                int duration = Integer.parseInt(attr.substring(i, next));
                result.put(new Integer(imageNum), new Integer(duration));
            } else {
                result.put(new Integer(imageNum),
                           new Integer(globalPause));
            }
            i = next + 1;
            imageNum++;
        }

        return result;
    }

    /**
     * Parse a String of form xxx@yyy and return a Point.
     */
    Point parsePoint(String s) throws ParseException {
        int atPos = s.indexOf('@');
        if (atPos == -1) throw new ParseException("Illegal position: "+s);
        return new Point(Integer.parseInt(s.substring(0, atPos)),
                         Integer.parseInt(s.substring(atPos + 1)));
    }


    /**
     * Parse the POSITIONS parameter.  It looks like
     * 10@30|11@31|||12@20, etc., where each item is an X@Y coordinate
     * corresponding to a source image.  Empty items mean that the
     * corresponding image has the same position as the preceding one.
     *
     * @return a Hashtable of Points keyed to Integer frame numbers.
     */
    Hashtable parsePositions(String param, Vector images)
    throws ParseException {
        Hashtable result = new Hashtable();

        int imageNum = 0;
        int numImages = images.size();
        for (int i = 0; i < param.length(); ) {
            if (imageNum >= numImages) break;

```

Figure 20-2 Continued.

```
            int next = param.indexOf('|', i);
            if (next == -1) next = param.length();

            if (i != next) {
                result.put(new Integer(imageNum),
                           parsePoint(param.substring
i, next)));
            }
            i = next + 1;
            imageNum++;
        }

        return result;
    }

    /**
     * Get the dimensions of an image.
     * @return the image's dimensions.
     */
    synchronized Dimension getImageDimensions(Image im)
    throws ImageNotFoundException {
        // Get the width of the image.
        int width;
        int height;

        while ((width = im.getWidth(this)) < 0) {
            try {
                wait();
            } catch (InterruptedException e) { }
            if (imageLoadError) {
                throw new ImageNotFoundException
(im.getSource());
            }
        }

        // Get the height of the image.
        while ((height = im.getHeight(this)) < 0) {
            try {
                wait();
            } catch (InterruptedException e) { }
            if (imageLoadError) {
                throw new ImageNotFoundException
                (im.getSource());
            }
```

```
        }

        return new Dimension(width, height);
    }

    /**
     * Stuff a range of image names into a Vector.
     * @return a Vector of image URLs.
     */
    Vector prepareImageRange(int startImage, int endImage)
    throws MalformedURLException {
        Vector result = new Vector(Math.abs(endImage - startImage) + 1);
        if (startImage > endImage) {
            for (int i = startImage; i >= endImage; i--) {
                result.addElement(new URL(imageSource, "T"+i+".gif"));
            }
        } else {
            for (int i = startImage; i <= endImage; i++) {
                result.addElement(new URL(imageSource, "T"+i+".gif"));
            }
        }
        return result;
    }


    /**
     * Initialize the applet.  Get parameters.
     */
    public void init() {

        try {
            String param = getParameter("IMAGESOURCE");
            imageSource = (param == null) ? getDocumentBase() :
new URL(getDocumentBase(), param + "/");
            dbg("IMAGESOURCE = "+param);

            param = getParameter("PAUSE");
            globalPause =
                (param != null) ? Integer.parseInt(param) :
defaultPause;
            dbg("PAUSE = "+param);

            param = getParameter("REPEAT");
            repeat = (param == null) ? true :
(param.equalsIgnoreCase("yes") ||
```

Figure 20-2 Continued.

```
param.equalsIgnoreCase("true"));

            int startImage = 1;
            int endImage = 1;
            param = getParameter("ENDIMAGE");
            dbg("ENDIMAGE = "+param);
            if (param != null) {
                endImage = Integer.parseInt(param);
                param = getParameter("STARTIMAGE");
                dbg("STARTIMAGE = "+param);
                if (param != null) {
                    startImage = Integer.parseInt(param);
                }
                images = prepareImageRange(startImage, endImage);
            } else {
                param = getParameter("STARTIMAGE");
                dbg("STARTIMAGE = "+param);
                if (param != null) {
                    startImage = Integer.parseInt(param);
                    images = prepareImageRange(startImage, endImage);
                } else {
                    param = getParameter("IMAGES");
                    if (param == null) {
                        showStatus("No legal IMAGES, STARTIMAGE,
or ENDIMAGE "+
                                   "specified.");
                        return;
                    } else {
                        images = parseImages(param);
                    }
                }
            }

            param = getParameter("BACKGROUND");
            dbg("BACKGROUND = "+param);
            if (param != null) {
                backgroundImageURL = new URL(imageSource, param);
            }

            param = getParameter("STARTUP");
            dbg("STARTUP = "+param);
            if (param != null) {
                startUpImageURL = new URL(imageSource, param);
```

```
            }

            param = getParameter("SOUNDSOURCE");
            soundSource = (param == null) ? imageSource : new
URL(getDocumentBase(), param + "/");
            dbg("SOUNDSOURCE = "+param);

            param = getParameter("SOUNDS");
            dbg("SOUNDS = "+param);
            if (param != null) {
                sounds = parseSounds(param, images);
            }

            param = getParameter("PAUSES");
            dbg("PAUSES = "+param);
            if (param != null) {
                durations = parseDurations(param, images);
            }

            param = getParameter("POSITIONS");
            dbg("POSITIONS = "+param);
            if (param != null) {
                positions = parsePositions(param, images);
            }

            param = getParameter("SOUNDTRACK");
            dbg("SOUNDTRACK = "+param);
            if (param != null) {
                soundtrackURL = new URL(soundSource, param);
            }
        } catch (MalformedURLException e) {
            showParseError(e);
        } catch (ParseException e) {
            showParseError(e);
        }



        setFrameNum(0);
    }

    void tellLoadingMsg(String file, String fileType) {
        showStatus("Animator: loading "+fileType+" "+abridge(file, 20));
    }

```

Figure 20-2 Continued.

```
    void tellLoadingMsg(URL url, String fileType) {
        tellLoadingMsg(url.toExternalForm(), fileType);
    }

    void clearLoadingMessage() {
        showStatus("");
    }

    /**
     * Cut the string down to length=len, while still keeping it readable.
     */
    static String abridge(String s, int len) {
        String ellipsis = "...";

        if (len >= s.length()) {
            return s;
        }

        int trim = len - ellipsis.length();
        return s.substring(0, trim / 2)+ellipsis+
            s.substring(s.length() - trim / 2);
    }

    void loadError(URL badURL, String fileType) {
        String errorMsg = "Animator: Couldn't load "+fileType+" "+
            badURL.toExternalForm();
        showStatus(errorMsg);
        System.err.println(errorMsg);
        error = true;
        repaint();
    }

    void showParseError(Exception e) {
        String errorMsg = "Animator: Parse error: "+e;
        showStatus(errorMsg);
        System.err.println(errorMsg);
        error = true;
        repaint();
    }

    void startPlaying() {
        if (soundtrack != null) {
            soundtrack.loop();
        }
```

```
    }

    void stopPlaying() {
        if (soundtrack != null) {
            soundtrack.stop();
        }
    }

    /**
     * Run the animation. This method is called by class Thread.
     * @see java.lang.Thread
     */
    public void run() {
        Thread me = Thread.currentThread();

        me.setPriority(Thread.MIN_PRIORITY);

        if (! loaded) {
            try {
                // ... to do a bunch of loading.
                if (startUpImageURL != null) {
                    tellLoadingMsg(startUpImageURL, imageLabel);
                    startUpImage = getImage(startUpImageURL);
                    try {
                        updateMaxDims(getImageDimensions
(startUpImage));
                    } catch (Exception e) {
                        loadError(startUpImageURL, "start-up image");
                    }
                    resize(maxWidth, maxHeight);
                    repaint();
                }

                if (backgroundImageURL != null) {
                    tellLoadingMsg(backgroundImageURL, imageLabel);
                    backgroundImage = getImage(backgroundImageURL);
                    repaint();
                    try {
                        updateMaxDims(
                           getImageDimensions(backgroundImage));
                    } catch (Exception e) {
                        loadError(backgroundImageURL, "background image");
                    }
                }

```

Figure 20-2 Continued.

```
                URL badURL = fetchImages(images);
                if (badURL != null) {
                    loadError(badURL, imageLabel);
                    return;
                }

                if (soundtrackURL != null && soundtrack == null) {
                    tellLoadingMsg(soundtrackURL, imageLabel);
                    soundtrack = getAudioClip(soundtrackURL);
                    if (soundtrack == null) {
                        loadError(soundtrackURL, "soundtrack");
                        return;
                    }
                }

                if (sounds != null) {
                    badURL = fetchSounds(sounds);
                    if (badURL != null) {
                        loadError(badURL, soundLabel);
                        return;
                    }
                }

                clearLoadingMessage();

                offScrImage = createImage(maxWidth, maxHeight);
                offScrGC = offScrImage.getGraphics();
                offScrGC.setColor(Color.lightGray);

                resize(maxWidth, maxHeight);
                loaded = true;
                error = false;
            } catch (Exception e) {
                error = true;
                e.printStackTrace();
            }
        }

        if (userPause) {
            return;
        }

        if (repeat || frameNum < images.size()) {
            startPlaying();
```

```
        }

        try {
            if (images.size() > 1) {
                while (maxWidth > 0 && maxHeight > 0 && engine == me) {
                    if (frameNum >= images.size()) {
                        if (!repeat) {
                            return;
                        }
                        setFrameNum(0);
                    }
                    repaint();

                    if (sounds != null) {
                        AudioClip clip =
                            (AudioClip)sounds.get(frameNumKey);
                        if (clip != null) {
                            clip.play();
                        }
                    }

                    try {
                        Integer pause = null;
                        if (durations != null) {
                            pause = (Integer)durations.get
(frameNumKey);
                        }
                        if (pause == null) {
                            Thread.sleep(globalPause);
                        } else {
                            Thread.sleep(pause.intValue());
                        }
                    } catch (InterruptedException e) {
                        // Should we do anything?
                    }
                    setFrameNum(frameNum+1);
                }
            }
        } finally {
            stopPlaying();
        }
    }

    /**
     * Paint the current frame.
```

Figure 20-2 Continued.

```
     */
    public void paint(Graphics g) {
        if (error || !loaded) {
            if (startUpImage != null) {
                g.drawImage(startUpImage, 0, 0, this);
            } else {
                if (backgroundImage != null) {
                    g.drawImage(backgroundImage, 0, 0, this);
                } else {
                    g.clearRect(0, 0, maxWidth, maxHeight);
                }
            }
        } else {
            if ((images != null) && (images.size() > 0)) {
                if (frameNum < images.size()) {
                    if (backgroundImage == null) {
                        offScrGC.fillRect(0, 0, maxWidth, maxHeight);
                    } else {
                        offScrGC.drawImage(backgroundImage, 0, 0, this);
                    }

                    Image image = (Image)images.elementAt(frameNum);
                    Point pos = null;
                    if (positions != null) {
                        pos = (Point)positions.get(frameNumKey);
                    }
                    if (pos != null) {
                        xPos = pos.x;
                        yPos = pos.y;
                    }
                    offScrGC.drawImage(image, xPos, yPos, this);
                    g.drawImage(offScrImage, 0, 0, this);
                } else {
                    // no more animation, but need to draw something
                    dbg("No more animation; drawing last image.");
                    g.drawImage((Image)images.lastElement(), 0, 0, this);
                }
            }
        }
    }

    /**
```

```
     * Start the applet by forking an animation thread.
     */
    public void start() {
        if (engine == null) {
            engine = new Thread(this);
            engine.start();
        }
    }

    /**
     * Stop the insanity, um, applet.
     */
    public void stop() {
        if (engine != null && engine.isAlive()) {
            engine.stop();
        }
        engine = null;
    }

    /**
     * Pause the thread when the user clicks the mouse in the applet.
     * If the thread has stopped (as in a non-repeat performance),
     * restart it.
     */
    public boolean handleEvent(Event evt) {
        if (evt.id == Event.MOUSE_DOWN) {
            if (loaded) {
                if (engine != null && engine.isAlive()) {
                    if (userPause) {
                        engine.resume();
                        startPlaying();
                    } else {
                        engine.suspend();
                        stopPlaying();
                    }
                    userPause = !userPause;
                } else {
                    userPause = false;
                    setFrameNum(0);
                    engine = new Thread(this);
                    engine.start();
                }
            }
            return true;
        } else {
```

Figure 20-2 Continued.

```
865                 return super.handleEvent(evt);
866             }
867         }
868
869 }
870
871
872 class ParseException extends Exception {
873     ParseException(String s) {
874         super(s);
875     }
876 }
877
878 class ImageNotFoundException extends Exception {
879     ImageNotFoundException(ImageProducer source) {
880         super(source+"");
881     }
882 }
883
884
885
```

First of all, this applet contains four distinct blocks of code that will be compiled into three class files. The first (after the copyright notice, that is) is the import section (lines 32 to 42), followed by the Animator applet class (lines 52 through 870). Lines 873 through 877 comprise the ParseException exception class, and lines 879 through 883 make up the ImageNotFoundException exception class. Almost all of the code, therefore, is contained in the applet itself; there are no panels, no canvases, and no other classes other than the exceptions that we need to look out for. The complexity of the Animator is in its applet methods, not in the number of classes that are created. Accordingly, the rest of this discussion focuses on the applet, with references to the exception classes as they come up in the code.

BREAKING DOWN THE ANIMATOR APPLET

The Animator applet is going to be a lot more manageable if you can break it down into its functional parts. To do that, you have to have

some idea of what the applet is trying to accomplish. Rather than stepping through the applet line by line, deciphering as you go, think about what you know about applets, and start by looking for the familiar pieces.

THE IMPORT STATEMENTS

Import statements, although not part of the applet code, still can tell you quite a lot about what the applet does. This applet has the following imports:

```
032 import java.io.InputStream;
033 import java.awt.*;
034 import java.awt.image.ImageProducer;
035 import java.applet.Applet;
036 import java.applet.AudioClip;
037 import java.util.Vector;
038 import java.util.Hashtable;
039 import java.util.Enumeration;
040 import java.io.File;
041 import java.net.URL;
042 import java.net.MalformedURLException;
```

You can deduce several things from this import list (assuming that the imports actually are required). The applet uses the AudioClip interface to streamline sound file processing, the Vector and Hashtable utilities indicate that there are going to be some lists stored for later retrieval (a list of filenames is a good bet), and the java.net classes are required because the applet is retrieving files across the Net (images and sound files).

THE APPLET DECLARATION

Because the Animator applet implements the Runnable interface, it has the capability to start and manage threads of execution. This is a logical approach to take with an animator, since you have a process that you may want to start and stop.

APPLET DATA DECLARATIONS

Most applets have some data declarations that are global to the applet, and Animator is no exception. The code from line 54 to line 213 is all applet data, including the data types listed in Table 20-1, which you might not have run into before.

TABLE 20-1 The Animator applet data types.

Data type	Description
Vector	Vectors are "growable" arrays that can contain any Java object.
Hashtable	Hashtables are indexed lists of objects, geared toward quick retrieval of data.
URL	URLs are objects that define a Uniform Resource Locator, such as the name of an HTML document or a .GIF file used by the Animator.
AudioClip	An AudioClip is a highly abstracted audio object that has **loop()**, **play()**, and **stop()** methods.
Graphics	Graphics is an offscreen graphics context in which you can assemble an image before writing the image out to the screen.

THE STANDARD APPLET METHODS

Once you're past the data section, you'll start seeing applet methods, and they'll either be overridden standard applet methods or completely programmer-defined methods. Because everything that an applet does has to start with one of the standard applet methods, you're often best off beginning your investigation there.

THE INIT() METHOD

As you'll recall, the **init()** method is the applet's startup method. When investigating somebody else's applet code, start here. The Animator's **init()** method is located from line 502 to line 598; a little inconveniently buried, perhaps, but there's no law as to where in a class a method has to appear.

init()'s main purpose here is to retrieve the parameters from the applet tag by using the **getParameter()** method. The first three parameters—IMAGESOURCE, PAUSE, and REPEAT—all employ code that uses the conditional operator, which is a ternary operator (meaning it takes three terms).

The code:

```
506 imageSource = (param == null) ? getDocumentBase() : new
URL(getDocumentBase(), param + "/");
```

defines three expressions. The expression to the left of the **?** is evaluated to true or false. If true, the result of the expression between the **?** and the **:** is returned; otherwise, the result of the expression to the right of the **:** is returned.

The code for **imagesource** (which is a URL object) translates as "if the param variable is empty, set the imageSource to the value of **getDocumentBase()**; however, if it isn't empty, set imageSource to a new URL made up of the document base URL plus the parameter.

Line 507 doesn't have anything to do with the operation of the applet per se. If you look at line 246, you'll see the dgb function declared, which just prints out the passed string to stdout. The dbg function just makes for a little less work than always typing out System.print.ln.

The code from line 518 to line 546 is a little more involved, as it allows for one of several possibilities for specifying images to use. First, the code checks for the **ENDIMAGE** parameter. If the parameter is found, the code retrieves the numeric portion of the image filename using **Integer.parseInt()** method. Next, some very similar code retrieves the numeric part of the **STARTIMAGE** parameter, if available, and calls the **prepareImageRange()** method, which starts on line 483. If **startImage** and **endImage** contain valid numbers, **prepareImageRange()** will build a vector (or list) of image names and store them in the images vector. There's a little more logic there to also allow the use of the **IMAGES** parameter, but there are no code surprises.

The rest of the **init()** method is devoted to getting the rest of the parameters, if present. Several of these parameters use parsing methods that are declared elsewhere in the applet (and discussed in the next section of this chapter). In all cases, the purpose of these methods is to convert a parameter that contains multiple values into a vector or hashtable of values, for easier retrieval.

Note that all of this **init()** code is enclosed in a **try{}** block. Before the animator can retrieve any graphics or sound files, it needs to have a valid URL for each file, so it's a good idea to enclose the code that creates URLs in a **try{}** block that catches the MalformedURLException. This block also checks for any problems when calling the parse methods (note that, because the parsing methods are custom code rather than Java library code, the ParseException is declared in this source file as well.

THE START() METHOD

The **start()** method, as you'll recall, is invoked automatically by the applet's context (typically a Web browser). In the case of applets that implement Runnable, it's also a suitable place to start a thread. The engine thread is declared in the applet's data section (see line 132), and it is instantiated if it hasn't already happened (this is an important check because **start()** might be called more than once).

THE STOP() METHOD

The **stop()** method is a parallel of **start()**, except that it shuts down the engine thread if it's been launched. See chapter 15, "Multithreaded applets and applications," for more on starting and stopping threads.

THE RUN() METHOD

The **run()** method, which starts on line 658 and ends on 778, is called after **init()** and is there by virtue of the Runnable interface. The **run()** method is invoked by the code:

```
825 engine.start();
```

run() will execute after the **init()** method has completed, so by this time, all of the URLs for the various images and sound files should be in place.

The first code to execute creates a copy of the current thread and uses it to set the thread priority lower than the applet's thread priority (which, by default, will be **NORM_PRIORITY**). This ensures that any user action, such as clicking the mouse, will take priority over the activity going on in the **run()** method.

The first part of the **run()** method is concerned with loading the images whose URLs were loaded in the **init()** method. The reason for doing this here is the time involved; actually loading files across the Internet will take an unknown amount of time, depending on the speed and efficiency of the user's connection and the size and number of the files. If you put this code in the **init()** method, the applet will be unable to accept any other processing until the files are all loaded. While you could put the URL retrieval code in **run()** rather than **init()**, the code does

not take a long time to execute, and putting it in **init()** ensures that the critical URL information is verified before anything else happens.

The code for loading the startup image (if present) is as follows:

```
666 if (startUpImageURL != null) {
667   tellLoadingMsg(startUpImageURL, imageLabel);
668   startUpImage = getImage(startUpImageURL);
669   try {
670     updateMaxDims(getImageDimensions(startUpImage));
671 } catch (Exception e) {
672     loadError(startUpImageURL, "start-up image");
673   }
674   resize(maxWidth, maxHeight);
675   repaint();
676 }
```

In this block of code, line 667 is just a call to a programmer-defined function that displays an appropriate message on the applet context's status bar. The display code looks like this:

```
showStatus("Animator: loading "+fileType+" "+abridge(file, 20));
```

Next, the **getImage()** method attempts to retrieve the image from the Web server. This is the bit that takes time, which is why it's nice to display a message to the user about what's going on.

Assuming the image file has arrived safely, it's time to find out how big it is. The **updateMaxDims()** method, which starts on line 268, is another programmer-defined method that simply takes the width and height dimensions from the library **getImageDimensions()** method, then tests these against the **maxWidth** and **maxHeight** variables (see lines 107 and 112), storing the greater of the two in **maxWidth** and **maxHeight**. You'll want these variables for resizing the applet to the size of the largest image to be displayed. You can run the animator without this code, but the applet will almost certainly take up too much or too little space on the page.

It's wise to make sure that **getImage()** retrieved a valid image. You might think that you should put the image retrieval inside a **try{}** block, and you could do that, but you'll also have to put the **getImageDimensions()** in a **try{}** block. You can be more efficient in your code by just testing for the exception after **getImageDimensions()**, because a failed image retrieval will result in an exception here as well.

After all of the images/sounds have been retrieved, set the loaded flag to true so that there's no possibility of this code executing again (in case **run()** gets invoked again) and do that final check for exceptions, remembering that all of the file-loading code is enclosed in a **try{}** block so that, if any problem occurs, the entire block will terminate.

The **e.printStackTrace()** method, by the way, belongs to Throwable and just prints out the Throwable object and that object's stack trace:

```
722 } catch (Exception e) {
723   error = true;
724   e.printStackTrace();
725 }
```

There are two short code blocks that execute just before the next major **try{}** block, which contains the animation loop. The first of these code blocks just checks for the status of a boolean variable called **userPause**, which has its state flipped each time the user presses the mouse key over the applet:

```
728 if (userPause) {
729   return;
730 }
```

The idea behind this code is that, if the user has clicked in the applet before the image loading is complete, the **run()** method will terminate. That means that the thread dies, and the **handleEvent()** method (discussed a little later) will detect this and restart the thread.

The second block of code starts up the continuous soundtrack, if present and if either the **REPEAT** parameter was passed in (see line 514) or the current frame counter (**frameNum**) is less than the total number of images (frames) to show.

THE ANIMATION LOOP

The animation loop is the second large **try{}** block (lines 736–770) inside the **run()** method. The first line of this block is a test to make sure that there are two or more images to show; there's no point in repeatedly displaying the same image:

```
737 if (images.size() > 1) {
```

The next line of code tests for several possible error conditions that might have slipped through. If no valid image width/height was recorded (remember that the **updateMaxDims()** method was called for each image), the animator loop will not be executed:

```
while (maxWidth > 0 && maxHeight > 0 && engine == me) {
```

The third test terminates the loop if the user has shut down the thread via clicking on the applet (see the **handleEvent()** discussion later in this chapter). At the start of the **run()** method, the me thread instance is set to the current thread; this code detects when the current thread has been set to null.

Finally, we're ready for the animation! Because the animator displays a series of images, it keeps a counter (**frameNum**) for the current image. The counter is incremented in each loop. If it exceeds the total number of images returned by **images.size()**, it has to be set to zero (if this is a repeating animation) or the thread should terminate:

```
if (frameNum >= images.size()) {
  if (!repeat) {
    return;
  }
  setFrameNum(0);
}
repaint();
```

Once the frame number is set, a call to the **repaint()** method invokes the applet's **paint()** method (discussed shortly), which displays the appropriate image.

If there's an audio clip for this image, retrieve and play it (the code that stores and retrieves audio clips is discussed later in this chapter):

```
if (sounds != null) {
  AudioClip clip =
    (AudioClip)sounds.get(frameNumKey);
  if (clip != null) {
    clip.play();
  }
}
```

That's about it for the animation loop, except that, left as it is, the loop will run at the maximum speed supported by the user's platform and probably won't produce the desired effect. Another **try{}** block encloses calls to the thread's **sleep()** method, with whatever default value or parameter value is appropriate:

```
try {
  Integer pause = null;
  if (durations != null) {
    pause = (Integer)durations.get(frameNumKey);
  }
  if (pause == null) {
    Thread.sleep(globalPause);
  } else {
    Thread.sleep(pause.intValue());
  }
```

There's one last code block at the tail end of this **try{}** block. This code, which turns off the background music (if any), always executes no matter how the animator loop terminates:

```
} finally {
    stopPlaying();
}
```

THE PAINT() METHOD

The **paint()** method is invoked automatically as needed (such as when the applet starts up or is unhidden). However, more to the point here, **paint()** is invoked via the **repaint()** call in the **run()** method's animator loop.

Like **run()**, **paint()** also tests for possible error conditions before beginning to draw images:

```
if (error || !loaded) {
  if (startUpImage != null) {
    g.drawImage(startUpImage, 0, 0, this);
  } else {
    if (backgroundImage != null) {
      g.drawImage(backgroundImage, 0, 0, this);
    } else {
      g.clearRect(0, 0, maxWidth, maxHeight);
    }
  }
```

The **error** variable is set to true in a number of places throughout the applet, whenever an error condition is detected. The **loaded** variable is set to true only after the **run()** method has successfully loaded up all needed files. **loaded** also acts as a flag to prevent the applet reloading the images each time the applet is paused and resumed. If the animator files are not ready to go, this startup code will draw the startup image (if available) or the background image. If all else fails, it will just clear the image area entirely.

If the animator is ready to roll, there should be more than one image in the image list, but the animator checks just to be sure:

```
791 if ((images != null) && (images.size() > 0)) {
792   if (frameNum < images.size()) {
```

This code also makes sure that the frame counter has not exceeded the total number of images available.

> You might think that the error checking in this applet is a bit excessive. For example, if the animator loop is written correctly, there should never be a case when the frame number exceeds the total number of images. That's fine as long as you never modify the code, or no one else does; however, as soon as you start revising code, you increase the likelihood that you'll start making it do things that you never originally intended. The more error checking you build into your code and the more error conditions you anticipate, the less hair you'll pull out in the long run.

The **paint()** method uses graphics double-buffering to avoid screen flicker when displaying images. If you look back to line 188, you'll see that offScrGC is an offscreen Graphics object that you can use just as you would an onscreen image. This allows you to do multiple operations on an image, while only writing it out to the screen once. Here the applet builds up a background image before applying the animation frame:

```
793 if (backgroundImage == null) {
794   offScrGC.fillRect(0, 0, maxWidth, maxHeight);
795 } else {
796   offScrGC.drawImage(backgroundImage, 0, 0, this);
797 }
```

The following code retrieves the image from the images vector (storing images in the vector is discussed later in this chapter):

```
799 Image image = (Image)images.elementAt(frameNum);
```

SPRITE ANIMATION

The animator is designed to allow you to do sprite animation, where you have a graphics background and a series of smaller graphics

images (sprites) that you can move across the background. This requires you to specify a series of display coordinates for the images, which, if present, will have been retrieved in the **init()** method:

```
Point pos = null;
if (positions != null) {
  pos = (Point)positions.get(frameNumKey);
}
```

If position data exists, it will be used in the **drawImage()** call that places the image on the background. Once the image is fully assembled, the **paint()** method invokes **drawImage()** to display the image on the screen:

```
g.drawImage(offScrImage, 0, 0, this);
```

THE HANDLEEVENT() METHOD

The **handleEvent()** method only traps the **MOUSE_DOWN** event and uses it as a pause button. If the animation hasn't been loaded, pressing the mouse key has no effect. If the animation is loaded, the method determines if the **run()** method is alive and kicking with the code:

```
if (engine != null && engine.isAlive()) {
```

If the **run()** thread is alive, then the code either resumes or suspends the thread, depending on the state of the **userPause** variable, then flips the state of **userPause**.

If there is no thread running yet, the **handleEvent()** method will launch a new thread:

```
userPause = false;
setFrameNum(0);
engine = new Thread(this);
engine.start();
```

That pretty much wraps up the standard applet methods. All of the remaining code in the applet is made up of support methods that do a variety of jobs, from simplifying debug statements to converting parameters to easily managed lists of URLs, images, and more.

APPLET INFORMATION METHODS

If you're distributing any applet, you should always override the **getAppletInfo()** and **getParameterInfo()** methods to display information about the applet and how it should be used. This is vital if you do not distribute the source with the applet (and, of course, still want people to use it). Any applet user should be able to call these two methods from your applet to know what the applet is and how (or whether) to use it. See lines 218 to 241 for the Animator's versions of these methods.

PROGRAMMER-DEFINED METHODS

Several of the programmer-defined methods added to the animator applet already have been discussed, but there are several important methods that are essential to understanding how the animator manages its data and that you can use as examples for many other programming tasks.

UTILITY METHODS

The **dbg()**, **updateMaxDims()**, **tellLoadingMsg()**, and **clearLoadingMsg()** methods already have been discussed. The **loadError()** method (line 625) and the **showParseError()** method (line 634) both simply display error messages (on the status line and to stdout) and repaint the applet. The **abridge()** method (line 613) simply cuts out the middle part of a too-long string and replaces it with an ellipsis.

THE IMAGE VECTOR

Throughout the animator code, you'll see references to the images vector, which contains a list of the image file URLs. The following code is called by the **init()** method if the tag specifies a range (as opposed to a list) of images to display:

```
483 Vector prepareImageRange(int startImage, int endImage)
484 throws MalformedURLException {
485   Vector result = new Vector(Math.abs(endImage–startImage) + 1);
486   if (startImage > endImage) {
487 for (int i = startImage; i >= endImage; i–) {
488       result.addElement(new URL(imageSource, "T"+i+."gif"));
489     }
490   } else {
491     for (int i = startImage; i <= endImage; i++) {
492       result.addElement(new URL(imageSource, "T"+i+."gif"));
493     }
494   }
495   return result;
496 }
```

The **prepareImageRange()** method returns a vector data type, so it needs to create a new vector to work with (line 485). Next, the method loops through the range of numbers representing the file, prepends a *T*, adds the .GIF extension, and uses that filename to create a new URL object that is added to the vector with the **addElement()** method (lines 488 and 492). (The imageSource URL is initially set at the start of the **init()** method and already will contain the current document location plus any subdirectory specified in the **imagesource** parameter.) Finally, the method returns the new vector, which gets copied to the images vector, as shown in this code:

```
images = prepareImageRange(startImage, endImage);
```

The image vector is used throughout the animator applet. For example, after you obtain the image URLs, you need to retrieve the images. This is the job of the **fetchImages()** method:

```
298 URL fetchImages(Vector images) {
299   for (int i = 0; i < images.size(); i++) {
300     Object o = images.elementAt(i);
301     if (o instanceof URL) {
302       URL url = (URL)o;
303 tellLoadingMsg(url, imageLabel);
304       Image im = getImage(url);
305       try {
306         updateMaxDims(getImageDimensions(im));
307       } catch (Exception e) {
308         return url;
309       }
310 images.setElementAt(im, i);
311     }
312   }
313   return null;
314 }
```

The **fetchImages()** method uses the **images.size()** method to obtain the number of objects (in this case URLs) in the image vector, then retrieves the URL with the **images.elementAt()** method. Note that the method creates a new URL and casts the image vector object to that URL so that the compiler knows the data type of the image vector object before calling **getImage()**.

If the call to **getImage()** is successful, the vector element, which was of type URL, is replaced with the actual image itself (line 310). Once all of the images have been stored in the vector, the animator only has to retrieve a vector element that contains a given image, rather than continually reload images across the Net.

The remaining methods in the animator are primarily hashtable methods.

HASHTABLE METHODS

The hashtable methods are those that create, manipulate, or retrieve data from a hashtable. *Hashtables* essentially are indexed lists of data that you can retrieve by specifying the data item that the hashtable entry was added with. Among other things, the Animator uses hashtables to store sound files for easy retrieval. In a similar approach to how images are retrieved, the sound file URLs first are extracted from the **SOUNDS** parameter via the **parseSounds()** method (line 324–346), then the sounds hashtable is passed to the **fetchSounds()** method:

```
354 URL fetchSounds(Hashtable sounds) {
355   for (Enumeration e = sounds.keys() ; e.hasMoreElements() ;) {
356     Integer num = (Integer)e.nextElement();
357     Object o = sounds.get(num);
358     if (o instanceof URL) {
359       URL file = (URL)o;
360       tellLoadingMsg(file, soundLabel);
361       try {
362         sounds.put(num, getAudioClip(file));
363       } catch (Exception ex) {
364         return file;
365 }
366     }
367   }
368   return null;
369 }
```

The **fetchSounds()** method employs an enumeration of the hashtable as an easy way to create a **for** loop that retrieves each of the hashtable elements. As with **fetchImages()**, the return type is URL so that the method can pass back any invalid URL that caused an error.

The hashtables and the image vector come into play in the **run()** and **paint()** methods. The second half of **run()** optionally queries the sounds hashtable for the appropriate audio clip:

```
747 if (sounds != null) {
748   AudioClip clip =
749     (AudioClip)sounds.get(frameNumKey);
750   if (clip != null) {
751     clip.play();
752   }
753 }
```

The **run()** method also optionally checks the durations hashtable for the pause length:

```
if (durations != null) {
  pause = (Integer)durations.get(frameNumKey);
}
```

The **paint()** method optionally checks the positions hashtable for special positioning information for the image (as when you are using the applet to do sprite animation):

```
if (positions != null) {
  pos = (Point)positions.get(frameNumKey);
}
```

ONE SMALL FIX...

If you're working with the Beta 2 JDK (and possibly later versions), then you'll see a rather annoying flicker when the Animator runs. This is happening because the **update()** method, which calls **paint()**, is clearing the applet window before displaying the next image. To solve the problem, just override **update()**, and only execute the **paint()** call:

```
public void update(Graphics g){
  paint(g);
}
```

This flicker problem might have been fixed in later releases of the JDK. In any case, be aware that you are preventing the applet's window from being cleared, and there might be some circumstances where not clearing the window could cause you other display problems.

SUMMARY

The Animator applet that comes with the JDK is a flexible, effective tool for doing frame-by-frame and sprite animation. You can use the applet out of the box, or if you want, you can modify it to suit your own needs. Either way, this applet demonstrates a number of useful techniques for safely retrieving images and sounds and presenting them to the user in a controlled manner.

TRANSFORMING THE WEB WITH JAVA

HOW WILL JAVA CHANGE the World Wide Web? Prediction is always a tricky business, doubly so when there's relatively little historical data on which to base your predictions. The Web itself is barely half a decade old, and at the time of this writing, Java is not yet in its first production release. Ultimately, it will be Java programmers like you who determine the shape of the future Web; however, in the meantime, it's possible to draw a few useful pictures of how the Web is changing and suggest where Java might come into play.

WEB SHOPPING

The concept of the Web as a place to shop is almost as old as the Web itself. There have been a variety of efforts over the years, some predating the Web by a decade or more, to bring shopping to the consumer via some computerized medium.

The big problem with shopping on the Web is lack of security. While banking systems are in place to handle electronic transfer of funds, the Internet, which is an essentially public network, is not a particularly safe place to pass around virtual cash. With the recent explosion of interest in the Web, a number of companies have invested resources in the encryption technology required to make Web shopping a relatively safe experience, including Netscape (*http://www.netscape.com*) and DigiCash (*http://www.digicash.com*). With its ability to deliver software to the user as an integral part of Web documents, Java is an ideal vehicle for such technology. Once (or, if you're a little more of a pessimist, if) consumer confidence in electronic purchasing is established, you can expect to see a rapid growth in the number of stores online.

Another factor that will encourage the development of Web storefronts is 3D technology. It's not that Web shopping doesn't have its advantages; if you know what you're looking for, by product or brand name, it's conceivable that the computer can find the item far faster than you can by physically searching through a store. Similarly, a computer store can have inventory in many different physical locations, can compare prices for you, and can even keep a running tally of how much you're spending (although it's unlikely that any store owner would be so honestly foolish as to provide that service).

Web stores still are pretty much two-dimensional, visually unrealistic experiences. Even television shopping, which has enjoyed remarkable success, has more depth. There's usually a human voice giving you the sales pitch over the picture of the product, or the product actually is demonstrated. You can see what you're getting, and if you can't comparison shop, well, the sales people will be happy to do it for you.

Really good 3D graphics software certainly has the potential to give Web stores a kind of depth and familiarity that they now lack. One of the major players in the 3D field is VRML, the Virtual Reality Modeling Language, which is a sort of three-dimensional HTML. Java has been chosen as the reference language for VRML, Of particular interest to Java programmers is the work being done by Dimension X, Inc. (*http://www.dimensionx.com*) to create a Java-based VRML browser. This technology blends 3D visualization with Java's interactive capabilities.

Despite such very interesting technology, it might take awhile for the Web to achieve the same level of picture resolution in 3D as it currently has in 2D. Images of any complexity require a tremendous amount of data, and for most users, Internet bandwidth still is quite limited.

THE JAVA-POWERED STORE

While you're not likely to have a visual (or tactile) experience in a Web store that's anything like the one you'd have in a physical store (at least not for some years), Java does make it possible for Web stores to interact with users in other ways that are both interesting and helpful.

If you're designing a storefront, give your imagination free reign. After all, the physical appearance of a store often is determined by the kinds of product that you're handling. You don't put new cars on bookshelves, and you don't stack best-sellers out in the parking lot. On the Web, all of those rules go out the door. There might be some value in keeping a familiar look and feel to your store, but there might be more value in finding some radically new way of presenting your information. Does your Web site sell used cars? Create a couple of cyber-salespeople and let your customers choose whether they want to hear from the sympathetic, no-pressure personality or the high-powered, deal-a-minute, marginally sleazy salesperson.

Animate your product demonstrations. Collect online testimonials, and (if you're feeling particularly daring) let customers talk to each other via e-mail about what they like or don't like about your products. Give out Java applets as prizes. For that matter, you could create a store that sells Java applets. Can you imagine a better "try before you buy" experience?

WEB PUBLISHING AND EDUCATION

At the close of the 20th century, there are a number of communication technologies—including the Internet, cable television, and satellite communications—that are merging into an information superstructure that has the potential to radically reshape all of our lives in ways that we can't yet imagine.

You already can get live audio and video on the Internet (although video refresh rates, in particular, tend to be fairly slow). Also, many publishers now are making portions of their paper publications (and, in some cases, additional computer-only materials) available on the Internet. For example, Ziff-Davis has a news service at *http://www.zdnet.com/~zdi/pview/pview.cgi* that filters the news according to parameters that you determine, which is something that's generally not possible with print media. You also can use a variety of paid information services to search databases worldwide.

JAVA-POWERED PUBLISHING AND EDUCATION

For information publishers, Java provides a point of integration for text, audio, video, animation, and commercial access.

One of Java's greatest strengths is its built-in ability to handle virtually any data stream that can flow over the Internet. This means that you can use a Java program to manage the flow of information in a publication. From a commercial point of view, this could mean restricting all or portions of a document to paid subscribers. From a creative point of

view, this means that you can easily integrate various interactive education tools into a document.

One good example of how a Java program can enhance published material is the SortItem applet (Figure 21-1), which you can find at *http://java.sun.com/./applets/applets/SortDemo/example1.html*.

Figure 21-1 The SortItem applet, with all three sorting algorithms running.

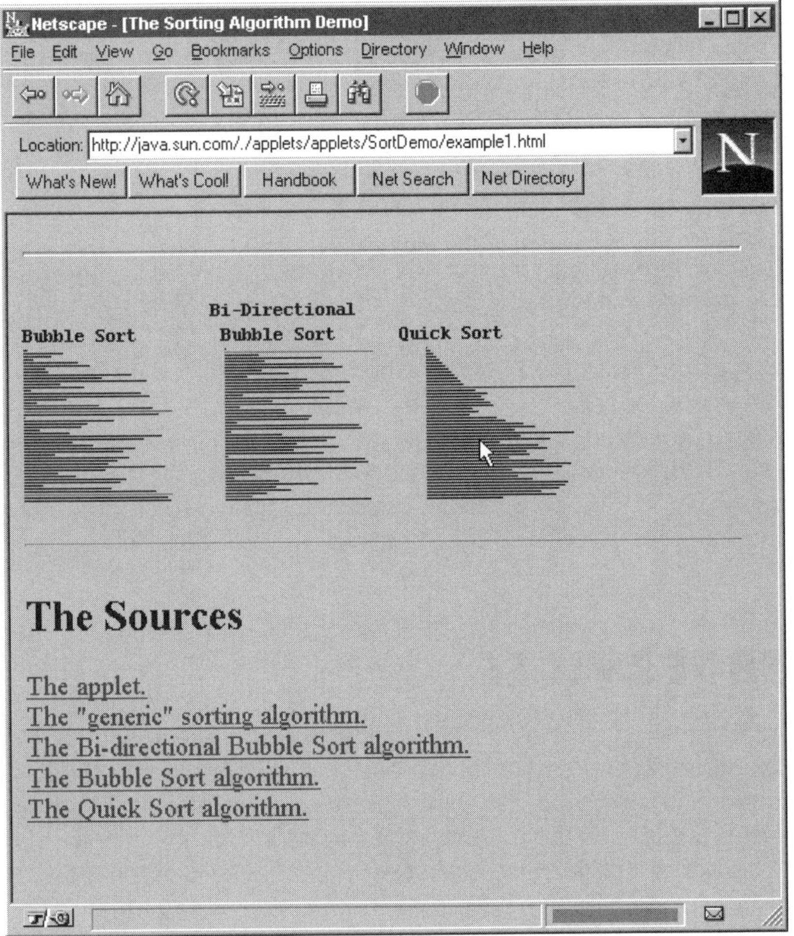

The SortItem applet shows three unsorted arrays of lines that need to be sorted from shortest to longest. While you certainly could approximate the activity of the sorting code by diagrams and descriptions, which is what all books must do, a document enhanced with Java actually can show you how these sorting methods work. Just click on the arrays in the document to start each sort going. This applet vividly demonstrates not just how each algorithm works, but also shows the dramatic differences in speed between the different algorithms.

> Not all information lends itself to this kind of animated demonstration, and it's important to know when to use an applet and when not to. It's a common mistake with beginning desktop publishers to use a wide variety of fonts in a wide range of sizes and styles, just because the fonts are there. Unfortunately, the result usually is visually distracting at best and garish and unreadable at worst. The same concepts applies to applets; they can greatly enhance a document when they have a specific purpose and fit within the style of the document as a whole. Applets for the sake of applets will rarely be successful. You won't make any friends if you have Duke dancing the rumba through every other paragraph on the page.

The SortItem applet by no means exhausts the possibilities for animating educational materials. Java integrates with a large number of other multimedia tools. For example, you could use the RealAudio real-time audio server (*http://www.realaudio.com*) and the VRML library from Dimension X (*http://www.dimensionx.com*) with Java to create a three-dimensional presentation to accompany a live broadcast of a training session.

WEB SERVICES

Companies are increasingly using the Web for product support, as well as product marketing and sales. Among the most popular of these services are those that give the user specialized information. For example, Federal Express uses the Web to let customers track the progress of their shipments (*http://www.fedex.com*), as does UPS (*www.ups.com*). Other companies, like Oracle Corp. (*http://www.oracle.com*) and, of course, Sun Microsystems (*http://www.sun.com*) provide software support and downloads of trial software.

JAVA-POWERED SERVICES

Most companies use FTP servers, HTML documents, and CGI scripts to get information out to their users. Java makes it possible to extend these kinds of services to provide better access to information.

For example, the Gamelan Web site (*http://www.gamelan.com*), which is a comprehensive directory of Java resources, has (at the time of this writing at least) a Java applet that allows you to easily navigate the site. One of the big problems with HTML documents as displayed in browsers is that they don't easily give you an outline of their organization. On the Gamelan site, you can click on the **Navigate** button on the index page, and you'll see a Java window appear, as shown in Figure 21-2.

Figure 21-2 {{ gamel1.bmp}} The Gamelan web site navigator window.

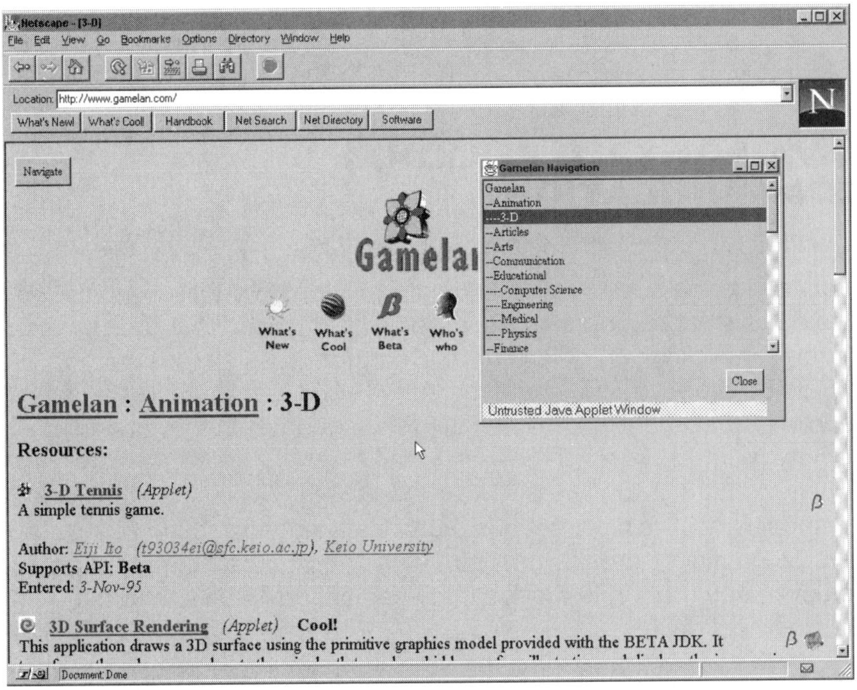

The navigator window presents an instantly available hierarchical listing of documents available on the site. Just double-click on an item to bring up that HTML page. This kind of navigation is considerably easier to use than stepping up and down through a series of HTML pages.

WEB PERSONAL COMMUNICATIONS

As chapter 2, "Essential Internet concepts," explains, the Web is just one of the services of the Internet. When it comes to personal communications (e-mail), most people still use the SMTP mail transfer protocol (whether they realize it or not) to handle their personal communications. As new Web technologies come online (such as real-time video, which lets you feed images from a video camera attached to your computer to another user on the Web), the communications software market probably will become more fragmented. New technologies often mean new protocols to handle the particular kind of data involved.

JAVA-POWERED PERSONAL COMMUNICATIONS

Java is designed specifically to accommodate new kinds of data streams. Just as a Java applet runs actual code on the client computer to display animations or present database information, so it can run code to transfer information according to a protocol designed by the applet's author. Before Java, any new protocol demanded that the Web browser have knowledge of the protocol; with Java, the protocol is part of the applet.

Developing new communications protocols is not something that most Java programmers are likely to do. As third-party toolkits proliferate, however, you might find that you do use new protocols that other programmers develop.

Java also is well-suited to enhancing, and even combining, existing communication protocols. Consider the Chat Touring applet at *http://www.cs.princeton.edu/~burchard/www/interactive/chat/*. This

applet sets up a chat session that lets you share your favorite Web sites with others participating in the chat.

When you log on to Chat Touring, you're asked to provide a nickname and optionally change some settings. Then you're able to use the chat window, as shown in Figure 21-3.

Figure 21-3 {{todo—kwest.bmp}} The Chat Touring applet.

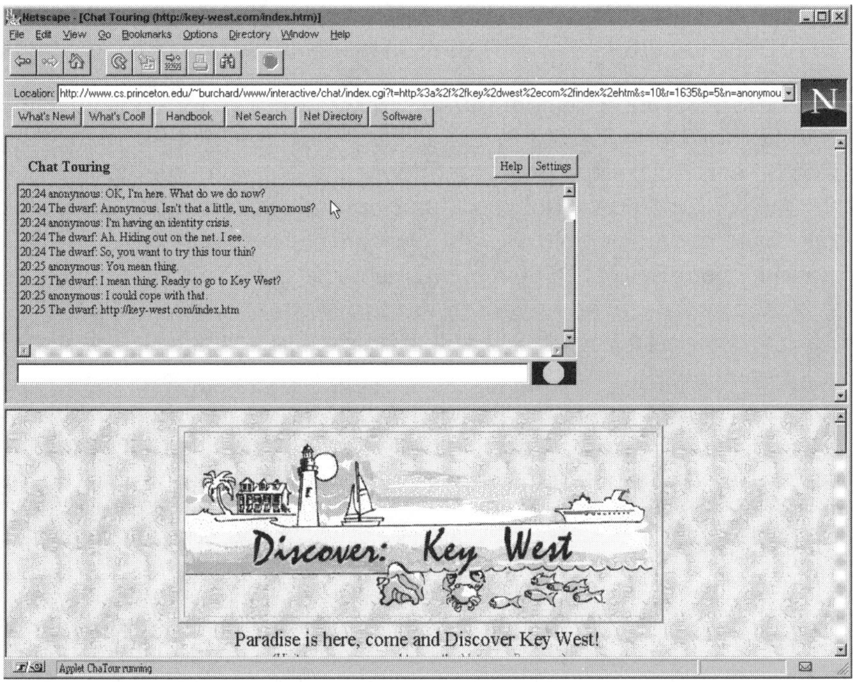

To chat, just enter your comment in the text window and press Enter. To take the other people in the chat to a Web site, enter in a URL instead of chat text. You'll see a **<<Teleporting>>** message, and shortly the Web page you've specified will appear in the bottom half of the browser window on your computer and on the computers of all those participating in the chat. You can "teleport" your fellow chat participants to anyplace on the Web that you like. The applet also lets you attach yourself to another chat participant so that person can be your tour guide, irrespective of where any of the other participants teleport to.

WEB ENTERTAINMENT

The Web is a popular (and sometimes notorious) place for fun and games, with everything from the Amazing Fish Cam (*http://www2.netscape.com/fishcam/fishcam.html*) to Multi-User Domain (MUD) games, such as Netropolis (*http://www.delphi.co.uk/netropolis/*). There also are many games that are available on the Net that will run on your local computer.

Java opens up a huge number of possibilities for various kinds of games and entertainment. One of the great advantages of Java is that you can create an entertainment applet that has many of the features formerly restricted to standalone, downloaded applications and make it instantly available to everyone on the Web. One of our favorites is the Electro Magnetic Poetry applet (Figure 21-4), which is available at *http://prominence.com/java/poetry/*. Electro Magnetic Poetry is perhaps more art than entertainment but still is an excellent illustration of the new possibilities Java brings to the Web. To use the applet, just drag words around on the screen until you've created your masterpiece!

Java also is ideally suited to multi-player games such as MUDs. Where as most Web communication now is done on a transaction basis (browser opens a channel to a server to request a document, receives the document, and closes the channel), it's relatively easy to create a Java game server that creates a continuous communication link with applets, updating information for all of the players in real time without requiring a resend of a Web page to display the new information. For more on Java servers, including a Java client applet and server application, see chapter 18, "Client/server, Java style."

FUTURE DIRECTIONS: THE INTERACTIVE 3D WEB

Although the previous list of Web application types is by no means fully representative, a few hours surfing on the Net will make it clear that there isn't a whole lot of business being done out there. Java has the potential to change all that.

Figure 21-4 The Electro Magnetic Poetry applet.

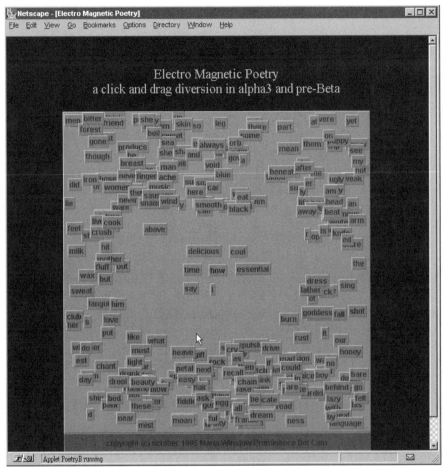

In each of these snapshots of the Web, Java brings the activity on the Internet into a closer parallel with the kinds of activities people do on standalone and LAN-connected computers. Internet software development is beginning the same kind of transformation that personal computer software has undergone over the past decade, from text-mode programs with relatively limited capabilities to graphical software capable of handling text, images, sound, animations, and more.

Personal computer software also has become progressively more interconnected. Even if you're running most of your programs on a

standalone computer, those programs are likely designed to be used in a shared (LAN) environment. Workgroup software, which is designed specifically to help with the distribution and management of tasks within a group of individuals, continues to grow in popularity.

With the introduction of Java, which is a true Web programming language, it now becomes possible to do the same kinds of software development for the Web that programmers have done for standalone and networked computers. Java programs do have some limitations. In particular, local connections to the Internet usually have drastically less bandwidth than even slow LAN connections. Java programs also lose some flexibility in not being able to address the hardware directly (without the use of native methods, which were discussed in chapter 16, "Linking native C code").

Java programs also enjoy some unusual advantages, as compared to platform-specific languages. Because Java programs are written to the Java Virtual Machine and not a specific hardware platform, each program, in theory, can be run on just about any computer that can connect to the Internet. The Java language also is a relatively easy language to learn and is considerably more forgiving in its syntax and implementation (and therefore is easier to debug) than languages like C++. Java programs need not make any assumptions about the computer that they'll be running on, except for the existence of the Java Virtual Machine. That gives Java programmers full control over the resources available to them, all without leaving the comfort of their own development platform.

SUMMARY

On the Web, everything is ultimately information. Because Java is a programming language developed specifically for the Internet, Java lets you harness the full power of the computer to present your information the way that you want it presented. Whereas the pre-Java Web is pretty much restricted to the text and graphics page-server model, the Java-powered Web can have most of the capabilities formerly restricted to a LAN-based operating environment.

22 INTRODUCTION TO WEB SITE PLANNING

IN THE FIRST CHAPTERS of the book, we talked about what it took to create the Internet and the World Wide Web. It is astonishing to see the instant effect that Java has had on the Internet and the Web in such a short time. We described how the overall infrastructure evolved over time to become what it is today: a worldwide means of mass communication in near real-time. In successive chapters, we took you through a detailed introduction to the Java language and gave some simple examples of how to use the language. Next, we showed you how to develop larger and more complex applets and applications that a web site programmer is likely to want or need. In this last part of the book, the next several chapters will provide you with the information necessary to plug yourself into the Internet and begin applying the principles that we've discussed so far. In essence, this part of the book is what Web site programming with Java is about.

Setting up a Web site can be a very simple task or a decidedly complex and convoluted effort. Plentiful choice of tools for the Web site programmer can make getting it right the first time require considerable preparation. Instead of being forced into a very narrow and predefined solution space by one company or organization, you are literally overwhelmed with choices. Choices of hardware platforms, operating systems, software packages, service providers, communications protocols, and information management technologies.

The next few chapters will give you the advice that you need to figure out who your target audiences are and what you'll need to do to create compelling Java-enabled Web sites. Setting up your first Web site can be a challenging task because it involves the convergence of several different technologies that might or might not be familiar to you, as an emerging Web-site programmer. As it is with any worthwhile task, it will take time, tenacity, and patience.

After reading through the remaining chapters, you should be able to follow the recommended design approaches, modifying the processes as you see fit, and arrive at your own version of a Java-enabled Web site. With the overwhelming amount of choices of hardware and software available, these chapters cannot cover every possible method. Instead, the methods most familiar to the authors are used, and

generalizations can and should be made from the basic assumptions behind the choice of tools.

We try to talk about each of the pieces that you will need to build your Web site as generically as possible. The choice of who makes or provides those pieces will be up to you. In studying the process of creating and maintaining Java-enabled Web sites, we have identified seven key steps.

Perhaps the most important thing to recognize about these seven steps is that they are both iterative and cyclical. In the iterative sense, you will need to do them again and again until you find what works the best. Once the Web site is complete, you are faced with the choice of starting over again or porting what you've learned to a new Web site. These steps, in approximate order, consist of the following:

1. User requirements—Defining your target audience and their requirements.
2. System requirements—Selecting the hardware and software platforms to implement on.
3. Web architecture design—Selecting the best tools and methods for delivering applets, applications, and data.
4. Authentication and privacy—Defining access methods and security measures for your Web site.
5. Web content creation—Designing the Web information structure and creating content.
6. Implementation—Bringing all of the tools together to create a working Web site.
7. Web site maintenance—Planning for the evolution and upkeep of the Web site.

At the completion of the maintenance phase, you essentially are ready to return to the start of the cycle as the next step in planning the evolution of your site. This almost always is driven by feedback from your users and analysis of their most prevalent patterns of browsing and using your Web site. The remaining chapters of the book will examine several of these areas in greater detail.

CHOOSING A WEB SITE TYPE

WEB SITE TYPES are as varied as Web sites themselves. For now, we will consider three types of Web sites that can be served by this book:

- Private, leased-access home page with simple to complex Java applets
- Internal and external corporate Web sites utilizing Java applets and applications
- Commercially developed Web sites with a mix of Java applets and other functional web content.

PRIVATE, LEASED-ACCESS HOME PAGE

To expand a bit on what we mean, a private, leased-access Web site usually is created by an individual working through a local Internet Service Provider (ISP). Most often, the Web pages are hosted on a machine that is not owned by the individual and is hosted by the ISP for a fee. This category also includes those lucky enough to have a permanent Internet connection or the more likely case of occasional Internet access via dynamic IP address allocation.

An individual home page hosted on a remote site is not likely to contain large amounts of sophisticated Java programming. However, it is where the lion's share of variety and ubiquity in applets and applications will most likely be.

CORPORATE WEB SITES: INTERNAL AND EXTERNAL

Beyond the individually owned and operated Web site is the corporate Web site, which almost always comes in two flavors: internal and external. In either context, the opportunity for Java programming on these kinds of Web sites is significant. Internally, almost any corporate information function or application can be coded in Java, potentially simplifying the software development and maintenance load of the IS department. On their external Web sites, corporations now are free to experiment with entirely new ways of engaging customers. In the case

of companies that sell software, a total revolution of the commercial software distribution model is about to take place. Let's take a closer look at both kinds of corporate Web sites.

EXTERNAL CORPORATE WEB SITE

The external corporate Web site is designed to best represent the corporation's public image. It usually tells visitors to the Web site about the company's products and services, sales and support, and anything else associated with the normal business operations of a corporation. It is the digital equivalent of what you would expect to see in a sales brochure. With the caveat that this paradigm provides for something that no printed brochure can provide (real-time, interactive feedback and dynamic content generation), the following snapshots of the Java home page and the Sun home page should give you some idea of what we're talking about (Figures 23-1 and 23-2).

The external corporate Web site usually has very strict and consistent security measures installed. Frequent visitors to the external corporate home page expect to see consistent content themes, presentation schemes, and information flow. The Web pages themselves usually are covered with the corporate logo and complementary text and imagery. It is as though you walked into the front door of the corporate headquarters for an interview or business meeting. (See Figure 23-3.)

INTERNAL CORPORATE WEB SITE

The internal corporate Web site is meant to be accessed only by company employees or specially authorized visitors. As a rule, security on the internal corporate Web page usually is much less restrictive, and content tends to vary widely in both quality and timeliness.

Most of these Web sites also are maintained by individuals within the company or are created by internal organizations that have a need to publish and distribute information or applications within the company. Almost every major computer software and hardware company in North America offer sites of every imaginable kind, from engineering to marketing and human resources to the personal home pages of every employee motivated to author their own Web site.

Figure 23-1 The Java home page.

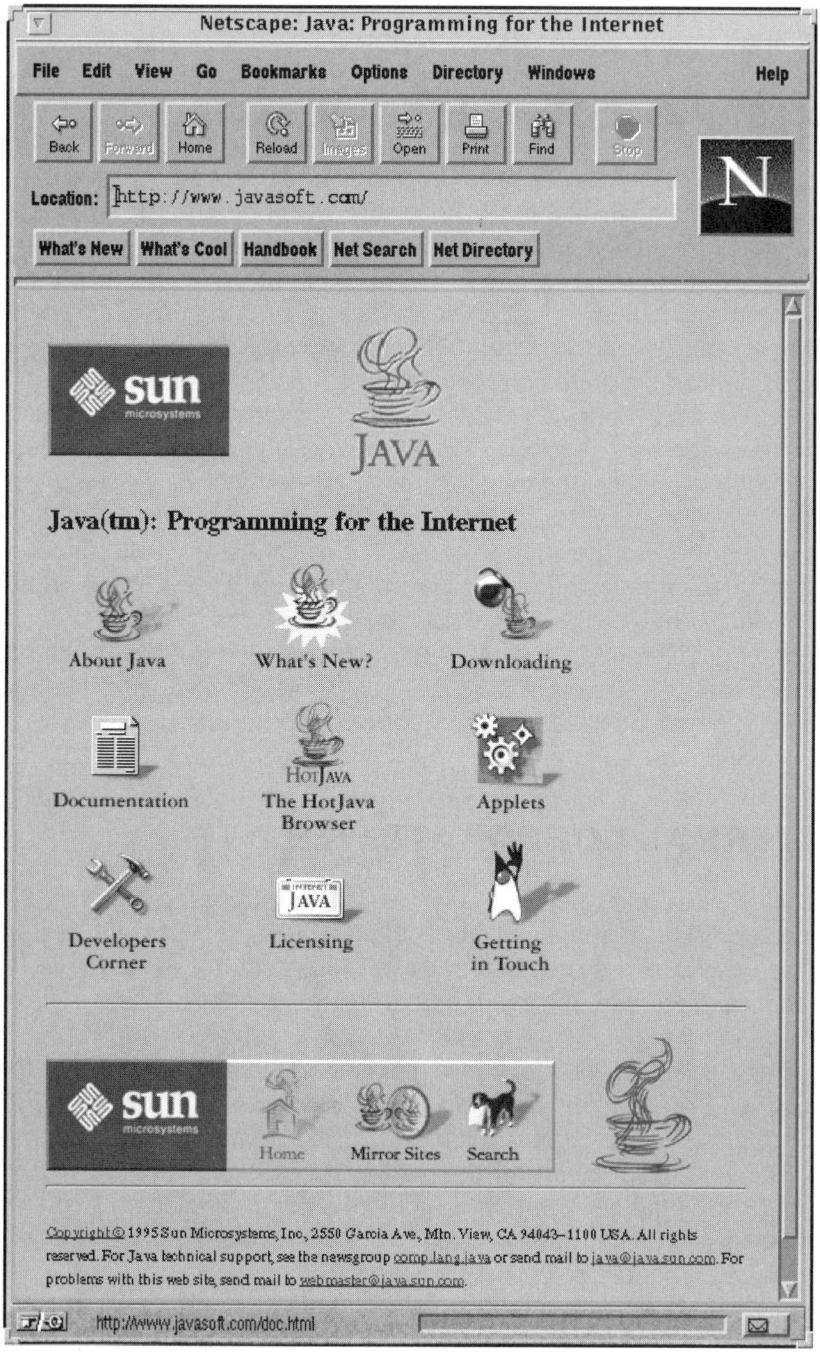

Netscape: Java: Programming for the Internet

File Edit View Go Bookmarks Options Directory Windows Help

Back Forward Home Reload Images Open Print Find Stop

Location: http://www.javasoft.com/

What's New What's Cool Handbook Net Search Net Directory

sun microsystems

JAVA

Java(tm): Programming for the Internet

About Java
What's New?
Downloading
Documentation
The HotJava Browser
Applets
Developers Corner
Licensing
Getting in Touch

sun microsystems
Home Mirror Sites Search

Copyright © 1995 Sun Microsystems, Inc., 2550 Garcia Ave., Mtn. View, CA 94043-1100 USA. All rights reserved. For Java technical support, see the newsgroup comp.lang.java or send mail to java@java.sun.com. For problems with this web site, send mail to webmaster@java.sun.com.

http://www.javasoft.com/doc.html

Figure 23-2 The Sun home page.

Figure 23-3 The external corporate home page.

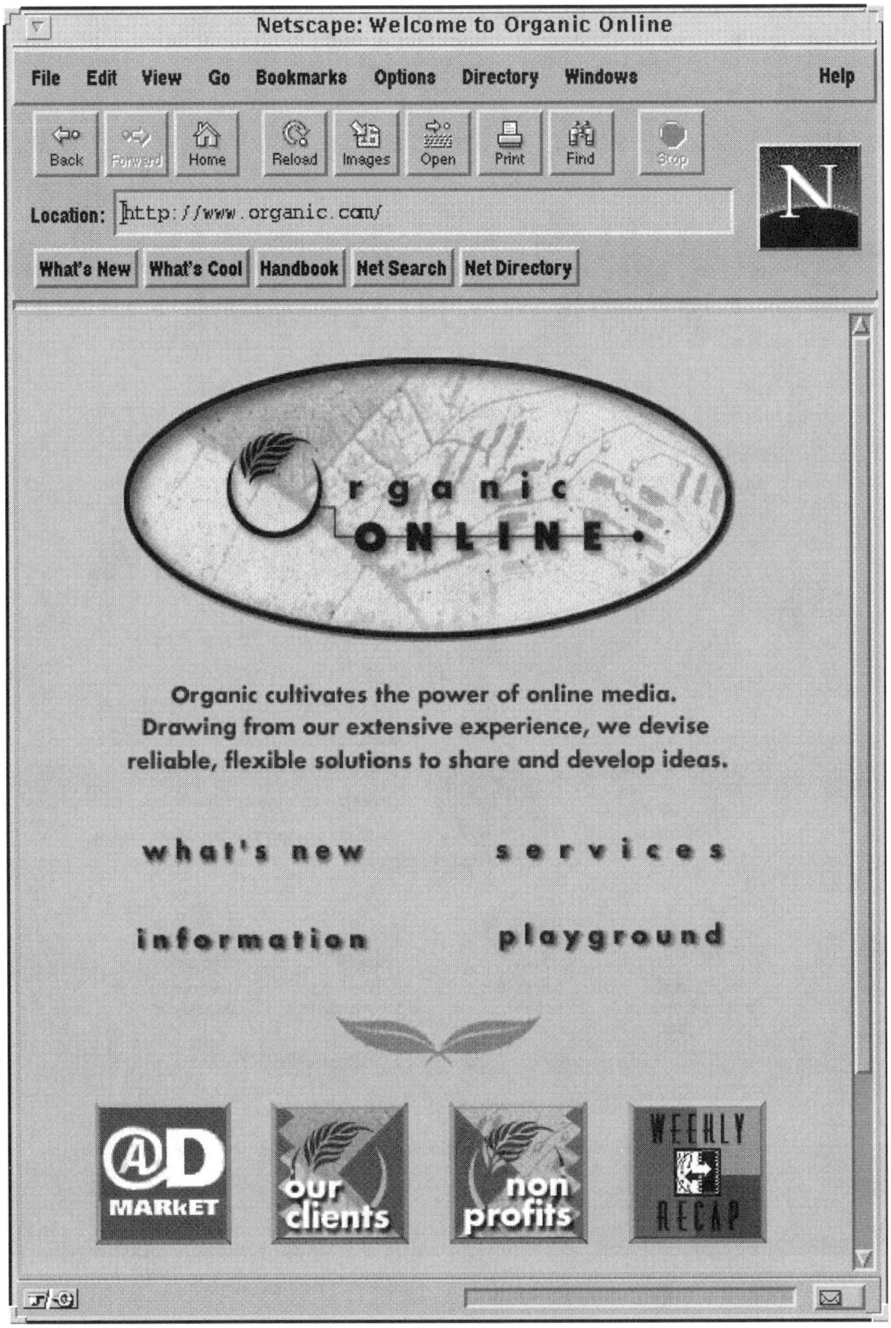

Netscape: Welcome to Organic Online

File Edit View Go Bookmarks Options Directory Windows Help

Back Forward Home Reload Images Open Print Find Stop

Location: http://www.organic.com/

What's New What's Cool Handbook Net Search Net Directory

Organic ONLINE

Organic cultivates the power of online media.
Drawing from our extensive experience, we devise
reliable, flexible solutions to share and develop ideas.

what's new services

information playground

@D MARkET our clients non profits WEEKLY RECAP

COMMERCIALLY DEVELOPED WEB SITES

Commercially developed Web sites are those that are developed for profit or prestige by professional Web site developers. Most often these are start-up companies with small but efficient staffs of graphic design professionals, multifunction executives, and Internet-centric software gurus.

As the popularity of the Internet exploded in the early to mid-1990s, so did an entirely new kind of techno-advertising agency industry. This overnight industry was created by thousands of women and men, formerly employed by major technology firms, who now are out on their own trying to make a go of it in an entirely new world.

Many of these new companies have corporate client portfolios that read like a combination of the Fortune 500 and the top clients of the Madison Avenue advertising giants. This revolution occurred practically overnight and completely deconstructed the traditional way of defining the corporate and commercial public image. Instead of relying on the three traditional staples of advertising—print, radio, and television—forward-thinking companies are hiring commercial Web "image" developers to create a digital presence for them on the Internet.

Commercially developed Web sites have very high professional design aesthetics, although they sometimes are lacking in practical user interface considerations. Worse, they also might lack sufficient security measures. Commercial Web site development firms will live or die by their ability to provide secure access to their client's sites without compromising their systems, data, or intellectual property. We will be talking about security in much greater detail in later chapters.

USER REQUIREMENTS

If you are designing a Web site that several thousand to potentially several hundred thousand Net surfers will visit, the best thing that you can do is to place the users' needs at the top of every list. Your site

might be solely devoted to telling others about you and the work that you do or the things that you're interested in. At the most basic level, if you cannot provide for people who come to the site to find out about you, they either won't come, or if they do, they certainly won't stay very long. For your personal home pages, this might not be much of a consequence, except perhaps to your ego.

However, if the business that you or your company is creating depends on people using your Web site, then your ability to anticipate their needs can make the difference between success and failure. Either way, plan for the people that will ultimately visit your site to be able to make the most of it.

Early in your design process, try to define your audience. Who will be using your pages?

- Employees of your company?
- Customers?
- People familiar with your subject matter?
- People just learning the things that you will be discussing?

The amount of prior knowledge that your audience has of your chosen subject matter will dictate how much background information you need to provide and the extent to which you must clearly define and explain your terminology.

Answer the question "What problem is my reader trying to solve?" If your documents will be read by your customers, familiarize yourself with the particular segments of your customer base that will find your information useful and the problems that they will be attempting to solve as they read your pages. Even if your pages are destined only for use within your company, you should try to do a similar categorization of the potential readers of your pages.

Weigh the advantages and disadvantages of using a browser-specific technique carefully, and try to make your documents usable and valuable to the broadest number of readers. Consider the following list of potential browser software that will be used to navigate your Web site:

- HotJava (alpha, beta, or 1.0)
- Netscape Navigator
- NCSA Mosaic (not Java-enabled)
- Spyglass Communications (not Java-enabled)
- Text-based (not Java-enabled)

Try to understand the consequences of optimizing for a particular Web browser. Usually, you should not make assumptions about how someone will be viewing your web pages. You should try to accommodate people with a wide range of viewing capabilities. This range includes those with text-only browsers on slow links to professionals with fast, 24-bit color displays served by high-bandwidth direct network connections.

There are at least four fundamental things that you will need to address to create enough design flexibility and availability of system resources to provide a usable and potentially interesting Java-enabled Web site. Offering up a responsive site with the right mix of content and functionality is a perpetual balancing act. In essence, it is a successively refined process of chasing performance bottlenecks and accommodating user requests. The four most important areas to concentrate on include:

- Response time
- Content quality and quantity
- Use of standard conventions and practices
- Reliability and security

RESPONSE TIME

The Internet is primarily about Interactivity, with a capital *I*. Interactivity and the presence or lack of it will directly affect the future of the Web revolution, as well as the future of any commercial site that you might be planning.

To say that the Internet is interactive can be a bit of a misnomer, especially if you are one of the many who connect via dial-in lines regularly. While you might be interacting with the computer and your connection to the Internet, it is hardly an experience one would call *interactive.*

Interactivity can be thought of as a condition, with various states or degrees of quality. Another way to say it is that it is the threshold of pain, visitors to your site are willing to bear, before giving up or leaving altogether. On average, how long does it take to do something that they can perceive as progress or activity? In this instance, Java can be as much of a boon as a bust. If you can get enough bytecode across the user's link quickly enough, the applets will run locally and enhance the appearance and interactive feel of your Web site. However, if you have so much bytecode to download that it prevents the user from doing anything at your site, you will have completely missed your target.

It is hard to overstate the importance of this issue to the success of your Web site. Reasonable response time and a sense of interactivity also will need to permeate into the design and specification of your Java content. The best way to solve this is to consider what the slowest platform and smallest configuration that you will reasonably assume and develop to that common denominator.

Also consider the bandwidth of the user's Internet connection. Generally, the slower the link over which your reader will be retrieving your Web pages, the more important it is that you maximize "value" and usable content and minimize document size and load time. Unfortunately, it is a fact of cyberlife that the unpredictability of Internet connections will affect your audience's perception of your product quality.

It's up to the efficiency of the currently configured Internet at that exact moment. As we discussed in Part 1 of this book, the Internet is never configured the same way twice on any given day, or ever. Dial-in lines are subject to noise storms that degrade compression ratios, and satellite links and transatlantic cables succumb to failures more often than their manufacturers would like to admit. Old equipment on the Net, such as a slow router with firmware bugs (likely written in C) can drop packets and force a wait for retransmission. On top of all that, each hop from machine to machine induces latency, slowing down the overall time to send and retrieve data. Because there's no guarantee that your messages will ever travel the same path, exactly how well a given Web site will perform is often a case of blind luck.

After a closer look, it's not as crazy, random, and hopeless as it seems. Web site connections tend to be relatively short, increasing the chances that the current route that you are taking advantage of will be sustained. When this is the case, you have a near constant rate to measure the current rate of data interchange. Knowing this can allow you to gauge how much data your Web server can provide and decide what to do with multiple connections.

On the up side, if you can provide reasonable or simply the best response time, natural migration to your site seems to occur in favor of better overall performance. Survival of the fittest definitely applies on the Internet.

CONTENT: QUALITY AND QUANTITY

Seasoned Web site consumers thrive on easy to read, easy to use, and *self-revealing* interfaces. If you are designing the panel layout of your applets from scratch using AWT, you need to think carefully about what layouts will work. The challenge of laying out your applets and the way that you blend them into the supporting HTML, imagery, and other helper applications presents an entirely new dimension of Web site interface design.

Perhaps the most impressive example of applet layout this year was demoed at the World Wide Web conference held in Boston, Massachusetts during December of 1995. Arthur Van Hoff, founding member of the Java team, gave a short preview of the features of the beta version of the HotJava browser. Using the panel feature of HTML 3.0, Arthur demonstrated three simultaneous applets running on the same page intertwined with active image maps and attractively rendered text in the other panels of the browser window.

Clearly, this was one of the most compelling Java-enabled Web pages yet demonstrated. With a bag of magic tricks like this to work with, Web site developers are poised to breathe life into old Web site content.

Each kind of Web site attracts very different Web site visitors. Large corporate sites need to be highly visible, easily accessible, and targeted at people who have a desire to do business with that corporation. Every little detail of the corporate Web site needs to be

examined. Will people like this font over that font? Can the proper corporate image and best face be put forward over the Net?

Consider the challenge that Web site designers for the federal and state governments face. How does an organization that usually is regarded as regimented, slow, and bureaucratic present itself as dynamic, connected, and in touch with its constituency?

Private individual Web sites can be as hard or as easy to figure out as you want them to be. After all, it's your Web site. In the case of Web sites done for hire, it almost always is a compromise arrived at between what the customer wants to do and what the Web site developer can deliver.

In this section, we have been talking qualitatively about content as it relates to user requirements and Web site types. We will have more to say on content issues as they relate to content creation in chapter 25, "Creating content."

USE OF STANDARD CONVENTIONS AND PRACTICES

Over the course of several centuries of sailing the world's oceans, mariners have developed consistent and standard methods of marking coastlines, waterways, maps, and charts. Perhaps the best known is "Red, right, returning," which tells the sailor to always keep red buoys (nuns) to the right when coming in to port from being at sea. It is a simple convention that has kept many a sailor free from hidden shoals and other dangers.As it is with sailing, it is just as vital that you consistently use a recognizable form of navigation markers throughout your Web site. Perhaps the biggest single complaint of first-generation Web sites (circa 1993/1994) was that it was impossible to figure out where anything was. HTML is not an inherently hierarchical information formatter, so it is up to the Web site developer to impose this structure on the information and accurately represent it. If every Web site developer uses their own standard, the only contribution that they will have made will be to provide a way to locate content on this particular site. This assumes that the standard even works.

By now, there are dozens of books on HTML layout conventions, standards, and practices. However, there probably is no better place to intuitively learn these things than the World Wide Web itself. By visiting scores of Web sites of every type, you can quickly tune into the devices and conventions that work best and the ones that do not. In this section, we will talk briefly about what concepts translate to including Java on a Web site.

There are three simple Web site components that will make navigating your content that much easier for the user:

- *Content map*—What's on the site and where.
- *Index Search*—How to locate a particular item on the site.
- *Well-behaved Java content*—All applets, interfaces, and conventions work consistently.

CONTENT MAP

One of the most important components of any mid- to large-sized Web site is the *content map*. For the purposes of this discussion, these would be Web sites that offer more than three pages of material to browse. It doesn't matter what size font your browser uses or how big your screen is, if users have to sort through more than three pages, you need a content map—something that tells people what's here and how to get to it. This is a perfect opportunity for the location and placement of your first applet on any Web site that you develop. Note, the latest version of Netscape Navigator includes an option to graph the current layout of the material that you've browsed, helping you to visualize the Web structure.

An excellent example of this is the Gamelan home page, which is itself an index of all of the currently registered Java applets and applications. (See Figure 23-4.) The very first button on the Gamelan home page is a navigation browser to all of the applets listed in the index. While this is something approaching overkill, it certainly gets the point across: Organize your information for easy access and navigation.

Figure 23-4 The Gamelan home page.

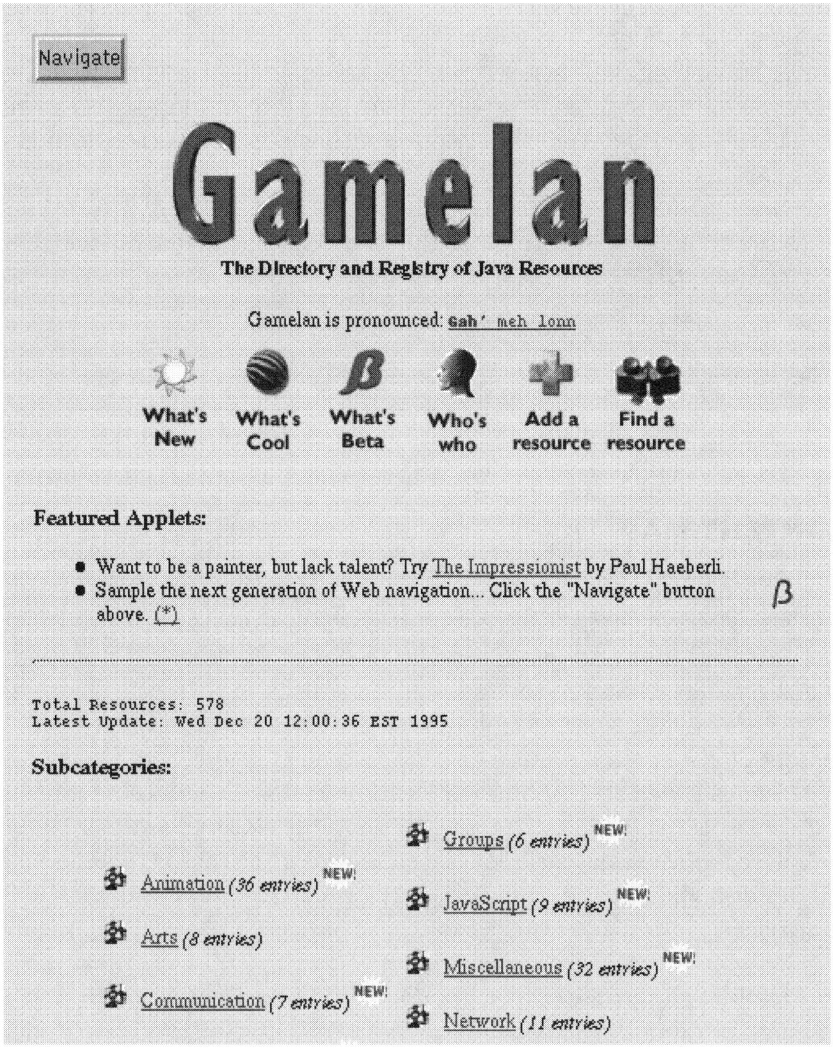

INDEX SEARCH

This is a bit of a specialization of the content map. The search facility provides visitors to your Web site an automated means of finding the exact information that they are looking for. Again, the Gamelan home page provides an excellent example of using a Java applet to perform the search for you, instead of the much maligned HTML form.

WELL-BEHAVED JAVA CONTENT

It is quite likely that the spectacular success of the Apple Macintosh user interface can be mostly attributed to the consistency of its application interfaces. While it might have seemed overtly strict, it served a purpose. Any Mac user, in many cases regardless of their native tongue, could drive just about any Mac application in minutes or at most a few hours. From the very beginning, all Macintosh applications worked the same way. This sometimes obstinate commitment to consistency gave people an unprecedented sense of confidence in using a personal computer.

It should and still can be the same way with Java. Sun Microsystems is not in the business of mandating all styles of user interface. The Java AWT will work within the Motif, OpenWindows, Windows, and Mac platforms this year, so Java-enabled Web site developers will be able to minimize the user interface confusion.

To the best of the ability of the Java programmer and the Web site developer, Java applets and applications should act consistently throughout. User interface precedents adopted in one applet should be adhered to in all applets. This might be obvious to you now, but it will not be so easy if you are working with several applet developers. Alternatively, this also applies if you are developing and maintaining several applets over a long period of time. These are issues common to any designer of software with a heavy investment in user interface.

Not only should user interface considerations be consistently applied, but applets themselves need to act within the context of the users and their environment. Applets developed under large Unix systems should not blindly assume that there is an unlimited pool of memory lying around. In the case of the minimum Java-capable Intel platform, a 40-MHz 386 DX PC with 8MB of RAM cannot be expected to have much left in the way of system resources to run memory-hungry applets (also known as *applumps*).

While it is difficult, and probably in bad taste, to point to any particular Java-enabled Web site as an example of bad user interface practice, we can offer the next best thing. We invite you to return to the excellently organized Gamelan Web site and try several of the applets

listed there with a new intention: Run as many different applets as you can as quickly as you can. The variation in applet behavior should be enough to give you the idea. In this instance, no one person or group can be held responsible. Because the Gamelan folks have no control over what a given applet will do, the writers of the applets and applications certainly don't plan to look and act like every other applet referenced by the Gamelan home page.

RELIABILITY

Reliability is the hallmark of a successful Web site. It is by far the most difficult area of Web site development to really get right. If you consistently provide a reliable and reproducible experience, people will come back to your site again and again. In some cases, even if you don't have the most interesting content, people will come back as long as it works the same way every time.

This certainly is the case with any industry trade show veteran whose job it is to demo Java. The ultimate test of being added to that all important hotlist is: "How reliable is this site?"

The following is a brief list of topics you can design in to ensure that your Web site passes the reliability test (remember them as the three Cs of reliability):

- Connected
- Continuous
- Complete

CONNECTED

If your site isn't available, it's rather difficult for people to get to it. While perhaps an obvious statement, the solution is not always so obvious. Despite the best of intentions, computer equipment fails with disparaging regularity. To be connected, your site needs to be fully up and running on at least a semi-regular basis.

Does this mean that you need to mirror your Web site? Not necessarily, but it certainly is a good question to ask your prospective Internet Service Provider, prior to choosing them as your link to the outside world.

As a Web site developer, you should consider the following issues when trying to design in high availability as part of your Web site:

- Disk mirroring
- Multiple network interfaces
- Regular system maintenance

Mirroring a site is just what it sounds like, an exact duplicate of the original image. If properly configured and a disk subsystem fails, the main server can recover and fall back to the mirrored disk. Under ideal conditions, it might happen while several users currently are connected without them ever noticing.

Fail-safe network connections also are an option to consider. Ask of your service provider. In this scenario, two or more network devices are allowed to map to the same IP address, thereby creating a redundant link should one of the network devices ever fail.Regular system maintenance is never needed, until something fails. Then you realize just how much you need it. There is no substitute for regular, complete, and correct system backups. In addition, it is worth the effort to routinely test the throughput and reliability of the primary interfaces that support your Web site, such as system memory, disk subsystems, networking devices, and power supplies. All it takes is a major system crash during a peak sales cycle to remind you how critical these issues are.

CONTINUOUS

If you are like most people constructing Web sites today, you are quite likely to reference other Web sites with embedded hyperlinks. This is a great concept when all of the sites that you've hyperlinked your Web pages to are up and responding. However, any site that fails to respond immediately becomes a pothole on the Information Superhighway. Choose links to other sites with care. Only send people to sites that you already have audited and know about or obviously declare these as untrusted sites.

Test every link and every applet or application thoroughly. If people hit dead ends, they get frustrated. People make a very direct connection between the perceived fit-and-finish of your pages and the perceived reliability of the information. If they get a lot of errors and cannot follow

your links, they will not stick around to read your pages. Verify your HTML syntax and construction. Until there are reliable WYSIWYG tools for creating HTML pages, use a utility to check your formatting. Note that the beta version of the HotJava browser demoed by Arthur Van Hoff at the 1995 World Wide Web conference included a full HTML 3.0 verifier—certainly an excellent tool for auditing Web sites.

Yahoo provides a great starting point for finding tools. Keep your pages up-to-date. Check regularly for external links that don't connect. To preserve your sanity, if you're maintaining a sizable Web site, explore using an automated mechanism to do your link checking. MOMspider is a publicly available example of such a tool.

A Web site that doesn't provide the user with a continuous flow of information or feedback ultimately will be judged as unreliable. Do everything that you can to minimize your risk of having unstable content at your site. Even if it means paring back your content, you can at least be certain that the content that you do have works.

COMPLETE

Design and implement a complete Web site experience. While it is reasonable to have one or more "under construction" zones on a given Web site, an entire home page full of hazard yellow road signs will send people away from your site as quickly as they got there.

Most of all, don't make references to nonexistent or incomplete Java applets and applications. There is nothing more frustrating than waiting for something to happen that was never meant to happen in the first place.

Leaving "stub" links to other HTML documents or applets is a useful way of developing the Web site on your own machine. When it is time to go live, you need to have all of this fleshed out or marked with some sort of under-construction alert as mentioned previously.

SUMMARY

This chapter has focused on the most basic and important aspects: selection of the type of Web site and the requirements of the people who will use it. We talked about three main kinds of Web sites: private, corporate, and commercial. As you design your site, stay focused on the kinds of user requirements that successful Web sites address completely: response time, content quality and quantity, standards, and lastly reliability. Now it is time to turn our attention to the details of selecting the hardware and software that you will need to create a home for your Web site.

CHOOSING A WEB SITE PLATFORM

THIS CHAPTER is intended for people who intend to actually build their own Web server. In many cases, perhaps even the majority of cases, the Web server already will be built for you. You just rent the space from the Web-site provider, which almost always is the same provider that you connect to the Internet through. If this is the case with the Web site that you intend to build, you can skip this chapter altogether. However, you might want to return to this material should you decide to upgrade your system or try your hand at building a Web server of your own. Too often Web site developers begin their journey to a complete Web site by starting immediately with the selection of the system components. In the "write once run many" world of Java, the importance of the hardware platform actually begins to diminish somewhat. While there is no question that the right choice of hardware and software for the job will make or break the success of the Web site, it is very easy to implement identical versions of highly usable sites on many different systems. This chapter focuses exclusively on the selection criteria for the basic hardware and operating systems that you will need.

It is not our intent to promote one system over another for anyone's benefit other than their own or yours. To say it another way, we are not being paid or even influenced to recommend one choice of system over another. In essence, this next chapter is as much a documentation of our existing sites as it is a reference guide for selecting Web site system components. We have done our best to err on the side of generality and go into specifics as needed to make a point. Yes, you will definitely need a computer to host a Web site, but the choice of which computer you use is entirely up to you.

You might notice that we will be talking significantly less about Java in this chapter. The system requirements for a Java-enabled Web site are identical to those of a non-Java Web site, with the single caveat that the platform that you are purchasing needs to run Java. Actually, this is incorrect, because it is quite possible to serve precompiled Java bytecodes from any Web server; however, it is not exactly clear why someone would want to do this.

The remaining sections of this chapter will focus on several areas that are paramount to selecting the right system for your needs. These areas

have been selected as the consistently encountered decision points that people in the Web site development industry are faced with. The following criteria represent the majority of research that you should be doing prior to choosing a system for Web site development:

- Setup, maintenance, and upgrade criteria
- Price and performance criteria
- Capacity planning

This list can be applied to virtually any kind of hardware and operating system available today. For a large number of readers, you already will have made these choices and probably can skip this chapter altogether. However, it might be worth at least skimming through this material for issues specific to serving Java content or developing Java software.

For the purposes of this book, we are going to focus on the two major platforms that Java has emerged on. These include the ubiquitous Intel 80x86 hardware platform coupled with the Windows NT and Windows 95 operating systems and the Sparcstation line of desktop Unix workstations coupled with the Solaris 2.4 or 2.5 operating system.

While there can be no question that the ultimate success of Java will be its widespread acceptance on several computing platforms, we can only document those hardware platforms and operating systems that Java runs on today. It is expected that, by the time this book is in your hands, the language will be fully supported in the Netscape Navigator product on several popular platforms including:

- Macintosh Power PC and System v7.*x*
- Silicon Graphics MIPS-based workstations running Irix v5.*x*
- Hewlett Packard PA-RISC-based workstations running HPUX v10.*x*
- Intel 80*x*86 PC's running Linux
- Digital Alpha-based workstations running DEC UNIX
- IBM RS6000-based workstations running AIX

The exact plan for Sun support of Java on all of these platforms is not yet publicly available. However, it has been said on several occasions at trade shows and industry conferences throughout the world that the

Mac and SGI ports probably are the most widely sought after. It is where the vast majority of content creators are. However, this should not be construed as a public statement of direction from Sun.

SETUP, MAINTENANCE, AND UPGRADE CRITERIA

Barely two years ago, it took a significant wealth of hardware and operating system familiarity to purchase, install, and configure a machine capable of acting as a Web site server. As the Internet has grown, this knowledge has spread far and wide as have the numbers of people who can make use of it.

In choosing a Web server platform, you immediately are faced with perhaps the biggest choice of all. Work with hardware and software that you already are familiar with, or expand your knowledge base and purchase equipment that you might not be proficient with. Because this book assumes that you already have some kind of computer and can use it to connect to some kind of network, it's fair to assume that you already have some level of hardware and software knowledge.

Most often these decisions have to be made under some amount of time and money pressure. If this is the case, go with what you know. However, if now is the time to take on a new hardware and software architecture, don't be afraid of taking this on in the context of building a Web server. You are virtually guaranteed that you will need to touch almost every piece of the new hardware and software architectures, thereby ensuring a complete education in the process of building something useful.

Once you've decided whether you will stay with the known or venture into new territory, you now are faced with another important decision. Will you opt for a preconfigured Web server solution or roll your own? Either way, you'll want to be very careful to fully consider the amount of time, patience, and money required in either case. The next few sections talk about the pros and cons of each path and what impact they have on ease of installation, ease of maintenance, and your ability to keep current with technology.

WEB SERVER BUNDLES

While it still is true that the more you know, the better off you are, computer hardware manufacturers have come a long way in packaging up existing pieces of hardware and software into specially designed "Internet bundles." These bundles are almost always the result of a hastily thrown together marketing effort designed to compete with similar bundled offerings from other vendors in the marketplace. Depending on the completeness of the solution, these bundled offerings can provide practically everything that you need to plug into and serve content on the Internet. Fortunately, many of these product lines have had time to mature and are becoming the standard method for purchasing and installing Web site servers.

Some good examples of such a bundled product offering are the Netra "I" Internet server from Sun Microsystems and the Webforce Internet server from Silicon Graphics, Inc. These systems come preconfigured from the factory ready to plug in and turn on. All you do is add the Internet connection. At least, that's how they are advertised. In many cases, they do work as advertised. Most often, people run into trouble when they want to do something else with the machine (such as using an unsupported networking interface or protocol or not having met the minimum criteria set forth by the vendor).

As for the Intel 80x86 version of the bundled Internet server, the most commonly found solutions are offered by third-party integrators or partners. Both Compaq and Gateway 2000 list several vendors who resell their systems preconfigured as Internet Web site servers. These days, the best place to start is at the Web site of the prospective solution provider that you are interested in.

What you are looking for in a bundled Internet server solution is a combination of hardware, software, and dedicated support that will be difficult if not impossible to find at the same price elsewhere. Because networking has been the lifeblood of the Unix workstation world for more than a decade and a half, it's no surprise that Unix workstation companies have jumped on this growing market.

The all-in-one approach solves two major problems in the quest for a fully functional Web site: ease of installation and maintenance. Bundled

Web server systems are extremely easy to install, set up, and configure as this is their key value over and above buying the equipment yourself. If it doesn't work, you also have some kind of support agreement that you should be able to use until things are working. Maintenance usually is quite straightforward, assuming that you have registered with the company that you bought the equipment from and make a reasonable effort to allow them to stay in touch with you.As for upgrading the equipment, you unfortunately will find that your options are not quite as open as the roll-your-own approach. Computer hardware vendors are just like any other business; they want your repeat business, which is where most of their money comes from. To ensure that this happens, service and support contracts usually specify that you must use vendor-approved products and that you follow their requirements for adding to the system. If you decide to add third-party memory or disks, you might violate the terms of your contract. If you decide to buy a bigger system, you will quickly find that you might have to accept whatever else comes with that bigger system, even if you don't want it or don't need it.

A desktop Internet server package usually includes:

- CPU
- Power supply
- RAM (usually just barely enough)
- Disk storage
- Built-in network interface
- Built-in floppy and CD-ROM drive
- Monitor and keyboard.
- Operating system and window system

The software that you get will depend significantly on the kind of configuration that you buy and whom you get it from. Most often, you should expect to get a native set of TCP/IP networking drivers, configuration and setup software, a licensed version of a Web server package (Netscape, for example) or a freeware CD-ROM that includes several of the popular tools that you will need to set up your machine as a web server. A possible list of tools would include:

- HTTPD server (CERN, NCSA, etc.)
- WAIS
- GOPHER
- Emacs
- GNU compilers and utilities
- XV image editor
- Socks
- PPP
- SLIP
- Web browser (NCSA, Netscape, HotJava, etc.)

DO IT YOURSELF

For people who have specific, hard-to-fulfill requirements, this approach will almost always yield a better solution. If you are just trying to save money and could make use of a preconfigured solution, it is rather unlikely that you will be able to come up with a better solution on your own. Take a very hard look at all of your options before deciding to go it alone.

Okay, so you've decided to put together the ideal configuration. How will you address the three main issues that we are dealing with in this section?

Buying a system that's easy to install and maintain is not hard to do these days. PCs now are a consumer-level product and are sufficiently well understood by the retail outlets that sell them. Almost any new PC that you buy today will have an operating system on it. The question then becomes: "Is it the one that you want?" A machine capable of acting as a Web server is a vastly different animal than a machine that only runs a Web browser. This is where your hours of research and prior experience will pay off. If you have designed your configuration on paper ahead of time, you will know exactly what to buy and what you will need it to do. This also will allow you to anticipate how well you will be able to maintain and upgrade each piece of the solution.

PRICE AND PERFORMANCE CRITERIA

This section deals specifically with the kinds of trade-offs that you will want to consider when making purchasing decisions. If money is not the primary factor, then it is acceptable to select systems and software solutions based solely on their features and the overall performance of those features. In this category, you will find the widest offering of systems. Because every vendor is out to make a profit, they will structure their best systems in the highest price categories. Even if you still have to deal with the bottomline, this is not a bad process to use for evaluating Web site system solutions.

If you are selecting your Web site based upon price/performance, your work gets considerably harder, because you now need to look a decidedly larger array of hardware, software, and permutations thereof. If you only want the best, it is easy to narrow down the real choices out there. If you want the best bang for your buck, you will need to wade through a significant amount of hype and featuritis that seems to abound in the price/performance market segment.

A good way to evaluate systems based on performance and functionality is to devoutly scour whatever relevant trade publications you can find. Try the *Computer Shopper*, *Unix World*, *PC Magazine*, *Network Computing Magazine*, and their associated Web sites, as well as the Web sites of the hardware and software vendors themselves. Look for any kind of benchmarking data that you can find that compares basic system properties feature for feature.

The best method is to actually compare systems side by side, feature for feature. Except in the case of large equipment acquisitions, this usually is not a feasible exercise. You will have a difficult time convincing your vendors that they should loan you the equipment to perform the comparisons.

Unfortunately, at this point in time, there still is no fully accepted Web server benchmark, although efforts are being made to standardize

around SGI's proposed Web site benchmark, which assigns relative performance values as Webstones. (To learn more about this benchmark, try connecting to *http://www.sgi.com.*) For now, here is a sample list of hardware and software feature and performance criteria that you can use to evaluate potential systems.

HARDWARE: CPU

Use the SPEC '95 numbers, not SPEC '92 or earlier. Look for Level 1 and Level 2 cache allocations and throughput. You are interested in a fast and reliable Level 1 cache (also known as *onboard cache*) and in the size and cache miss penalty (in clock cycles) of level 2 caches.

HARDWARE: I/O

For disk subsystems, look for read *and* write performance from memory to disk, disk to disk, and disk to memory. Don't simply rely on vendor-quoted disk speed rates, as they almost always refer to the read-only transfer rate on the motherboard of the disk, not through the entire system.

For memory systems, be sure to compare the maximum possible memory configurations and the transfer rate of data from one section of memory to another (i.e., the performance of a call to the C **memcpy()** function).

NETWORK

If you are connected to the Internet or to an internal corporate network via Ethernet or some other LAN technology, you will want to be very critical of the performance of your network interface cards. Not all 10-megabit-per-second Ethernet cards will deliver the same performance. They are certified to work on networks that can deliver that kind of performance, but this says nothing about what the network interface actually can deliver. The same is true for 100-megabit Ethernet cards, ATM cards, FDDI cards, and token-ring network cards. Be ruthless in this regard. The ability of your system to provide optimal network performance is of the utmost importance.

Home-based, dial-up phone lines present a somewhat different and more challenging puzzle because they tend to be of a lower overall bandwidth and have wildly varying line qualities. Two possibilities exist for dial-up connections: POTS and ISDN. POTS stands for Plain Old Telephone System, and ISDN stands for Integrated Services Digital Network. ISDN is essentially a "cleaner" line than regular voice-grade lines and is certified to deliver a minimum bandwidth (two 64-kilobit channels and one 16-kilobit channel).

Because of their lower bandwidth, both ISDN and POTS utilize a wide array of data-compression technologies to fit more data in the same space. The compression algorithm used is not as important as the compatibility of a given device. You will want to evaluate modems on their ability to support a good selection of compression and connection protocols. If someone is connecting to your Web site from a different modem than the one that you have, you will want to invest in a modem that has the greatest possible chance of speaking whatever flavor of data compression the incoming caller is using.

In most cases, the modem compatibility issue really needs to be resolved between you and the Internet service provider that you are using because the majority of people visiting your site will be using the equipment of their service provider to get to your site. However, if you connect to multiple service providers or are providing dial-in service for others, you will want to look at this in more detail than we can cover in this chapter. More than likely, the best place to look is on the Internet itself.

GRAPHICS AND DISPLAY

Strangely enough, in the case of the Web site server, the display and the adapter card probably will be the least of your worries because no one really cares what your system is capable of displaying, only in how fast and how well it can deliver the data. The one exception to this is in the area of content creation, which we will have significantly more to say about in a later chapter.

The logic is as follows: If you have a poor quality or old display adapter on the machine that you use to create content, you are only going to create content that can be displayed on your machine. On the other side

of the coin, if you have a state-of-the-art display card that allows you to create extremely large and color-rich images, you might be tempted to use these high-quality images that are significantly larger than lower-quality images. This choice will almost certainty reduce your server's throughput. You also should be aware that the majority of visitors to your site have economy display capability at best.

Either way, this is an arbitrary limitation imposed on your Web site and on the visitors to your Web site that can adversely affect the perceived quality of your content or response time. It will be up to you to decide how much you should invest in display technology, but rest assured that it will have no immediate impact on the performance of your Web site.

SOFTWARE: OPERATING SYSTEMS

Because this chapter is devoted to the selection of hardware and software platforms only, the only real thing to discuss with regard to software is your choice of an operating system. Unfortunately, at this point in time, there are only two choices if you are going to be creating a Java based Web site: Windows NT 3.*x* from Microsoft or Solaris 2.*x* for Sparc-based platforms from SunSoft. It is important to note that, just as NT has been ported to several hardware platforms (Intel 80*x*86, Digital Alpha, PowerPC, and Intergraph Sparc), SunSoft has ported Solaris 2.*x* to Sparc, Intel 80*x*86, and PowerPC. Unfortunately, Java has not yet been ported to each of these operating systems on each of these chips. However, SunSoft has assured the Java community that Java for Solaris on Intel and Solaris on PowerPC will be available in the very near future.

The choice between the NT or Solaris is almost certain to be dictated by your personal preference or prior experience with one operating over the other.

A strong case can be made for selecting Windows NT based purely on the disproportionate ratio of Intel boxes to Sparc boxes in the real world. Additionally, there are significantly more Web-authoring packages available under Windows NT than Solaris. For private individuals with existing investments in Intel-based computing equipment and Redmond-based operating systems, migrating to Windows NT (if you're not already there) probably is the best way to go. This might require some expensive upgrades in system memory and

disk but probably will be worth it in the long run. To effectively act as a Web site server, a Windows NT box should have a minimum of 16MB of memory (32MB is recommended) and at least 500MB of disk space.

For corporate Web sites that will handle large volumes of traffic and will need to be rock-solid secure, Solaris is a better candidate. The same is true for commercially developed Web sites that also are likely to have large traffic volumes and require the highest possible security. Windows NT has been shown to have significant problems scaling reliably in early versions, and it's not entirely clear those problems are gone.

The decidedly small choice of Java-capable operating systems will change rather drastically in the next year as several Java ports are slated to ship in 1996. For now, the best that we can say is that it will provide significant cause for rework in a future edition of this book.

CAPACITY PLANNING

This section will help guide you through the basics of selecting system components and configuration based upon what kind of Web site you've chosen to implement and how much traffic you intend to support.

There is a saying that goes: "Be careful of what you wish for because you just might get it." Nowhere could this be more applicable when it comes to designing an Web site that you want to be successful.

When the Java team released the first version of Java for public consumption on the Internet, success was defined as having a few thousand users and several hundred applets in six months. Very few people suspected that there would be tens of thousands of users and thousands of applets in the same time span. Overnight the Web site used to make Java available was swamped with users busily downloading the alpha versions. This was alpha code, and people were treating it like product! Sun's T1 line was completely overloaded between the popularity of the central Sun home page and the demand for Java through that link.

One of the first emergency counter measures enacted to cope with the demand was to mirror the Java releases on other servers, such as the

site at *http://www.blackdown.org*. Even this was not sufficient, and many people grew frustrated at their inability to get the free software. This has happened time and time again with successful Web sites the world around. After reading this section, you hopefully will be prepared to match your system's capabilities with the demand of your users.

As we've mentioned elsewhere, performance and capacity planning are iterative processes that usually are not much more than chasing bottlenecks. The bottlenecks are network, server CPU, and server disks. The key points to remember are:

- Peak bandwidth
- Peak operations
- Users and accounts

Peak bandwidth is measured in bytes per second and will directly determine the network data rate that you will need. This number represents the maximum amount of network traffic that can be moved through your system.

Peak operations is measured as the number of protocol operations (HTTP, NNTP, or SMTP) performed per second and directly determines what kind of performance your server will be capable of delivering.

The total number of users and associated user accounts will determine what disk subsystem is needed.

The number of operations per second that any given Web server can do is approximately the same for average file sizes up to 10K. As an approximation, we can assume that NNTP, SMTP, and HTTP operations create equal load on the server. The peak operations-per-second rate typically is 5 to 10 times the average rate for a day.

Now that we've defined the basic units of measurement, here are some important ways that we can characterize the work to be done:

- *Bandwidth per user*—How much of the total data rate is available to any given user at any given time?
- *Operations per second per user*—How many server operations per second can any given user expect to execute?

- *Average file size*—The kilobyte total of all files to be served divided by the number of files to be served.
- *Number of total users*—Fairly obvious. The total number of users that you expect to support.
- *Number of active users*—More important than the total number of users, this represents the total number of users actually using the system at any given time.

Now that you have the quantities that you want to know, the following formulas can be used to calculate them:

- Bandwidth per user = (operations per second) per user × average file size
- Operations per second = (operations / second) / user × (number of active users)
- Bandwidth = bandwidth / user × (number of active users)

Finally, here are the target performance metrics that you will want to satisfy when designing or upgrading your Web site:

- *Throughput*—The number of Web server operations per second. For example, when retrieving HTML files, this number represents the number of discrete operations performed by the HTTPD daemon per second.
- *Response time*—Measured as the number of milliseconds that it takes to perform a given Web server operation, this quantity is perhaps the most important variable to minimize, because it will directly affect the user's impression of the responsiveness of the Web site.
- *Maximum operations per second*—Based upon the available bandwidth, this quantity is important to maximize because it defines the upper limit on what your web server will be able to achieve.

Table 24-1 contains examples of precomputed maximum HTTPops/second for a given network bandwidth and average file size.

TABLE 24-1 Examples of precomputed maximum HTTPops/second.

Network Connection	Bandwidth (per sec)	If average file size is 1KB	10KB	100KB
9.6 modem	9.6Kb	1.2	0.1	0.0
14.4 modem	14.4Kb	1.8	0.2	0.0
28.8 modem	28.8Kb	3.6	0.3	0.0
56KB frame relay	56Kb	7.0	0.7	0.1
ISDN 1	64Kb	8.0	0.8	0.1
ISDN 2	128Kb	16.0	1.6	0.2
T1	1.5Mb	187.5	18.7	1.8
Ethernet 10BaseT	10Mb	1250.0	125.0	12.5
T3	45Mb	5625.0	562.0	56.2
Ethernet 100BaseT	100Mb	12500.0	1250.0	125.0
ATM 155Mb/sec	155Mb	19375.0	1937.0	193.0
ATM 622Mb/sec	622Mb	77750.0	7775.0	777.0

EXAMPLE: CORPORATE AND COMMERCIAL WEB SITE SIZING

In this section, we offer a hypothetical analysis methodology for determining the number of systems that will be needed to support the stated requirements of a midsize to large Web server. In the typical corporate and commercial Web site, a collection of incoming Web surfers pass through the firewall and connect to the Web server that is offering several Web services, such as HTML with caching enabled, e-mail, Net news, FTP, and DNS.

Consider a site with the following characteristics:

- Bandwidth per user = (100 kilobit / second) / user (Assume a cable modem)
- Average file size = 5 Kilobit / operation
- Operations per second per user = 20 (This is an upper bound)

- Number of users = 500 users
- 20% of the users are active at any given time = 100 active users

Then the requirements for the systems are:

- Bandwidth = 10 megabits per second = 80 megabytes per second required
- Operations per second = 2000
- Network subsystem requires 155-megabit-per-second ATM

Suppose system X can do 400 operations per second, then you will need 5 such systems.

EXAMPLE: PRIVATE INDIVIDUAL WEB SITE CAPACITY PLANNING

For the majority of home-based Web sites, the best that you can expect to provide in the way of networking throughput will be the current state-of-the-art in serial line modem technology: 28.8 kilobits per second.

Referring to Table 24-1, we list an ideal figure of 3.6 kilobytes per second with an average file size of 1 kilobyte. Unfortunately, this is not what we've observed in actual usage. Under Solaris 2.5 beta and Netscape Navigator 2.03b (admittedly, both are beta), the actual data rate works out to roughly 1.1 to 1.3 kilobytes per second. Much of this has to do with all of the networking hardware and software between the sending machine and receiving machine, which are guaranteed to induce latency.

We have seen peak throughputs as high as 3 kilobytes per second, but sustained throughput stays around the 1.1 to 1.3 kilobyte range. That's not exactly blazing speed, but then again, it is almost three times as fast as the state of the art from three years ago, which was 9.6 kilobits per second. (Be careful not to confuse the terms *kilobit* and *kilobyte*. To calculate kilobytes per second, simply divide the kilobit rate by 8.)

Let's do some math to help you decide how much content that you will want to offer and what you can expect your users to live by. To do this,

we'll make some initial assumptions, such as the length of time that you can expect a given user to stay on your Web site, the average reasonable size of the HTML content and bitmap images, and the average size of a Java applet.

Based upon our experience, the average attention span of the prototypical Internet surfer falls between 5 minutes and 30 minutes, assuming that there is a clean link between your site and their machine and everything is working well. For the sake of discussion, we'll put this at 20 minutes of time spent retrieving data from your site, as opposed to the wall clock time, which includes the time that it takes to read and process the information. Assuming this is the case, 20 minutes yields 1200 seconds. At roughly 1.2 kilobytes per second transfer speed, you can expect the average user to consume no more than 1.41MB of data—approximately the size of one double-sided, double-density PC-formatted 3.5" floppy disk. Rather disheartening isn't it? But wait, let's have another look. It's actually not as bad as it seems.

The average reasonable file size that you can expect to set as the limit for bitmapped images should be no more than 75 kilobytes, and 50 kilobytes is ideal. You will need to decide whether you want to use a lossless or lossy compression method (GIF versus JPEG) and what kind of image depth that you want (8 bit versus 24 bit).

> If you aren't familiar with the difference between 8- and 24-bit images, You should take the opportunity to compare the two side by side on your next visit to a computer store that has them in stock. As they say, you won't believe your eyes.
>
> 8-bit images allow for a maximum of 2^8, or 256, unique colors to describe an image. 24-bit images allow for 2^{24}, or 16 million, total colors. As you would expect, 24-bit images require three times the data of an 8-bit image for the same image width and height.

Let's assume that you will be using 65-kilobyte images that already are JPEG compressed and are 8-bits deep. JPEG compression ratios vary wildly, but 4-to-1 is not considered too bad for loss of image quality. Properly decompressed, this means that the destination image expands to almost 250 kilobytes—an approximate image size of 500×500 pixels. (The beta version of the HotJava browser and the Java-enabled Netscape browser both support JPEG image types; the alpha version of Java did not).

Although crude, it is possible to arrive at the average size of a Java applet by calculating the geometric mean of every class in the demo directory of the Java developer's kit, which comes out to roughly 3 kilobytes per applet. The Java group wasn't kidding when they said that Java was compact!

Using this information, you now can calculate the rough amount of data that you can expect to put into your Web site before it becomes too big for most people to navigate in one sitting.

If you were to offer nothing but image data, you could put approximately 20 images on your site.

If you were to offer nothing but applets on your Web site, you could place just under 500 applets on your home page.

If you were going to offer only HTML text, you could place approximately 1MB of text, assuming that you will have to account for some overhead in the actual HTML formatting commands that are not visible to the user but that must be transmitted just the same.

As a good rule of thumb, we suggest that you use the following ratio of text to images and applets: 25:40:35. That is, 25% of your Web site data should be text, 40% should be bitmapped images, and 35% should be Java classes or bytecodes. This provides for a good balance of the different data types and takes advantage of each of their strengths and weaknesses. For example, text is cheap, so don't be afraid to use lots of it to engage the user and explain what your site is all about. Images are not cheap and should be used sparingly. The old saw is that a picture is worth a thousand words, so this is roughly the metric that is used. Lastly, Java applets are relatively cheap, and leaving a good chunk of the data space for Java allows you to offer several very small applets or at least a few good-sized applets.Using these metrics, you can expect to put approximately 250 kilobytes of text, 9 strategically chosen images, and lots and lots of little 3-kilobyte applets, or you can just beef up your applets to a more realistic size, say 30 kilobytes, which allows you to serve 15 good-sized Java applets.

HTML AUTHORING PACKAGES

When it comes time to begin creating the content for your Web site, you will want to make your job as easy as possible. HTML authoring packages simplify your life by providing a tool for WYSISWYG content creation (what you see is what you get). What you see on your screen is a modifiable version of what your users will see on their screen, with the layout tools and window borders of the authoring package replaced by the familiar navigation controls and borders of the browser window. This brings us to an interesting dilemma in the state of the art of Web browsers today.

To date, almost all Web browsers are read-only with respect to the content that they are browsing. You can look, but you can't touch. To put it mildly, this is a bit of an inconvenience. Wouldn't it be better if you could author the content with the same tool that you view it with? Would it have been reasonable, 10 years ago, to ask users of MacWrite to create all of their documents with one tool, leave that tool, fire up another, and view the results of their work in another window altogether? Certainly not, but it's where we are today. Fortunately this problem will be solved, and in the next year, you will see several Web browsers that are capable of modifying content on the fly, including the 1.0 version of the HotJava browser itself, which will fully support HTML 3.0.

While it is guaranteed that HTML authoring packages will vary in features and functionality, they will all have one thing in common: simplifying the task of generating HTML content. The HTML language, while relatively simple in its scope, is not something that nontechnical and creative types yearn to master. If you've never written HTML before, the best way to describe it would be to imagine that you were a modern day combination of a creative writer and typographer. The HTML format defines a palette of typography commands (referred to as *format tags*)—such as font size, color, line breaks and paragraph breaks—that must be specified within the actual text of the document being generated.

Once complete, this document is saved as a file and stored as part of the Web content structure. All Web browsers implement an HTML parser, which understands the HTML format and converts it to a readable image. As the HTML parser reads the file, it applies all of the specified attributes to the text and converts that to a readable image that can be displaced on a monitor or sent to a printer for hardcopy output.

Unfortunately, there are no commercially available packages that will insert Java applets into your HTML source automatically. Therefore, at some level, you will need to get your hands dirty. Basically, all of this really consists of is editing the HTML output from a given HTML authoring package and inserting the applet tags as necessary.

You can use the examples throughout the book as well as the example Web page that comes on the companion CD-ROM to guide you through inserting your own applets tags. Be sure to refer back to the examples in Part 2 of this book for examples of inserting applets into HTML. Also, assuming that you have installed the Java Developers Kit, each of the demos includes a sample HTML file that shows you how to inline tag an applet and specify the arguments for an applet. You can expect to see Java authoring packages within the next year from companies such as Macromedia, with their ShockWave line of Web content creation plug-ins for Netscape Navigator. You also will want to give your attention to Javascript from Netscape Communications, which provides a high-level programming interface to Java applet authoring. See the Netscape home page at *http://www.netscape.com.*

Given the wealth of HTML authoring packages available today, it probably is better to provide a starting point for your research than an exhaustive list of applications available today that will be out of date tomorrow. Our favorite list of commercial authoring packages and shareware packages is hosted on the WWW organization's main site at *http://www.w3.org/hypertext/WWW/Tools/Overview.html.*

HTTP SERVERS

The HTTP server space probably is not as large as the number of HTML authoring packages, but it is a growing market and one that you will need to be familiar with as a Web site developer. Specifically, you will

want to be able to understand the trade-offs between the offerings in the commercial HTTP server space and the shareware HTTP server space. For a complete index of currently available shareware and commercial HTTP servers, we'll refer you to Yahoo's complete list of known offerings *http://www.yahoo.com/Computers/World_Wide_Web/HTTP/Servers/*.

SHAREWARE VERSUS COMMERCIAL HTTP SERVERS

The most important trade-off between shareware and commercial servers is the availability of product support. All shareware packages will clearly state that there is no dedicated support and that you are on your own. Almost all shareware packages include some form of README support file. Most often, this file will direct you to the person or persons responsible for their answering questions and maintenance. Failing that, you at least should get a pointer to the newsgroup or e-mail address of the entity that can assist you with your specific problem.

Shareware servers, in the ideal sense, are designed and created to facilitate the growth of the Internet, the World Wide Web, and perhaps the widespread use of specific features or functions that the server's authors have designed into their offering. They usually are not meant as direct revenue generators. Because of this lack of profit incentive, shareware servers are not likely to offer guarantees of performing faster, better, or more reliably than any other shareware server on the Internet. Simply put, they usually do the job, with some offerings working better than others.

The best advice that we can give you is that, if you are developing a commercial or corporate Web site, it probably is best to spend the money on a commercial Web server product. Get a package that comes with specific performance and security features that are legally enforceable by you, the customer. While there is no guarantee that the product that you are purchasing is any better than what is freely available (and many are not), you at least will have some form of recourse should the product not perform as advertised.

If you simply are developing your own Web site for hobby or academic interests, using shareware HTTP servers is more than appropriate. The

two best-known Web servers out there today also are the oldest ones. Both the CERN httpd and the NCSA httpd servers have been ported to literally every commercially available hardware platform and operating system in existence today. Support is liberally available in the form of online documentation, newsgroups, and e-mail.

CACHING AND PROXY WEB SERVERS

In the early 1990s, as the demand for information at the most popular Web sites went through the roof, it became obvious that Web servers were doing way too much repetitive work in the form of retrieving documents, even if the document that was just retrieved had been accessed by someone else just minutes before. The concept of Web server caching says that, as users request documents and images, the Web server should keep track of these requests. As each chunk of data is sent to the user, a copy is stored locally in case they are referenced again in the near future.

This technique makes a good deal of sense, because it conserves bandwidth on the Internet and provides significantly faster response time for the end user. Bandwidth is conserved on the Internet by virtue of the fact that the Web server now has a local copy of the document to refer to. This is much better than having to continually request the same document from the original Web server. User response time is increased because it is only a matter of communicating with the local HTTP server. This effectively eliminates any network latency induced as a result of having to transport the data across the Internet to the user's machine.

Proxy HTTP servers go one step beyond caching by taking advantage of the cache pool of other servers that it knows about. Proxy caching works by making connections to other caching servers to retrieve documents instead of going to the original source. This is sort of like a Web within a Web—a dynamically configured array of cooperating HTTP servers that will offer content from their store of cached documents.

SUMMARY

As you have seen, the process of choosing a Web server platform is not trivial. There are several factors to be concerned with, and some of them conflict with one another, forcing you to make trade-offs in the implementation process. There is no substitute for adequate preparedness and prior experience. Hopefully this chapter has given you some idea of what you need to know and how to go about acquiring that knowledge.

CREATING CONTENT

ON THE INTERNET, Content is everything. You have only one chance to get the point across, and that chance usually is a handful of fleeting moments when your ability to get the message across will either lure Web surfers deeper into your lair or scare them off never to return.

Early in the process of creating your Web pages, you should spend some time thinking about the goals for your documents. Web pages can be categorized by purpose. Being responsible to a specific purpose can help you make specific design choices. Are you providing a user interface to a service? If so, you'll need to decide whether you want to use Java for your input forms or rely on the HTML forms feature. Are you presenting information to an already interested audience? If so, then you might not have to spend as much time on glitz and glitter and more time on real content.

Sometimes, you can assume that many of your readers will arrive at your page because they need and want the information that you're presenting. You can use longer pages, present more detail, and worry less about "channel-switching" behavior on the part of your audience. There's a tension between the amount of "packaging" that you do to your content and your audience's desire to get the information that they need as efficiently as possible. What might be a good format for a product advertisement could fail dismally when presenting product documentation because of the frustration incurred when people are forced to navigate and visualize a Web page of short segments and are given tantalizing but incomplete glimpses of the answers that they need.

Are you trying to sell products or services? Information presentation on the Web has many guises. If you're selling something, you need to present your pages very succinctly, especially if you're trying to "hook" a person who might be a reluctant reader. Everything that you do in your design that forces a person to search, navigate, or otherwise use their browser's controls will reduce your chances of getting them to read to the end of your pitch. Lots of detail and presenting many branches (which might work well for other types of Web information) can confuse and frustrate your audience.

With regard to incorporating Java applets as part of your Web site content, weigh the trade-off between load time and value delivered. Until mainstream network bandwidth finally catches up with interactive needs, Java content developers need to carefully understand the balance between the time that a person has to wait for an applet to download and the perceived value received from that applet. If a user loads something once at the beginning of a session and uses it for the rest of their workday, the time spent waiting for the download is deemed worthwhile. However, if they spend four minutes waiting for an animation that takes only five seconds to run, only appears once, and contributes no information content, they'll probably press the **Stop** button and move on.

OBJECTIVE CRITERIA

You might want to apply the following objective criteria before deciding to implement a given Web page feature in Java.

INTERACTIVE

Will your Web page require give and take? That is, do you require your users to interact with the content on the page? Interactive applets loaded into a Web browser can present a much more satisfying interactive experience, without the long pauses and timing uncertainties that other, HTML-based Web applications exhibit. If the problem that you're trying to solve can't wait for better input range-checking, smarter image map targets, or more intelligent list selectors, you can build the needed widgets in Java.

PORTABLE

Do you have a heterogeneous or homogenous user system profile? If you know that all visitors to your Web site will be using the same platform and the same browser, you can "hardwire" certain features that are supported only on that platform with that version of the Web browser. However, if you cannot be certain of the platform or the browser, Java becomes appealing because you can guarantee the same behavior despite differing hardware platforms and Web browsers. (This presumes that Java already is supported).

ACCESS TO NETWORK DATA

Do you have a requirement to work with other data and applications on the network? If this is the case, with Java you have the native networking support built in, which greatly simplifies multiplatform networking access.

WEB AUTHOR'S STYLE GUIDE

The remaining portion of this chapter consists of a style guide for Web content authors adapted for reuse in this book. The original style guide was authored by Rick Levine of Sun Microsystems and appears with the kind permission of Mr. Levine. We present this for your consideration when designing what content you will place on your Web site. The original style guide is accessible by accessing *http://www.sun.com /styleguide/tables/welcome.html*.

PAGE LENGTH

For presentations that must grab people's attention to be successful, don't make the page longer than the window. Like the fold in a newspaper, the bottom edge of the browser window will stop some people from reading further. If the page is only as long as the default browser window, your reader will see all that you present in a glance and won't have to guess about what's below the edge of the window. Some content must be presented in one screen because the user cannot tell if there's more to be seen below the edge of the window.

If you need to present short, clearly segmented chunks of information, you should try to keep your pages short so that people won't miss things that fall off the end of the page. If the content that you present is in the form of short, loosely connected blocks, you must depend more heavily on layout and typography to organize your presentation. Keeping pages short will reduce the possibility that a block will be "orphaned" beyond the bottom edge of the browser window.

If your pages present text that people will want to read at length, it's all right to use longer, scrolling pages. Scrolling the browser window allows a reader to advance in the text with less loss of mental "context"

than does following a link. This advantage lasts up to about four screenfuls of text. After that, there is a tendency for people to lose their context and get frustrated with the mechanism of scrolling and their inability to keep track of what's elsewhere on the page.

There is a rhythm established for a reader by your text, typography, and layout. Retrieving a new page by clicking on a link introduces a delay that will break that rhythm. This unavoidable pause of a few to many seconds is something that you must take into account when deciding how long a page should be.

As a general rule of thumb, try to make the majority of your pages no longer than one-and-a-half screenfuls of text, and you probably will not get into too much trouble. If you have doubts, ask for feedback from members of your intended audience. For printing or saving, provide a separate link to a complete document. If you have long documents that people will want to print or save in one operation, provide a link to a complete, printable, or savable document, rather than trying to cram lots of content into one page.

Use shorter pages to make your Web more maintainable. If you're going to be changing your documents frequently, it's usually easier to swap several short files than change the middle segments of longer ones. (If you break something, your whole Web isn't out of commission!)

HYPERLINKS

The presence and placement of links affects the utility of your pages. Links provide connections to other content, organizational markers and a means to define terms and provide references. Links can support or detract from your presentation.

Write about your subject as if there were no links in the text. Don't refer to the mechanism of the Web, and don't attempt to guide or instruct your reader.

Having said that, Web-based user interfaces to services or procedural tasks, Java-based or otherwise, do need to provide guidance and

instruction for users of the interface. Decide which you are about—providing content or procedural guidance—and design appropriately.

Choose meaningful words or phrases for links. Your reader should be able to scan the text of your links and learn something about their destination without much reference to the surrounding text. "Telegraphic" links, those that use cryptic or obscure language, force the reader to follow the link before they're sure whether the information at the other end is worth reading. If it's not what they want, their time is wasted, and they often have to back up to continue.

Choose an appropriate length for the link text. A single word might be too small of a target and might not be meaningful. Using an entire sentence for a link might prove difficult to read, especially if the text extends over multiple lines.

Create context for the link. Write surrounding text so as to help people understand what the link does. Help your reader understand where links lead and what sections contain. They're paying a time penalty for every link that they follow. Help them understand what value that they will receive if they traverse a link. Be critical of each link; if your surrounding text does not accurately predict the destination, examine that text or, more fundamentally, the reason for having the link.

Choose your links so that they support your sentence and concept structure. Adding a link to text does emphasize the word or phrase containing the link and can actively make the text more difficult to read.

Try to match the link text that someone clicks on with the title of the resulting page. It's an impossible task to make the text displayed in a link match the title of the destination page. It also makes for maintenance headaches as the titles of documents change. Try to choose link text that has a conceptual similarity to the title and headers of the destination document.

Highlight text that is different. When using lists of links with similar text, use links to highlight those words or phrases that are different, rather than highlighting the entire phrase:

Application summaries for **Engineers**
Application summaries for **Architects**
Application summaries for **Masons**
Application summaries for **Excavators**
Application summaries for **Interior Decorators**

as opposed to:

Application summaries for Engineers
Application summaries for Architects
Application summaries for Masons
Application summaries for Excavators
Application summaries for Interior Decorators

An even better solution might be to eliminate the redundant prefix text.

Don't change text link colors! It's bad enough if you're monkeying with the body text color. Are you sure that people with varying forms of color blindness still can read your message on the interesting background that you've chosen? The convention that's evolved among creators and users of Web browsers is that links that have not yet been followed use a brighter or higher luminance color than those that already have been traversed. (For many browsers, they're shown in shades of purple or blue). When you change the link colors, you can easily reverse this brightness mapping, or worse, choose colors that read at the same level of brightness.

GRAPHIC IMAGES

Images can add a lot to the visual appeal and information content of a page. Unfortunately, they also can add a lot to the time that it takes to load a page. Many people viewing your pages won't have high-bandwidth access to the Internet. Images also can confuse your audience and distract from your message.

Use graphics that add to the information content of your page. Provide images that help explain or demonstrate your subject. Each image that you include in a page will slow down the person loading the page. Give them value for the time that they wait.

In traditional print and especially broadcast media, the inclusion of images is a safe way to capture and hold your audience's attention. Web pages are different in that many people will hit the **Stop** or **Cancel** button on their browser if images are too slow in downloading. With today's technology and network connections, the user has to wait for images to load. If your content takes too long to arrive, people will give up before the page completes.

Limit large images that are used solely for visual appeal. We've all seen the flashy sites (*www.sun.com*, for example) that use full-page graphics with image maps as the top-level "welcome page" for the site. Your readers will put up with this technique if it's used very sparingly. Using it once on the top level might be appealing, appearing on two levels will raise eyebrows, and three or more levels will frustrate people. If the top-level image isn't an image map used as a navigational visualization of the site, or a critical content-related image, consider eliminating it or making it much smaller.

Keep the total size of all images used on a page to less than 50K. If a single image is critical to the information being presented, it's okay to be larger, but consider using a thumbnail of the image and linking to the full-size copy of the master image. If the image won't survive being scaled down to thumbnail size, try using a small part of the image for the thumbnail, instead.

Take care with background images. If you must use background images, keep them very small (to minimize download time), and use the low-resolution JPEG format. If you're fond of creating your backgrounds on a computer with a high-color display, make sure you try living with them on an 8-bit tube. Text legible on a 16- or 24-bit screen is very often unreadable on a 256-color system.

Keep backgrounds pale and muted to avoid interfering with text. Better yet, don't use a background image.

IMAGE MAPS

In today's Web browser implementations, image maps, the clickable graphics used on Web pages, present a rather poor user interface. Unless the image itself has well-delineated "active" regions, there is no

clear indication of where a user should click. Having clicked, there is no feedback to indicate that a user's click has been recognized by the browser. The only sure cure with current browsers is to not use image maps. Having said this, if you do decide to use image maps, try to follow these guidelines.

Clearly delineate the clickable regions in an image map. The navigation bar at the top of many of the best Web pages have clearly defined rectangular regions.

If possible, make the clickable regions in an image map look like "buttons."

Explain image-map ambiguities.

If there is any ambiguity about where to click on an image map or what the destination of the links will be, describe the actions that are required and the effects of following the link to your audience.

Provide alternate text links elsewhere on the page for image-map destinations. This helps the people using text-only browsers, those who choose to browse with their images turned off, and those of us who might not be able to figure out what your image is supposed to do. If there are a large number of image-map destinations and including links to all of them force using short link descriptions, you might be better off moving the list to another page.

Include alternate text for each image. Use the **<...ALT="*description*"...>** parameter in your HTML source to specify the text to be seen by people with text-only browsers or those who choose to turn off image display while they're browsing. (It also will help visually impaired folks using screen-reading software.) The text description should be succinct and summarize the content or purpose of the image.

Use images with transparent backgrounds to better integrate your images. By setting the background area of a GIF image to transparent, you allow the browser's background color to show through, giving the appearance of a nonrectangular image.

CONTENT

Provide value that gets people to add your offering to their HotJava hotlist or GoTo page. The richer your pages are in needed information, the more likely people will be to return to them.

Pare down your text. One of the more interesting results from usability tests conducted on the Web is that people sometimes don't like to read Web pages. They will skip over text that they consider nonessential. They don't like to scroll. Often, your audience will skim your text, only reading the text of the hypertext links before they choose their next destination. It's not clear how much of this behavior is linked to the relatively crude legibility of computer displays or the extent to which it's tied to personal browsing style or situational context.

The pages that seem be the most successful are those that use a "bursty" style. Short, factual, well-written, prose with interesting links seems to attract the biggest audience.

Provide "context" links to satisfy a wide range of audience needs. It usually is quite difficult to predict how knowledgeable your audience will be of your subject matter. Provide links to information that can help a less knowledgeable person bring themselves up to the level of your presentation.

Provide clues to the dynamic nature of your content. Much of the information that you'll see on the Web is static. It changes seldom, if at all, after it's written. Some information is intended to be updated over time, possibly frequently. Give your users clues about how that information will be updated, especially if you're mixing static and dynamic data. If you have changed the behavior of a Java applet, do your best to document these changes *before* the user clicks on the link.

Don't assume that all of your readers will use the same browser features and defaults as you do. Visually impaired users might have selected much larger fonts. Many users will turn off backgrounds and color and font overrides. Browsers differ in how they implement rendering of white space. Some browsers will give end users far greater control over the use of colors, fonts, spacing, and other presentation attributes. A classic abuse of headers is to use <H5> or <H6> to mean

"smaller font," which is not what the HTML specification defines or what some browsers implement.

SELLING

Minimize the effort required to learn about your product. Put answers to the obvious questions that people will ask close at hand, either on one page or under well-labeled links. A focused presentation will allow people to efficiently get the information that they need. Optimize around shorter pages. Don't make people scroll or unnecessarily use their browser controls. Provide an easy way to get more information. If your product is complex enough that you cannot provide all of the information that someone needs in one presentation (and most of ours are that complex), make it easy for them to get more information. Provide links to more resources, and a mail link with a fill-in form that allows them to state the questions to which they need answers. Provide a path to make a purchase.

If you're going to talk about a product that your company sells, explain how to order one. You can point to somewhere else but make very sure that the destination is the place with succinct, accurate information on how to order the product that you were describing. If your business depends on selling things, talking about a product without providing the opportunity to make a sale is bad. Think twice about offering links to competitors' sites. When someone follows a link to another site, they might not come back. If you link to a subpage of a competitor's site that has their (presumably inferior) competitive offering, you're begging them to customize that page to effectively counter your pitch. It won't take long for the targeted competitor to find out about it.

NAVIGATION

Include document and chapter headings on long, multipart documents. If yours is an essentially hierarchical document having chapters or other predictable sections, consider adding a heading on each page that links back to beginning of the document. Also, for pages within each chapter or section, add a secondary header that takes readers back to the beginning of that chapter.

Consider duplicating navigational headers at the bottom of your pages. If your pages are consistently longer than one-and-a-half screens, it might be valuable to repeat any navigational links at the bottom of a page as well as putting them at the top to help readers navigate without forcing them to always scroll to the top of your pages. If repeating the same navigational aid would look awkward, try a simplified version, offering only essential destinations.

Avoid **Return to** or **Back** buttons and links. You have no way to predict where someone came from. Describe the destination of the link in absolute terms, rather than using implied destinations. **Previous** and **Next** assume that people can predict your structure and that they can quickly return if the destination wasn't what they expected. Neither of these assumptions is likely to be true. Your document structure probably will be foreign to many of your readers, and many of them will be running over low-bandwidth connections.

A phrase that describes where your link leads, such as "Ahead to Chapter 5: Quality," is better than an unadorned "Next." A better technique is to use a navigation scheme that employs concrete navigation links connecting a small number of topics.

Avoid using a palette of graphic navigation buttons. Most people will not be spending enough time looking at your pages to learn the meaning of the buttons. In addition, people will be creating links to your pages from other pages with dissimilar navigation landmarks. Icon palettes work in large, widely used, closed systems and often are combined with other, textual navigation hints. If you must use graphic navigation buttons, use "redundant" text labels as well. That way, it will be easier for people to decode your symbols.

Supply alternate text for graphic navigation buttons. Even if you do so for no other images, supply text labels for any graphical navigation buttons. If appropriate, add a brief table of contents at the top of the page. If the page is long, with several distinct sections that are not visible from the first screenful, add a short list of the sections. On a long page or a Web of related pages, this serves two purposes. First-time readers get a sense of what to expect from a section. Returning readers can quickly tell if a page contains what they need, then navigate rapidly to the destination that they want.

Put a title header on each page. It doesn't need to be large and bold, as long as it's recognizable as a title, separate from the rest of the page content. Choose the HTML title to reflect the textual page title. The title that appears in the header of the browser window should match the HTML page title. Try to have a unique title for each page. On pages that are essentially similar to their peers, such as the possibly machine-generated pages in catalog offerings, unique titles can be a reader's navigational lifeline.

Choose a title that accurately summarizes the content of the page. You'll frustrate your audience if you try to use the title as a "bait and switch" tactic to get them to read your page. Meaningful titles save your readers time when they are included in hotlist or search result lists.

Keep in mind that your pages will likely be scanned by Web crawling programs, such as the MOMspider, to extract titles, addresses, link text, and other data for indexing purposes.

Provide a search service. For sizable document webs, or even smaller Webs with nonobvious structure, provide a search service if that will improve retrieval and accessibility. Clearly state the scope of the collection being searched.

Put as much content towards the top of a hierarchy as is possible. When creating a Web offering that lends itself to a hierarchical style of organization, it's fairly easy to arrive at a presentation that requires a person to navigate several thinly populated "menu" or "index" pages before they get to real information. It is beneficial to "flatten" your hierarchy, providing more information sooner. In addition, try to avoid value-free intermediate pages.

Provide useful content on each page seen by your audience. Given that at least two levels of hierarchy probably are unavoidable (a top-level index and second-level content pages), try to provide valuable content on your top-level page.

SUMMARY

Content creation is much more of an art than a science. It probably is the most rewarding part of the whole Web site development process and certainly is the most important. Without content, there is nothing but a collection of very expensive software and hardware doing not very much at all. While the medium for delivering content has changed radically, many of the basic rules of presenting it have not. Above all else, put the reader's needs first. A successful Web site will be judged almost entirely on its content and very little by what hardware and software pieces you've chosen to deliver it with.

SECURITY

SECURITY represents a myriad of potential hot areas with respect to Web-site programming and development. Issues of security and privacy can affect almost all of your hardware, software, and data-access decisions. Will you leave your Web site wide open so that people can login to it from afar? Will you just rely on the base level of security provided with your operating system? Perhaps you will need to go so far as to create a full-blown firewall with packet-sniffing security hardware and encrypted transactions.

These matters are far beyond the scope of this book. For the purposes of this chapter, we will be focusing solely on security as it relates to the Java language and Java-enabled browsers. There are several texts that can assist you in establishing secure firewalls and system-access protection from the outside world. One of the better known texts in this regard is *Firewalls and Internet Security: Repelling the Wily Hacker*, by Cheswick and Bellovin.

Two things usually happen when people recognize the potential of dynamic content with Java. The first is the "aha!" reaction that comes when they understand that Java bytecodes are just like any other form of Web data, until they are processed by the runtime interpreter whereby they "come alive." Without fail, almost immediately afterward is the naturally paranoid question, "If this is really a program that I've downloaded onto my machine, what can it do to my machine?" Then begins a seemingly endless discussion of Java and security in Java. It's inevitable, and it should be, in this security-conscious world.

Like any complex and time-consuming subject, the Java security model takes some getting used to. The best description of the security model is that of an onion, which is composed of several successively smaller layers until you arrive at the core of the beast.

Security in the Java language and in the applied world of Java-enabled browsers will be the subject of at least one, if not many, other books. For the time being, the best references that we can provide for you are on the Java home page itself. The first document to read from top to bottom is the Java Security FAQ. This is a list of frequently asked questions that pertain to security issues in Java. This excellent document

has been carefully compiled by Marianne Mueller of the JavaSoft development team and reprinted here with kind permission.

> Please note: The Java Security FAQ should be regarded as a living document, as it will continue to evolve and change. For the latest information and list of security-related questions and answers, you should refer to the URLs listed in this section.
>
>

The second important security-related document to read is the Java Security Story. This technical white paper is a very good layman's discussion of the various levels of security in Java and how they are implemented. It details how these levels work with one another and how they support trusted data access methods and prevent unwanted methods from executing.

Figures 26-1 and 26-2 give you a good idea of what these pages look like. We recommend them as the best available and most accurate guide to getting started on the path of understanding the Java security model.

The Java Security FAQ can be found at *http://java.sun.com /sfaq/index.html*. (See Figure 26-1.) The Java Security Story can be found at *http://java.sun.com/1.0alpha3/doc/security/security.html*.

JAVA SECURITY FREQUENTLY ASKED QUESTIONS

WHAT ARE APPLETS PREVENTED FROM DOING?

In general, applets loaded over the Net are prevented from reading and writing files on the client file system and from making network connections except to the originating host.

Figure 26-1 The Java Security FAQ at *http://java.sun.com/sfaq/index.html.*

Netscape: Frequently Asked Questions – Applet Security

File Edit View Go Bookmarks Options Directory Window Help

Back Forward Home Reload Images Open Print Find Stop

Location: http://java.sun.com/sfaq/index.html#summary

What's New What's Cool Handbook Net Search Net Directory Software

Home About New Download Docs Browser Applets Developers Licensing In Touch

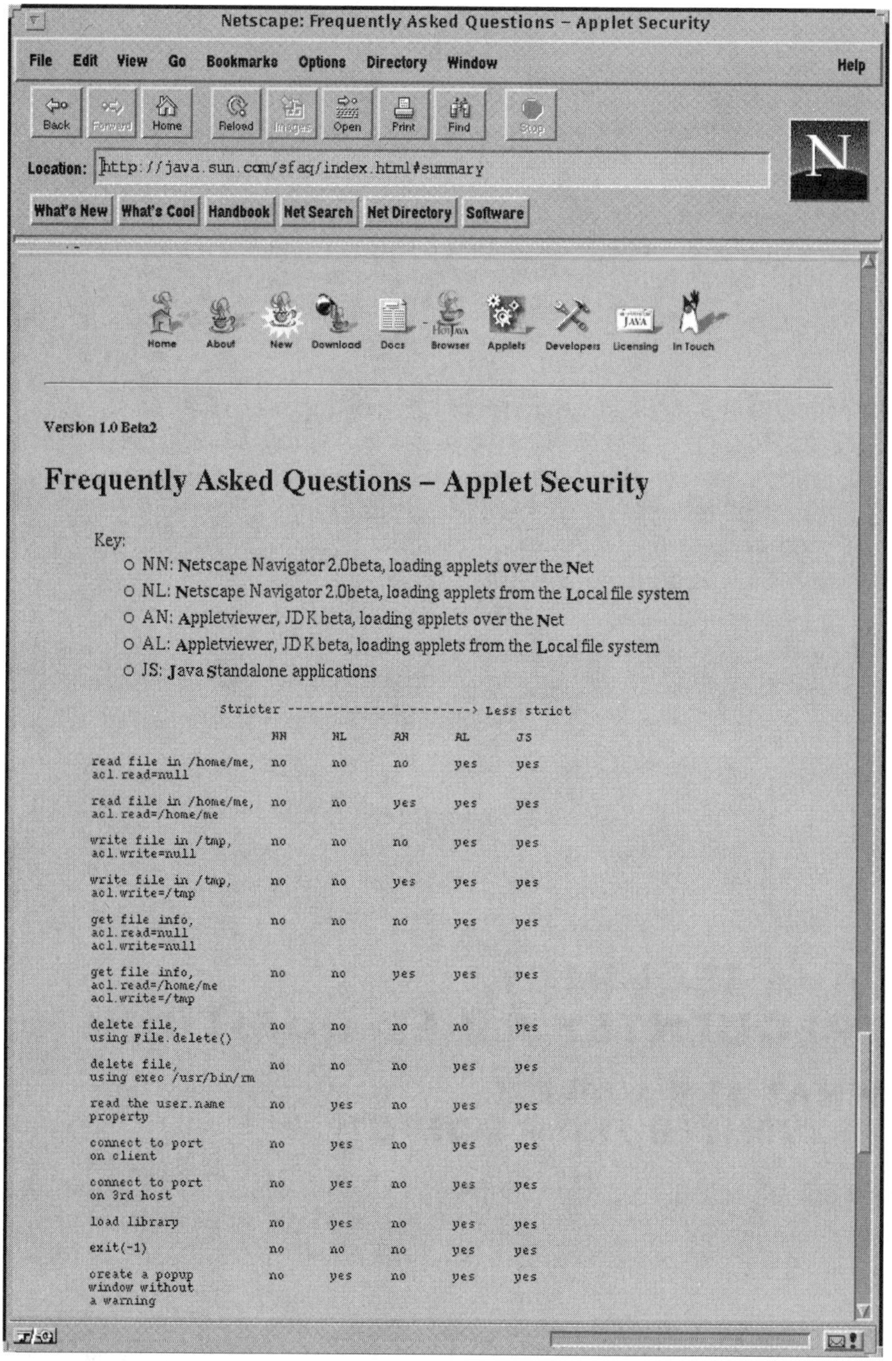

Version 1.0 Beta2

Frequently Asked Questions – Applet Security

Key:

- NN: Netscape Navigator 2.0beta, loading applets over the Net
- NL: Netscape Navigator 2.0beta, loading applets from the Local file system
- AN: Appletviewer, JDK beta, loading applets over the Net
- AL: Appletviewer, JDK beta, loading applets from the Local file system
- JS: Java Standalone applications

Stricter -----------------------> Less strict

	NN	NL	AN	AL	JS
read file in /home/me, acl.read=null	no	no	no	yes	yes
read file in /home/me, acl.read=/home/me	no	no	yes	yes	yes
write file in /tmp, acl.write=null	no	no	no	yes	yes
write file in /tmp, acl.write=/tmp	no	no	yes	yes	yes
get file info, acl.read=null acl.write=null	no	no	no	yes	yes
get file info, acl.read=/home/me acl.write=/tmp	no	no	yes	yes	yes
delete file, using File.delete()	no	no	no	no	yes
delete file, using exec /usr/bin/rm	no	no	no	yes	yes
read the user.name property	no	yes	no	yes	yes
connect to port on client	no	yes	no	yes	yes
connect to port on 3rd host	no	yes	no	yes	yes
load library	no	yes	no	yes	yes
exit(-1)	no	no	no	yes	yes
create a popup window without a warning	no	yes	no	yes	yes

Figure 26-2 The Java Security Story at *http://java.sun.com/1.0alpha3/doc/security/security.html.*

HotJava(tm): The Security Story

HotJava(tm) is a world wide web (WWW) browser, built using a new language called Java. Perhaps the most significant new facility that HotJava implements is the ability to import code fragments across the net and execute them. One of the most important technical challenges in building a system like HotJava is to make it safe. Importing code fragments across the network, installing, and running them is an open invitation to security problems.

The question of how to provide a secure environment for code to execute in doesn't have a single answer. HotJava has layers of interlocking facilities that provide defenses against a variety of attacks. These layers are:

- The JavaTM language, which was designed to be a safe language and the Java compiler which ensures that source code doesn't violate the safety rules.
- A verification of the byte codes imported into the runtime to ensure that they obey the language's safety rules. This layer guards against an altered compiler producing code that violates the safety rules.
- A class loader which ensures that classes don't violate name space or access restrictions when they are loaded.
- Interface-specific security that prevents applets from doing destructive things. It depends on the security guarantees of the previous layers. This layer depends on the integrity guarantees from the other three layers.

Security layer one: the language and compiler

The Java language and the compiler comprise the first line of security for HotJava. Java was designed to be a safe language.

In addition, applets loaded over the Net are prevented from starting other programs on the client. Applets loaded over the Net also are not allowed to load libraries or to define native method calls. If an applet could define native method calls, that would give the applet direct access to the underlying computer. There are other specific capabilities denied to applets loaded over the Net.

CAN APPLETS READ OR WRITE FILES?

In Netscape Navigator 2.0, applets cannot read or write files at all.

Sun's JDK 1.0 AppletViewer allows applets to read files that reside in directories on the access control lists. If the file is not on the client's access control list, then applets cannot access the file in any way. Specifically, applets cannot:

- Check for the existence of the file
- Read the file
- Write the file
- Rename the file
- Create a directory on the client file system
- List the files in this file (as if it were a directory)
- Check the file's type
- Check the timestamp when the file was last modified
- Check the file's size

HOW DO I LET AN APPLET READ A FILE?

Applets loaded into Netscape Navigator 2.0 can't read files.

Sun's AppletViewer allows applets to read files that are named on the access control list for reading. The access control list for reading is null by default (in JDK 1.0beta2 and later.) You can allow applets to read directories or files by naming them in the acl.read property in your ~/.hotjava/properties file.

Note: The tilde symbol is used on UNIX systems to refer to your home directory. If you install a Web browser on your F:\ drive on your PC and create a top-level directory named .hotjava, then your properties file is found in F:\.hotjava\properties.

For example, to allow any files in the directory home/mrm to be read by applets loaded into the AppletViewer, add this line to your ~/.hotjava/properties file:

```
acl.read=/home/me
```

You can specify one file to be read:

```
acl.read=/home/me/somedir/somefile
```

Use colons to separate entries:

```
acl.read=/home/foo:/home/me/somedir/somefile
```

Allowing an applet to read a directory means that it can read all of the files in that directory, including any files in any subdirectories that might be hanging off that directory.

HOW DO I LET AN APPLET WRITE A FILE?

Applets loaded into Netscape Navigator 2.0 can't write files.

Sun's AppletViewer allows applets to write files that are named on the access control list for writing. The access control list for writing is empty by default.

You can allow applets to write to your /tmp directory by setting the acl.write property in your ~/.hotjava/properties file:

```
acl.write=/tmp
```

You can allow applets to write to a particular file by naming it explicitly:

```
acl.write=/home/me/somedir/somefile
```

Use colons to separate entries:

```
acl.write=/tmp:/home/me/somedir/somefile
```

Bear in mind that, if you open up your file system for writing by applets, there is no way to limit the amount of disk space an applet might use.

WHAT SYSTEM PROPERTIES CAN BE READ BY APPLETS, AND HOW?

In both Netscape Navigator 2.0 and the AppletViewer, applets can read the system properties listed in Table 26-1 by invoking **System.get Property(String *key*)**. Applets are prevented from reading the system properties listed in Table 26-2.

TABLE 26-1 The system properties that the applet can read.

Key	Meaning
java.version	Java version number
java.vendor	Java vendor-specific string
java.vendor.url	Java vendor URL
java.class.version	Java class version number
os.name	Operating system name
os.arch	Operating system architecture
file.separator	File separator (e.g., "/")
xpath.separator	Path separator (e.g., ":")
line.separator	Line separator

TABLE 26-2 The system properties that the applet is prevented from reading.

Key	Meaning
xjava.home	Java installation directory
java.class.path	Java classpath
xuser.name	User account name
user.home	User home directory
xuser.dir	User's current working directory

To read a system property from within an applet, simply invoke **System.getProperty(*key*)** on the property that you are interested in. For example:

```
String s = System.getProperty("os.name");
```

HOW DO I HIDE SYSTEM PROPERTIES THAT APPLETS ARE ALLOWED TO READ BY DEFAULT?

There's no way to hide the system properties listed in Table 26-1 from applets loaded into Netscape Navigator 2.0. The reason is that

Netscape Navigator 2.0 doesn't read any files, as a security precaution, including the ~/.hotjava/properties file.

From the AppletViewer, you can prevent applets from finding out anything about your system by redefining the property in your ~/.hotjava/properties file. For example, to hide the name of the operating system that you are using, add this line to your ~/.hotjava/properties file:

```
os.name=null
```

HOW CAN I ALLOW APPLETS TO READ SYSTEM PROPERTIES THAT THEY AREN'T ALLOWED TO READ BY DEFAULT?

There's no way to allow an applet loaded into Netscape Navigator 2.0 to read system properties that they aren't allowed to read by default.

To allow applets loaded into the AppletViewer to read the property named by key, add the property **key.applet=true** to your ~/.hotjava/property file. For example, to allow applets to record your user name, add this line to your ~/.hotjava/properties file:

```
user.name.applet=true
```

HOW CAN AN APPLET OPEN A NETWORK CONNECTION TO A COMPUTER ON THE INTERNET?

Applets are not allowed to open network connections to any computer, except for the host that provided the .class files. This is either the host where the HTML page came from or the host specified in the codebase parameter in the applet tag, with codebase taking precedence.

For example, if you try to do this from an applet that did not originate from the machine foo.com, it will fail with a security exception:

```
Socket s = new Socket("foo.com", 25, true);
```

HOW CAN AN APPLET OPEN A NETWORK CONNECTION TO ITS ORIGINATING HOST?

Be sure to name the originating host exactly as it was specified when the applet was loaded into the browser. That is, if you load an HTML page using the URL *http://foo.state.edu/~me/appletPage.html*, then your applet will be able to connect to its host only by using the name foo.state.edu. Using the IP address for foo.state.edu won't work, and using a "shorthand" form of the host name, like foo.state instead of foo.state.edu, won't work.

HOW CAN AN APPLET MAINTAIN PERSISTENT STATE?

There is no explicit support in the JDK 1.0 applet API for persistent state on the client side. However, an applet can maintain its own persistent state on the server side. That is, it can create files on the server side and read files from the server side.

CAN AN APPLET START ANOTHER PROGRAM ON THE CLIENT?

No, applets loaded over the Net are not allowed to start programs on the client. That is, an applet that you visit can't start some rogue process on your PC. In UNIX terminology, applets are not allowed to **exec** or **fork** processes. In particular, this means that applets can't invoke some program to list the contents of your file system, and it means that applets can't invoke **System.exit()** in an attempt to kill your Web browser. Applets also are not allowed to manipulate threads outside the applet's own thread group.

WHAT FEATURES OF THE JAVA LANGUAGE HELP PEOPLE BUILD SECURE APPLETS?

Java programs do not use pointers explicitly. Objects are accessed by getting a handle to the object. Effectively, this is like getting a pointer to an object, but Java does not allow the equivalent of pointer arithmetic on object handles. Object handles cannot be modified in any way by the Java applet or application.

C and C++ programmers are used to manipulating pointers to implement strings and to implement arrays. Java has high-level support for both strings and arrays, so programmers don't need to resort to pointer arithmetic to use those data structures.

Arrays are bounds-checked at runtime. Using a negative index causes a runtime exception, and using an index that is larger than the size of the array causes a runtime exception. Once an array object is created, its length never changes.

Strings in Java are immutable. A string is zero or more characters enclosed in double quotes, and it's an instance of the String class. Using immutable strings can help prevent common runtime errors that could be exploited by hostile applets.

The Java compiler checks that all type casts are legal. Java is a strongly typed language, unlike C or C++, and objects cannot be cast to a subclass without an explicit runtime check.

The **final** modifier can be used when initializing a variable to prevent runtime modification of that variable. The compiler catches attempts to modify final variables.

Before a method is invoked on an object, the compiler checks that the object is the correct type for that method. For example, invoking **t.current Thread()** when **t** is not a Thread object causes a compile time error.

Java provides four access modifiers for methods and variables defined within classes and makes sure that these access barriers are not violated.

PUBLIC A public method is accessible anywhere that the class name is accessible.

PROTECTED A protected method is accessible by a child of a class as long as it is trying to access fields in a similarly typed class. For example:

```
class Parent { protected int x; }
class Child extends Parent { ... }
```

The class Child can access the field "x" only on objects that are of type Child (or a subset of Child).

PRIVATE A private method is accessible only within its defining class default. If no modifier is specified, then by default, a method is accessible only within its defining package.

For example, programmers can choose to implement sensitive functions as private methods. The compiler and the runtime interpreter checks to ensure that no objects outside the class can invoke the private methods.

WHAT IS THE DIFFERENCE BETWEEN APPLETS LOADED OVER THE NET AND APPLETS LOADED VIA THE FILE SYSTEM?

There are two different ways that applets are loaded by a Java system. The way that an applet enters the system affects what it is allowed to do.

If an applet is loaded over the Net, then it is loaded by the applet class loader and is subject to the restrictions enforced by the applet security manager.

If an applet resides on the client's local disk and in a directory that is on the client's CLASSPATH, then it is loaded by the file system loader. The most important differences of applets loaded via the file system are:

- Allowed to read and write files
- Allowed to load libraries on the client
- Allowed to exec processes
- Allowed to exit the virtual machine
- Not passed through the bytecode verifier

For these reasons, Netscape Navigator 2.0 does not load applets via file URLs. This means that, if you specify the URL in the text field at the top of Netscape Navigator, like so:

```
Location: file:/home/me/public_html/something.html
```

and the file something.html contains an applet, Netscape Navigator 2.0 won't load it. You need to specify the URL using the http protocol, like so:

```
Location: http://someserver/~me/something.html
```

WHAT'S THE APPLET CLASS LOADER, AND WHAT DOES IT BUY ME?

Applets loaded over the Net are loaded by the applet class loader. For example, the AppletViewer's applet class loader is implemented by the class sun.applet.AppletClassLoader.

The class loader enforces the Java namespace hierarchy. The class loader guarantees that a unique namespace exists for classes that come from the local file system and that a unique namespace exists for each network source. When a browser loads an applet over the Net, that applet's classes are placed in a private namespace associated with the applet's origin. Thus, applets loaded from different network sources are partitioned from each other.

Also, classes loaded by the class loader are passed through the verifier. The verifier checks that the class file conforms to the Java language specification; it doesn't assume that the class file was produced by a "friendly" or "trusted" compiler. On the contrary, it checks the class file for purposeful violations of the language type rules and namespace restrictions. The verifier ensures that:

- There are no stack overflows or underflows
- All register accesses and stores are valid
- The parameters to all bytecode instructions are correct
- There is no illegal data conversion

The verifier accomplishes that by doing a data-flow analysis of the bytecode instruction stream, along with checking the class file format, object signatures, and special analysis of **finally** clauses that are used for Java exception handling.

Details on the verifier's design and implementation were presented in a paper by Frank Yellin at the December 1995 WWW conference in Boston.

A Web browser uses only one class loader, which is established at startup. Thereafter, the system class loader cannot be extended,

overloaded, overridden, or replaced. Applets cannot create or reference their own class loader.

WHAT'S THE APPLET SECURITY MANAGER, AND WHAT DOES IT BUY ME?

The applet security manager is the Java mechanism for enforcing the applet restrictions described earlier. The AppletViewer's applet security manager is implemented by sun.applet.AppletSecurity.

A browser can have only one security manager. The security manager is established at startup and thereafter cannot be replaced, overloaded, overridden, or extended. Applets cannot create or reference their own security manager.

IS THERE A SUMMARY OF APPLET CAPABILITIES?

Table 26-3 is not an exhaustive list of applet capabilities. It's meant to answer the questions that we hear most often about what applets can and cannot do.

IF OTHER LANGUAGES ARE COMPILED TO JAVA BYTECODES, HOW DOES THAT AFFECT THE APPLET SECURITY MODEL?

The verifier is independent of Sun's reference implementation of the Java compiler and the high-level specification of the Java language. It verifies bytecodes generated by other Java compilers. It also verifies bytecodes generated by compiling other languages into the bytecode format. Bytecodes imported over the Net that pass the verifier can be trusted to run on the Java virtual machine. To pass the verifier, bytecodes have to conform to the strict typing, the object signatures, the class file format, and the predictability of the runtime stack that are all defined by the Java language implementation.

TABLE 26-3 A list of applet capabilities.

	Stricter	———————>		Less strict	
	NN	**NL**	**AN**	**AL**	**JS**
Read file in /home/me, acl.read=null	No	No	No	Yes	Yes
Read file in /home/me, ,acl.read=/home/me	No	No	Yes	Yes	Yes
Write file in /tmp, acl.write=null	No	No	No	Yes	Yes
Write file in /tmp, acl.write=/tmp	No	No	Yes	Yes	Yes
Get file info, acl.read=null acl.write=null	No	No	No	Yes	Yes
Get file info, acl.read=/home/me acl.write=/tmp	No	No	Yes	Yes	Yes
Delete file, using File.delete()	No	No	No	No	Yes
Delete file, using exec /usr/bin/rm	No	No	No	Yes	Yes
Read the user.name property	No	Yes	No	Yes	Yes
Connect to port on client	No	Yes	No	Yes	Yes
Xconnect to port on third host	No	Yes	No	Yes	Yes
Load library	No	Yes	No	Yes	Yes
exit(-1)	No	No	No	Yes	Yes
Create a popup window without a warning	No	Yes	No	Yes	Yes

Key:

NN: Netscape Navigator 2.0beta, loading applets over the Net

NL: Netscape Navigator 2.0beta, loading applets from the local file system

AN: AppletViewer, JDK beta, loading applets over the Net

AL: AppletViewer, JDK beta, loading applets from the local file system

JS: Java standalone applications

SUMMARY

As someone on the Java team recently said, "We are only interested in accurate information being published when it comes to security in Java, and right now there's a lot of inaccurate information out there." Be very careful what you take as fact from other articles (e.g., USENET, technical journals, etc.).

This does not mean that you shouldn't rely on USENET. This is a perfectly valid forum for making announcements, raising software development issues, and the like. For your reference, the comp.lang.java newsgroup is recommended for these purposes.

IMPLEMENTATION

BRINGING IT ALL TOGETHER

THE TIME HAS COME to bringing together all of the individual pieces that we've talked about thus far. As with any complex subject, the best way to approach it is through a series of simplifications. The goal of this chapter is to describe, in a general way, the sequence of things that you will need to do to arrive at a functioning Web site. This is meant to be more of a discussion or "lecture" than it is a tutorial. We can't tell you the exact sequence of things to do because we cannot presume to know every piece of hardware and software that you've got. However, we can at least tell you the approximate sequence of steps and give you some idea of how we did it ourselves.

The process of building a Web site can be described in 10 steps, starting with the installation and configuration of the hardware to going live and testing and tuning your site:

- Installing and configuring the Web site hardware
- Testing the Web site hardware
- Installing and configuring the operating system
- Testing the operating system configuration
- Installing and configuring the HTTP server
- Testing the HTTP server
- Creating the Web information structure
- Testing the Web information structure
- Going live
- Web site maintenance

USING THE COMPANION CD-ROM

Note: For complete details on the CD-ROM, please refer to appendix C.

Throughout the remaining sections, we will be referring to various pieces of the companion CD-ROM that is included with the book. This

CD-ROM has been mastered in the ISO 9660 standard format, which means that you can mount and read the CD using almost any PC or UNIX workstation. The CD-ROM has been laid out as a prototype Web site. We have constructed a simple Web site to serve as the coding tutorial for many of the earlier chapters. Unfortunately, we are unable to include a beta Java-capable Web browser at this time. Sun had not released the beta version of the HotJava browser at the time of publication, and we are unable to freely ship Netscape's product. We recommend that you download the Netscape Navigator Java-capable browser, which can be downloaded from *http://www.netscape.com*, or look on the Java home page at *http://www.javasoft.com* to see if the beta-capable HotJava browser has been released. You should expect to see a beta version of the HotJava browser release some time in the spring of 1996.

The CD-ROM is broken down into three main directories: web, sparc, and x86. Sparc and x86 stand for the Sun Microsystems Sparc hardware architecture and the Intel 80x86 hardware architecture, respectively. This way, depending on which platform you are using, you can locate the right piece for your machine. The web directory is architecture-neutral, which is what Java is all about. Under the web directory, you will find all of the HTML files, GIF image files, and, most importantly, every class of every Java applet or application written for the book.

> *Note*: The CD-ROM also includes both the alpha 1.3 version of the Java language and the HotJava browser. More importantly, the beta 2.0 release of the language and the AppletViewer are included in their original zipped or compressed format, but also are fully installed on the CD-ROM so that you can work directly from the CD-ROM. We also have included the PostScript and HTML documentation for the Java API. All of the code developed for this book should work with Java 1.0, as all of the code has been developed with respect to that API.

STEP 1: INSTALLING AND CONFIGURING THE WEB SITE HARDWARE

We will assume at this point that you have the following pieces of hardware ready to go:

- Desktop or server package with all of the immediate peripherals, such as the keyboard, mouse, display, hard drives, floppy drives, etc.
- Networking hardware and cables, potentially including a network interface card, modem, serial cables, twisted pair or coaxial network cabling, phone lines, or a network connection.

The best place to begin will be with the manuals that came with your system. Failing that, you will need to find someone who knows the ins and outs of the system that you've got to help you get to a functioning configuration.

The goal is to get the system sufficiently assembled that you can power it on and begin the process of bootstrapping the operating system, either across the network or with a floppy disk or CD-ROM. We realize that this sounds like pretty basic stuff, and it is, but we have to start somewhere.

STEP 2: TESTING THE WEB SITE HARDWARE

Again, this is not terribly exciting or sophisticated stuff, but it will be of greater value to you later on in the process, when problems arise and you need to know what's working and what's not.

Testing the motherboard, CPU, keyboard, monitor, and basic system peripherals is as obvious as it sounds. When plugged in and powered

up, do they operate as expected? Almost all computers have some form of POST (Power On Self Test), which tests the most basic system functions for correct behavior. In the case of an Intel PC or Sparcstation, this includes a full memory test, peripheral system bus test, keyboard test, and storage drives test, including hard disk, floppy disk, and CD-ROM.

As for the modem or network interface, this might involve slightly more work. A modem is very easy to test if you have access to a dumb ASCII terminal that you can hook up to the modem with a serial null modem cable. (The null modem cable reverses the appropriate pins between terminal and modem to allow for proper communication between the two devices). If you don't have access to a dumb terminal, you can test the modem on a PC by booting from floppy and simply sending the modem's initialization string through the proper COM port on the PC.

Almost all modems today implement some basic set of the Hayes AT command set. The reset command for Hayes compatible modems is **ATZ**. If you can send this command to the modem and get an **OK** prompt back, your modem is at least functioning as it should. Testing a modem on a Sparcstation is not quite as easy, so we recommend that you try to test your modem using the means described previously.

However, if you are using a "real" network to support your site, chances are that you have multiple systems at the site, implying the presence of a network hub connecting multiple systems together from a single network connection.

The most basic test of an Ethernet network using either category 3 or hopefully category 5 twisted pair (what 99.9% of most Ethernet networks use today) is the network link integrity test. When successful, this test almost always results in the lighting of the link light for the given port on the network hub. If you don't get a link light when connecting your hub to the network connection supposedly carrying the Internet connection, you definitely have got a problem. Without the aid of a more sophisticated diagnostic device, this is about as far as you can go. You will need to contact the service provided on the other end of your network connection and enlist their aid in solving the problem.

Assuming that your system has passed its internal power on diagnostics and that your modem and/or network is functioning properly, you are ready to proceed with the operating system.

STEP 3: INSTALLING AND CONFIGURING THE OPERATING SYSTEM

This is where things start to get significantly more detailed. Installing a multitasking, network-aware, virtual memory-based operating system is not a trivial task, no matter what the operating system vendor tells you. If you know what you're doing and know all of the services and features that you need, you can install just about any operating system after a few attempts. If you don't even know what pieces you need, it's a formidable task. Here are the basics of what you'll need to be aware of as you go through this process.

All multitasking, multiuser, virtual memory-based operating systems are broken up into several different subsystems that work together to provide a complete system solution. In the case of Solaris 2.*x* and Windows NT, there is a "core" operating system component that handles the most basic operations, such as process scheduling, memory management, system I/O, and device management. You definitely will need these components, and there's no need to worry, because they'll get installed no matter how you proceed.

If you have sufficient disk space, always install the entire operating system from soup to nuts. This greatly simplifies the installation process and ensures that, if you need component "X," it will be there. You can avoid having to search for the OS install disks in your maniacally neat and tidy office so that you hopefully can post-install the necessary drivers and utilities when you discover you need them. If, after you have got the Web server up and running, you decide you don't need a given component, you can always delete it from the system to recover valuable disk space.

At some point in the install procedure, you will be asked whether or not your system will be connected to a network and, if so, what kinds of

interfaces and protocols you will want to use. In the case of a Web server, we're going to make the broad and implicit assumption that you are either using a modem or an Ethernet-based network interface. This implies that you will need to load the drivers for these interfaces as part of the total operating system installation. All Sparcstations come with a built-in Ethernet interface, so this makes your life somewhat easier. Intel based 80x86 PCs usually do not come with an Ethernet card, so you will need to have the disk or CD-ROM that was provided with your card when you purchased it. Hopefully you remembered to tell the person at Computer City that you were using Windows NT or Solaris before they sold you that card or modem.

It will be up to you when you want to configure the machine for connecting to the network. If possible, it is advisable to do it during the operating system install, because this is part of the process. If you don't have the complete information or are not able to configure the network until after the install, so be it. Either way, you will need to be prepared at some point to configure your machine to run the TCP/IP network protocol. As described in Part 1 of this book, this means that you will need to know:

- The Internet IP address for your machine (e.g., 38.2.54.102)
- The Internet domain name that you will be part of (e.g., interramp.com)
- The domain naming service that you will use (e.g., DNS for Windows NT or NIS+ for Solaris)
- The Internet address of your default router (e.g., 38..1.1.1)
- The name of at least one or more name servers that you will use (e.g., 38.8.17.2)

The first item presumes that you are using a dedicated address. If you are using PPP, for example, your IP address might be assigned dynamically when you connect to your Internet provider or corporate Internet server.

Assuming that you have gotten the operating system installed properly on the machine and that you are able to boot it completely and cleanly, you are ready to move on to testing the configuration.

STEP 4: TESTING THE OPERATING SYSTEM CONFIGURATION

Once you are able to successfully boot and shutdown your machine with no errors and are able to login to the machine as an authenticated user, you can begin testing the various pieces of the operating system to check for proper functioning.

With respect to creating a Web site, you are interested in the integrity and functioning of your file systems, the network interfaces, and the basic system utilities that you will need to support them. Examples of these include backup and restore, all the traditional file system navigation commands or GUI-based file managers, Ethernet card drivers, TCP/IP stacks, PPP stacks, serial port drivers, and the virtual memory system.

Every operating system comes with some form of diagnostic checking tool. It is worth the time and effort to run through these tests to check that all of the basic features of the hardware and software operating system are functioning.

Once you have run the system diagnostics, you can begin testing the network interfaces if they're not already functioning. In the case of a networked Web server, try bringing up the network stack. On a Windows' system, this might involve running a GUI-based network initialization utility. On a Unix system, the system administrator edits a number of system files with the network address information listed in the previous step. (The Solaris install process uses a GUI to request and configure this information.)

The most basic network functionality tests to run are to successfully initiate the **ping**, **ftp**, and **telnet** utilities.. Assuming that you have gotten your network interface functioning (or serial line modem connected to your service provider), you should try to ping the default name server or default router for your network. If you can successfully ping these machines, try FTPing to a known anonymous FTP site, such as

java.sun.com (206.26.48.100), *sunsite.unc.edu* (198.86.40.81), and *ftp1.netscape.com* (198.95.249.66). (*Warning:* These IP addresses are not permanent and are subject to change.)

If you cannot successfully ping using the machine name, try using the IP address listed previously. If you can ping using the IP address but not the system name, then you have a problem with your naming server. If you cannot successfully ping using either, then you have a more fundamental problem. If you can ping using the name but not the IP, then either the IP has changed or something is very wrong.

At this point, if you are successfully able to ping other machines on your corporate network or on the Internet, you will want to reconfigure your machine as a standalone device for the next few steps until you are ready to go live.

STEP 5: INSTALLING AND CONFIGURING THE WEB SITE HTTP SERVER

You've made it this far, which means that you have a functioning system that is properly connected to the Internet or to some sort of network. The next thing to do is to install the various Web site utilities that you've chosen to use. During the development of this book and the accompanying Web site, we tested freeware HTTP servers from CERN, NCSA, and EMWAC for Windows NT. Each of these packages has its own merits and shortcomings.

Unfortunately, due to copyright infringment concerns, we are prevented from redistributing these pacakges on the CD-ROM at this time. Here is the list of URL's for each package that we tried:

- Tools for Internet Providers: *http://www.w3.org/hypertext/WWW/Tools/Overview.html*. This page will point you to EMWAC, which is a Windows NT HTTPD freeware server from the Univeristy of Edinburgh, as well as several other servers, including the others included in this list.
- NCSA HTTPD home page: *http://hoohoo.ncsa.uiuc.edu/*

- CERN HTTPD home page: *http://www.w3.org/hypertext/WWW/Daemon/*
- Windows 95 HTTPD: *http://www.w3.org/hypertext/WWW/Daemon/*

Assuming that you will be using one of these software packages, the next step is to download it to your machine. Uncompress and install the files into the destination directory on your hard drive. From here, it will be a matter of reading the README files and associated documentation that comes with each kit.

> *Note*: Almost everyone has settled on the convention of including minimal documentation in hopes of reducing overall file size, thereby decreasing downloading time. Full documentation usually is provided as a separate archive that you can download or is kept on a Web server that you can access. The latter is useful, assuming that you can connect to the site in the first place.

Be careful to pay close attention to the documentation for modifying the Web server configuration file. Modifying this file is the key to providing the pointer to the beginning of your Web site. If you have the CD-ROM mounted, you might want to begin by setting the entry in this file for the "web server root" to be the path name of the index.html file in the web directory of the CD-ROM. This will at least get you started with a simple HTML file that you can work with.

STEP 6: TESTING THE HTTP SERVER

Assuming that you have properly configured the HTTP server on your machine, as well as any other utilities that you have chosen to add, (e.g., WAIS, SOCKS, and GOPHER), you now can begin to test the server for proper functioning.

The easiest test for connecting to the Web server on your machine is to try to open a telnet session to your machine on the well-known TCP/IP port number 80. (This assumes that you have used the default port for the HTTP server in the server configuration file). Here is an example of connecting to our Web site machine using telnet:

```
daria% telnet localhost 80
Trying 127.0.0.1...
Connected to localhost.
Escape character is '^]'.
<CR>
<HTML>
<HEAD>
<TITLE>Error</TITLE>
</HEAD>
<BODY>
<H1>Error 400</H1>

Invalid request "" (unknown method)

<P><HR><ADDRESS><A HREF="http://info.cern.ch/httpd_3.0/">CERN httpd
3.0</A></ADDRESS>
</BODY>
</HTML>
Connection closed by foreign host.
daria%
```

The use of the hostname **localhost** essentially tells the network software that we want to connect to the local machine through the loopback port of the local machine. This does not require any extra hardware. The loopback port is an internal data path that is used to abstract the local hardware into the network paradigm employed by the protocol drivers. You also can use the hostname of the machine or the IP address that you've assigned to the machine.

The **<CR>** has been inserted to indicate that you will need to press the Return key after establishing the telnet connection to your HTTP server. The errors following the HTML tags actually indicate that the server is working properly, because you are not the kind of client that this server understands (i.e., you are a TTY-based user, not a Web browser), so it terminates the connection.

If you are able to successfully connect to the HTTP server, you now will want to try connecting to your local machine with your chosen Web browser. If you already have initialized the HTTP server configuration file to use your own HTML files or the ones on the CD-ROM, then your browser should be able to make the connection and parse and display whatever HTML that you have set up as the default.

If you cannot connect to the HTTP server, you should begin troubleshooting backward from the attempt to connect to the server. For

example, if you are using Solaris, is the Web server daemon up and running? Or in the case of using the inetd.conf method, is there an appropriate entry in the file to start the connection. The file inetd.conf is essentially a look up of network services that is accessed when a particular network service is requested of the machine. If the configuration file has an entry for the requested service, it will pass the information along to the inetd daemon to start the requested service. In this case, it would be the HTTP server.

If the HTTP server appears to be intact or properly configured, is your TCP/IP protocol stack up and running? You can check this by pinging yourself or a local machine that you know to be connected on your local network.

If the network stack is not functioning properly, you are starting to get into a broad range of problems that can be only guessed at here. At this point, you should begin troubleshooting from the system boot sequence forward until you find the problem. Be careful to check for more than one hardware or software problem masking yet another problem.

STEP 7: CREATING THE WEB INFORMATION STRUCTURE

If you do not already have HTML and Java applets written and ready to go, this process is where the majority of your time will be spent. The proper layout of your Web content will greatly simplify your ability to manage and maintain this content over the lifetime of the Web site.

As a starting point, we suggest that you examine the layout of the directories and files on the companion CD-ROM. This will give you some idea of where to begin laying out your HTML documents, bitmap images, and Java applets and applications. While there is no single best way to solve this problem, we have tried to group like objects into separate directories. For example, all HTML files are collected into a single directory called /html, all Java class files have been collected into a single directory called /classes, and so on.

Others prefer simply to lump the entire Web information structure into a single directory.

For now, try copying the Web directory of the companion CD-ROM to your hard drive, then begin some minor modifications to the files that we have supplied so that you can customize it for your own tastes. Try replacing references to GIF image files with your own image files, or rewrite the HTML content to suit your own tastes.

STEP 8: TESTING THE WEB INFORMATION STRUCTURE

Once you have established the directory and file structure that best suits you, with the appropriate HTML content, images, and Java applets in place, you can begin testing it. Try using either the Netscape browser or, if it's available, the beta-capable HotJava browser.

> *Note*: The performance of the Web browser and the local network connection will be about as good as it gets at this point. This is because you are running 100% local, so you have zero overhead in the way of network delays or server latency. The only exception to this would be that the system that you are using is so busy that a significantly faster remote client can process the data faster than you can. In this case, it is your machine that is the bottleneck and not the network interface.

STEP 9: GOING LIVE

Okay, you've got your machine fully installed and configured, and you've gotten the HTTP server functioning and serving content to your browser by connecting to your machine locally (e.g., if your machine name is beavis, you can open the URL **http://beavis**). Now it's time to put yourself on the Internet or the corporate backbone and advertise your site to the rest of the world.

Assuming that you've been successful up to this point, you should reconfigure your machine to be an Internet client and bring the system up with the HTTP server also functioning. Up until now, you've been developing and testing everything on a machine that was running the TCP/IP protocol but that was not physically connected to a real network.

To complete the testing, you will need to find another machine that also is connected to the Internet or a local subnet. This machine needs to be connected to the same network that you are attached to. Try connecting to your machine with a Java-capable browser running on the remote machine. If all goes well, you should see the exact same output and interactive behavior with the browser on the remote machine as you did locally. Depending on the throughput and performance of your network connection, your interactive "mileage" will vary.

At this point, you can consider yourself approximately 20% complete with respect to building and running a Java-enabled Web site. As we have mentioned elsewhere in the book, Web site development is very much like software development, which adheres to the 80%/20% rule. This rule states that approximately 80% of the total time and money spent developing any worthwhile software project is expended in the maintenance phase of the project.

STEP 10: WEB SITE MAINTENANCE

This step ultimately will lead you back to each of the previous steps outlined in some form or another. At some point, you will want to upgrade your system components. Perhaps it's as simple as adding more memory to the system or adding a larger hard drive. Maybe it's time to upgrade the entire motherboard or operating system. Each of these processes will potentially impact your Web site, and you will need to plan this out prior to making any changes.

As for the Web site content, such as the Java applets that you've chosen to offer or the currency of the information embedded in the HTML source, these too will need to undergo life cycle changes and modifications.

If you are maintaining a particularly large or actively changing Web site, we strongly recommend that you have a good look at Web management applications and the coming wave of Java development tools that will help you to enforce versioning and change-control techniques. A good place to look is on the Sun Microsystems home page at *http://www.sun.com* or the JavaSoft home page, which you should have memorized by now (*http://java.sun.com*). Other good places for this kind of information are the Gamelan home page at *http://www.gamelan.com* or the World Wide Web home page at *http://www.w3.org*.

A Web site is a living, breathing entity. If allowed to grow stale and wither on the vines of the Internet, fewer and fewer people will come to your Web site over time. Keeping current with the ever-changing pace of the Internet and Web technology is time consuming and challenging. Then again, that's why you got into this business in the first place, isn't it?

SUMMARY

In less than six months, the Java language and the HotJava browser have managed to permanently alter the way that people think and work on the Internet. What once was a static collection of text and images has now come alive, thanks to the hard work and years of experience of a very special and talented group of people on the Java development team.

The authors are indebted to the JavaSoft team and to Sun Microsystems for creating the Java language and to you the reader for buying and using this book.

THE HOTJAVA BROWSERS

AS OF THE TIME of this writing, Sun was preparing a release of the beta HotJava browser. With the Java team focusing its development efforts on the beta JDK, work on the beta HotJava browser had to be delayed, and one of the consequences of that delay is that we are not able to include any significant information on the beta browser in this book.

Accordingly, the focus of this appendix is on the alpha HotJava browser, which, as of early 1996, still is available on the Sun Web site (*http://java.sun.com*). While there are substantial changes to the beta browser's interface, many of the fundamental concepts remain the same.

Aside from getting a general idea of Sun's idea of a browser and satisfying your historical curiosity, you also might be interested in the alpha browser because there's a significant amount of code out there that was written for alpha and that hasn't yet been ported to beta or 1.0. The alpha browser will, at least, let you run those older applets.

HOTJAVA INSTALLATION

If you don't already have HotJava up and running on your computer, appendix C will show you how to install and configure HotJava. The accompanying CD contains versions of HotJava for Solaris, Windows 95, and Windows NT.

By the time you read this, HotJava might be available for other platforms as well, which are not discussed in this book. You should check the README.TXT file on the root directory of the CD-ROM for final information on what the disk contains. If your platform is not supported, you also should check the Java home page at *http://java.sun.com* for current release information.

However, all platforms have essentially the same needs, so while the specifics of installing HotJava might vary slightly, this appendix should give you enough information to get you started.

HOTJAVA IS FREE!

HotJava is copyrighted, freely distributed software; that means that you don't have to register it or pay anyone a fee to use it. There are some

restrictions on HotJava's use (generally intended to prevent anyone except Sun from making a profit on HotJava), but these restrictions should in no way prevent you from getting the fullest use out of HotJava.

DOWNLOADING HOTJAVA

Because HotJava is freely distributed, the latest version is available by download from a number of World Wide Web sites, chiefly Sun's own Java site at *java.sun.com*. (You also can get a list of mirror FTP sites via the Java home page.) You are certainly encouraged to use the version of HotJava that is on the CD, at least for your initial installation, but you probably will want to download updated software at some point.

The easiest way to download HotJava is via the World Wide Web. That means that you need to have a Web browser already up and running, so if HotJava is your only Web browser, just install it from the CD-ROM and come back to this section after you have everything up and running and know how to connect to the Java home page.

If you do have a Web browser running, you can surf to *http://java.sun.com*. Click on the downloading icon to get instructions on downloading and installing the latest copy of HotJava.

If you don't have a Web browser, you still can obtain Java via FTP (assuming you know how to use one of the many available implementations of FTP, which is beyond the scope of this book). Connect to *java.sun.com* and look in the *pub* directory for a single self-extracting archive (an executable program) with a descriptive name that leaves little doubt as to what the file is for. For example, the alpha 3 file for Windows NT and Windows 95 is called hotjava-alpha3-win32-x86.exe. The x86 indicates that this release is for the Intel 80x86 series of chips (486 and higher).

HARDWARE AND SOFTWARE REQUIREMENTS

HotJava now is available for Sun workstations running the Solaris operating system and Intel 80x86 computers running Windows NT or

Windows 95. HotJava also is being ported to Macintosh and Windows 3.*x* platforms as of this writing. To get the latest information on which platforms currently are supported, check out the Java home page at *www://java.sun.com.*

Details of Java's requirements for the various supported operating systems are given in the following sections. In general, however, HotJava requires you to have a supported multimedia sound device installed on your computer (at least if you want to be able to hear any audio components of applets), and the video system must be capable of displaying at least 256 colors.

Your computer also will need to be capable of making a TCP/IP connection to the Internet. TCP/IP is not part of HotJava; it is available for a variety of platforms from a number of vendors. If you're one of the lucky few with a permanent Internet connection, then you already have the TCP/IP protocol running, and all you need to do is install, configure, and run HotJava. It's more likely, however, that you'll be using a dial-up connection, in which case you need to install TCP/IP first. Newer operating systems come with TCP/IP capability built in; see the following sections for details on your particular type of installation.

INSTALLING HOTJAVA ON WINDOWS 95

HotJava will run on a minimal Windows 95 installation with 8MB of RAM; however, as with most other applications, you'll be happier with the performance if you have 12MB or more. Install the HotJava browser according to the instructions in appendix C.

CREATING A SHORTCUT

After HotJava is installed, create a shortcut for the HotJava browser. One way to do this (there are several) is to right-click with the mouse on an empty space on the desktop. Choose **New¦Shortcut**. You'll see the **Create Shortcut wizard** window, as shown in Figure A-1.

Click on the browse button to bring up a file dialog window. Use that file dialog to select **\hotjava\bin\hotjava.exe**, and follow the remaining wizard instructions to finish with the wizard.

Figure A-1 The Create Shortcut wizard.

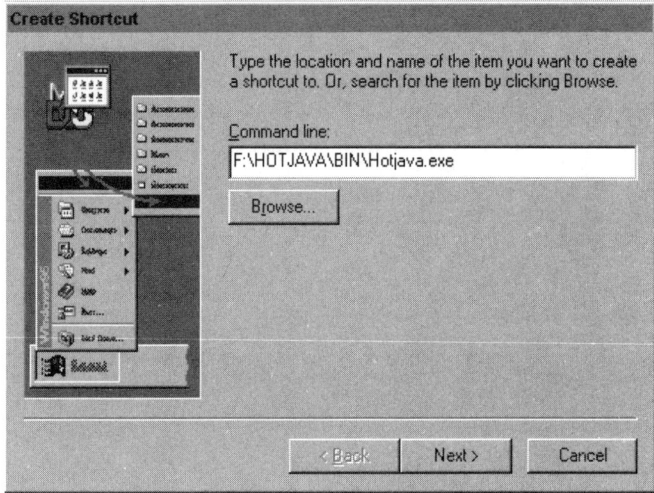

That's all there is to installing HotJava itself. You can run it now, if you want, and you will be able to browse the Web pages that came with HotJava. However, to get on the Internet, you need to install/configure your TCP/IP connection and the Dial-Up Networking software, both of which can take quite a bit more work.

INSTALLING TCP/IP AND DIAL-UP NETWORKING

As discussed earlier in this appendix, HotJava communicates with the Internet via the medium of a TCP/IP connection. To find out if you installed TCP/IP when you loaded Windows 95, go to the Control Panel and click on the Network folder. (If you don't have a Network folder, you'll need to run the Windows 95 setup again and, when you're presented with the list of options to install, select **Accessories** and **Dial-Up Networking**.) Make sure the Configuration tab is selected, and you'll see a list similar to that in Figure A-2.

If you don't see TCP/IP in the list, you'll need to add it. Click on **Add**. You'll get a listing of Network Component Types. Choose **Protocol**. Click on **Add** again for the Select Network Protocol dialog. From this dialog, select **Microsoft** from the Manufacturer's list on the left-hand side of the dialog. The dialog now should look similar to that shown in Figure A-3.

Figure A-2 The Network Configuration dialog window.

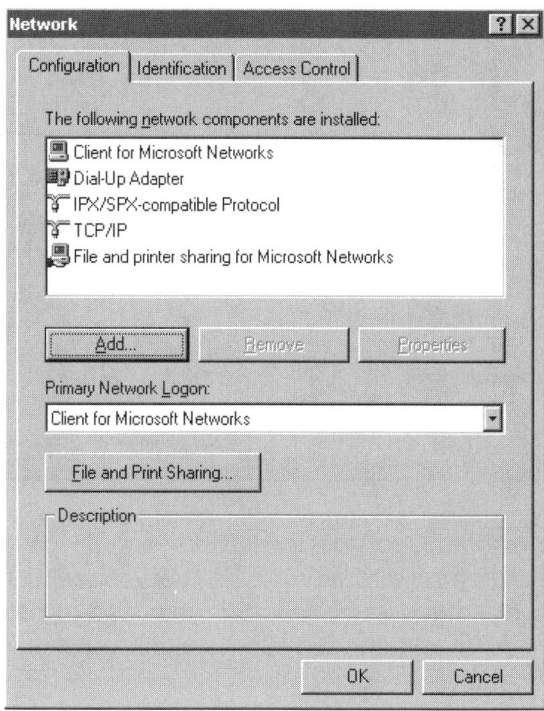

Figure A-3 The Select Network Protocol dialog window.

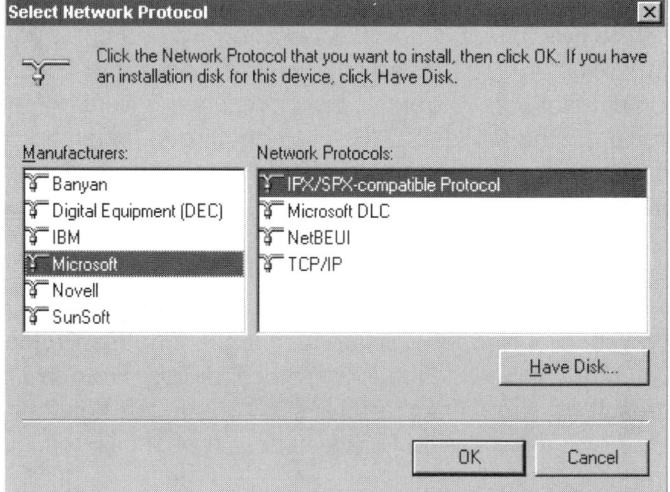

Choose **TCP/IP** from the list of Microsoft Network protocols, and click **OK**. Follow the instructions (if any are given) for locating the required files. If you installed from a CD-ROM, you'll need to put the Windows 95 disk in the drive. If you installed from floppies, you will be prompted for the required disks. You'll need to restart your computer before the changes to your configuration take effect.

If you're going to be dialing into your service provider, you also should make sure that the Dial-Up Networking software is installed. From the taskbar, choose **Programs**¦Accessories, and look for the Dial-Up Networking folder on the Accessories menu. If it isn't there, go to the Control Panel, click on **Add/Remove Programs**, and select the Windows setup tab. From the list of Windows components, choose **Communications**, and click on the **Details** button. Choose **Dial-Up Networking** from the list of Communications components, click on **OK**, then click on **Apply** and follow the instructions that you are given.

CONFIGURING TCP/IP FOR WINDOWS SYSTEMS

Click on the Network icon in the Control Panel, choose **TCP/IP** from the list of network components, and click on the **Properties** button. Select the IP Address tab on the TCP/IP Properties dialog. You'll see the dialog shown in Figure A-4.

There are six pages (tabs) of settings here, and some of the information that you enter will have to come from your Internet service provider. The following section gives general information only; your particular installation might vary slightly.

BINDINGS Check the Bindings tab, and make sure that **Client for Microsoft Networks** is checked.

ADVANCED You can leave settings on this tab at their default values.

DNS CONFIGURATION The DNS configuration tab contains information required to make your computer visible across a TCP/IP-based network and to tell TCP/IP where to find the domain name service (DNS) that translates string IDs to IP addresses. If you're only using TCP/IP to connect to the Internet as a user (as opposed to being an ongoing presence other computers should be aware of), you have the option of disabling DNS here and recording the DNS information from within the Dial-Up Networking software.

Figure A-4 The TCP/IP properties dialog.

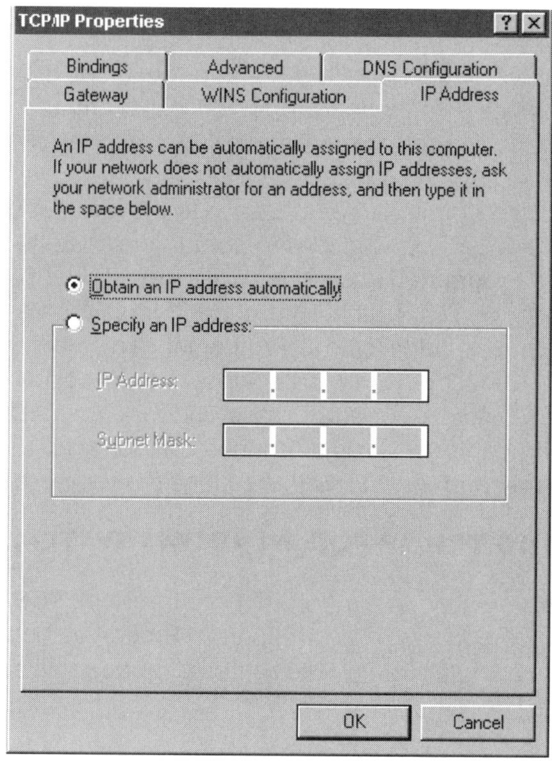

If you are using TCP/IP across a network connection, your system administrator can tell you how to configure this page. If you're dialing up your Internet provider and you would like to store your DNS information here instead of in the Dial-Up Networking software (and if in doubt, you should do so), you can use the following information as a guideline.

Click on **Enable DNS**. Enter your ID in the Host field and the name of your provider's computer in the Domain field. For example, given the Internet address of *dharms@mts.net*. **dharms** would go in the Host field, and **mts.net** in the Domain field.

Your provider will have given you one or two IP addresses for DNS servers. Enter them one at a time in the DNS Server Search Order field, and click on **Add** after adding each entry. DNS servers are always stored as IP addresses rather than names because, without a DNS, there's no way to translate a name to an address.

Enter the domain name in the Domain Suffix Search Order field, and click on **Add**.

GATEWAY Unless you've been given specific information for a gateway, you can leave this information blank.

WINS CONFIGURATION For most dial-up connections, you will check the **Disable WINS Resolution** box. If you're connecting across a network, check with your system administrator.

IP ADDRESS In most cases, the computer that you connect to to get access to the Internet will assign your computer an IP address (IP addresses are explained in chapter 2). If this is not the case (your Internet provider might have given you an IP address in the form 111.111.111.111, as well as an ID like *dharms@mts.net*), you will need to tell Windows 95 what that address is.

Click on **OK** from the TCP/IP properties window to return to the Network dialog, and click on **OK** again. Follow the instructions for restarting your computer so that the changes can take effect.

DIAL-UP NETWORKING FOR WINDOWS 95 AND NT

If you're connecting to the Internet via a dial-up connection, you'll also need to configure Dial-Up Networking, because there's yet another protocol involved when you interpose a pair of modems between two computers.

Your dial-up connection will be either a *Point-to Point Protocol* (*PPP*) or a *Serial Line Interface Protocol* (*SLIP*) connection. PPP is the newer of the two protocols, and if your Internet provider offers it, you should use this option.

> If you're installing SLIP, you should request specific instructions from your Internet provider. SLIP is *not* automatically installed along as part of the Dial-Up Networking software.

In either case, the software that handles the phone connection for Windows 95 is called Dial-Up Networking. From the Windows 95 **Start** button, choose **Programs**|Accessories. You should see Dial-Up Networking as one of the options in the Accessories menu. If you don't,

you'll need to go to the Control Panel, click on **Add/Remove Programs**, and choose **Windows Setup**. When you see the list of options shown in Figure A-5, choose **Accessories**, and click on the **Details** button. Choose **Dial-Up Networking**, then proceed with the setup process.

Figure A-5 The Add/Remove Programs Properties dialog window.

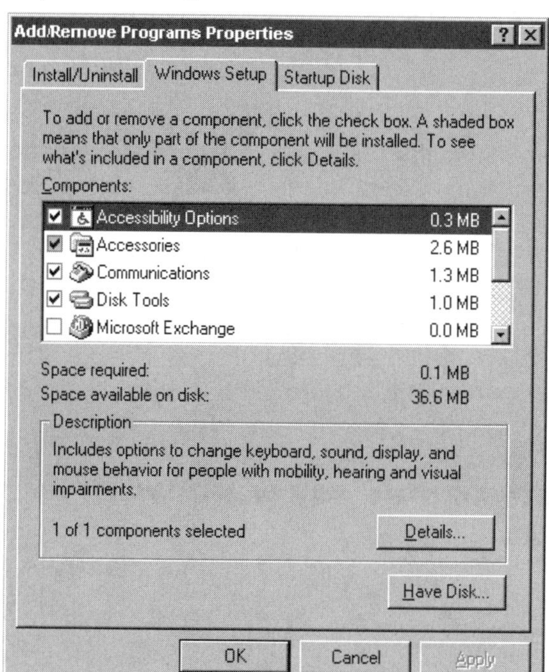

Once you have Dial-Up Networking installed, you'll need to configure it to connect up to your local provider. The first time that you use Dial-Up Networking, you'll get a wizard that helps you through the modem installation process. After the modem is successfully installed, the wizard begins to ask you for information related to the connection that you want to make. The steps that you need to take from that point on are described in the next section. If you have previously run Dial-Up Networking, when you run it again, you'll see a folder that looks something like the one shown in Figure A-6. From the folder menu, choose **Connections**¦Make New Connection to run the Make New Connection wizard.

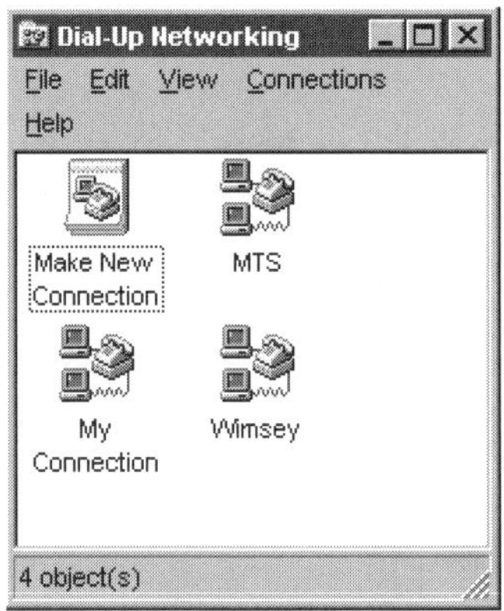

Figure A-6
The Dial-Up Networking folder.

MAKING A NEW CONNECTION The first page of the Make New Connection wizard asks you for a name for the connection and gives you the option of configuring the connection as well. In most cases, you should be able to use all of the defaults. However, if you have difficulties, ask your service provider for details on setting up the connection.

CONFIGURING THE CONNECTION After you've created the connection, you do need to configure it to recognize your Internet service provider's computer. Right-click on the shortcut that you've just created to bring up the shortcut's menu, and choose **Properties**. Click on the **Server Type** button. Choose the type of Internet connection that you will be making (it will be either SLIP or PPP, preferably the latter).

If you didn't enter the DNS IP address information when you configured TCP/IP, you can do so now. Your Internet provider should have given you this information when you opened your account. If the connection software doesn't know the address of the DNS, it won't be able to resolve IDs and URLs into actual IP addresses. Click on the **TCP/IP** button to bring up the TCP/IP Settings dialog. Click on **Specify Name Server Addresses**, and enter the primary DNS address (and any other DNS addresses and any WINS addresses that you have been given).

For most dial-up connections, you won't specify an IP address for your computer, as the server assigns addresses from an available pool each time that you log on. If you have been given a fixed IP address, you will need to enter it on the TCP/IP Settings dialog.

USING THE CONNECTION To use the connection, just double-click on the connection shortcut that you've created. The Dial-Up software will dial out through your modem and establish the connection with your service provider. After the modems connect, the software will attempt to negotiate the logon, unless you've opted to display a terminal so that you can enter your user ID and password and perhaps choose the type of protocol (SLIP or PPP) to use during that session. If you do use a terminal window, press F7 when you're done, and you should shortly be ready to run HotJava on the Internet.

DIRECT INTERNET CONNECTIONS

If you have a direct Internet connection and don't need to go through the hassle of dialing in, then you're one of the blessed few! Chances are TCP/IP already is properly installed and configured for your network. If it isn't, you should see your system administrator for specifics on getting TCP/IP set up.

RUNNING HOTJAVA ON WINDOWS 95

To run HotJava, just double-click on the HotJava shortcut that you created for *\hotjava\bin\hotjava.exe*. You also can run hotjava.exe from a DOS window, if the window properties permit programs to detect Windows. You don't need to make your TCP/IP connection before running HotJava, because HotJava loads a local HTML document on startup and only attempts to use TCP/IP when you request a document with a nonlocal name. (Because HotJava comes with a number of documents covering everything from using the browser to demonstrations of Java Applets, you can see Java in action without ever dialing up the Internet.)

INSTALLING HOTJAVA ON WINDOWS NT

HotJava installs on NT much the same way it installs on Windows 95. The difference is that, while Windows 95 uses Network services and Dial-Up Networking, NT uses Remote Access Services (RAS) to handle most aspects of the TCP/IP and PPP or SLIP connection.

If you're running the Windows 95 shell for NT (available in beta at the time of writing, for version 3.51), you also can create the shortcut the

same way as is described in the Windows 95 section of this appendix. If you're using Program Manager, use **Program**|New to create a new program item.

INSTALLING REMOTE ACCESS SERVICES

If you haven't already set up RAS for an Internet connection, click on the Network icon in the control panel. If NT Networking services are not already installed, you'll get a dialog box asking if you want to install them now. Answer **Yes**. For purposes of this discussion, you do not want to install a network card. Instead, choose the option that lets you install RAS, which is essentially network software that uses the phone lines (or other cable connection) rather than a dedicated network card. Follow the instructions on the dialog windows that you are presented with, and choose RAS (most likely a button labeled **Remote**) when it comes up.

The Windows TCP/IP Installation process automatically installs the TCP/IP stack, but it also lets you optionally install a number of related services that you might find useful. The Connectivity Utilities option includes FTP (for file transfers), Telnet (for terminal sessions), and Finger (for getting information on other users on the Net). There also are a number of other utilities that are automatically installed along with TCP/IP.

In general, you can find better (read more user-friendly) versions of these programs elsewhere, often at no or little charge. However, you might want to install the utilities anyway so that you have them as a last resort. FTP in particular is quite useful for downloading software, such as the latest version of HotJava (although you also can get it via the HotJava browser by going to the Java home page at *java.sun.com*.

Most of the other TCP/IP options are server (host) options. Because you will be using HotJava as a client, rather than a server, it's unlikely you will need these options (and if you do need them, you will know enough to disregard this advice).

The RAS setup program will take a few moments to install the required network components, then will attempt to detect your modem. If the program does not correctly identify your connection port (comm port and modem), you have the option of adding this information yourself.

Assuming you're satisfied that the connection information is correct, continue with the installation. The setup program then will copy all of the required code from your installation disks and create a program group. It also will present you with a network configuration dialog. Click **OK** to complete network configuration.

Once RAS installation is complete, the installation program will require you to reboot the computer. After you restart NT, you'll need to go to the newly created Remote Access Service Program Manager group and run the Remote Access icon to load RAS. You'll see the dialog window shown in Figure A-7.

Figure A-7 The Remote Access dialog window.

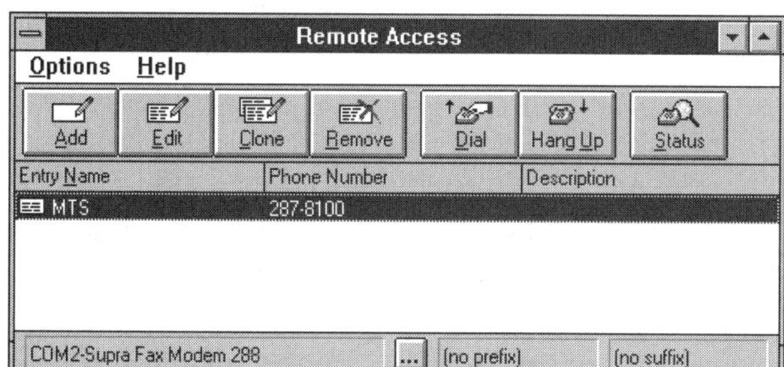

CONFIGURING RAS Take a deep breath; you're most of the way there! All that remains is to configure RAS to dial up your Internet provider, and use the appropriate protocol (SLIP, or Serial Line Interface Protocol, or PPP, Point-to-Point Protocol) for the connection.

> Both SLIP and PPP are well-established protocols for managing TCP/IP connections over telephone lines. If you have only one or the other option, don't worry; both will serve HotJava's purpose equally well. If you have the choice, however, you should use PPP, as this is the newer and slightly better protocol.

Make sure that you're at the Remote Access dialog window as shown in Figure A-7. To add a new RAS connection, click on the **Add** button. You'll see the Add Phone Book Entry, shown in Figure A-8.

Give the entry a name indicative of the provider that you're calling, and fill in the phone number of the service provider that you are calling.

Figure A-8 The RAS Add Phone Book Entry dialog.

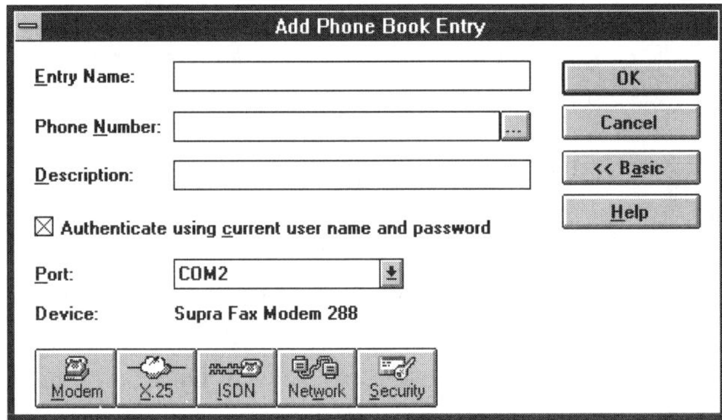

There are five buttons arranged along the bottom of the phone book entry dialog. You'll most likely be able to use the default settings for all of these buttons except **Network**. Click on **Network** to bring up the window shown in Figure A-9.

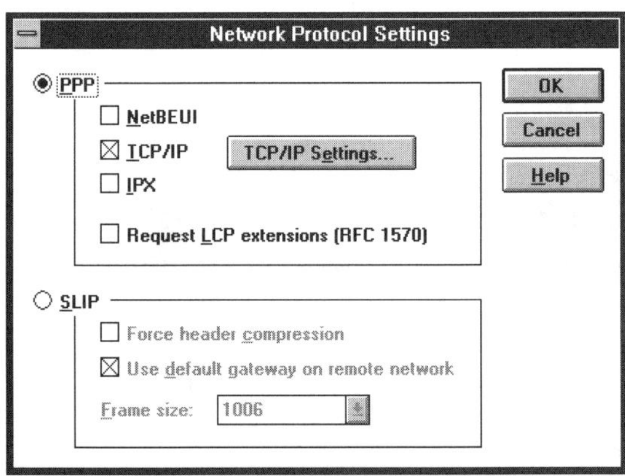

Figure A-9 The Network Protocol Settings dialog window.

Choose the protocol that you will use to connect to your Internet provider. Most likely this will be PPP, using the TCP/IP protocol, in which case you will need to click on the **TCP/IP** button to specify how IP addresses are to be handled. As described in chapter 2, for most dial-up connections, the server will assign you a temporary IP address, so you should enter a specific address for your computer only if your provider has instructed you to do so. If you have not been assigned a specific address, make sure **Server assigned IP address** is checked.

While dial-up computer addresses usually are variable, name server addresses usually are fixed. If your provider has supplied you with one or two numeric DNS or WINS addresses, make sure **Use specific name server addresses** is checked, and enter the values in the appropriate fields.

Click **OK** on the TCP/IP settings window, on the Network Protocol settings window, and finally on the Edit Phone Book entry.

You've now stored the phone number and the network settings required by RAS. You now can select the entry that you've created from the Remote Access dialog window and click on the **Dial** button. RAS will attempt to connect to your Internet service provider. If the modem dials out and makes a connection but is unable to log on, then you'll probably need to modify the dialing script, which is a text file that RAS uses as a template for its interaction with the host computer.

THE DIALING SCRIPT All of the RAS software is kept in \WINNT35\SYSTEM32\RAS. Along with the executable files is a text file called SWITCH.INF. This file is used to automate RAS logins, and a portion of it is shown in Figure A-10.

You can add your scripts to SWITCH.INF, if you like; this file is heavily annotated and actually contains a sample script that you can tailor to your own needs. It's possible that the standard script will do the job, but most likely you'll need to change the prompts (some systems use a "Logon:" or "User ID:" prompt instead of "Login:") or perhaps add a check for another question, such as the type of protocol used or perhaps whether compression should be used. You can find additional help on creating login scripts in RASPHONE.HLP.

> SWITCH.INF does allow you to put a literal password in the script, rather than use the one that you enter from RAS just before you dial in. Only do this if you're absolutely sure of the security of your system because, for anyone who knows where to look, it's in plain view.

HOTJAVA CONFIGURATION: SECURITY

Anytime that you transfer data over the Internet, you run the risk of someone intercepting that data and/or presenting you with bogus or harmful data. HotJava deals not only in the standard kinds of Internet

Figure A-10 A portion of the SWITCH.INF file used to automate RAS logins.

```
; SWITCH.INF for Windows NT Remote Access Service version 3.51
; Copyright 1995 Microsoft Corporation

[Generic login]

; This script will automate many logons when the remote computer
; prompts only for login (username) and password. This script requires
; Windows NT 3.51 or later.
;

; Start communication with remote computer by sending COMMAND=

  COMMAND=

  OK=<match>"ogin:"

  LOOP=<ignore>

  COMMAND=<username><cr>

  OK=<match>"assword:"
  LOOP=<ignore>

  COMMAND=<password><cr>

  OK=<ignore>ÆMDNMØ
```

data (hypertext documents and their associated files), but also in actual program code in the form of Java applets embedded in Web documents. Because Java applets have capabilities far beyond regular hypertext documents, it's particularly important to have mechanisms that help guarantee that the applet in question is a genuine Java applet that follows Java's security rules and/or is coming from a trusted source. Accordingly, the first time that you run HotJava you'll be asked to set a number of security options.

SECURITY MODE

HotJava's security applet addresses two issues. First, an applet from another computer might attempt to read documents from your computer, or from another computer on your system, when you wish those documents to be private. You can restrict applets from doing this or

specify only the files that are to be read. Second, an applet from an unknown source might perform some other action that you don't want to allow. You can specify which hosts you trust enough to provide you with applets.

HotJava's default security setting allows any applets to load but only allows those applets to retrieve documents that are on the system where the applet resides.

THE NO ACCESS OPTION The No Access option prevents applets from loading any documents at all, no matter where the applet is or where the documents are. However, this does not prevent an applet from doing other kinds of file access, so it is not a complete guarantee against infiltration.

If the Apply security mode to Applet box is checked, then HotJava is effectively prevented from loading any Java applets at all, and it becomes a "dumb" Web browser, able only to read standard HTML documents.

THE APPLET HOST OPTION The Applet Host option specifies that applets can only load documents from their own host computers. This generally is a good setting to use, unless you have absolutely no HTML documents on your system that you consider private. If the Apply security mode to Applet box is checked, then only applets that reside on your computer can be loaded, and therefore only documents on your computer can be loaded by Java applets.

THE FIREWALL OPTION The Firewall option lets you specify a group of hosts that you will allow the applet to load documents from. If the Apply security mode to Applet box is checked, then only Java applets from within the firewalled area will be loaded. This is a particularly useful option if you want to restrict Java use to your own networked organization, perhaps for an internal communications system.

THE UNRESTRICTED ACCESS OPTION Unrestricted Access means that Java applets can load URL documents from any system at all (although on your computer, the read and write areas available to applets are restricted by the HOTJAVA_READ_PATH and HOTJAVA_WRITE_PATH environment variables, which are discussed later

in this appendix). If the **Apply security mode to Applet** box is checked, this also means that applets from anywhere can be loaded by the browser.

DOMAIN TYPES: NIS AND DNS

Because HotJava is a product of Sun Microsystems Inc., it's designed to be able to take advantage of some of Sun's own technology. NIS is Sun's Network Information Services, which performs a service analogous to the Domain Name Servers that are prevalent on the Internet. If you're not running on a Sun network, choose **DNS**.

HOTJAVA PROPERTIES

After you've determined which security options you'll use, you might want to have a look at HotJava's other configuration settings. From the main menu, choose **Options**¦Properties. You'll see the window shown in Figure A-11.

Figure A-11 The HotJava properties window.

HotJava Properties

Firewall Proxy — Port: dudette.eng — 80

FTP Proxy — Port: 80

Caching Proxy — Port: sunweb.ebay — 80

Read Path: F:\HOTJAVA\BIN\..;~\public_html\

Write Path: \temp\

Underline anchors: [x]

Delay image loading: [ ]

Delay applet loading: [ ]

Apply — Cancel

The first part of this window is concerned with various kinds of proxies. Proxies normally are not important to people who have dial-up connections to Internet providers. If you're connected to the Internet via a network, however, a *proxy* is a trusted machine that acts as a go-between, managing and regulating the flow of information. In short, if you're not sure what you should do with these settings, check with your system administrator. If you don't have a system administrator, you almost certainly don't need these settings.

A Firewall proxy is a server with security responsibilities. You'll hear the term *firewall* bandied about a lot. As more companies get on the Internet, the need for safeguards against unwanted intrusion becomes more important. Firewalls help provide those safeguards.

An FTP proxy handles File Transfer Protocol requests, and a Caching proxy stores recently retrieved information, so a reload of a Web page, for example, doesn't require a resend from the original server.

The Read Path and Write Path fields are default settings for the environment variables by the same name, which are discussed in the following section. These values determine where Java applets can read and write files, so they have important consequences for security.

The **Underline Anchors** options simple tells HotJava whether or not to underline hyperlinks to other documents.

Delay Image loading and **Delay Applet loading** are options to speed up the display of text. Images and applets are loaded after all the text has arrived and is formatted for display.

ENVIRONMENT VARIABLES

HotJava uses a number of optional environment variables to control its configuration. For information on setting environment variables, see your operating system documentation.

HOTJAVA_HOME

The **HOTJAVA_HOME** variable specifies the base directory from which HotJava will look for its resources. The default value for this variable is the directory where HotJava was installed (for example, c:\hotjava on a Windows 95 or Windows NT system).

WWW_HOME

The **WWW_HOME** variable tells HotJava which HTML document it should load as its home page when it starts up. You also can specify a home page by typing a URL on the command line when you start up HotJava.

HOTJAVA_READ_PATH

The **HOTJAVA_READ_PATH** variable tells HotJava which directories Java applets are permitted to read files from. Use this variable in conjunction with the HotJava security settings discussed earlier in this appendix to ensure that applets from other systems do not read private documents on your computer.

On Sun systems, for example, the default read path for Sun installations is:

```
&lt;hotjava-install-dir&gt;:$HOME/public_html/
```

The read path can contain both directories and file specifications. When you specify a directory, you also grant access to all of that directory's subdirectories. When you specify a file, all files that match that file will be readable as well, no matter where they are.

Setting the **HOTJAVA_READ_PATH** to * disables all read checking. You should *not* use this setting except for directories where you are prepared to let any Java applet read any file on your system.

HOTJAVA_WRITE_PATH

The **HOTJAVA_WRITE_PATH** variable tells HotJava which directories Java applets are permitted to write files to. Use this variable in conjunction with the HotJava security settings discussed earlier in this appendix to control where applets write files.

As with the **HOTJAVA_READ_PATH** variable, **HOTJAVA_WRITE_PATH** lets you specify both directories and files. The default value for Sun installations is:

```
/tmp/:/devices/:/dev/:~/.hotjava/
```

Setting the **HOTJAVA_WRITE_PATH** to * disables all write checking. You should *not* use this setting except where you have absolute confidence

that all Java applets that could potentially run on your system will behave themselves. This is never advisable except on closed systems (i.e., a network with a local Web server and no connection to the Internet).

INSTALLATION SUMMARY

HotJava is relatively easy to install and run. The trickiest part of the business usually is getting TCP/IP installed and running correctly, particularly if you're hooking up to the Internet via a dial-up connection. The most essential part of the installation process, and usually not a tricky one at all, is setting up HotJava's security options so that incoming Java applets don't get into any parts of your system that you don't want them getting into.

If you do get stuck installing HotJava, first be as sure as you can be that TCP/IP is installed correctly. If you can use another Web browser or Telnet or any other Internet tool, then you can be confident that TCP/IP is working correctly. If it turns out that the problem is with HotJava, use one of your other Internet tools to post a question to the *comp.lang.java* newsgroup.

USING HOTJAVA

As Web browsers go, HotJava is fairly simple in its design. Don't let that simplicity fool you, however. After all, HotJava is the first Java-capable browser, and that means that whatever functionality it lacks can, in all probability, be obtained from the growing number of Java-ized Web sites around the world.

This section will take you on a brief tour of the HotJava browser. If you've installed HotJava and TCP/IP as described earlier in this appendix, then you're almost ready to take it out on the I-highway. All you need to know is where to find the gas, brake, and turn signals. Read on.

RUNNING HOTJAVA "STANDALONE"

Without yet connecting to the Internet, run HotJava according to the instructions given for your particular platform earlier in this appendix. You'll see something similar to Figure A-12. This is HotJava with its

Figure A-12 The HotJava browser running on Windows '95.

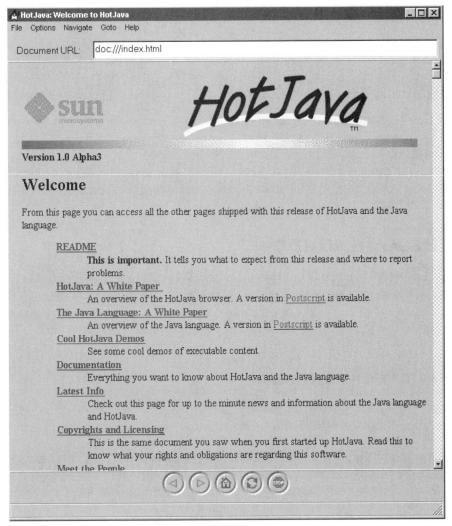

home page loaded. Unlike some other browsers that you might have used, HotJava loads a local document as its home page. It's quite possible, and sometimes useful, to run HotJava without being connected to the Internet at all. This has the benefit of giving you time to get used to HotJava without incurring Internet charges (even though those charges are likely to be quite low).

The HotJava browser is fairly basic in design, as compared to some other browsers. Its two primary functions are to navigate the World Wide Web via HTML documents and URLs and to retrieve and execute Java applets. It's quite possible to extend HotJava with Java applications, so rather than focus on adding enhancements, the authors of Java (and HotJava) have concentrated their energies on providing the underlying, enabling technology.

HotJava was designed out of necessity. There was no point in creating the first Java applets without a browser to display them. However, as other Web browser vendors are incorporating Java support, it's possible that, with time, the HotJava browser might become less important. It's equally possible that it will become the base product of a very interesting and innovative set of Java Internet programs.

THE MAIN WINDOW

The main window (as shown in Figure A-12) is where you'll spend the vast majority of your time when using HotJava. There are several configuration and usage options, which are discussed later in this appendix. However, for the most part, browsing with HotJava means looking in at the Web through that main window.

NAVIGATION CONTROLS

There are two kinds of Web page navigation controls: those that let you manage pages and those that appear within pages.

At the top of the window is the Document URL text field. You can type in the URL of the document you want to view, in the format *http://server/directory/document*. If you're navigating via links in the document, the field will display the URL of the current document.

HotJava has five page-management buttons arranged along the bottom of the main window.

The button with the left-pointing triangle is the **Back** button. It allows you to quickly view a previously displayed page.

The button with the right-pointing triangle is the **Forward** button. This button is disabled unless you've used the **Back** button to retrieve an

earlier page. The **Forward** button lets you retrace your steps forward in the list of viewed pages.

The button with the icon of a house is the **Home Page** button. The button with two circulating arrows is the **Reget** button. The button with the red stop sign is, appropriately enough, the **Stop** button.

THE LOCAL HOTJAVA PAGES

For now, let's take a tour of the local HotJava documentation. If you're not familiar with Web browsers, take a moment to familiarize yourself with HotJava documentation home page, as shown in Figure A-12. Note the format of the default home page's document URL. The prefix is not *http:*, but *doc:*, indicating that this is a local documentation file.

> You can tell HotJava which Web page to load on startup either by specifying the document URL on the command line (as in **HotJava http://java.sun.com/**) or by setting the environment variable **WWW_HOME** to the URL of the desired page. To load a local page, use the form *doc://directory/file*. If you do not specify a start-up page, HotJava will load the documentation home page by default.

Click on the link labeled Cool HotJava Demos. You should get a page similar to that displayed in Figure A-13.

Choose the Bouncing Heads link. This page is a demonstration of simple Java applet that animates a head shot of the program's author, sending the head ricocheting and spinning around the page.

Take a few minutes to explore some of the other links on the local pages. If you accidentally select a hotlink to a nonlocal document, you'll get a message saying that the URL could not be found. Press the **Back** button to return to the previous page or the **Home** button to get to the documentation home page.

MANAGING WEB DOCUMENTS FROM THE MENU

In addition to locating and displaying documents via hypertext links, you can use several main menu commands to open, reload, and inspect Web documents.

Figure A-13 The HotJava demo page.

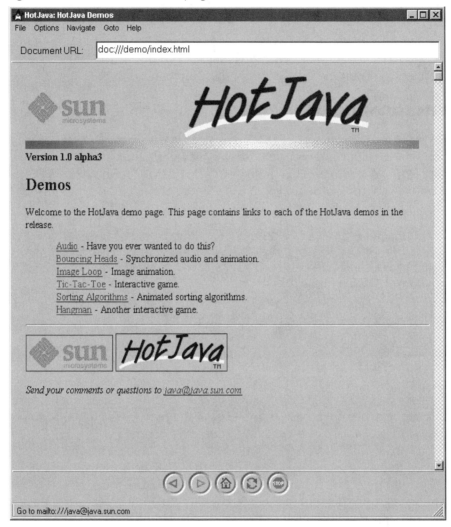

The **File**¦Open command brings up a dialog window that lets you enter a document URL directly. In the beta, this dialog has exactly the same functionality as the URL entry field on the main menu but should have a file lookup dialog in the final release.

File¦Reload has the same function as the **Reload** button on the bottom of the main window.

File¦Print brings up the standard print dialog, which lets you send the current HTML document to the printer or to a print file.

File¦View Source displays the HTML source for the document that you're currently viewing. You then can save the document to a file. This two-step process currently is the only way to save a Web document from another computer on your own computer in HotJava. **View** can be very useful when you're surfing the Web; if you come across a page that has accomplished some particularly nice effect, viewing the source might give you some ideas on how to do something similar. Of course, if the effect is due to one or more Java applets, you might have to ask the applet author for the Java source to really know what's happening.

CONNECTING TO THE INTERNET

Because HotJava is an application that runs on top of TCP/IP, the only thing that you need to do to connect to the Internet is to run your TCP/IP application and, if you have a dial-up line, use your dial-up software to connect to the provider. Once you're logged on to the Internet, HotJava will make use of the TCP/IP connection to retrieve HTML documents. If you attempt to retrieve a nonlocal document without being connected, you'll see the message shown in Figure A-14.

Figure A-14 The URL Not Found error window.

You'll also see the message shown in Figure A-14 if your HTTP request to view a Web page cannot be resolved by any Domain Name Server that was involved in processing the request.

> If you do get this message while connected and you know that the URL is valid, it's possible that the routing protocol (see chapter 2) currently in use just doesn't have this address in any of its available DNS servers. Try again after you've moved to another server. By moving onto a different network, you might open up a routing that was not previous available.

If you haven't already made your connection to your Internet provider as described earlier in this appendix, do so now.

Once you're connected to the Internet and logged on, switch back to HotJava. Click on the **Home Page** button to bring up the Java documentation home page. Find the hypertext link called **Latest Info**, and click on it. This will take you to the Java home page.

THE JAVA HOME PAGE

The Java home page, at *http://java.sun.com*, is a place that you'll be visiting often. Although this page focuses more on Java the language than Java the browser, it's also the place to get information on the latest versions of Java and HotJava, find out about related sources of information (like the *comp.lang.java* newsgroup), get updated documentation, and of course, check out some cool Java programming demos.

COOL JAVA SITES

One of the problems with publishing paper books is that they're static, while the world that they're about (especially if they're about the Internet) is in a rapid state of flux. Accordingly, some of the links described in this chapter might or might not exist by the time that you read this. It's a fair bet that *java.sun.com* and *www.sun.com* still will be the same, however, so if all else fails, make these your starting points and go exploring!

Note: Some of the alpha applets already might have been ported to beta or 1.0. Check out the Gamelan directory at ***www.gamelan.com*** for a list of alpha applets.

CONTEST WINNERS As of this writing, there's a link on the Java home page (remember, that's the Java home page—*http://java.sun.com*—at Sun Microsystems, not the documentation home page that is local to your computer) called HotJava Applet Programming Contest Results! One of my favorites from this contest is the Dining Philosophers applet, by Brian Gloyer, which you can find on the list of contest winners or directly at *http://www.eng.uci.edu:80/~bgloyer/hotjava/DiningPhilosophers.html*. Figure A-15 shows the Dining Philosophers in action (well, so to speak; that's another problem with print versus electronic media; you can't see the action).

The purpose of this applet is to demonstrate a classic problem in synchronizing multiple processes, in this case represented by a group of philosophers who divide their time between eating and thinking about the rules that govern who eats and when. The goal is to have all philosophers getting equal table time. The implementation is highly entertaining. What's even more interesting than the cute animations is the fact that the viewer has control over the applet's parameters, so you can experiment with different settings and get a very immediate and graphic feedback on how the balance between thinking and eating affects the activity around the table.

Another nice applet is the LED sign applet, by Darrick Brown. You can find this one via the HotJava Applet Programming Contest Results page or go direct to *http://www.cs.hope.edu/~dbrown/java/LED/WWW/LED.html*. Figure A-16 shows the LED applet demo page. The applet simulates an LED panel with scrolling characters and is driven entirely by scripts, so you don't actually need to change the source code to change the panel's appearance.

If you're into games, check out the crossword puzzle at *http://www.starwave.com/people/haynes/crosswordEntry.html* (also available from the contest page). This is a terrific implementation of a daily crossword, which even goes so far as to tell you if the letter you've typed in is correct.

Figure A-15 The Dining Philosophers Java applet.

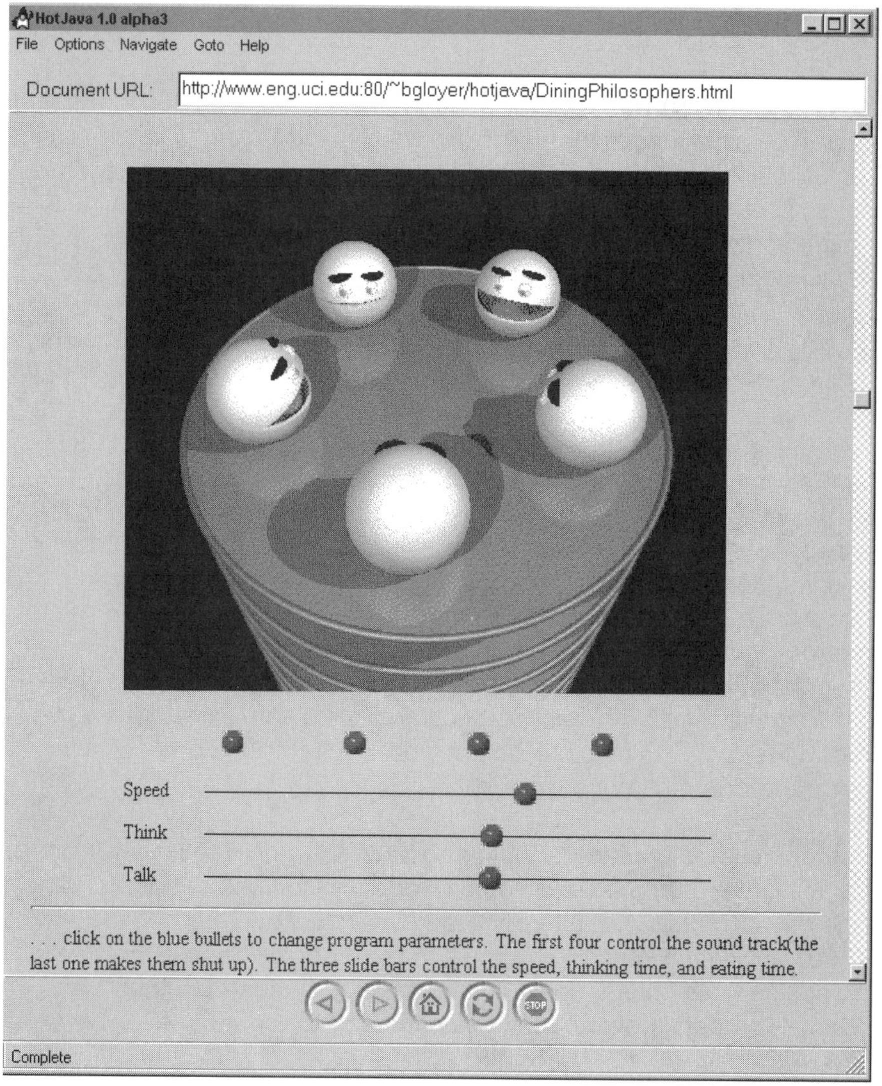

CUTTING-EDGE GRAPHICS For 3D graphics, you'll want to check out the Dimension X home page at *http://www.dimensionx.com*. From the home page, go to the Our Java page, which has links to a number of interesting demonstrations.

Figure A-16 The LED sign applet.

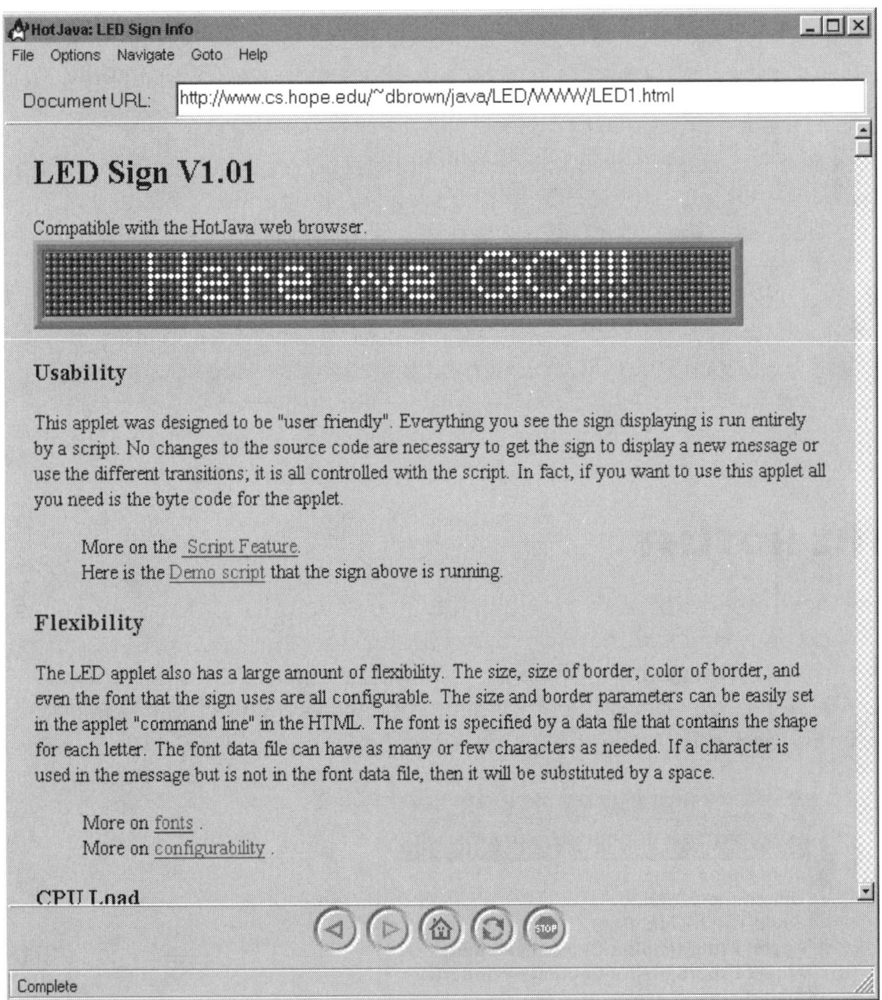

If you have a fast modem (or a good network connection to the Internet), check out the streaming animation player, which decodes animations as they arrive, meaning you don't have to wait for a lengthy file to arrive before you can see what's in it. Even if your connection isn't fast enough to give a proper illusion of motion until the file arrives, you'll have some idea of what the animation is like, and if you decide you don't want to sit through the entire animation, you can just press the **Stop** button or go to a different page.

There are several other demos at Dimension X that show various image manipulation effects, such as fading and embossing. The starfield simulation is scrolling credits on a changing starfield background, but unfortunately that applet comes with a rather massive (800K) sound file, which makes for a slow load.

Dimension X also is home to several interesting products, including Iced Java, which is a portable 3D-graphics library, written in C, but with a Java class interface to make the process of writing 3D applications much easier. Dimension X also produces Liquid Reality, which is a Virtual Reality Modeling Language (VRML) browser and toolkit based on the Iced Java library. This effectively blends Java's programmability with VRML's three-dimensional representations. Because Iced Java is designed for speed (a planned future version will offer support for hardware graphics accelerators), it's possible to do interactive 3D right on an HTML page. For more on 3D graphics and VRML, see chapter 20.

THE HOTLIST

Like most other browsers, HotJava lets you save a list of favorite places on the Web. Anytime that you find a Web page that you particularly like, choose **Navigate**|Add Current to Hotlist to save it to a permanent list. To revisit an item on your hot list, choose **Navigate**|Show Hotlist to activate the Hotlist window, which is shown in Figure A-17.

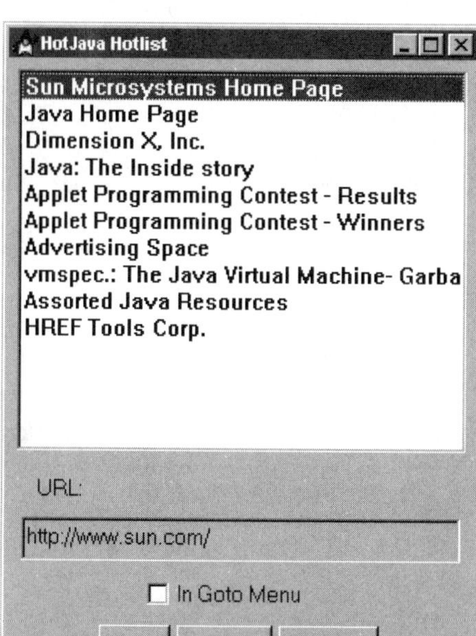

Figure A-17
The HotJava Hotlist window.

The Hotlist shows the page title, which it saved from the Web document itself. In the URL field at the bottom of the window, it displays the URL for the currently selected Hotlist item. Click on the **Visit** button to retrieve the selected page.

MODIFYING THE GOTO MENU

If you spend much time surfing the Web, you might find your Hotlist growing to unmanageable proportions. Rather than let pages that you visit frequently get lost in the list, you might want to add them to the GoTo menu on the main window. Just select the Hotlist item, click on **View** to make it the current document, then select **GoTo**|Add Current. The text for that Web page will appear thereafter on the GoTo menu.

> Information about which items are to be kept on the GoTo menu is stored in the *hotjava\.hotjava\hotlist-default file.* This is a straight text file that you can edit (though you should shut down HotJava before doing so). The **inMenu** identifier at the end of a line of text indicates that the item is to appear on the GoTo menu.

THE PROGRESS MONITOR

When HotJava is retrieving a Web page (or other data), the only indication that it gives you of its progress is the text in the status bar at the bottom of the main window. If you'd like a little more detailed information, choose **Options**|Progress Monitor from the main menu. You'll see the window shown in Figure A-18.

To see the progress monitor in action, visit the Sun Microsystems home page at *http://www.sun.com*, which contains a lot of graphics and Java applets with the progress monitor active. As each file is transferred, the progress monitor displays a progress bar, color coded as to type and labeled with the file's URL and the file size in bytes.

The progress window is resizable, and you'll almost certainly have to lengthen it to view all of the activity that goes on when you visit the Sun home page. Because HotJava is written in Java, which is a multitasking language, it can process multiple file requests at the same time. You might see half a dozen or more files being transferred at one time.

Figure A-18 The progress monitor.

HotJava Progress

html | image | class | audio | other | connecting

http://www.sun.com/audio/dialog/prod_and_solutions.au 11 Kb
http://www.sun.com/classes/ClickArea.class
http://www.sun.com/audio/phone.au 8345 bytes
http://www.sun.com/audio/dialog/sales_and_service.au 12 Kb
http://www.sun.com/audio/gears.au 15 Kb
http://www.sun.com/audio/dialog/technology_and_developers.au 19 Kb
http://www.sun.com/audio/jive.au
http://www.sun.com/audio/building_light.au 14 Kb
http://www.sun.com/audio/dialog/corp_overview.au 10 Kb
http://www.sun.com/audio/jive.au

Note also the types of files being transferred. A few, such as the main home page .GIF file, are images, but most are either .AU files (audio), or .CLASS files. CLASS files are compiled Java code and often are only a few thousand bytes in size each. Most of the time required to load the Sun page is due to the size of the graphics and audio files, not the size of the Java code.

FLUSHING THE CACHE

HotJava keeps the most recently viewed Web pages in memory, so if you want to return to a previously viewed page and you want to ensure that you get a fresh copy of that page (perhaps it contains some rapidly changing information), choose **Flush Cache** from the Options menu. That will empty out the Web page cache, and the next request for a document will result in a new copy being sent from the Web site (unless, of course, you happen to be using a caching proxy as described earlier in this appendix).

HOTJAVA HELP

HotJava comes with online help in the form of HTML documents. There are a variety of help file formats in use by different operating systems, so rather than have to accommodate these differences in the many versions of the HotJava browser, the designers wisely chose to use HTML. This also allows the documentation to be partly on the local machine and partly on the Sun Web server, which is particularly useful for information that could change at anytime, such as a list of known bugs, teaching examples, or a list of Web sites of interest to Java programmers.

If you're at the documentation home page (you can get there quickly by clicking on the home icon at the bottom of the page), click on **Documentation**, and you'll load the document *index.html*, which normally is on your computer in the directory hotjava\doc (some operating systems might use different directory and file names). Return again to the documentation home page, and click on **Latest Info**. This time the HotJava browser retrieves the home page document at *java.sun.com* via http from the Sun server.

SEARCHING THE DOCUMENTATION

HotJava gives you the ability to search the HTML help documents, which cover both the HotJava browser and the Java programming language. Choose **Help**¦Search HotJava Documentation from the main menu to bring up the help search window, as shown in Figure A-19.

Java help pages are grouped together into what HotJava calls *books*. The topics covered include the Java language specification, the Java class libraries, the manpages (user manual pages), writing and using HotJava applets, the Java Virtual Machine specification, and implementing native (usually C/C++) methods. You can search any one book or all of the books at once.

The help search window lets you enter a search string, then returns a list of Java help pages that meet the search requirements.

If you enter one or more words with no operators between the words, the help search engine assumes that you are doing a logical OR and

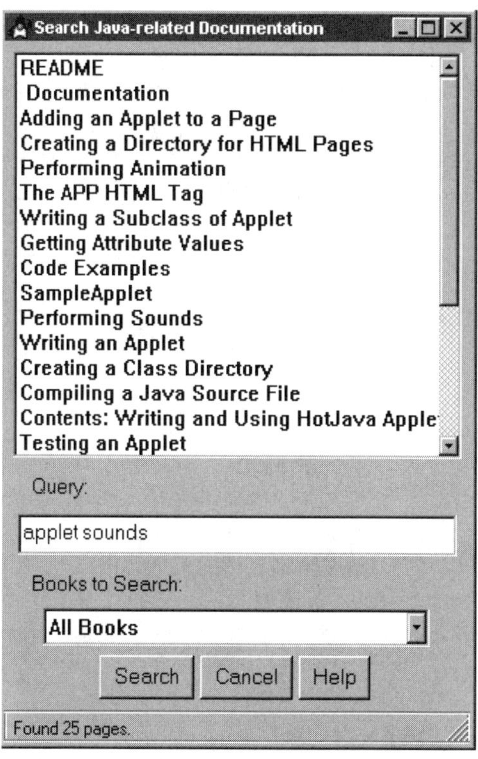

Figure A-19
The help search window

will find pages that contain any one of the words you have specified. For example, entering **applet sounds** will get you approximately 25 pages, which contain either the word *applet* or the word *sounds*.

To speed searches, the engine ignores common words that do not usually communicate anything meaningful about the document's content, including *a, an, and, as, at, be, but, by, do, for, from, have, he, in, it, not, of, on, or, she, that, the, there, to, we, which, with,* and *you*. This is called a *stoplist*. Because words on the stoplist will be ignored, if you want, you can use them in the query. This is to allow you to type a more natural English expression and still have the search return a result.

You also can specify the Boolean AND, OR, and NOT operators. (Although the word *and* is in the stoplist, the search engine does recognize it as a Boolean operator.) The operators work as follows:

- **Word1 AND Word2** will find all pages that contain both *Word1* and *Word2*.
- **Word1 OR Word2** works the same as **Word1 Word2**. It will find all pages that contain either *Word1* or *Word2*.
- **Word1 NOT Word2** will find all pages that contain *Word1* but that do not contain *Word2*.

You can use more than one Boolean operator in a query. The search engine will start with the first pair of words, find the search result, then apply the next operator and word to that search result. The query **Word1 Word2 NOT Word3** would first find all documents with *Word1* or *Word2* (remember that, if the operator is omitted, it is assumed to be OR), then remove from that list any documents that contained *Word3*.

Search terms must be more than one character long, and the only valid punctuation character is the apostrophe. When an HTML document is indexed, all punctuation characters except the apostrophe, all words on the stoplist, and all HTML tags are replaced with whitespace. The resulting words (duplicates are ignored) make up the list of words in the index.

Although a search might return any number of found documents (searching on "Java" will get you over 300 hits), only the first 100 documents will be displayed in the search result window.

To view a found document, simply double-click on the list item that you want to view, and that document will be displayed in HotJava's main window.

SUMMARY

Although HotJava, on the surface, is a fairly simple Web browser, its ability to execute Java applets means that its functionality is limited only by the imagination and skill of the Java programmers whose Web sites that you visit. For that matter, as you learn how to program in Java, HotJava will be limited only by your imagination and skill.

JAVA RESOURCES

ALTHOUGH JAVA still is a young language, there's a burgeoning supply of applets, classes, development tools, and other products that can make your programming/Web page design work easier. This appendix discusses some of those resources, as well as the growing industry support for Java.

APPLETS WITH SOURCE CODE

In the finest tradition of Internet programming, there is a lot of free Java source code available just for the asking. You should familiarize yourself with as much of it as possible, because it's almost always cheaper to buy a wheel than reinvent one.

All of the applets discussed here have source code available. However, you must check with the applet authors for any restrictions on the use of the applets and/or source code. The inclusion of applets on this list also is not in any way a guarantee of their quality or usefulness.

In addition to the URLs listed here, be sure to check out the Gamelan directory at *http://www.gamelan.com* and the comp.lang.java newsgroup (both are discussed later in this appendix).

EDDY-CURRENT SENSOR SIMULATION

Visit *http://www.uni-kassel.de/fb16/ipm/mt/java/javae.html* for an eddy-current sensor simulation applet. This applet is available for noncommercial use (contact *becker@mt.e-technik.uni-kassel.de* if you'd like to use this applet for commercial purposes).

The Kassel page also is available in German at *http://www.uni-kassel.de/fb16/ipm/mt/java/java.html.* Both versions contain hot links to other German Java sites. (You also might want to check out *http://java.pages.de/.*)

EXPIRING SIGN

Expiring Sign is an applet that shows text in the foreground and a series of triangles sliding by in the background. It is fully resizable and is available at *http://www.uni-kassel.de/fb16/ipm/mt/java/javae.html.*

This applet is available for noncommercial use (contact *becker@mt.e-technik.uni-kassel.de* if you'd like to use this applet for commercial purposes).

THE FLIPPER APPLET

If you find the Animator applet that comes with the JDK a little too complex, check out the Flipper applet at *http://www.greyassoc.com/java/apps/flipper.html*. Flipper dispenses with all of the display options and just loads a series of images and "flips" through them.

THE SAMPLE DISTRIBUTIONS APPLET

The Sample Distributions applet (Figure B-1) is an educational applet for the statistically minded that "shows how sample means tend to the population mean as the sample size." Like the sort demonstration at the Sun site, this applet is a good example of how Java can be used to animate concepts. It is available at *http://www.thomtech.com/~suresh/java/sample.html*.

THE SLIDE PROJECTOR APPLET

The slide projector at *http://www.thomtech.com/~suresh/java/beta/* is much like an animator but gives you frame-by-frame control over the images, with a button to play the associated audio. There are several other useful applets at this site, including the previously mentioned sample-distributions applet and a couple of graphics applets.

ANIMATED LOGO

A variation on Sun's ImageLoop applet, the Animated logo applet loads a single image that is a combination of all of the images you want to display. Loading one large image can be considerably faster than loading many small images because only a single http request is needed. This applet is available at *http://www.uni-kassel.de/fb16/ipm/mt/java/javae.html* for noncommercial use (contact *becker@mt.e-technik.uni-kassel.de* if you'd like to use this applet for commercial purposes).

Figure B-1 The Sample Distributions applet.

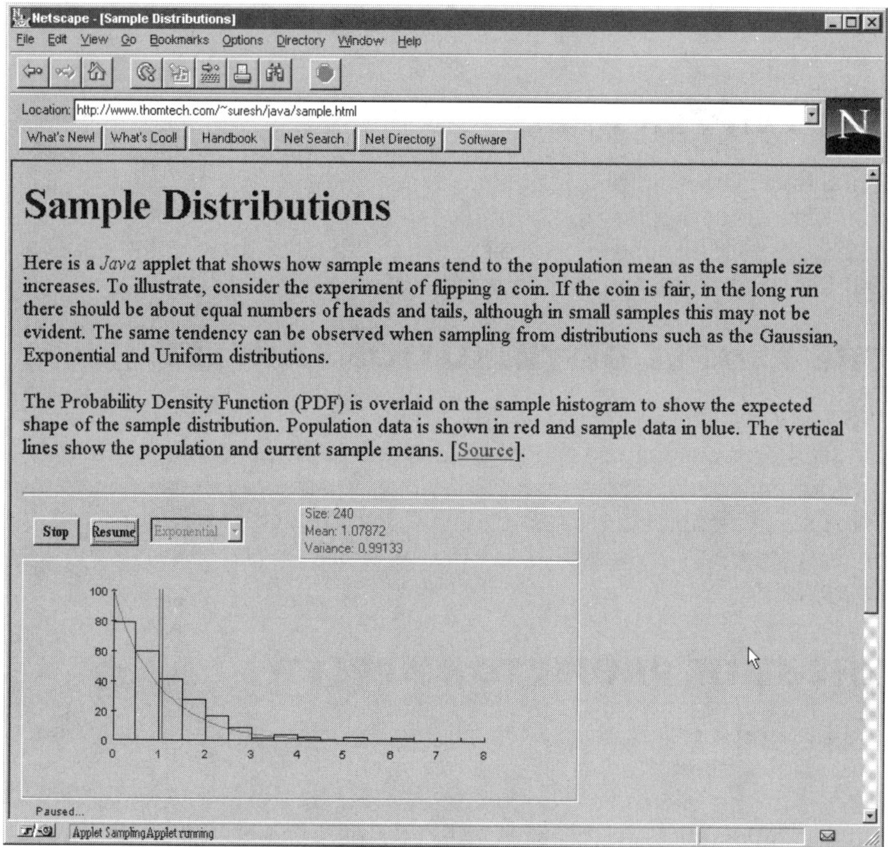

ELECTRO MAGNETIC POETRY

If you're looking for inspiration for your next gig at the local poetry reading, check out *http://prominence.com/java/poetry/*. This applet, shown in Figure B-2, lets you assemble a poem by dragging words around on the screen. It is an unusual and creative Internet application.

THE LED SIGN APPLET

The LED sign applet (Figure B-3) already is something of a classic and is regularly updated and enhanced by its author, Darrick Brown. You can

Figure B-2 Electro Magnetic Poetry.

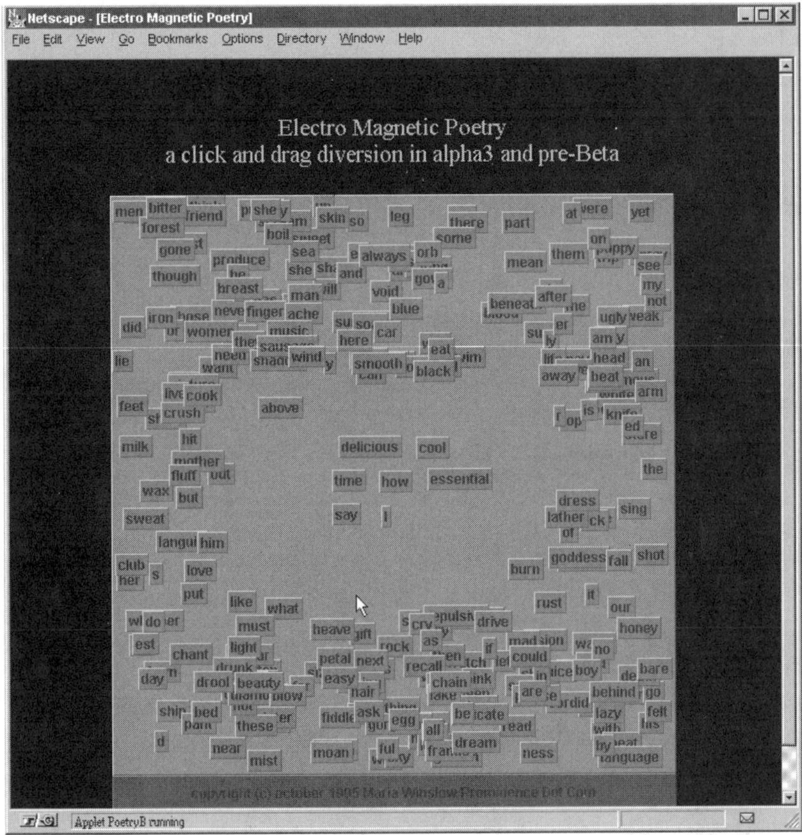

get the applet (and see it in action) at *http://www.cs.hope.edu/~dbrown/java/LEDSign/WWW/LED.html*. The LED sign has an extensive scripting language that lets you tailor it to just about any use without resorting to programming, but source code is available.

ASTERNOID!

For those of us old enough to remember and love Asteroids, here's a Java version that's sure to please (*http://www.crocker.com/~sigelman/java/aster/aster.html*). (See Figure B-4.) If you're interested in writing games, the fully commented source code is a huge help and is a good place to pick up some Java programming techniques.

Figure B-3 The LED sign applet.

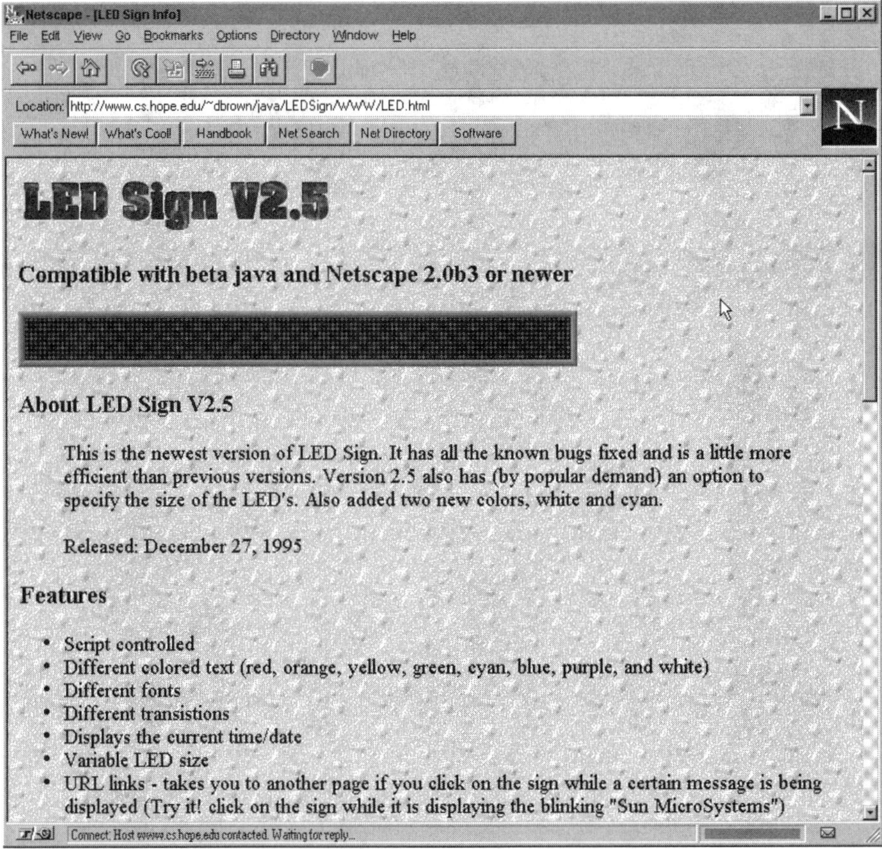

TICKERTAPE

TickerTape is a flicker-free and fully resizable ticker tape applet and is available at *http://www.uni-kassel.de/fb16/ipm/mt/java/javae.html*. This applet is available for noncommercial use (contact *becker@mt.e-technik.uni-kassel.de* if you'd like to use this applet for commercial purposes).

E-MAIL FORM

This applet collects information from the user, then sends the data as e-mail. As most browsers don't allow applets to send e-mail directly,

Figure B-4 Asternoid!

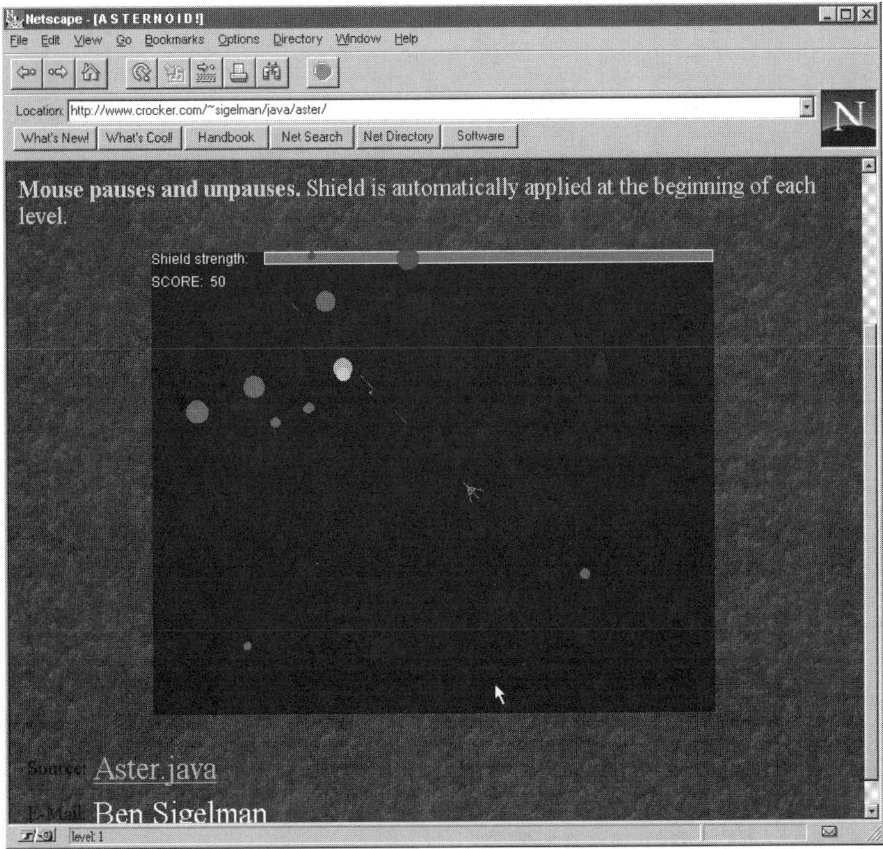

this one opens a connection to a dummy page and delivers the data there. E-mail Form is available at *http://www.uni-kassel.de/fb16/ipm/mt/java/javae.html*. This applet is available for noncommercial use (contact *becker@mt.e-technik.uni-kassel.de* if you'd like to use this applet for commercial purposes).

RUBIK'S CUBE

If the real Rubik's cube wasn't frustrating enough for you, have a look at the Java version, at *http://www.student.informatik.th-darmstadt.de/~schubart/rc_applet.html*. This page also contains links to a number of other Java resources, including Gamelan and the comp.lang.java FAQ.

NETWORKED WHITEBOARD

The networked whiteboard applet at *http://www.vpro.nl/interaktief/java/beta/whiteboard/intro.html* allows several people to draw on the same workspace together, across the Internet. The applet handles local input and display; the communication between the whiteboard applets is handled by a Java application running on the server. To browse the source and class files go to *http://www.vpro.nl/interaktief/java/beta/whiteboard/*.

SURF-O-MATIC

As the author of the Surf-o-matic applet (*http://www.xco.com:80/java/surfomatic/*) says, if you're already wasting too much time on the Internet, "try Surf-o-matic! In just seconds, you'll be wasting time far more efficiently than you could ever imagine." Surf-o-matic (love that name!) makes use of a number of URLs that server random URLs. A good introduction to retrieving Web pages.

WEB CRAWLER

Looking for a Web crawler written in Java? Check out *http://www.cs.mu.oz.au/~daa/pgs.html*. This applet does keyword searches and displays its progress in the Java console.

JAVA HTTPD SERVER

As an Internet programming language, Java is admirably suited to creating Web server software. One such project can be found at *http://www.vpro.nl/interaktief/java/beta/httpd/sources.html*. It's a work in progress but will be useful to anyone working on server software.

JAVA MIDI

Yes, someone is working on adding MIDI support to Java. Currently this involves using native methods, which means that the libraries have to be explicitly distributed because applets often aren't allowed to download native method code automatically. Check out the current work at *http://www.users.interport.net/~mash/javamidi.html*.

NAVIGATOR SOFTWARE THAT SUPPORTS JAVA

As support for Java grows, so does the number of Web browsers that have incorporated the ability to execute Java applets. The following is a partial list.

NETSCAPE NAVIGATOR

With the Netscape Navigator owning a reported 80% of the Web browser market, Netscape's decision in the spring of 1995 to license Java probably was the single most important factor in Java's acceptance as the *de facto* standard for crossplatform Internet programming. As of this writing, Navigator version 2 is in late beta and has support for Java 1.0 applets. That means that the majority of Web users either already are able to view applets that you create for your own pages or will be able to as soon as they upgrade to Netscape 2.0.

MICROSOFT'S EXPLORER

The big Java news in late 1995 was Microsoft's decision to license Java. The Internet programming community had been expecting Microsoft to unveil competing technology, and the move to license Java was widely read as an accession to Sun's dominance of the Internet language market. Aside from cementing Java's position as the standard Internet programming, Microsoft's licensing of Java for its Explorer navigator also promises to bring a number of new Java users online. Microsoft plans to improve the Windows 95 version of Java and will provide Sun with a reference implementation.

ORACLE'S POWERBROWSER

Oracle Corp. has entered the Web browser fray with its PowerBrowser, which uses Network Loadable Objects technology to add new capabilities to the browser. Among other things, NLOs allow for the support of Java applets. PowerBrowser also features BASIC programmability, an HTML authoring environment, and a personal

WebServer. As of late 1995, the PowerBrowser beta was available for download from the Oracle FTP server. Surf to *http://www.oracle.com /mainEvent/webSystem/powerBrowser/* for more information.

THE BETA HOTJAVA BROWSER

It had been Sun's intention to release a beta version of the HotJava version along with the beta release of the JDK, but the Java team didn't have the resources to do both projects, so the browser got put on the back shelf. With Netscape's support for Java, the work on HotJava has not been as critical to the success of Java, but you can expect to see an updated HotJava browser from Sun in the first half of 1996. For more on HotJava, see appendix A.

JAVA PORTING PROJECTS

SILICON GRAPHICS WORKSTATIONS

As of December 1995, a port of the beta Java compiler for Silicon Graphics workstations was available from SGI. This JDK consisted of the beta compiler, runtime environment, and the debugger and required either IRIX 5.3 or 6.2. It was available from *http://www.sgi.com/Products /cosmo/cosmo_instructions.html* at no charge. Because the kit was due to expire on January 15, 1996 (before this book hits the streets), these arrangements probably have changed.

The compiler is the first component of SGI's Cosmo Code Java development environment, which is part of the larger Cosmo project, which was announced on December 4, 1995. Cosmo is "a powerful set of advanced technologies bringing interactive multimedia and 3D graphics to the World Wide Web" and includes multimedia HTML and VRML authoring tools and support for a number of third-party plug-ins.

Cosmo Code includes a graphical Java source debugger and a visual source browser, as well as the Cosmo Motion and Cosmo MediaBase libraries.

The Cosmo code tools, including the debugger and browser, are scheduled for first customer shipment on March 15, 1996. For further information, check out the Cosmo page: *http://www.sgi.com/Products /cosmo/index.html*.

AMIGA

The Amiga Java/HotJava porting project is called P'Jami and has a Web page at *http://metro.turnpike.net/N/NiallT/hotjava.html*. There wasn't a lot of activity on this site over the fall, and as of the end of 1995, no software had been delivered. However, word has it that the port is progressing. If you'd like to be kept up-to-date, you can subscribe to the following mailing lists:

- *amiga-hotjava@mail.iMNet.de*
- *amiga-hotjava-announce@mail.iMNet.de*

To subscribe, send mail to *majordomo@mail.iMNet.de* and place a line that looks like:

```
subscribe <list-name> [<your-e-mail-address>]
```

in the body of the message. The P'Jami folks ask that you *not* send subscription requests to either of the mailing lists.

OS/2 AND AIX

IBM has announced that it will port Java to OS/2 and AIX, with products becoming available in the first quarter of 1996. As of late 1995, one of the alpha versions had been ported to both operating systems, and the beta version, with the exception of AWT, had been ported to OS/2. For more information, you can visit *http://ncc.hursley.ibm.com/javainfo* or e-mail *java@hursely.ibm.com*. IBM also has licensed Java technology for use in Lotus Notes. In 1996, the Release 4 Notes server will support the main World Wide Web protocols including HTTP and HTML, as well as Java.

MVS AND OS/400

IBM has reported that work is in progress on a port to MVS and OS/400. Visit IBM's Hursely site at *http://ncc.hursley.ibm.com/javainfo* for more information.

WINDOWS 3.1

IBM has announced that it will port Java to Windows 3.1, with the same projected delivery date as its other Java ports. This port is a little more

difficult than the others, however, as Windows 3.1 does not natively support either threading or long, mixed-case filenames.

LINUX

Visit *http://substance.blackdown.org/java-linux.html* for the latest on the Java-linux project. As of this writing, Randy Chapman's port of the Java beta was available at *ftp://java.blackdown.org/pub/Java/linux*. You also can check out the linux mailing list at *http://www.linux.ncm.com/java-linux/*.

> Blackdown (*http://substance.blackdown.org/java-linux.html*) is a well-maintained site with links to a number of interesting Java resources. It's also one of Sun's mirror FTP sites and well worth keeping on your hotlist.

DEVELOPMENT TOOLS

Java still is a little behind languages like C++ when it comes to choosing an integrated development environment. However, Java's popularity has prompted many vendors to either adapt existing environments to Java or design entirely new environments.
The following is a partial listing.

ROASTER FOR MACINTOSH

Natural Intelligence has announced that it will deliver the Roaster Java development environment for Power PC Macs. This integrated environment includes a colored-syntax source editor, a project facility, a fast compiler, a disassembler, a debugger, and a runtime environment for applet testing. Roaster looks to be the first Java opportunity. For more information visit *http://www.natural.com/pages/products /roaster/flyer.html*.

SUN'S JAVA DEVELOPMENT TOOLS

At the time of this writing, the Java development tools offered by Sun are pretty basic. You need to supply your own editor, and the compiling/debugging tools are more command-line than GUI. However, all of that will change sometime in 1996. Sun has announced that they will be providing a complete Java development environment, and you

can read the full text of that announcement at *http://www.Sun.COM:80/cgi-bin/show?951201/feature3/feature3.html*.

BORLAND'S LATTE

Borland has announced support for Java development in the form of Latte, a development environment developed in Java. Latte will be released in stages beginning in the first half of 1996. Current plans call for the complete product to include the usual visual RAD tools, plus scalable distributed database access. For more information, have a look at *http://netserv.borland.com/Product/java/java.html*. You also can join the Java e-mailing list at *http://netserv.borland.com/Product/java/javalist.html*.

SYMANTEC'S ESPRESSO

Symantec was the first major vendor to come out with a Java development environment. Not a standalone environment, Espresso is an add-on to Symantec's C++ development environment, version 7.2, and contains Sun's complete Java Development Kit. Espresso includes a Class Editor, a Java application development "wizard" called AppExpress, and a programmer's editor with macros and color syntax and keyword highlighting. Espresso also includes a source parser that creates a visual representation of applets and applications and any library classes used.

ETL HORB

Just to set things straight, ETL is the company, and HORB is the language. Specifically, HORB is a Java-compatible language that lets you create server objects from the client (applet) side, essentially turning Java into a distributed language. Among other things, HORB is an alternative to socket communications and doing CGI scripts. For more information, check out *http://ring.etl.go.jp/openlab/horb/*.

J2C: THE JAVA-TO-C TRANSLATOR

If you want to develop in Java but can't wait for the just-in-time compiler to get the executable speed of C, you should check out

http://www.webcity.co.jp/info/andoh/java/j2c.html, the home of j2c. j2c reads class files and generates C programs that do not need the Java interpreter. Of course, this completely voids the multiplatform capability and security features of Java. However, if you're not developing for the Web, that's not your worry. j2c currently is available for Solaris. Ports to FreeBSD, Win32, Linux, SGI Irix, HP-UX, and other platforms are under development.

THE BLACK STAR PUBLIC JAVA COMPILER

So you want to write Java applets, but you don't have a platform that supports Java. No problem; just visit the Black Star public compiler at *http://mars.blackstar.com/*. You'll be asked for the file to compile, as shown in Figure B-5.

Once the file has been uploaded and compiled, you'll be shown an HTML document like the one shown in Figure B-6.

The output document contains hotlinks to the files that result from the compile, and you download them either by clicking on the hotlinks or by using FTP.

JAVAMAKER

JavaMaker is a minimalist Java applet development environment, consisting of a source code editor with integrated calls to the compiler and the applet viewer. JavaMaker used to be available from *http://net.info.samsung.co.kr/~hcchoi/javamaker.html* and might yet be; however, as of this writing, the site was unavailable. You also could check out the JavaMaker link at Gamelan, at *http://www.gamelan.com*.

DIMENSION X'S 3D VRML

Dimension X (*http://www.dimensionx.com/lr*) has a Java VRML toolkit called Liquid Reality, which is expected to go into beta in January of 1996. A supported version is to be released soon after Netscape 2.0 is released. To keep abreast of developments, send a message to *majordomo@dnx.com* with the following text in the message body:

```
subscribe lr-announce your e-mail address
```

Figure B-5 The public compiler input window.

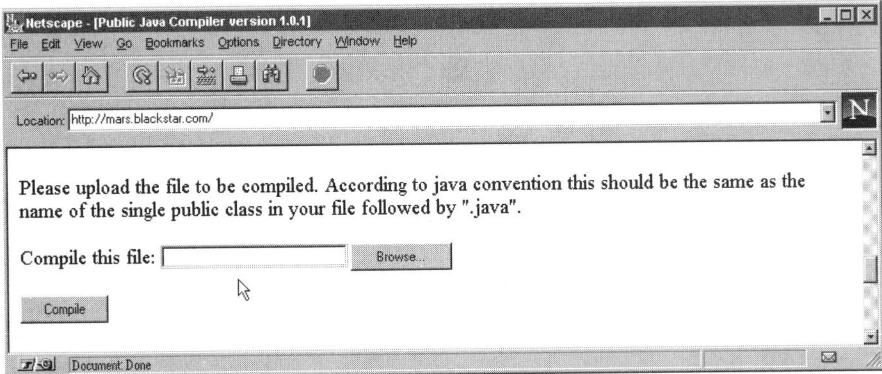

Figure B-6 The public compiler's output.

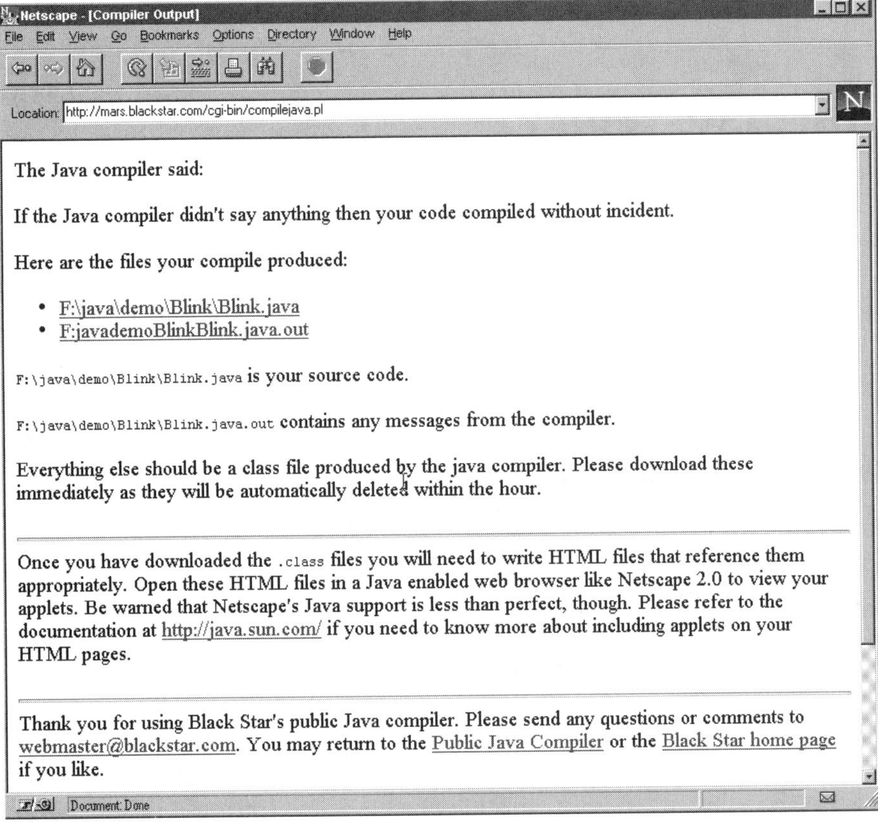

ADOBE SYSTEMS' PAGEMILL

In December of 1995, Adobe Systems, Inc. announced that it had licensed Java for integration into the PageMill Web authoring package, as well as the popular Acrobat electronic document software. Adobe also has indicated that it is considering supporting the Java API in its products, which would mean that developers could use Adobe products to develop Java applets and/or applications.

MISCELLANEOUS

GAMELAN

Gamelan is one of the best Java resources on the Net. Surf to *http://www.gamelan.com/*, and you'll discover a directory of everything Java, from animation applets and database applications to games, educational resources, and interesting Java-powered sites.

SUN'S JAVASCRIPT

JavaScript (formerly Netscape's LiveScript) is a crossplatform scripting language for Web content development. As a script language, JavaScript is considerably less powerful than Java but also is somewhat easier to use and doesn't require the same knowledge of programming techniques or object-oriented programming concepts. An impressive list of companies has endorsed JavaScript, including major players such as Borland, Oracle, DEC, Hewlett-Packard, SGI, SCO, and Novell.

VRML AND JAVA

In November of 1995, the VRML Architecture Group opted to make Java the reference language for VRML (Virtual Reality Modeling Language) development. VAG is the group that developed VRML, and while this endorsement doesn't mean that you can't use another language (the standard is an open one), it does mean that Java will get that much more attention from VRML developers. The fit between VRML and Java is a natural one, because Java's crossplatform capability is one of the keys to a successful Web-wide VRML implementation. Coupled with Netscape's support for Java, the pieces for useful Web VRML

applications finally look to be in place. For more on VRML, check out *http://vrml.wired.com.*

COMP.LANG.JAVA

The most active online Java discussion area is the comp.lang.java newsgroup. With hundreds of messages scrolling by each day, there's been regular discussion about splitting up the newsgroup into a number of subnewsgroups. When this happens, the new newsgroups should appear under comp.lang.java (e.g., comp.lang.java.new-user).

JAVA ON COMPUSERVE

For Java discussion on Compuserve, GO JAVAUSER. Sun is officially represented in JAVAUSER, and you also can download some of the files that are available from the Sun FTP server.

THE COMPANION CD-ROM

THIS APPENDIX details what's on the companion CD for this book.

If all you want to do is run the applets on the CD-ROM, you need to mount the CD-ROM on your machine and use the **Open local file** option of your Java-enabled browser to load the following, for Solaris 2.*x*:

```
$ browser /cdrom/cdrom0/mcghill/web/index.html
```

and, for Windows 95 and Windows NT:

```
C:\browser.EXE  D:\mcghill\web\index.html
```

assuming that your CD-ROM is mounted on drive D:. ***browser*** can be interchanged for commands such as **netscape**, **hotjava**, or some other Java-capable browser.

If you are having problems, read the rest of this appendix and the README files on the CD-ROM.

For updates to the contents of this CD-ROM, you should browse one of the following Web sites, where we are maintaining the CD-ROM on the web: *http://www.mts.net/~dharms/websitejava/* or *http://www.mcgraw-hill.com/*.

> Note: The use of the Java-powered logo indicates that the CD-ROM contains Java code in the form of applets and applications. Use of this logo should not be construed as an endorsement of the contents by JavaSoft or Sun. The Java Powered image is a standard branding logo that can be licensed from JavaSoft and is used to indicate the presence of Java content.

The companion CD-ROM is designed to serve several purposes. The primary purpose is to provide a known and "frozen" version of Java that should work with all of the example applets and applications included on the CD-ROM. Because it is impossible to know exactly when you will buy this book and what version of Java will be available when you get it, we are including it here to help ensure that the examples provided in the book will work as described in the text. All code on the CD-ROM is expected to work with the 1.0 release as of January 23, 1996.

The Java Developer's Kit (beta 2) has been completely unpacked and installed on the CD-ROM for both hardware architectures described on

the book. Additionally, the Java API documentation also has been installed on the CD-ROM. All of the zipped or compressed tar archives also are included on the CD-ROM. The contents of these archive files are exactly what's installed on the CD-ROM without change, so you can be certain that you have an identical copy of what was on the Java home page.

The CD-ROM also is laid out as a Web site in the form of a tutorial. As you read a chapter in the book, you can look at the accompanying tutorial code and follow along with your browser. To browse this Web site and see the Java applets in action, you will need a Java-capable Web browser. You can read the HTML-formatted text with any browser, but the applets will not run if you aren't using a Java-capable browser, such as Netscape Navigator 2.0.

The CD-ROM has been mastered as an ISO 9660 (full specification) format using long filenames for both the Solaris 2.*x* and Windows 95/Windows NT 4.0 directories. We have successfully tested the CD-ROM with these operating systems. We can certify only that the CD-ROM is readable and can be used with the previously named operating systems. In theory, the web directory should be readable by *any* Java-capable browser, because Java and HTML are platform-independent. If you have a version that runs on Apple, SGI, or HP, give it a try. It *should* work, but we have only been able to test it as mentioned previously.

> If you use NT 3.51 and have difficulty reading the CD-ROM, you can download the NT tutorial files from http://www.mts.net/~dharms/websitejava/index.html.

README files have been put in several of the subdirectories of the CD-ROM to assist in understanding what's in a given directory. To the best of our ability, we have made the CD-ROM as simple and self-documenting as possible.

As a final note, we have included the alpha 1.3 versions of the HotJava browser and Java utilities for both architectures. This will allow you to browse "legacy" applets on the Internet that might be of interest to you. The files are provided as is and without further documentation. They are identical copies to the versions on the Java Web site as of January, 1996 and are included for your convenience.

INDEX

A

570

573

Y

ABOUT THE AUTHORS

David Harms is president of Cove Communications, Inc., a software research and development company that provides services to the television industry. He is a magazine columnist and co-author of *Developing Clarion For Window Applications* and has been involved in the development of online information systems since 1991.

Barton C. Fiske specializes in computer graphics, multimedia, and imaging for Sun Microsystems. He has used Java and HotJava to create state-of-the-art interactive multimedia Web sites that link audio, UNIX applications, VRML browsers, and virtual reality authoring tools.

Jeffrey C. Rice is a senior systems engineer for Sun Microsystems, specializing in applications-development frameworks, object-oriented programming, user interface design, and Java.

CD-ROM WARRANTY

This software is protected by both United States copyright law and international copyright treaty provision. You must treat this software just like a book. By saying "just like a book," McGraw-Hill means, for example, that this software may be used by any number of people and may be freely moved from one computer location to another, so long as there is no possibility of its being used at one location or on one computer while it also is being used at another. Just as a book cannot be read by two different people in two different places at the same time, neither can the software be used by two different people in two different places at the same time (unless, of course, McGraw-Hill's copyright is being violated).

LIMITED WARRANTY

McGraw-Hill takes great care to provide you with top-quality software, thoroughly checked to prevent virus infections. McGraw-Hill warrants the physical CD-ROM contained herein to be free of defects in materials and workmanship for a period of sixty days from the purchase date. If McGraw-Hill receives written notification within the warranty period of defects in materials or workmanship, and such notification is determined by McGraw-Hill to be correct, McGraw-Hill will replace the defective CD-ROM. Send requests to:

McGraw-Hill, Inc.
Customer Services
P.O. Box 545
Blacklick, OH 43004-0545

The entire and exclusive liability and remedy for breach of this Limited Warranty shall be limited to replacement of a defective CD-ROM and shall not include or extend to any claim for or right to cover any other damages, including but not limited to, loss of profit, data, or use of the software, or special, incidental, or consequential damages or other similar claims, even if McGraw-Hill has been specifically advised of the possibility of such damages. In no event will McGraw-Hill's liability for any damages to you or any other person ever exceed the lower of suggested list price or actual price paid for the license to use the software, regardless of any form of the claim.

MCGRAW-HILL, INC. SPECIFICALLY DISCLAIMS ALL OTHER WARRANTIES, EXPRESS OR IMPLIED, INCLUDING, BUT NOT LIMITED TO, ANY IMPLIED WARRANTY OF MERCHANTABILITY OR FITNESS FOR A PARTICULAR PURPOSE.

Specifically, McGraw-Hill makes no representation or warranty that the software is fit for any particular purpose and any implied warranty of merchantability is limited to the sixty-day duration of the Limited Warranty covering the physical CD-ROM only (and not the software) and is otherwise expressly and specifically disclaimed.

This limited warranty gives you specific legal rights; you may have others which may vary from state to state. Some states do not allow the exclusion of incidental or consequential damages, or the limitation on how long an implied warranty lasts, so some of the above may not apply to you.